Profitable Small Scale Manufacture of COSMETICS (Synthetic and Herbal)

Profitable Small Scale Manufacture of COSMETICS (Synthetic and Herbal)

Written By

EIRI BOARD OF CONSULTANTS & ENGINEERS

ENGINEERS INDIA RESEARCH INSTITUTE

4449, Nai Sarak, Main Road, Delhi - 110006 (India)
Ph: 91-11-23918117, 23916431, 23840361
Fax: 91-11- 2391 6431, 2391 8117
*** E-Mail: eirisidi@bol.net.in**
***Website: www.eiriindia.org**

Sole Distributor :

INDIAN INSTITUTE OF CONSULTANTS, 4/27 ROOP NAGAR, DELHI -110007

PRINTED & PUBLISHED BY

ENGINEERS INDIA RESEARCH INSTITUTE

4449, Nai Sarak, Main Road, Delhi - 110006 (India)
Ph: 91-11-23918117, 23916431, 23840361
Fax: 91-11- 2391 6431, 2391 8117
* E-Mail: eirisidi@bol.net.in
*Website: www.eiriindia.org

DISTRIBUTED BY

*SMALL INDUSTRY RESEARCH INSTITUTE
*INDIAN INSTITUTE OF CONSULTANTS

ISBN: 81-86732-81-0

Printed in New Delhi (INDIA)

Rs. 950

Printed & Published by Sudhir Gupta for "Engineers India Research Institute" 4499 Nai Sarak, Main Road, New Delhi -110006

Preface

Since Ancient times women have been using flowers and herbs to enhance their beauty and the science of herbal cosmetics is as old as our history. A herbal cosmetics is a herb-based preparation intended to beautify and improve complexion, skin and hair by its external application. Nature has given us a wide variety of herbs which are of immense value as far as the nourishment of human body is concerned. The herbal cosmetics made after years of analysis of tropical conditions, body mechanisms and pollution effects are unique blends of several natural ingredients.

A finished cosmetic is not likely to preserve all its properties for ever. On ageing changes may occur in it. With this thing in mind, Bureau of Indian Standards have specified in case of certain cosmetics that words, "*Best use before.......*" should appear on the lable of cosmetics preceding the month and the year by which cosmetic is likely to preserve all its properties. To determine this date, a cosmetic chemist is required to carry out stability studies.

The book **Profitable Small Scale Manufacture of Cosmetics** covers almost all the basic and advanced details to setup own Cosmetic industry/Unit. The new edition of the book is covering latest technology including: *Drugs and Cosmetics Acts and Rules, Most Commonly Used Cosmetics Raw Materials, Hair Structure and Its Chemistry, Hair Shampoos, Hair Tonics and Conditioners, Hair Wave-Sets, Lacquers and Rinses, Hair-Grooming Preparations, Permanent Hair Waving Preparations and Hair Straighteners, Hair Bleachers and Hair Colourants, Depilatories, Shaving Soaps and Creams, Skin Creams and Lotions, Suntan and Anti-Sunburn Preparations, Skin Bleach Creams, Astringents and Skin Tonics, Antiperspirants and Deodorants, Face Powders* *and Other Coloured Make-up Preparations, Body Powders (Talcum Powders), Face Packs and Masks, Nail Lacquers and Removers, Toothpastes, Tooth Powders, Mouthwashes, Hair Oils & Hair Lotions, Preservation of Cosmetics, Plant and Equipment for Herbal Cosmetics Manufacture, Packaging of Herbal Cosmetics, Miscellaneous Formulae, Indigenious Materials & Technologies for Herbal Cosmetics, Present Manufacturing of Cosmetics Products, Suppliers of Plant and Equipments, Cosmetics Consultants, Raw Material and Chemical Manufacturers/ Suppliers, Manufacturers/Raw Materials Suppliers of Herbs/Plants and their Extracts.*

The book has been compiled for the benefit and to prove an asset and a handy reference guide in the hands of new entrepreneurs and well established industrialists.

Director

ENGINEERS INDIA RESEARCH INSTITUTE

Nai Sarak, New Delhi (INDIA)

E-Mail: eirisidi@bol.net.in

Contents-cum-Index

1

Drugs and Cosmetics Acts and Rules

At present there are several acts relating to manufacture and sale of drugs and cosmetics in India. There are also rules framed under the provisions of these laws which govern the production and sale.

The following are some of the laws operate at present in the country:

(i) The Drugs and Cosmetics Act of 1940 as amended by the Drugs (Amendment) Act, 1955 the Drugs (Amendment) Act, 1960, the Drugs (Amendment) Act, 1962, the Drugs and Cosmetics (Amendment) Act, 1964, the Drugs and Cosmetics (Amendment) Act, 1972, the Drugs and Cosmetics (Amendment) Act, 1982, and Drugs and Cosmetics Acts 1986.

(ii) The Drugs and Cosmetics Rules of 1945.

(iii) The Drugs and Cosmetics (Amendment) Act of 1964.

(iv) The Drugs and Cosmetics (Amendment) Act of 1972.

(v) The Drugs and Cosmetics (Amendment) Act of 1982.

(vi) The Drugs and Cosmetics (Amendment) Act of 1982.

(vi) The Drugs and Cosmetics (Amendment) Act of 1986.

A summary of above mentioned acts and rules is given as under covering important points:

THE DRUGS AND COSMETICS ACT OF 1940

The object of, the Act is to regulate the import, manufacture, distribution and sale of drugs.

Under the provisions of this Act the Central Government appoints the Drugs Technical Advisory Board to advice the Central Government and the State Governments on technical matters arising out of the administration of this Act. The Board Can constitute subcommittees for the consideration of a particular matter.

The Central Government has also to establish a Central Drugs Laboratory under the, control of a Director to carry out the functions entrusted to it by this Act.

The Central Government may also constitute the Drug Consultative Committee to advise the Central Government, the State Governments and the Drug Technical Advisory Board or any matter tending to secure uniformity throughout India in administration of this Act.

THE DRUGS AND COSMETICS ACT PROHIBITS IMPORT OF

(a) any drug (or Cosmetic) which is not of standard quality; (b) any misbranded drug (or misbranded or spurious cosmetic); (c) any adulterated or spurious drug; (d) any drug (or cosmetic) for the import of which a licence is prescribed; (e) any patent drug if it is not labelled in prescribed manner displaying its true formula; (f) any drug which claims to cure and mitigate disease prescribed (g) any cosmetic containing unsafe or harmful ingredient; and (h) any-drug the import of which is banned under the Act.

For contravening above mentioned provisions of the Act the prescribed punishment varies from six months R.I. and fine upto Rs. 5,000 or three years R.I. and fine upto Rs. 5000. Those convicted a second time have been prescribed punishment varying from one year R.I. to five years R.I. and fine tip to Rs. 10,000.

The Drugs and Cosmetics Act further prohibits manufacture for sale or for distribution or sale, or stock or exhibit or offer for sale; (i) any drug which is not of standard quality or is misbranded, adulterated or spurious, (ii) any cosmetic which is not of standard quality or is misbranded or spurious, (iii) any patent drug which does not bear on the label true 'Crmula or list of active ingredients together with quantities; (iv) any drug which claim to Cure and mitigate prescribed diseases; (v) any cosmetic containing any ingredient making if unsafe for use (vi) any drug the manufacture of which is prohibited under the Act; and (vii) any drug the manufacture of which is prohibited under the Act; and (viii) any drug or cosmetic manufactured in contravention of any of the provisions of the Act or rules made thereunder.

For any contravention of above mentioned provisions of the Act the punishments prescribed vary from one year R.I. and fine to life imprisonment and with fine depending on the nature of the offence.

The Central Government has been given powers to ban import and manufacture for sale or sale distribution of such drugs which are therapeutically irrational or which involve risk to human beings or animals.

It shall be no defence to plead merely that the accused was ignorant or the nature, substance or quality of the drug in respect of *whkii* the offence has been committed or of the circumstances of its manufacture or import

The Central Government and the State Governments can appoint Analysis with prescribed qualifications for specified drugs. The government may also appoint Inspectors who possess the requisite qualifications. The Inspectors can inspect any premises wherein any drugs is being manufactured and take sample for which he will pay fair price. He can also enter and search at all reasonable times any place where he believes any offence is being committed and seize stocks of drugs. Obstruction to the work of an inspector is punishable with imprisonment upto 3 years or fine.

The inspector on suspecting the Quality of drug Will get it tested by the Government Analyst who will deliver his report which will be taken as conclusive evidence in a court. If challenged by the accused the drug will be sent to the Central Drugs Laboratory whose decision will be binding on both parties.

Any person who purchases a drug can get it analysed on payment of the prescribed fee by the Government Analyst and receive a report of such test or analysis.

The report of the Government Analyst or the Central Drugs Laboratory should not be used as an advertisement of a Drug. Anyone doing so can be punished with a fine upto@-Rs. 500.

When a person has been convicted under the provisions of the Drugs and Cosmetics Act the stock of the drugs in respect of which the contravention has been made shall be liable to confiscation.

Section 34 of the Drugs Act lays down that where an offence has been committed by a company every person who at the time of the offence held charge and was responsible to the company shall be deemed guilty. To be exonerated, the person shall have to prove that the offence was committed without his knowledge or that he exercised all due diligence to prevent its commission.

THE DRUGS AND COSMETICS RULE OF 1945

In exercise of the powers conferred by the Drugs and Cosmetics Act the Central Government has made a number of Rules for the manufacture, sale and distribution of drugs in India. With the promulgation of these Rules, the Rules made by several States in India were repealed. Most of these Rules lay down the procedures and details of the enforcement of the provisions of the Act. There are prescribed forms of which different applications are to be presented or reports made for different purposes. Also there are schedules framed under different Rules.

Brief summary and the purpose of the schedules is given here:

Schedule A gives specimens of prescribed forms.

Schedule B states fees for test or analysis by the Central Drugs Laboratory or the Government Analyst. Schedule C and CI deals with biological and special products.

Schedule D is devoted to exemption regarding import of drugs.

Schedule EI gives a list of poisonous substances under Ayurvedic, Siddha and Unani Systems of medicine.

Schedule F and F(a) give details of the standards of bacterial vaccines made from any micro-organism pathogenic to man or other animals and also the vaccines made from other microorganisms which have any antigenic value.

Schedule FF gives details of the standards for ophthalmic preparations.

Schedule F(11) gives details of standards for surgical dressings, and bandage cloth. Schedule F (III) gives standards for umbilical tapes.

Schedule G details of drugs to be Labelled with words 'Caution-it is dangerous to take this preparation except under medical supervision'.

Schedule H deals with drugs and medicines which must be sold by retail only when a prescription by registered medical practitioner is produced.

Schedule J gives the list of ailments for which no drug should claim prevention or cure.

Schedule K lays down the condition under which certain cases are exempted from the provisions of Chapter IV of the Drugs Act.

Schedule M deals with Good Manufacturing practices and requirements of premises, plant and equipment. Part I deals with good manufacturing practices and factory premises. Part II deals with plant and equipment.

Schedule MI prescribes in detail requirements of factory premises for the manufacture of Homoeapathic drugs.

Schedule N deals with the minimum equipment of a pharmacy and gives directions regarding: (a) entrance of pharmacy, (b) premises, (c) furniture and apparatus, and (d) general provisions.

Schedule O deals with the provisions applicable to Back Disinfectant Fluids.

Schedule P deals with the life period of drugs including combinations with other drug. It gives periods in months for which the drug is expected to retain is Potency under the conditions of storage notified by the licensing authority.

Schedule Q gives the list of Coal Tar Colours permitted to be in cosmetics.

Schedule R describes the Standards for mechanical contraceptives.

Schedule T lays down the requirements of factory premises and hygienic conditions for Ayurvedic and Unani drugs.

Schedule U and UI give the particulars to be shown in manufacturing records.

Schedule V gives details of Standards for patent and proprietary medicines.

Schedule W gives the names of the drugs which shall be marketed under generic names only.

Schedule X gives the names of Psycbotropic drugs requiring special licences for manufacture and sale.

Schedule Y specifies requirements and guidelines on clinical trails, import and manufacture of new drugs.

THE MAIN DRUG RULES FRAMED BY THE UNION GOVERNMENT ARE AS FOLLOWS:

It shall be the function of the Central Drugs Laboratory to analyse or test such samples of Drugs as may be sent to it and report on payment of the prescribed fee.

An import licence shall be required for the import of any biological or other product specified in schedule C or CI.

Licence will be granted to such Persons who have proper storage place for drugs to be imported. There are other conditions attached to the licence such as licence shall allow an inspector to enter, with or without notice, premises where imported drugs ai-e stored, the licensee shall furnish samples of the drugs to the authorities, shall maintain a record of sales, shall not offer the drugs for sale if directed etc. The licence remains ordinarily in force for one to two years, depending on the date when it is granted, but can be suspended or cancelled by the Authority *if* the licensee fails to abide by requirements of the law.

No drug, the manufacture, sale or distribution of which is prohibited in the country of origin, shall be imported. No Biological or other special product shall be imported unless it complies with the standard or strength, quality or purity specified in Schedule F. Prohibited drugs can be imported only for the purpose of test and analysis. Under certain conditions new drugs can be allowed to be imported for personal use.

The Drug Rules lay down in detail the qualifications, functions, Powers and responsibilities of the Governor Analyst and Drugs Inspector.

One part of the rules is devoted to the sale of drugs describing how the licensing authority will grant licence on what conditions and payment of what fee. Licences are granted to sell stock or exhibit for sale or distribute drugs specified in Schedule C and CI by retail; on restricted licence or by wholesale. Licences are also granted to sell, stock or distribute drugs other than those specified in Schedule C and CI. Restricted licenses are granted to dealers in respect to drugs whose sale does require the supervision of a qualified person or in exceptional cases to itinerant vendors or travelling agents of a firm. Licences to sell drugs shall be, unless sooner suspended or cancelled valid upto 31st December of the year follow 'c' the year in which it is granted or renewed.

Application for grant of licence for sale of schedule 'X' drug is to be made in form 19-C. Wholesale licence for Schedule 'X' drugs is granted on form 20-G and for retail sale on Form 20-F.

If a licence is granted certain conditions have to be satisfied, notable among these being adequate premises equipped with proper storage space for preserving the properties of drugs and competent person in charge to supervise and control the sale, distribution and preservation of drugs. Other important conditions are that the supply of any drug on a Prescription shall be recorded and a register specially maintained for this purpose giving serial number of supply, name and address of prescriber, name of the patient, name of the drug, name of the manufacturer, if the drug is specified in Schedule C and the signature of the qualified person whose supervision the medicine was made up and supplied. Such records shall be maintained in case of supply of drugs, specified in Schedule C as well as purchases and sales by way of wholesale dealing of drugs in Schedule C. These records shall be preserved for three years from the date of the sale of the drug.

A drug specified in Schedule H should not be dispensed more than once unless the prescriber has given definite directions to do so.

The licensee should maintain an inspection book to enable an Inspector to record his impressions and the defects noticed by him.

If the licences fails to comply with any of the conditions of the licence or with any provision of the Act or Rules the licence is liable to be suspended to cancelled.

For manufacture of drugs, licences can be granted either for the manufacture of drugs specified in Schedule C and Cl of the Drugs Rules or for the manufacture of drugs not specified in these Schedules. In case of repacking of drugs for sale application is to be made in Form 24-B and in any other cases in Form 24-1 if an applicant does not have his own arrangements for manufacture but intends to avail himself of the manufacturing facilities owned by licence, he can apply for a loan licence in Form 24-A. This system of loan licensing is proposed to be abolished.

The conditions for the grant of manufacturing licence are that the manufacture is conducted under the active direction and personal supervision of a competent technical staff consisting of at least one person who is a whole time employee and who is either a graduate in Pharmacy or Pharmaceutical Chemistry, or a graduate in Science or a graduate in Chemical Engineering. The factory premises shall comply with the conditions prescribed in Schedule M. The applicant shall provide and maintain adequate staff, adequate premises and adequate laboratory equipment for carrying out tests.

The manufacturing unit and the testing unit should be separate under independent persons. There should be adequate arrangements for the storage of the manufactured drugs.

A licence in Form 25 shall remain valid up to 31st December of the year following the year in which it is granted or renewed unless sooner suspended or cancelled.

Those applying for manufacture of drugs for sale specified in the Schedule C and Cl shall submit their application in form 27 in this case also loan licences are granted (when) applied for in Form 27-A. Applications for the grant of licence to manufacture Schedule 'X' drugs have to be made on 24-F in case of drugs other than Schedule C, Cl but specified in Schedule 'X' on 27-B for those specified in Schedule C, Cl and 'X'. The conditions for obtaining these licences are those mentioned above in case of licence for manufacturing of drugs for sale other than those specified in Schedule C and Cl. Besides, the licensee shall have to keep the records of the details of manufacture of each batch of the substance which issued for sale and of the application of the tests in such form as to be available for inspection. The licensee shall allow any authorised inspector to enter with or without prior notice any premises, where the manufacture is carried on and inspect the plant and the process of manufacture or to examine all registers and records maintained under these Rules. The licensee shall notify changes in expert staff, supply samples of drugs, shall not sell any batch of drugs or will withdraw any batch of drugs from sale when called upon to do so. The licensee shall maintain an inspection book to enable the inspector to record his inspection and the defects noticed.

Before a licence is granted the Licensing Authority shall cause the establishment to be inspected in order to Check that all the prescribed conditions are met with.

If the licensee fails to comply with any of the conditions the Licensing Authority may cancel the licence after it was granted.

The license valid for one year can be granted to persons who want to manufacture drugs merely for examination, test or analysis but such drugs cannot be sold and the Inspector can inspect the premises to find that the drugs are manufactured only for the purpose mentioned. The licensee shall not only allow the inspector to enter the premises but also maintain register record of the manufacture and comply with requirements of the law.

LABELLING OF DRUGS

No drug can, be sold or distributed unless it is labelled in accordance with prescribed rules. Generally, the container of a drug should be labelled with (a) name of the drug (b) name and address of the manufacturer (c) batch or lot number, and (d) date of manufacture and expiry, the latter if required.

In case of the medicine made up ready for use, the label should give name and address of the licensee by whom it is supplied. If it is for external application it shall be labelled with the word, "Poison" and with the word "For external use only".

Further if the medicine contains a substance specified in Schedule G, it be labelled with the word "Caution". "It is dangerous to take this preparation except under medical supervision". If it contains a substance specified in Schedule H, it shall be labelled with the word "Schedule H drug and a warning" To be sold by retail on the prescription of a registered medical practitioner only.

The labels of Schedule H, Schedule X and Narcotic (Schedule H) drugs should bear symbols Rx, XRx and NRX respectively.

In the case of preparations included in the British Pharmacopoeia or the British Pharmaceutical Codex, the letters "B.P." or "B.P.C." respectively should be put on.

The letter "I.P.," "B.P." "B.P.C." and "U.S.P." shall be entered on the label of a drug only for the purpose of indicating that the drug is in accordance with the standard set out in the Indian Pharmacopoeia, the British Pharmacopoeia, the British Pharmaceutical Codex or the United States Pharmacopoeia as the case may be.

The label of the container of any preparation containing not less than 3 per cent of volume of alcohol shall include a statement to this effect. Non-Sterile surgical ligature or suture should be-declared on the label as such in indelible red ink. The lable of a patent or proprietary medicine should carry the name and address of the manufacturer and the true formula or list of ingredients. No drug should claim to prevent or cure any of the diseases specified in Schedule J. No drug should claim to procure or convey any idea that it may procure miscarriage in women.

BIOLOGICAL OR OTHER SPECIAL PRODUCTS

If any substance specified in Schedule C is advertised or sold as a proprietary medicine the proper name of substance shall appear on the label of every vial, ampoule or other container. On the label of any substances specified in Schedule C should be given (a) the proper name of the substance (b) the number; of licence under which it is manufactured, a distinctive batch number, statement of the potency unit and the date up to which the substance is expected to retain potency. No person shall sell, exhibit for sale any substance alter, obliterate or deface the inscription of mark recorded on the container, label or wrapper of manufactured drug.

STANDARDS

Every substance specified in Schedule C and C, intended for sale shall conform with the standard of strength, quality and purity specified in Schedule F and F. The test required for determining the strength and quality of each of the substances shall be those set out in Schedule F and F.

For the purpose of the Drugs and Cosmetics Act the Indian Pharmacopoeia, the Pharmacopoeia of the United Stated, the National formulary of the United States, the International Pharmacopoeia and the State Pharmacopoeia of the Soviet Socialist Republic shall be deemed to be prescribed pharmacopoeias. For the drugs for which no standard of identity, purity and strength are specified in latest edition of Pharmacopoeia but are specified in the earlier editions or in the British Pharmaceutical Codex the standards should be those given in the British Pharmacopoeia or British Pharmaceutical Codex as the case may be.

THE DRUGS AND COSMETICS (AMENDMENT) ACT OF 1964

An amendment of the Drugs and Cosmetics Act, 1940 was passed by the Indian Parliament in 1964. The object of the amendment was two-fold. First, to bring Ayurvedic and Unani drugs which were till then not covered by the law, within the scope of the Act. Secondly, to prohibit the import, manufacture, sale etc., of adulterated, misbranded, spurious or sub-standard drugs.

Under the provisions of the amendment a drug shall be deemed to be adulterated if it consists, in white, or in part filthy putrid or decomposed substances, or if it has been prepared, packed or stored under insanitary conditions, if its container is composed of any poisonous or deleterious substances, if any substance is mixed or packed therewith so as to reduce its quality or strength.

The punishment for contravening the provisions of the law has been enhanced. Any one convicted second time of an offence under clause (a) of section 27 will be imprisoned for not less than two years. It may extend to ten years and he will also be liable to fine. In clause (b) of the same section for the words "five years" the words "ten years" have been substituted.

Furthermore, it has been provided under this act that any implements or machinery used in the manufacture of adulterated drugs and any receptacles, packages or coverings in which such drug is contained and the animals, vehicles, vessels or other conveyances used in carrying such drug shall also be liable for confiscation.

THE DRUGS AND COSMETICS (AMENDMENT) ACT OF 1972

The Drugs and Cosmetics Act was amended in 1972 and thereby it was extended to the state of Jammu and Kashmir.

THE DRUGS AND COSMETICS (AMENDMENT) ACT OF 1982

The Drugs and Cosmetics (Amendment) Act 1982 received the assent of the President in November, 1982. It came into force with effect from 1st February 1983. The main amendment made are:

(i) The definition of the term 'drug' has been enlarged. Preparations used for repelling insects like mosquitoes, all substances intended for use as components of drugs including empty gelatin capsules and devices used in diagnosis, treatment etc. of diseases (to be notified) are drugs.

(ii) Toilet soaps are cosmetics and required to be manufactured under licence.

(iii) Definitions of misbranded, adulterated drugs have been rationalised. A new term spurious Ayurvedic, Siddha or Unani drug has been provided for the first time. Similar misbranded and spurious cosmetics and, misbranded and adulterated Ayurvedic, Siddha drugs have been defined.

(iv) The Central Government has now acquired powers to ban, by notification, import and manufacture of such drugs which involve risk to human beings or animals or are therapeutically unsound.

(v) Punishments for various contraventions of the provisions of the Act have been rationalised. For a drug, which is adulterated and is likely to cause death or grievous hurt, imprisonment of not less than 5 years which may extend to a term of life has been provided.

For Adulterated and *spurious drugs the punishments are upto three and five years respectively.*

(vi) Powers of Inspectors have been enhanced. They can now stop and search any vehicle or vessel or any other conveyance.

(vii) Provision has been made for summary trial of offences under this Act.

(viii) Central Government can constitute an Advisory Committee to be called the Ayurvedic, Siddha and Unani Drugs Consultative Committee.

THE DRUGS AND COSMETICS (AMENDMENT) ACT OF 1986

Sections 26 and 32 have been amended and this empowers any person or a consumer association to take samples of drugs for test/analysis and they can also prosecute firms for manufacture/sale of substandard drugs.

MANUFACTURE, SALE AND DISTRIBUTION OF [DRUGS AND COSMETICS]

Standards of quality

(1) For the purposes of this Chapter, the expression "standard quality" means—

(a) in relation to a drug, that the drug complies with the standard set out in [the Second Schedule], and

(b) in relation to a cosmetic, that the cosmetic complies with such standard as may be prescribed.]

(2) The [Central Government], after consultation with the Board and after giving by notification in the Official Gazette not less than three months' notice of its intention so to do, may be a like notification add to or otherwise amend [the Second Schedule] for the purposes of this Chapter, and thereupon [the Second Schedule] shall be deemed to be amended accordingly.

Comments

The standards of qualities are fixed by the Government after due deliberation and after consulting a committee of competent men, it is for them to give due allowance for probable errors before fixing a standard. When a standard has been fixed it has to be observed strictly; *State of Kerala* v. *Vasudevan Nair,* 1974 KLT 617 (FB): 1975 Cri LJ 97.

Misbranded drugs

For the purposes of this Chapter, a drug shall be deemed to be misbranded,—

(a) if it is so coloured, coated, powdered or polished that damage is concealed or if it is made to appear of better or greater therapeutic value than it really is; or

(b) if it is not labelled in the prescribed manner; or

(c) if its label or container or anything accompanying the drug bears any statement, design or device which makes any false claim for the drug or which is false or misleading in any particular.

Adulterated drugs

For the purposes of this Chapter, a drug shall be deemed to be adulterated,—

(a) if it consists in whole or in part, of any filthy, putrid or decomposed substance; or

(b) if it has been prepared, packed or stored under insanitary conditions whereby it may have been contaminated with filth or whereby it may have been rendered injurious to health; or

(c) if its container is composed, in whole or in part, of any poisonous or deleterious substance which may render the contents injurious to health; or

(d) if it bears or contains, for purposes of colouring only, a colour other than one which is prescribed; or

(e) if it contains any harmful or toxic substance which may render it injurious to health; or

(f) if any substance has been mixed therewith so as to reduce its quality or strength.

Spurious drugs

For the purposes of this Chapter, a drug shall be deemed to be spurious,—

(a) if it is manufactured under a name which belongs to another drug; or

(b) if it is an imitation of, or is a substitute for, another drug or resembles another drug in a manner likely to deceive or bears upon it or upon its label or container the name of another drug unless it is plainly and conspicuously marked so as to reveal its true character and its lack of identity with such other drug; or

(c) if the label or container bears the name of an individual or company purporting to be the manufacturer of the drug, which individual or company is fictitious or does not exist; or

(d) if it has been substituted wholly or in part by another drug or substance; or

(e) if it purports to be the product of a manufacturer of whom it is not truly a product.

Misbranded cosmetics

For the purposes of this Chapter, a cosmetic shall be deemed to be misbranded,—

(a) if it contains a colour which is not prescribed; or

(b) if it is not labelled in the prescribed manner; or

(c) If the label or container or anything accompanying the cosmetic bears any statement which is false or misleading in any particular.

Spurious cosmetics

For the purposes of this Chapter, a cosmetic shall be deemed to be spurious,—

(a) if it is manufactured under a name which belongs to another cosmetic; or

(b) if it is an imitation of, or a substitute for, another cosmetic or resembles another cosmetic in a manner likely to deceive or bears upon it or upon its lable or container the name of another cosmetic unless it is plainly and conspicuously marked so as to reveal its true character and its lack of identity with such other cosmetic; or

(c) if the label or container bears the name of an individual or a company purporting to be the manufacturer of the cosmetic which individual or company is fictitious or does not exist; or

(d) if it purports to be the product of a manufacturer of whom it is not truly a product.]

Prohibition to manufacture and sale of certain drugs and cosmetics

From such date as may be fixed by the State Government by notification in the Official Gazette in this behalf, no person shall himself or by any other person on his behalf—

(a) [manufacture for sale or for distribution, or sell, or stock or exhibit or offer for sale,] or distribute—

(i) any drug which is not of a standard quality, or is misbranded, adulterated or spurious;

(ii) any cosmetic which is not of a standard quality or is misbranded or spurious;]

(iii) any patent or proprietary medicine, unless there is displayed in the prescribed manner on the label or container thereof [the true formula or list of active ingredients contained in it together with the quantities, thereof];]

(iv) any drug which by means of any statement design or device accompanying it or by any other means, purports or claims [to prevent, cure or mitigate] any such disease or ailment, or to have any such other effect as may be prescribed;

(v) any cosmetic containing any ingredient which may render it unsafe or harmful for use under the directions indicated or recommended;

(vi) any drug or cosmetic in contravention of any of the provisions of this Chapter or any rule made thereunder;

(b) sell or stock or exhibit or offer for sale, or distribute any drug or cosmetic which has been imported or manufactured in contravention of any of the provisions of this Act or any rule made thereunder,

(c) manufacture for sale or for distribution, or sell, or stock or exhibit or offer for sale,] or distribute any drug [or cosmetic, except under, and in accordance with the conditions of, a licence issued for such purpose under this Chapter:

Provided that nothing in this section shall apply to the manufacture, subject to prescribed conditions, of small quantities of any drug for the purpose of examination, test or analysis:

Provided further that the [Central Government] may, after consultation with the Board, by notification in the Official Gazette, permit, subject to any conditions specified in the notification, the [manufacture for sale or for distribution, sale, stocking or exhibiting or offering for sale] or distribution of any drug or class of drugs not being of standard quality.

Comments

(i) The practitioners of the Indian system of medicate that is Ayurvedic (including Siddha) or Unani are not entitled to keep allopathic drugs for administering to the patients; *Swaran Singh* v. *State of Punjab,* AIR 1987 Punjab 81.

(ii) The section casts a vicarious liability. But the relationship between the two persons should be regular or viable than casual; *State (Delhi Admn.)* v. *I.K. Nangia,* AIR 1979 SC 1977.

(iii) The expression "himself or by any other person on his behalf" must imply that the person contemplated is the master or the principal and not the servant; *Bhagwandas* v. *State,* AIR 1962 Punj 419: (1962) 2 Cr LJ 400.

Disclosure of the name of the manufacturer, etc.

Every person, not being the manufacturer of a drug or cosmetic or his agent for the distribution thereof, shall, if so required, disclose to the Inspector the name, address and other particulars of the person from whom he acquired the drug or cosmetic.]

Comments

On a reading of section 18A and sub-section (4) of section 23 together, it is clear that out of the four portions into which the sample has been divided one portion should be sent to the person, if any, whose name and address and other particulars have been disclosed under section 18A; *In re: R. Dayalan,* 1978 Cri LJ 1852: (1979) 1 FAC 29.

Maintenance of records and furnishing of information

Every person holding a licence under clause (c) of section 18 shall keep and maintain such records, registers and other documents as may be prescribed and shall furnish to any officer or authority exercising any power or discharging any function under this Act such information as is required by such officer or authority for carrying out the purposes of this Act.]

Pleas

(1) Save as hereinafter provided in this section, it shall be no defence in a prosecution under this Chapter to prove merely that the accused was ignorant of the nature, substance or quality of the drug [or cosmetic] in respect of which the offence has been committed or of the circumstances of its manufacture or import, or that a purchaser, having bought only for the purpose of test or analysis, has not been predicated by the sale.

(2) For the purposes of section 18a drug shall not be deemed to be misbranded or [adulterated or spurious] or to be below standard quality nor shall a cosmetic be deemed to be misbranded or to be below standard quality only by reason of the fact that—

(a) there has been added thereto some innocuous substance or ingredient because the same is required for the manufacture or preparation of the drug [or cosmetic] as an article of commerce in a state fit for carriage or consumption, and not to increase the bulk, weight or measure of the drug [or cosmetic] or to conceal its inferior quality or other defects; or

(b) in the process of manufacture, preparation or conveyance some extraneous substance has unavoidably become intermixed with it; provided that this clause shall not apply in relation to any sale or distribution of the drug [or cosmetic] occurring after the vendor or distributor became aware of such intermixture.

(3) A person, not being the manufacturer of a drug or cosmetic or his agent for the distribution thereof, shall not be liable for a contravention of section 18 if he proves—

(a) that he acquired the drug or cosmetic from a duly licensed manufacturer, distributor or dealer thereof;

(b) that he did not know and could not, with reasonable diligence, have ascertained that the drug or cosmetic in any way contravened the provisions of that section; and

(c) that the drug or cosmetic, while in his possession was properly stored and remained in the same state as when he acquired it.]

Comments

All that the prosecution is required to prove in order to establish the contravention of section 18 is the fact that the accused had sold or exhibited for sale the drug which was not of standard quality or which was a misbranded drug. If the accused want to get rid of the effect of the prosecution evidence then it is for them to establish the defences which are available to them under sub-section (3) of section 19 of the Act; *Public Prosecutor* v. *Hatambhai*, AIR 1969 AP 99.

Government Analysts

(1) The State Government may, by notification in the official Gazette, appoint such persons as it thinks fit, having the prescribed qualifications, to be Government Analysts for such areas in the State and in respect of such drugs or [classes of drugs or such cosmetics or classes of cosmetics] as may be specified in the notification.

(2) The Central Government may also, by notification in the Official Gazette, appoint such persons as it thinks fit, having the prescribed qualifications, to be Government Analysts in respect of such drugs or [classes of drugs or such cosmetics or classes of cosmetics] as may be specified in the notification.

(3) Notwithstanding anything contained in sub-section (1) or sub-section (2), neither the Central Government nor a State Government shall appoint as a Government Analyst any official not serving under it without the previous consent of the Government under which he is serving.

(4) No person who has any financial interest in the import, manufacture or sale of drugs or cosmetics shall be appointed to be a Government Analyst under sub-section (1) or sub-section (2) of this section.

2

Most Commonly Used Cosmetics Raw Materials

Such a large number of materials are used in the manufacture of cosmetics that covering all types of materials will be difficult in one chapter. Therefore, only those materials will be covered under this chapter which are used in several types of cosmetics. Some of the most commonly used materials include water, preservatives, antioxidants, humectants, surface active agents, oils and waxes, colours, and perfumes. These have been covered in proceeding paragraphs.

WATER

One of the most widely used raw materials in the manufacture of cosmetics is water. Since the water is available cheap and in abundance, not much importance is given to this material. It is also thought that it is an innocuous material. But it is not so. Water is an extremely reactive substance. But surprisingly, physiologically, it is innocuous This is demonstrated by the fact that a dead material rottens in the presence of water while living material does not. Four types of reactions take place in biochemical processes, i.e., oxidation, reduction, condensation and hydrolysis. Water is an essential requisite of all living things. There can not be any life without water.

In cosmetics, water is used as solvent for many ingredients of cosmetics. The water which is available from water mains contains traces of contaminations. These contaminations are a cause of concern to a cosmetic chemist. Contaminants that may be present in water which reaches manufacturing plants will depend upon the purification process being carried out at the water works of municipal authorities. Water from urban areas contains inorganic traces like ammonia, phosphates, arsenates, borates, chromium, zinc, beryllium, cadmium , copper, cobalt, nickel, iron, manganese and organic contaminants like petrol, chlorinated solvents, surface active agents such as alkyl benzene sulphonic compounds. Water from rural areas contains inorganic ions like calcium, magnesium, sodium, potassium, bicarbonate, sulphate, chloride, silicates and organic substances such as humic and fulvic acids, amino acids, carbohydrates, proteins etc. With purification, the levels of these contaminants are brought to such limits as are not harmful to human begins and animals. Whatever may be the source of water, it is certain to contain micro-organisms (bacteria, viruses, moulds and yeasts).

At one time, the cosmetics were being manufactured with water from mains. But to meet the today's standards water from mains can not be used. Two types of contaminations in water should be looked into, if it is to be used in the manufacture of cosmetics. Of these, the first is inorganic ions. A number of cosmetics are emulsions. Presence of inorganic ions such as magnesium and zinc can interfere with balance of static charges responsible for proper functioning of some surfactants and can bring about separation of emulsions. In colognes, traces of calcium, magnesium, iron and aluminium present in water can lead to formation of insoluble residues. If present, phenolic organic compounds such as antioxidants can be the cause of discolouration in the presence of trace metals. The second type of contamination is presence of micro-organisms. If micro-organisms present in the water are introduced into cosmetics and are allowed to thrive, there would be development of foul odour, visible colonies of bacteria, moulds or fungi. The product will be spoiled with potential of harm to the consumer. Therefore, treatment of water from mains is necessary.

Purification of Water

Minerals from water can be removed with the help of ion-exchange systems, reverse osmosis or distillation. Of these the most commonly employed method is ion-exchange system.

Ion-exchange Systems

To remove all ions, two types of resins are used. One type of resin removes anions and the other type of resin removes cations. There are two columns, one column contains cation resins and the other column contains anion resins. Water from mains is first passed through one column and then through other column. Thus cations and anions are removed and water becomes free from inorganic ions. However, these resins have limited capacity to bind anions or cations as the case may be. Therefore, when their capacity is exhausted, inorganic ions are not removed and water passing through columns does not lose its inorganic ions and is passed through them as such. This can be detected by a conductivity meter as the conductivity is directly proportional to inorganic ions present in water. A conductivity meter is attached to these columns. Conductivity can be seen in this meter. When the conductivity is more than the recommended for water free from inorganic ions, inlet of water is stopped. Resins of these columns are regenerated with strong mineral acid and sodium hydroxide. After regeneration, the resins again become fit for de-mineralisation of water.

A number of manufacturers are manufacturing ion-exchange systems. For regeneration cycles, manufacturer's instructions should be followed.

De-ionised water on exposure to atmosphere absorbs carbon dioxide and forms carbonic acid. Therefore, pH of de-ionised water is acidic.

Distillation

In this process, water is heated and boiled which causes formation of steam. The steam thus produced is condensed and water again produced is collected. Inorganic materials being non-volatile remain in the still and condensed steam produces water free from minerals. Several types of water stills are available in the market. Equipment as well as operation of distillation plant is costly and distillation plant is seldom used by the cosmetics manufacturers. Distillation plants are more commonly used in pharmaceutical industry particularly by those units which manufacture sterile products.

Reverse Osmosis

In this process, feed water passes across and through membrane and is collected as purified water on the other side of the membrane. About 75 per cent of feed water is collected as purified water and 25% of it is continuously discarded as concentrate. In this process membrane does not play a passive role and its nature and structure is of great importance to the efficiency of the process. Several types of membranes are available. But the most commonly used membranes are anisotropic cellulose acetate and the hollow polyamide fibre. The latter, however, can be attacked by bacteria. A typical cellulose acetate membrane consists of relatively dense non-porous layer which is also called as 'active' layer (thickness about 1500-2000 Å) supported on highly porous substructure which is the bulk of the membrane. Membranes are made in the form of cylinders which can withstand pressures of 400-600 psi.

Though the reverse osmosis water purification equipments are costly, but these can be used for purification of water for cosmetics use.

Microbiological Purification

The above-mentioned three processes of purification remove minerals only. Since the water is purified at water works of municipal corporations, the type of bacteria that can thrive in tap water is limited to *Pseudomonas, Achromobacter* and *Alkaligenes* type. Other type of micro-organism if introduced in the water supply may survive chlorination and may adopt non-proliferating form until suitable substrates are available to them.

Ion-exchange resins are good breeding ground for micro-organisms particularly, if ion-exchange systems are not run every day.

It is because of these reasons that water should be treated to bring down the number of micro-organisms. Methods which can be employed to control micro-biological quality of water are given hereunder:

(a) Chemical Treatment

Ion-exchange resins and distribution systems can be treated with dilute solutions of formaldehyde or sodium hypochlorite. Ion-exchange beds should be exhausted with prolong contact with brine before treating them either of the two solutions. The usual practice is to leave the beds and distribution systems with 1% solution of either chemical. This treatment will greatly reduce the number of micro-organisms in water that is passed through ion-exchange systems. But this treatment will not take care of deionized water which is stored. Microbial count of stored water can be kept under control by dosing it with small amount of either formaldehyde or sodium hypochlorite. Usually the later is used. A concentration of 1 to 4 ppm of chlorine is sufficient to preserve deionised water. Levels of chlorine should be monitored in the stored water. It should not fall below 1 ppm.

(b) Heat Treatment

Heat Treatment to deionized water is often given in the process vessel itself in the cosmetic industry. An adequate quantity of water is transferred to the vessel and water is heated to boiling and is held at this temperature for at least 20 minutes. This treatment will destroy all water borne bacteria except spore forming.

However, if it is suspected that spore forming bacteria are present, the treatment should be repeated after two hours and for absolute safety a third time after two hours.

In an alternative method the water is heated to 120°C in thin film and then instantaneously cooled. This is an in-line device and is called as ultra high short term (UHST) treatment.

(c) UV Radiation

UV radiation (below 300 nm) are known to have lethal effect on micro-organisms. Since the radiation of this wavelength do not penetrate very far through water, water has to be brought very close to the source of radiation in thin film. Some manufacturers of ion-exchange system supply ion-exchange units having UV radiation system also. Efficiency of UV exposure to water goes down with the formation of slime as well as with deterioration of UV radiation source. UV radiation treatment is not completely effective-a few micro-organisms manage to escape even from most efficient UV radiation system.

(d) Filtration

Membrane filters of pore size 0.2 mμ or less are known to retain bacteria. Though these filters can effectively remove bacteria but have a number of drawbacks. The drawbacks are:

- because of high resistance to flow, running costs are very high;
- with the gradual built-up of micro-organisms in the filter matrix, the resistance to flow increases to a point where either the flow stops or some micro-organisms break through membrane;
- some micro-organisms like moulds are able to grow in filter matrix and literally go through the other side of the filter.

For this reason many people think that this method is not suitable for treating water for cosmetics.

If deionized and treated water is stored in a tank and distributed through distribution pipe to the points of use, the nature of materials used for construction of distribution system becomes important. The material may leach into water substances or water may react with material of construction itself. The ideal material for construction of distribution pipe work is stainless steel. But the cost of such work is high. Many distribution systems employ plastic pipe work particularly pipes fabricated from unplasticized poly vinyl chloride, poly propylene and acrylonitrile-butadiene-styrene. All these materials have the drawback that these cannot be sterilized with steam and also has potential of leaching of additives.

In this book, in the formulae in subsequent chapters, wherever, term water appears, it means deionized water which has been treated for microbial contamination.

PRESERVATIVES

Preservatives are used to prevent spoilage of cosmetic products. There are two main reasons for spoilage of cosmetics, i.e., oxidation of oils and fats and microbial growth. A cosmetic preparation may require addition of substances to prevent either of them or both of them.

Most of the cosmetics preparations are likely to deteriorate if preservatives have not been added. Water promotes growth of micro-organisms, therefore, all cosmetic preparations containing water as ne of the ingredients are susceptible to microbial growth. Microbes can attack even most anhydrous preparations like lipsticks. Cosmetic preparations containing oils and fats are susceptible to oxidative reactions also. In view of this, cosmetic preparations containing oils and fats must be preserved with antimicrobial agents and antioxidants. Both, antimicrobial agents and antioxidants will be dealt with in the following paragraphs.

Anti-Microbial Agents

Microbes (bacteria, fungi, yeasts) are widely distributed in the nature. Near the earth, there may be hardly any places where microbes are not present. Sources of microbial contamination are many and include raw materials, environment, equipment, packaging materials and personnel. As such, microbial contamination is inevitable. But steps should be taken to minimize microbial contamination. Microbes multiply by utilizing materials in their immediate surroundings. Microbes multiply very fast. During the multiplication of microbes, complex chemical reactions occur and a variety of metabolites are formed. If microbes are allowed to multiply in finished cosmetics, they will utilize cosmetic ingredients for their growth and metabolites produced will interfere with the ingredients present and thus the product will be spoiled. In a product not adequate preserved, moulds and fungi can be seen on the surface of the product as they grow macroscopically. Bacteria in liquid preparations may be visible and may be seen as turbidity and sedimentation. Colour changes may occur due to change in pH. Colour change may also be due to pigments produced by bacteria. Some bacteria cause formation of gas which may be seen as bubbles or froth in liquid preparations.

Pathogens (disease producing microbes) if present in cosmetics can cause infection and this is a serious consequence. It is imperative, therefore, to check the growth of microbes in cosmetics.

Surveys carried out by various workers revealed presence of a variety of micro-organisms in used and unused cosmetics. Used cosmetics were found contaminated with *staphylococci, diphtheroids, fungi and yeast.* In unused cosmetics, *pseudomonas* were most frequently present.

Many chemical compounds exhibit antimicrobial properties. A list of salient compounds which are used as preservatives in cosmetics and pharmaceutical preparations is given in Table 2.1. But the number of compounds that can be used in cosmetics as preservatives is quite limited. The reasons for this limitation are that they may impart an undesirable odour or colour or may be toxic, irritant or allergenic or they may be active only in a narrow pH range.

An ideal preservative must possess the following attributes:

* it should be compatible with the formulation.
* It should be soluble to such an extent that effective concentration is achieved.
* It should remain stable to provide sustained anti-microbial effect.
* It should be colourless and odourless or nearly so.
* It should be non-toxic, non-irritant or non-allergic in concentrations used.

The ideal preservative having all the requisite attributes is yet to be found. At the time of development of formulation a detailed study should be carried out regarding suitability of preservative.

There are several factors which affect effectiveness of preservatives. These factors will be discussed in brief.

(i) Dissociation and pH

Different types of cosmetics have different pH and different micro-organisms can grow at different pH. One type of micro-organisms can grow in acidic medium while other type may grow in alkaline pH. There are very many micro-organisms which can grow in neutral pH. An ideal preservative should be effective in wide range of pH. However, in practice, majority of preservatives are active in acidic range than in alkaline range. Preservatives which are active in both acidic and alkaline pH ranges have the disadvantage of being highly reactive in nature. For example, formaldehyde and formaldehyde releasing compounds. These compounds can react with other ingredients of formulation. There are many preservatives which are greatly influenced by pH. For example, weak acids. Activity of weak acids depend on their undissociated amount of acid which in turn depends on the dissociation constant and pH of the system. This can be illustrated by the fact that at pH 6, the quantity of benzoic acid will be about 60 times of the quantity of benzoic acid at pH 3. Methyl parabenzoic acid is approximately 50% dissociated at pH 8.5. Simon has demonstrated that effectiveness of weak acids is influenced in a regular manner by changes in pH.

Table 2.1: Preservatives which are used in Cosmetics and Pharmaceutical preparations

Organic Acids	Benzoic acid
	p-Hydroxy benzoic acid
	Dehydro acetic acid
	Formic acid
	p-Chloro benzoic acid
	o-Chloro benzoic acid
	Propionic acid
	Sorbic acid
	Salicylic acid
	Vanillic acid
Alcohols	Ethyl alcohol
	Isophropyl alcohol
	Phenylethyl alcohol
	Chlorbutanol
Aldehydes	Formaldehyde
	Cinnamic aldehyde
Phenolic Compounds	Cresol
	p-chloro-m-cresol
	p-chloro-m-xylenol
	Dichloro-m-xylenol
	Methyl Chloro thymol
	Phenol
	Bis-phenols (e.g., hexachlorophene)
	o-phenyl phenol
Esters	Methyl p-hydroxy benzoate
	Ethyl p-hydroxy benzoate
	Proppyl p-hydroxy benzoate
	Butyl p-hydroxy benzoate
	Benzyl p-hydroxy benzoate
Mercury Compounds	Thiomersol
	Nitromersol
	Phenyl mercuric salts e.g., acetate, nitrate, gluconate

Surface Active Agents	Benzathonium chloride
	Benzalkonium chloride
	Cetyltrimethyl ammonium bromide
	Cetyl pyridinium chloride
	Dimethyl di-iododecenyl-ammonium bromide
Miscellaneous Compounds	5-Bromo-5 nitro-1, 3-dioxan
	Vanillin
	Ethyl vanillin
	Tetramethyl thiuram-disulphide (TMTD)

On the other hand, there are preservatives which are active only in dissociated from. For example, cationics. Quaternary ammonium compounds are effective in higher pH (alkaline) but these become ineffective in lower pH (acidic).

Some preservatives may be pH dependent because of the stability problem. For example, 2-nitro-2-bromo-propanediol (Bronopol) start deteriorating at pH higher than 7.

(ii) Concentration

There are no set rules for the concentration that should be used. There are several factors which influence the effectiveness of preservatives. Some materials used in cosmetic formulations have antimicrobial action and, therefore, concentration of preservatives required may be very less. While there may be ingredients in cosmetics which promote growth of micro-organisms, for example, mucilages of natural gums. Concentration of preservatives, obviously will be more in such products. Recommended effective concentration range from as little as 0.001% (organic mercury compounds) to 0.5-1.0% (weak acids). Availability of preservatives to micro-organisms is more important than overall concentration of preservatives which may depend upon permeability across cell wall, diffusion rate, and degree of absorption and partition coefficient of the preservative depending on the mechanism of action.

Concentration of preservatives may be reduced if more than one preservative is used in combination.

Some commonly used preservatives and their recommended concentrations are given in Table 2.2

(iii) Susceptibility of organisms

Different antimicrobial agents have different activity against microbes. For example, hydroxy benzoates are active against moulds, fungi and yeasts but less active against bacteria. Chlorobutanol has antibacterial and anti-fungal activities. Phenyl mercuric nitrate is active against bacteria, fungi, moulds and yeasts.

Table 2.2: Names and usual strengths of commonly used anti-microbial agents

Name	concentration %
Benzoic acid	0.5
Esters of p-hydroxy benzoic acid	
Methyl, Ethyl, Propyl, Butyl, Benzyl	0.1
Salicylic acid	0.5
O-phenyl phenol	0.6
Chlorbutanol	0.5
Dehydroacetic acid	0.5
Formaldehyde	0.5
Phenyl mercuric	0.1
– acetae, – nitrate	0.002
5-Bromo-5-nitro-1, 3 dioxane	0.1
Bronopol	0.1
4-Isopropyl-m-cresol	0.1
4-Chloro-m-cresol	0.1
4-Chloro-3, 5-xylenol	0.1
Phenoxyethanol	0.5
Sorbic acid	1.0
Hexamethylene tetramine	0.2
Benzyl alcohol	0.1
Alkyl trimethyl ammonium bromide	1.0
Chlorphenesin	0.2
Benzalkonium chloride	0.25
Glutaraldehyde	0.1

(iv) Interference by Ingredients of Cosmetics

Several non-ionic surfactants such as Tween 80, Polyethylene glycol 1000 monocetyl ether, Polyethylene glycol 400 laureate interfere with activity of preservatives by exerting protective effect on micro-organisms.

Soaps and anionic surfactants in lower concentrations promote growth of Gram-negative bacteria. Hydrophilic polymers like polyethylene glycols, gum tragacanth, methyl cellulose, carboxymethyl cellulose and polyvinyl-pyrolidone have only marginal effect in reducing efficiency of majority of anti-microbials.

Addition of certain materials to the aqueous phase of emulsions help in minimizing adverse effect of non-ionic surfactants on preservatives. Materials like propylene glycol, glycerin and hexylene glycol have been found useful in this respect.

(v) Influence of Solid Particles

A number of cosmetics preparations contain insoluble solid particles. Salient of these are kaolin, chalk, zinc oxide, talc and pigments. Preservatives can be absorbed on the surface of solid particles. The extent of adsorption will depend on nature of solid particles and pH of the preparation. Preservatives can also interact with plastics. Phenolic and quaternary ammonium compounds have been reported to react with polyurethane.

Guidelines for Selecting Preservatives

It is not possible to lay down guidelines which preservative will suit every formulation. But the guidelines given below will give an idea about probable preservatives which could be used and thus saving time and money. The following steps will help in selecting preservative(s) for developing a cosmetic formulation. All the ingredients of a formulation should be checked for their likelihood of contamination.

* Identify the materials which could promote the microbial growth, e.g.
  - glycerin, sorbitol etc. (in concentration less than 5%);
  - soaps and anionic surfactants below 15%;
  - proteins;
  - carbohydrates;

- cellulose derivatives;–
- gums

* pH of aqueous phase should be found out as some preservatives are active in acidic pH and others are active in alkaline pH.
* It should be estimated whether preservative will be partitioned between two phases depending on formula of the preparation. If the preservative is likely to leave aqueous phase leaving insufficient quantity to be effective, see whether there is any material which is will reduce the partition coefficient (e.g., propylene glycol, hexylene glycol).
* The ratio of total to free preservative should be estimated in presence of macromolecules present in the formulation.
* The least toxic of the possible preservatives should be selected.

The Indian Standard IS 4707 (part 2): 1993 lays down two lists of preservatives; one of those which are allowed to be used and the other of those which are provisionally allowed to be used.

Anti-Oxidants

Cosmetic preparations containing fats and oils particularly those which have unsaturated linkage are susceptible to oxidative deterioration. Even a very small quantity of highly unsaturated ingredient is sufficient to start a typical oxidative deterioration.

The term, rancid, is used when the fats and/or oils contain sufficient amount of oxidation products which can be detected by organoleptic tests. Since the consumer applies cosmetics to body, any deterioration detectable by organoleptic tests (smell, touch, etc.) will be immediately known to him. Therefore, addition of antioxidants is most logical solution to the problem of rancidity of fats and oils in cosmetics. Although in fats and oils, natural antioxidants occur (usually tocopherols) but these are destroyed during the process of refining.

It will be worthwhile to deal in brief the factors affecting rancidity.

(i) Presence of Pro-oxidants

Some fats and oils may contain pro-oxidants or oxidizing enzymes, known as oxidases. As soon as, favourable conditions are available, the enzymes present will become active and will cause rancidity. Favourable conditions can be provided by presence of moisture, light and oxygen.

(ii) Oxygen

Unsaturated fats and oils react with atmospheric oxygen and small quantities of peroxides are formed. These peroxides attack glycerides of fats and oils. Decomposition products of randicity have autocatalytic effect. As such, deterioration, initially, is slow but later, the deterioration is fast. During the decomposition process, various chemical compounds are formed, e.g., alcohols, aldehydes, ketones, hydroxy acids, lactones etc.

(iii) Moisture

Moisture attacks glycerol esters producing fatty acids, short chain fatty acids, in particular. Moisture also acts accelerator to auto-oxidation. Besides these, moisture also provides favourable atmosphere for microbial growth.

(iv) Light

It cannot be said conclusively that which wavelengths of visible light have deleterious effect on cosmetics. It seems that light does not cause oxidative reaction itself but it acts as accelerator once the oxidative reaction starts.

(v) Heat

Heat generally accelerates reaction. The reaction that can be accelerated by heat in rancidity of fats and oils is hydrolysis of fatty acid constituents of cosmetics. Besides this, higher temperature also provides conducive conditions for growth of micro-organisms.

(vi) External Pro-oxidants

There are a number of external pro-oxidants. If these are incorporated in cosmetics these external pro-oxidants destroy naturally occurring pro-oxidants first then oxidants which have been added in cosmetic preparation. External pro-oxidants include metals and their alloys, peroxides, oxidized fats, unsaturated fatty substances and organic compounds like isosafrole, benzyl alcohol, benzaldehyde, acetophenone etc. Of the metals, copper is most effective catalytic agent. Other metals in decreasing activity order are iron, lead, zinc, tin and aluminium.

(vii) Micro-organisms

Many bacteria, moulds and yeast grow on fatty materials. As a consequence of their growth many fatty glycerides are split into glycerol and fatty acids. Moulds like penicillia, aspergilli attack fats with carbon atoms less than 14. These moulds produce ketones.

From the foregoing account it is very clear that cosmetics containing fats and oils must be preserved by adding antioxidants besides antimicrobial agents.

Classification of Antioxidants

A number of chemical compounds have antioxidant properties. The most commonly used antioxidants can be classified as follows:

(i) Phenolic Type

A number of phenolic compounds exhibit antioxidant property. A list of compounds which have been used as antioxidants is given below:

Gallic acid

Methyl gallate

Ethyl gallate

Amyl gallate

Beylated hydroxy anisole (BHA)

Butylated hydroxy toluene (BHT)

2, 5 Di-tert-Butyl hydroquinone

Nordihydro guaiaretic acid (NDGA)

Di-hydro phenols

Methyl p-hydroxy benzoate

Propyl p-hydroxy benzoate

Butyl p-hydorxy benzoate

Gallates is one of the most important class of antioxidants. Propyl gallate is usually used in food stuffs, but there is no bar to use propyl gallate in cosmetics. Besides propyl gallate, other gallates like methyl-, ethyl-, dodecyl-gallate, are used in cosmetics. Gallic acid, though is powerful antioxidant, but has the disadvantage of developing colour in presence of traces of iron.

Solubilities of propyl-octyl- and dodecyl gallate in ground nut oil, castor oil and mineral oil are given in the Table 2.3.

Table 2.3: Solubilities of gallates in some oils

	Propyl gallate %	Octyl gallate %	Dodecyl gallate %
Groundnut Oil	0.05	0.300	0.40
Castor Oil	22.00	18.000	21.00
Mineral Oil	0.50	0.005	0.01

A mixture of gallates or gallates in combination with other antioxidants such as BHA can be used. Propyl gallate in concentration of 0.01% to 0.1% is superior to many oxidants.

Butylated hydroxy toluene (BHT) and butylated hydroxyanisole (BHA) are useful antioxidants. BHT is used for fatty acids and oils. It has advantage over other phenolic compounds such as freedom from phenolic smell, stability towards heating and low toxicity. In cosmetics, it should be used in concentration of 0.01% to 0.1% preferably with a sequestering agent like citric acid or EDTA. BHA, generally is not used alone. It forms synergistic useful mixtures with gallates. A mixture that can be successfully used in cosmetics is:

BHA	20.0
Propyl gallate	6.0
Citric acid	4.0
Propylene glycol	70.0

Alkyl parahydroxy benzoates are used more for their antimicrobial properties than antioxidants.

(ii) Quinone Type

Quinone type antioxidants which are of some value include the following:

Tocopherols

Hydroxy chromans

Hydroxy coumarones

Solvent Extracted wheat germ oil

Tocopherols occur in nature. These are not used widely in cosmetics because of their high cost and little usefulness in preservation of vegetable oils. However, they have antioxidant effect in animal fats (e.g., tallow). If used, these are combined with synergist like citric acid, lecithin or phosphoric acid. The same hold true of wheat germ oil which contains tocopherols.

(iii) Amine Type

Antioxidants of amine type include substances like:

- ethanolamine;
- lecithin;
- glutamic acid;
- hydroxamic acid;
- purines;
- kephalin etc.

Antioxidants of this group are usually used in combination with other antioxidants.

(iv) Organic Acids, Alcohols and Esters

A large number of organic acids, alcohols and esters act as antioxidants. Some of the important antioxidants of this group are:

- ascorbic acid;
- iso-ascorbic acid;
- citric acid;
- malonic acid;
- oxalic acid;–
- propionic acid;
- malic acid;
- tartaric acid;
- thiopropionic acid;
- sorbitol;
- mannitol;
- isopropyl citrate;
- di-lauryl thiopropionate;
- di-stearyl thiopropionate.

Many of these substances act as antioxidant synergist and are used in combination with other antioxidants.

(v) Inorganic Acids and Their Salts

Some acids and their salts are used as antioxidants. The most common example of this group of antioxidants are:

- phosphorus acid and its salts;
- sodium sulphite;
- sodium metabisulphite.

Out of these, acids of phosphorus are used as antioxidant synergist.

Choice of Antioxidant

All cosmetics which have oils and fats as their ingredients should be protected against oxidative deterioration. Unsaturated fats and oils are more prone to oxidative reactions. The selection of anti-oxidant(s) depend on the following:

* The nature of fat and/or oil present as ingredient of cosmetic.
* The physical form of cosmetic.
* pH of cosmetic.
* Intended use of cosmetic.
* Expected shelf life of cosmetic.
* Conditions of storage of cosmetic.

An ideal antioxidant would be one which is stable and effective over a wide range of pH and is soluble in its oxidized form. The reaction products of antioxidant should be colourless and odourless. The best approach in the preservation of cosmetic is empirical. It does not mean that any published data will not help in selecting an antioxidant. The guidelines given below will be helpful in selecting antioxidants.

* Antioxidants which can be used in aqueous systems include:
  - Sodium metabisulphite;
  - Ascorbic acid;
  - Cystenic hydrochloride;

- Iso-ascorbic acid;
- Sodium bisulphite;
- Sodium formaldehyde sulphoxylate;
- Sodium thiosulphate.

* Antioxidants which can be used in non-aqueous systems include:
  - Ascorbyl palmitate
  - Butylated hydroxy anisole (BHA)
  - Butylated hydroxy toluene (BHT)
  - Hydroquinone
  - Lecithin
  - Nordihydroguaiaretic acid
  - Phenyl-2 naphthylamine
  - Propyl gallate
  - α-tocopherol
* Certain chemical substances act as synergists to antioxidants. Some antioxidants and synergists are given below:

Table 2.4: Antioxidants and their synergists

Anti-Oxidant	Synergist
Propyl gallate	Citric acid and phosphoric acid
α-Tocopherols	Citric acid and phosphoric acid
Nordihydroguaiaretic acid (NDGA)	Ascorbic, phosphoric and citric acids and BHA
Hydroquinone	Lecithin, citric acid and phosphoric acid, BHA, BHT
Butylated hydroxyanisole (BHA)	Citric and phosphoric acids, lecithin, BHT, NDGA
Butylated hydroxy toluene (BHT)	Citric and phosphoric acids

Concentrations of antioxidants which are usually employed for preservation are given in Table 2.5. However, efficiency of antioxidant should be found out with suitable method.

Table 2.5: Anti-oxidants and concentration in which they are usually used

Name of anti-oxidant	Usual Concn. %
Prophy gallate	0.005-0.15
Butylated hydroxy-anisole	0.005-0.01
Butylated hydroxy-toluene	0.01
α-Tocopherols	0.05-0.1
Nordihydroguaiaretic acid	0.01-0.1
Mono-octadecyl ester of corboxy mercapto-succinic acids (MECSA)	0.005
Mono-octadecyl ester of thiosuccinic acids (METSA)	0.005
Sodium metabisulphite	0.01-1.0
Sodium sulphite	0.01-1.0

UV-Absorbers

Some products are vulnerable to visible or UV-light. This type of deterioration is called photo-deterioration. It is usually manifested by fading of colour of product or development of off colours. Such deterioration can be avoided by packing cosmetics either in opaque containers or coloured containers like amber colour bottles. But, at times, this is not desirable for consideration of appearance, elegance etc.

To prevent photo-deterioration, UV-absorbers can be incorporated in the formulation. By incorporating UV-absorbers colourless containers can be used, if deterioration is due to UV-light. Often UV-light deterioration involves the presence of traces of metals like iron. It is therefore, useful to use chelating agent. Sometimes, the chelating agent alone prevents photo-deterioration by chelating metallic ions. EDTA is one of the most commonly used chelating agent. EDTA also affects the cell membrane of *pseudomonas aeruginosa* and thereby enhances antibacterial activity of antimicrobials, phenolic antimicrobials in particular in concentration of 0.05%. Uric acid in concentration of 0.02-0.5% acts as UV-absorber.

HUMECTANTS

Drying out of cosmetic can occur due to vapourization of water. It depends on temperature, its degree of exposure to air and the relative humidity of air to which the product is exposed. Humectants are hygroscopic materials. These absorb water vapours from atmosphere till a certain degree of dilution is attained. Aqueous solutions of humectants can reduce the rate of loss of moisture. Humectants are added to cosmetics like oil in water type creams (vanishing creams) to prevent their drying out. In addition to this, when cosmetics containing humectant are applied on skin, a thin film of humectant is formed which influences texture and condition of the skin. It is for this reason that all moisturizing preparations contain humectants.

The problem of drying out of cosmetic, however, cannot be overcome by addition of humectant alone. The nature of container in which product is packed and closures are important factors which should be looked into to prevent drying out of cosmetics.

An ideal humectant should have the following attributes:

* It must absorb moisture from atmosphere and retain the same under the normal conditions of atmospheric humidity.
* It should cause a little change only in water content with the change of relative humidity within normal relative humidity range.
* It should be compatible with a large number of raw materials which are generally used for manufacture of cosmetics.
* It should be colourless or not of too intense colour and it should have good odour and taste.
* If should be non-toxic and non-irritant.
* It should be non-corrosive to packaging materials which are normally used for packing of cosmetics.
* Under normal conditions, it should not solidify or crystallize.
* It should not be too costly.
* Its viscosity and temperature curve should be relatively flat.

Types of Humectants

Humectants can be classified in to three general classes, namely, inorganic, metal-organic and organic.

Inorganic Humectants

Calcium chloride is a typical example of inorganic humectants. But because of compatibility problems and corrosive nature, it is not used that frequently in cosmetics. Inorganic humectants, in general, find a very limited use in cosmetics.

Metal-Organic Humectants

The example of this class of humectant is sodium lactate. Although it has greater hygroscopic powers than glycerin, but because of compatibility problems, corrosive nature and pronounced taste it is not widely used in cosmetics. It can be used in skin creams as the lactates occur naturally in the body. So there is no risk of toxicity. An admixture of sodium lactate and lactic acid can be used to overcome pH problems. In general, metal-organic humectants find a limited use in cosmetics.

Organic Humectants

Organic humectants include polyhydric alcohols, their esters and ethers. Organic humectants are widely used in cosmetics. Of organic humectants which are most commonly used in cosmetics are given below:–

- ethylene glycol,
- propylene glycol,
- glycerol,
- sorbitol,
- polyethylene glycol.

Polyethylene glycols of varying molecular weight are available. Multiple ether linkages reduce hygroscopic properties. A humectant will have different efficiency at different concentration. A list of humectants which find use in cosmetics is given below:

- Diethylene glycol
- Ethylene glycol
- Triethylene glycol
- Polyethylene glycols
- Propylene glycol
- Di-propylene glycol

– Glycerin
– Polyoxyethylene glycerin
– Alpha methyl glycerin
– Xylitol
– Sorbitol
– Mannitol
– Sorbitan
– Sorbide
– Polyoxyethylene sorbitol
– Glucose
– Propylene glycol glucoside
– Triethanolamine
– Sodium lactate
– Triethanolamine lactate
– Urea.

SURFACTANTS

Surfactants or surface-active agents lower one or more boundary tensions at interface in the system. These can also stabilize one or more interfaces by formation of absorbed layers. These effects are taken advantage of in preparation of cosmetics. There are five main uses for which surfactants are used in cosmetics and these are:

– detergency;
– wetting;
– foaming;
– emulsification;
– solubilization.

The above-mentioned properties of detergents are not mutually exclusive. All these properties are shared to some degree by all the surfactants. Depending up on these properties and the end use of cosmetics, selection of surfactant is done.

One common feature of all surfactants is that they all are amphipathic molecules. By amphipathic it is meant that the molecule has two distinct parts, one, a hydrophobic part and two, a hydrophilic part. Hydrophobic part of a molecule of a surfactant usually is a hydrocarbon chain, ring or a mixture of two and hydrophilic part usually is a polar group such as carboxylic, sulphate or sulphonate group. Non-ionic surfactants contain a number of hydroxyl or ether groups. It is because of this feature that they adsorb at interfaces.

Classification of Surfactants

Surfactants can be classified on the basis of their physical properties, chemical structure or on the basis of their uses. But none of the above-mentioned classification is satisfactory. The most logical classification of surfactants is on the basis of their ionic behaviour in aqueous solution. On the basis of this classification, the surfactants can be classified into four types:

- anionic;
- cationic;
- non-ionic;
- ampholytic.

A brief discussion on each type of surfactants will follow in proceeding paragraphs.

Anionic Surfactants

Those surfactants in which surface-active ion is negatively charged in solution, are anionic surfactants. One of the commonest examples is soap (sodium oleate, $C_{17}H_{33}COO^{-}Na+$). Anionic groups may be directly connected to hydrophobic part or these may be connected through ester, ether, amide or amidine links. On the basis of this, a sub-classification can be made. The classification, as well as the general formulae of the materials are given below. In the formulae, R denotes a hydrophobic chain (usually C_{12}–C_{18}) or a ring or a system or rings and M denotes a cation (usually sodium, potassium, ammonium, or organic base).

(i) Surfactants having anionic groups connected directly to the hydrophobic unit

Group	General Formula
Fatty acid soaps	$R{-}COO^{-}\ M^{+}$
Alkyl sulphates	$R{-}OSO_3^{-}M^{+}$

Alkyl sulphonates	$R{-}SO_3{-}M^+$
Alkyl aryl sulphonates	$R{-}C_6H_4SO_3{-}M^+$
α-Sulphonyl fatty acids	$R{-}CHCOO{-}M^+$ | $SO_3{-}M^+$
Secondary alkyl sulphates (Tergitols)	$R{-}CH\,(OSO_3^-)R^1\,M^+$
Alkyl phosphates	$R{-}OPO_3{-}2M^+$

(ii) **Surfactants having anionic groups connected through ester links**

Group	General Formula
Monoglyceride sulphates (Monolaurin)	$R{-}COO{-}CH_2$ | $CH{-}OH$ | $CH_2OSO_3{-}M^+$
Dialkyl sulphosuccinates	$ROCO{-}CH_2$ | $ROCO{-}CHSO_3{-}M^+$
Polyethylene glycol ester	$RCO{-}(O{-}CH2{-}CH_2)_nOSO_3{-}M^+$
Sulphates isoethionates	$R{-}COO{-}CH_2CH_2SO_3{-}M^+$

(iii) **Surfactants having anionic groups connected through ether links**

Group	General Formula
Alkyl ether sulphates	$R(O{-}CH_2{-}CH_2)_nOSO_3^-M^+$
Phenol ether sulphates	$R{-}C_6H_4{-}(O{-}CH_2{-}CH_2)_nOSO_3^-M^+$
Alkyl ether carboxylates	$R{-}(O{-}CH_2{-}CH_2)_n{-}O{-}CH_2{-}COO^-\,M^+$

(iv) **Surfactants having anionic group connected through amide links**

Group	General Formula
Alkanolamide sulphates	$R{-}CO{-}NH{-}CH2{-}CH_2{-}OSO_3^-M^+$
Taurines	$R{-}CO{-}NH{-}CH_2{-}CH_2{-}SO_3^-M^+$
Sucrosinates	$R{-}CO{-}N{-}CH_2{-}COO^-M^+CH_3$

(v) **Surfactants having anionic groups connected through amidine links**

Group	General Formula
Imidazole sulphates	

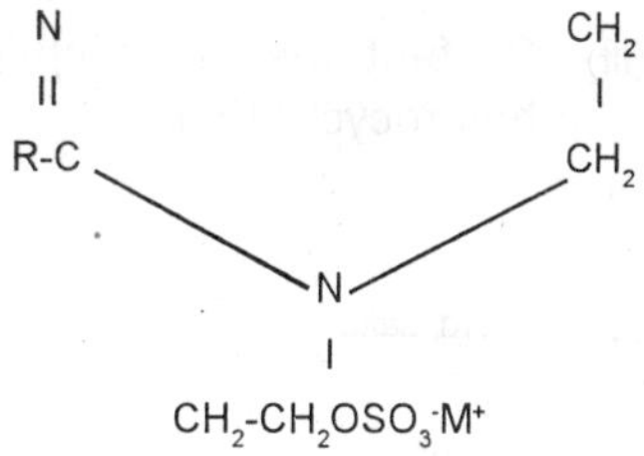

Cationic Surfactants

Those surfactants in which surface-active ion is positively charged in solution, are cationic surfactants. These can be further subdivided into nitrogenous cationic surfactants and non-nitrogenous cationic surfactants. Nitrogenous cationic surfactans can be grouped on the basis of a placement of cationic group. This sub-classification and general formulae of the materials are given below. R denotes a hydrophobic chain (usually C_{12}–C_{18}) or an aromatic ring and X denotes a suitable anion (usually chlorine or bromine).

A. Nitrogenous Surfactants

(i) Quaternary ammonium salts in which nitrogen is directly attached to the hydrophobic part

Group	General Formula
Alkyl trimethyl ammonium salts	$R–N^{+} (CH_3)_3 X^{-}$
Dialkyl dimethyl ammonium salts	$RR'–N (CH_3)_2 X^{-}$
Alkyl dimethyl benzyl ammonium salts	$RN+ (CH_3)_2 X^{-}$ | $CH_2C_6H_5$
Ethoxylated alkyl-dimethyl ammonium salts	$R–N+ (CH_3)_2 X^{-}$ | $(OCH_2–CH_2)_n$

(ii) Surfactants in which cationic group separated from the hydrophobic group

Group	General Formula
Quaternized amides of etylenediamine	$RCO\ NH–CH_2–CH_2N+(CH_3)_3 X^{-}$
Quaternized amides of polyethylenediamine	$R–CO\ NH(CH_2–CH_2N)_n– CH_2N^{+} (CH_3)_3$ | CH_3X^{-}

(iii) Surfactants in which cationic group is located in a heterocyclic ring

Group	General Formula
Alkyl pyridinium salts	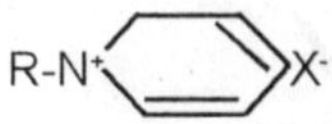
Alkyl morpholinium salts	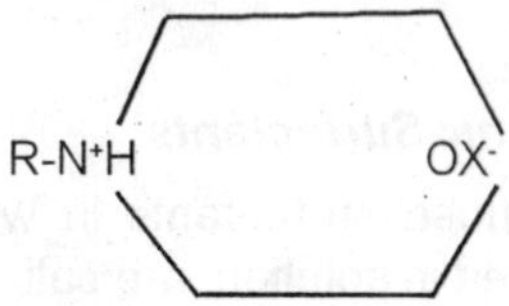
Alkyl imidazolinium salts	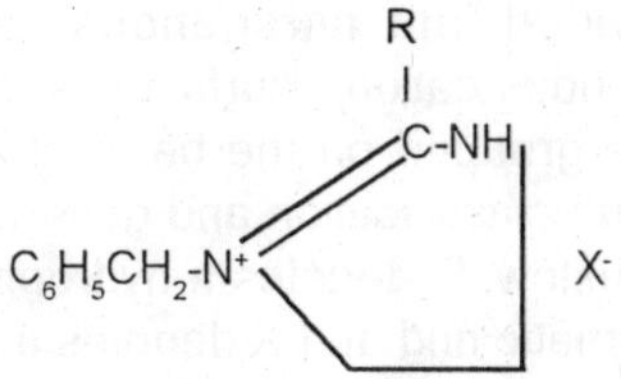

(iv) Dicationic Surfactants

Group	General Formula
Quaternized diamine salts	$R–N+ (CH_3)_2–CH_2–CH_2–N(CH_3)_3\ 2X^-$

B. Non-nitrogenous Surfactants

Group	General Formula
Sulphonium salts	$R–S+ (CH_3)_2\ X^-$
Phosphonium salts	$R–P+ (Ch_3)_3\ X^-$

Non-ionic Surfactants

In non-ionic surfactants hydrophilic part of the molecule is made up of multiple uncharged polar groups, for example, hydroxyl groups or ether linkages in ethylene oxide chains. Non-ionic surfactants can be further sub-classified on their chemical nature. The groups of compounds and general formulae are given below. In the formulae, R denotes a hydrophobic chain (usually $C_{12}–C_{18}$). The letter n denotes a whole number.

(i) Alkanolamides

Group	General formula
Fatty acid alkanolamide	$RCONH–CH_2–CH_2–OH$
Fatty acid dialkanolamide	$RCON(CH_2–CH_2–OH)_2$

(ii) Polyethylene glycol derivatives

Group	General formula
Alkyl polyglycol ether	$R(OCH_2{-}CH_2)_n\ OH$
alkyl aryl polyglycol ethers	$RC_6H_4(OCH_2{-}CH_2)_n\ OH$
Polyglycol esters	$RCO(OCH_2{-}CH_2)_nOH$
Thioethers	$RS(CH_2{-}CH_2O)_nH$

(iii) Polyethyleneimine derivatives

Group	General formula
Alkyl polyethyleneimine	$R\ (NHCH_2{-}CH_2)_nNH_2$
Polyethyleneimine amides	$R\ (CONH(CH_2{-}CH_2NH)_nH$

Ampholytic Surfactants

The characteristics of ampholytic surfactants is that they are able to form a surface-active ion with both positive and negative charges. These surfactants can be sub-classified on their chemical nature. Groups of compounds and their general formulae are given below. In the formulae, R denotes a carbon chain of 12-18 atoms (C_{12}-C_{18}).

(i) Alkylamino acids

Group	General formula
Alkyl β-amino-propionates	$RN^+H_2{-}CH_2{-}CH_2{-}COO^-$
Betains	$RN+(CH_3)_2CH_2COO^-$
	$RN+(CH_3)_2{-}CH_2CH_2COO^-$

(ii) Acylamino acids

Group	**General formula**
Acyl β-amino-propionates	$RCON+H_2{-}CH_2{-}CH_2{-}COO^-$
Acyl peptides	$RCON+H_2C{-}CHCONH{-}CH{-}COO^-$
|	|
R'	R"

(iii) Alkylimidazolines

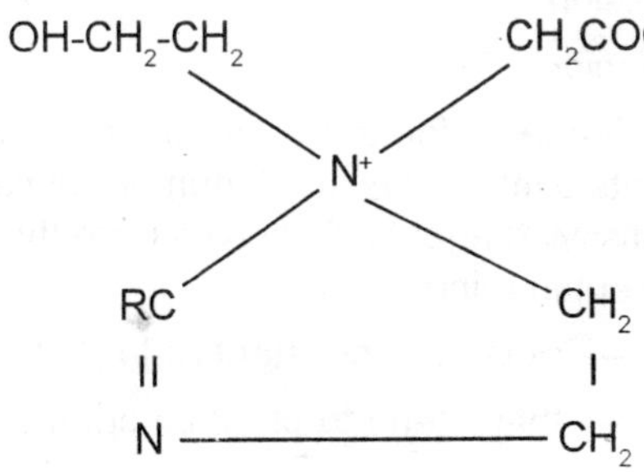

Properties of Surfactants

As mentioned earlier surfactants cause changes in surface properties. With the rise of concentration of surfactant there is rise in effect (e.g., interfacial tension, electrical conductivity). But at certain level, there is no more rise in effect. The concentration at which this discontinuity occurs is called critical micelle concentration (CMC).

As surface tension falls, foaming and wetting properties are increased. With the fall in surface tension, usually there is fall in interfacial tension also. Fall in interfacial tension results in better emulsifying and detergent properties. All surface-active agents, above CMC have some solubilizing properties.

Uses of Surfactants

Emulsifying Agents

A large number of cosmetics are emulsions and surfactants have been used as emulsifying agents. Three types of surfactants are usually used as emulsifying agents, i.e., anionic, cationic and non-ionic surfactants.

Anionics

This group of emulsifying agents have been used extensively in the formulation of hand creams and lotions. Anionics which have been used in hand creams and lotions include fatty acid soaps. polyol fatty acid mono esters containing fatty acid soaps, sulphuric esters (sodium salt), polyol fatty acid monoesters containing sulphuric esters.

Fatty acid soaps and sodium salts of sulphuric ester are strongly hydrophilic and will tend to produce oil-in-water type emulsion while the polyol fatty acid monoester soap mixtures are only slightly hydrophilic and therefore, will tend to produce dual emulsion.

Cationics

These surfactants have not been widely used as emulsifying agents. Only a very small number of cationics have been used as emulsifying agents. Cationics have three properties which should be kept in mind:

- these are substantive to protein at acid pH.
- these tend to produce emulsions with acid pH;

– these are germicidal if not inactivated by anionics or other incompatible materials.

Non-ionics

Since these surfactants do not ionize these are compatible with a large number of cosmetics ingredients when these are used as emulsifying agents, even cationics can be incorporated in formulation for taking advantage of their germicidal properties. Some of the common non-ionics which are used as emulsifying agent include:

* Polyoxyethylene fatty alcohol ethers (e.g., Polyoxyethylene lauryl alcohol)
* Polyoxyethylene fatty acid esters (e.g., Polyoxyethylene stearate)
* Polyoxyethylene sorbitan fatty acid ester (e.g., Polyoxyethylene stearate)
* Polyoxyethylene sorbitan fatty acid ester (e.g., polyoxyethylene sorbitan monostearate)
* Sorbitan fatty acid ester (e.g., sorbitol monostearate)
* Polyoxyethylene glycol fatty acid ester (Polyoxyethylene glycol mono-and di-sterates)
* Polyol fatty acid ester (e.g., propylene glycol monostearate).

Foaming and Cleansing Agents

Surfactants for their foaming and cleansing properties are used in shampoos.

Anionics

Anionics like soaps, alkyl sulphonates, alkyl benzene sulphonates are not used in shampoos. But anionics like α-olefin sulphonates, alkyl sulphates are used in shampoos. Sulphosuccinates have low incidence of eye irritation and sting and therefore are used in mind shampoos. The other anionics which have been used as auxiliary to shampoo are methyl taurides, acyl sarcosinates and acyl peptides.

Cationics

In general, cations have inferior cleansing and foaming properties. Further, these have affinity for proteins which may result in re-deposition of dirt on hair fibre. These are irritant to eye and can also react with anionics. Therefore, their use has been limited. These have been used as additives in small quantities (below 5%). Some of the commonly used cations are alkyl trimethyl ammonium, steryl dimethyl benzyl ammonium, cetyl pyridinium salts.

Non-ionics

Of the non-ionics polyglyceryl ethers have good foaming properties. These are devoid of irritation to eye muscosa. These can be used as main surfactants for shampoos. Fatty acid alkanolamides are of no great use as shampoo detergents but these are of great importance as additives to anionic detergents. Other non-ionics which have been used as auxiliary to shampoo base include:

- ethoxylated fatty alcohols,
- pluronics,
- sorbitol esters.

Amphoterics

Amphoteric surfactants are used in preparation of mild shampoos. Their compatibility with other detergents allow them large flexibility of use. These may also contribute to the conditioning effect on hair surfactants which have been used in shampoos include:

- N-alkyl amino acids,
- betains,
- imidazoline derivatives.

N-alkyl amino acids exhibit best foaming properties in slightly alkaline pH.

Betains are cationic in acidic and anionic in alkaline solutions. Betains are effective cleansers with high foaming properties. Foam performances are not affected by pH variations. Betains are compatible with cationics, anionics and non-ionics. Because of these characteristics, betains have wide range of use.

Alkyl imidazolines exhibit fair foaming properties and are mild to the skin. These are stable within a wide range of pH (pH 2.0 to 12.0). These find use in baby shampoos.

Wetting Agents

All surface-active agents have wetting properties, the degree of wetting may, however, differ. Short chain alkyl sulphate (C_{12} alkyl sulphates), alkyl ether sulphate and alkyl aryl sulphonates are commonly used for their wetting properties.

Solubilization

As mentioned earlier, all surfactants above the CMC have solubilizing properties. This property of surfactants is employed when perfume or an insoluble organic material is to be incorporated in a clear product. Most of the surfactants have been used for this property in one situation or the other.

OILS, FATS AND WAXES

Oils, fats and waxes are extensively used in cosmetics. Creams, lotions, brilliantines, hair oils, lipsticks are the cosmetics where their use is inevitable. Fixed oils of vegetable origin mainly consist of triglycerides. These glycerides may be simple in which three hydroxyl groups of glycerol may be esterified with same acid or mixed triglycerides in which three hydroxyl group of glycerol may be esterified with different fatty acids. The fatty acids in triglycerides in oils generally are unsaturated fatty acids. Saturated fatty a acids glycerides generally result in fats.

A number of compounds derived from mineral sources are used in cosmetics. These include mineral oils, petroleum jelly and other paraffins. Chemically these are hydrocarbons.

A number of fats and waxes obtained from animal source are used in cosmetics. For example, wool fat, bees wax, spermaceti wax, etc.

It is beyond the scope of this book to deal with these substances in detail. An overview of these substances will be given in following paragraphs.

Oils

Oils from vegetable origin as well as from mineral origin are used in cosmetics. Commonly used oils from both the sources will be covered briefly.

Vegetable Oils

A number of vegetable oils are used in cosmetics preparations. Salient of them are given below:

Almond Oil

It is a pale yellow oil with slight characteristic odour. It consists of glycerides chiefly of oleic acid with smaller amounts of other acids namely, linoleic, myristic and palmitic. It has emollient properties and is used in creams and lotions.

Arachis (Ground nut) Oil

It is a pale yellow oil with faint nutty odour. Refined ground nut oil is colourless clear oil. It consists of glycerides chiefly of oleic and linoleic acids with smaller amounts of other acids. It becomes cloudy at 3°C. At lower temperature it solidifies. It is used in hair oils and brilliantines.

Castor Oil

It is faintly yellow or colourless transparent viscid oil with slight odour. It is a mixture of triglycerides out of which 80% is ricinoleic acid. It remains clear even at 0°C. It is emollient. It is commonly used in lipsticks. It can also be used in hair oils, brilliantines, creams and lotions.

Olive Oil

It is pale yellow or greenish yellow oil consisting of glycerides of mainly of oleic acid with smaller amounts of palmitic, linoleic, stearic and myristic acids. It has slight odour. At low temperatures, its solid or partly solid. Olive oil is emollient and soothing. It is used in bath oils, creams and lotions.

Coconut Oil

A white or pearl white unctuous mass in winter and colourless oil in summer. It has an odour of coconut. Melting point of coconut oil is 23-26°C. As such, in winter it solidifies.

Mineral Oils

Of the mineral oils which are commonly used in cosmetic preparations are light liquid paraffin and heavy liquid paraffin.

Light Liquid Paraffin

It has lower weight per ml (0.83 to 0.87 g) and has lower viscosity. It is a mixture of liquid hydrocarbons. It is colourless and odourless oily liquid. It has very good spread. It is used in bath oils, hair oils, brilliantines, lotions and creams.

Heavy Liquid Paraffin

It is a mixture of hydrocarbons. The composition of heavy liquid paraffin varies according to the source of petroleum from which it has been obtained. It is colourless or almost colourless and odourless oily liquid. It is emollient in nature. It is used in creams, lotions, brilliantines, hair oils, bath oils.

Mineral oils are much more stable than vegetable oils. However, it is advisable to use 10 ppm of tocopherol or butylated hydroxy toluene (BHT) as stabilizer.

Fats

A variety of fatty materials are used in cosmetics. These materials may be from vegetable, animal or mineral origin or these may be synthetic materials. Only those materials which have outstanding distinction of being used will be covered here in brief

Fatty Acids

Although fatty acids having carbon chain ranging from C_{12}-C_{18} have been used in cosmetics but stearic acid is the fatty acid of choice. Commercially available stearic acid is a mixture of palmitic acid and stearic acid. "Triple pressed" stearic acid is a mixture of 55% palmitic acid and 45% of stearic acid. Unsaturated fatty acids are liquids. Thus from a mixture of fatty acids commercial stearic acid is obtained by pressing the mixture to exclude unsaturated fatty acids. The names single, double or triple pressed are given on the basis of pressing given in the process.

Good quality of stearic acid can also be manufactured by solvent crystallization or hydrogenation.

The only other fatty acid which has been used is oleic acid. It is unsaturated fatty acid and has potential for rancidity. Adequate preservatives should be used when oleic acid is used. Oleic acid is used for enchancing pearly sheen in lotions and creams. It is also used to overcome the problem of gel formation which is associated with stearates.

Fatty Alcohols

Fatty alcohols are widely used in creams and lotions. Most commonly used fatty alcohols like lauryl and myristyl have also been used. The latter fatty alcohols are usually incorporated in combination either with cetyl or steryl alcohol.

Cetyl and steryl alcohols are effective emollient. These are hydrophobic and therefore produce occlusive films which help in hydration of dry skin. Their melting point being high, they also deposit non-greasy films on the skin.

Fatty Acid Esters

Fatty acids esters of lower molecular weight such as butyl stearate, isopropyl stearate, isopropyl palmitate, isopropyl myristate have been widely used in creams and lotions. These are oily in character and have low viscosity. When product containing these substances is applied to the skin, they deposit a thin, oily film which is not tacky or greasy.

Polyol esters of fatty acids have also been used in creams and lotions. Examples of this group of materials are glyceryl monostearate, propylene glycol monostearate. These materials are used either as emollient or emulsifying agents. Glyceryl monostearate and ethylene glycol monostearate cause increase in viscosity with rise in their concentration. Therefore, their concentration should be decided on the basis of final consistency desired in the product. These materials are generally used in concentration of 0.5% to 5% in lotions and 1% to 10% in creams. The nature of polyethylene glycols monostearate depends on the length of ethylene oxide chain. The longer the chain, the more solid the product and the more hydrophilic the product. In oil-in-water (o/w) emulsions long chain polyethylene glycols are used in concentration of 0.5% to 5%. A combination of long chain and short chain polyethylene glycol ester can also be used.

Lanolin and Its Derivatives

Lanolin and its derivatives have been used in cosmetics very widely. Lanolin is natural fat consisting mainly of esters formed by higher fatty alcohols and higher fatty acids. It is a good emollient because of its hydrophobic and adhesive character. However, its use hardly exceeds 5% concentration because higher concentration imparts tackiness to the final product. Besides its emollient property, it has emulsifying property. When used as an emulsifier it produces w/o type emulsion.

Lanolin alcohols are derived from lanolin. Lanolin alcohols are a mixture of alcohols which fall into three groups:

– sterols,

– triterpene alcohols,

– aliphatic alcohols.

As a matter of fact, this classification is incomplete, because about 20% of alcohol fraction remains unknown. Commercially, these are available either as solids or liquids (solution of lanolin alcohols in mineral oil) or unctuous bases (of ointment consistency prepared with materials like lanolin, petroleum jelly, mineral oil and paraffin). These bases when mixed with water form water-in-oil emulsion spontaneously.

Some cases of hypersensitivity to lanolin led to the development of lanolin derivatives. Of these two derivatives are used in cosmetics and these are:

– acetylated lanolin

– propionyl lanolin derivative.

Lanolin is quite hydrophobic. Efforts were made to make it hydrophilic which resulted in a class of compounds which were less viscous, more soluble in water than natural lanolin. Solubility varies directly with the length of the ethylene oxide chain. These are known as polyoxyethylene lanolins.

Soft Paraffins

Soft paraffin is a purified mixture of hydrocarbons obtained from petroleum. It is pale yellow to yellow, translucent, soft, slightly fluorescent mass. It is odourless when rubbed on skin. It is known as yellow soft paraffin or yellow petrolatum or yellow petroleum jelly. Its melting point is 38°C to 56°C.

When bleached it becomes white. It is known as white soft paraffin or white petrolatum or white petroleum jelly.

Soft paraffins are emollient. They probably function by covering the skin with a hydrophobic occlusive film which prevents water loss from skin thereby promoting its hydration.

Waxes

Bases of many cosmetics are prepared with a mixture of oils, fats and waxes, e.g., lipsticks. Commonly used oils and fats have been briefly covered in foregoing paragraphs. Some of the waxes which are widely used will be covered here.

Bees Wax

Bees wax is a secretion formed by the hive bee (species of Apis) for making the cells of honey comb. Bees wax contains 70% of esters mainly muricyl palmitate. It is yellowish brown solid having honey like odour. It becomes brittle when cold. The melting point of bees wax is 62°C-65°C. When bleached, it becomes yellowish white solid with a faint characteristic odour. It enables water to be incorporated and form w/o emulsion.

Spermaceti

A solid wax obtained from mixed oils from the head, blubber and carcase of spermaceti. It is translucent, crystalline pearly white unctuous mass with little odour. It mainly consists of cetyl palmitate and cetyl myristate. Its melting point is 42°C-50°C.

Synthetic spermaceti is also available and it is a mixture of esters of saturated fatty alcohols (C_{14}-C_{18}) and saturated fatty acids (C_{14}-C_{18}). available as white to off white translucent flakes with crystalline structure and pearly luster. Its melting point is 43°C-47°C.

Paraffin Wax

Paraffin wax or hard paraffin is a mixture of solid hydrocarbons consisting mainly of n-paraffins and to some extent their isomers. It is obtained by distillation from petroleum.

It is colourless or white odourless, translucent wax like solid. It is slightly greasy to touch. Its melting point is 50°C-57°C. Paraffins of other melting points are also available.

Ceresin and Ozokerite Wax

Ceresin is also known as Mineral wax and Purified Ozokerite. It is a mixture of hydrocarbons obtained by the purification of ozokerite, a naturally occurring solid paraffin. It is colourless, odourless, crystalline wax resembling bees wax. It has melting range of 50°C-75°C.

Carnauba Wax

Carnauba wax is obtained from the leaves of the Brazilian wax palm (*Copernicia cerifera*). Various grades are available. The highest grade is light brown to pale yellow either a moderately coarse powder or flakes. It has characteristic bland odour. It has melting range of 81°C-86°C. It is one of the hardest wax.

PERFUMES

There may be only a few types of cosmetics which may not contain perfume. There are many products which are sold for their perfumes, e.g., perfumes, toilet waters. Thus perfumes form a part of this chapter. Perfumery is a subject in itself and there are many books on it. The reader may refer to W.A. Poucher's Perfumes, Cosmetics and Soaps (volume I and II) for detailed information on perfumes.

History

The word perfumes has been derived from "per" which means through and "fumum" which means smoke. It suggests that early perfumes were pleasant smells obtained by burning wood and grass etc. Since the earliest times the man has been searching plant and animal origin materials which could be used for medicinal purposes. The early search for fragrant materials must have been for their medicinal values. Even today fragrant materials are used for medicinal purposes. In fact, aroma therapy is being practised in many countries. Some of the fragrant materials were later found to be useful as perfumery compounds. It is estimated that here are about 4,00,000 odorants which include pleasant and unpleasant odours. Perfumes are made with pleasant odours.

In India fragrant materials have been used from ancient times. Fragrant materials were included in "Havan Samigri" for "Yajna" and Yajna was associated almost with every religious ceremony. Havan samigri was burnt along with wood pieces, while doing so, each "Ahuti" was offered to some God or Goddess to propitiate Him/Her. Apart from the religious benefits, it resulted in fragrant smell in the environment around Yajna.

In history also mention is found of use of floral waters by kings and riches. The early Romans used to enjoy perfumes. They used rose water extensively after bathing. The city of ancient Rome had shops which sold perfumes. In India, Kannauj (a city in Uttar Pradesh) has been famous for perfumes. In fact, the desire to use pleasant perfumes from flowers and fruits had been common to all human beings irrespective of region. In the eleventh century, Islamic alchemists invented the steam distillation methods and also discovered how to concentrate and separate ethyl alcohol. Ethyl alcohol played an important role in the development of the culture of perfume. However, the technology for manufacturing natural perfumes developed in the 17th and 18th century. In the 19th century many aroma chemicals were synthesized. The 20th century has witnessed fast developments and has brought a wealth of fragrances and perfumes.

Human beings have been using vegetable oils and animal fats from animals. Some of these oils and fats were scented with flowers to make balms and pomades. Some of them are used even today. Similarly floral waters have also been used by mankind for a long time. Other early cosmetics in which perfumes were used include perfumed bath oil and massage oils. Today, there will be hardly any cosmetic in which perfume has not been used.

Natural Perfumes

Natural perfumes are obtained either from plant sources or animal sources. Natural perfumes from animal sources are generally derived from animal glands. Musk from Musk Dear is the most expensive perfuming compound. But now, it is banned item as the Musk Dear is, now, an endangered species. Other natural extracts from animal sources include civet, castoreum and ambergris. Ambergris is as important as musk. It is obtained from pathological secretion from the intestines of the sperm whale. Civet is collected as a secretion from the glands of the civet cat living in Ethiopia and its odour changes when diluted in the same way as musk. Castoreum is obtained from the glands near the reproductive organs of the beaver. In view of the Washington Treaty which bans international trade in protected species of wild animals and plants, availability of natural perfumery compounds has been reduced to almost nil. As such, aroma chemicals with same odour as natural are used in place of natural perfumery compounds obtained from protected species of animals and plants.

Natural perfumes from plant are obtained from different parts of plants like flowers, fruits, seeds, leaves, branches, bark, wood, root etc. Different procedures are used for isolation of perfumes from plants. Most commonly used methods include distillation, solvent extraction and expression. Names of plants, parts used, extraction methods and main components of the perfume appear in Table 2.6.

Table 2.6: Some natural essences

Name of Essence	Plant and plant part used	Extraction method	Main components of essence
Rose oil	Rosadama scena and rosa centifolia, flowers	Steam distillation, solvent extraction	l-citronellol, geraneol, l-linalool, damascone, damascenone, β-phenyl ethyl alcohol, farneosol, nonyl aldehyde, rose oxide
Jasmine oil	Jasminium officianale, flowers	Solvent extraction	Benzyl acetate, α-linalool jasmine, inidole, phytol, cis-jasmone, benzyl alcohol, benzyl benzoate, jasmine lactone
Neroli oil	Citrus aurantium subspamara, flowers	Steam distillation	l-linalool, linalool acetate, d-nerolidol, geraniol, nerol, terpinol, pinene, camphene
Lavender oil	Lavandula officianalis, flowers	Steam distillation, solvent extraction	Linalyl acetae, limonene, cineole, nerol, linalool esters, geraneol esters d-borneol, lavandulol
Ylang ylang oil	Cananga odorata formagenuina, flowers	Steam distillation, solvent extraction	Linalool, geraneol, benzyl alcohol, sesquiterpenes, farneosol
Tuberose oil	Polyanthes tuberosa, flowers	Solvent extraction	Geraneol, farneosol, benzyl alcohol, benzyl benzoate, methyl salicylate, methyl anthranilate, nerol
Clarysage oil	Salviasclaria, flowers and leaves	Steam distillation, solvent extraction	Linalyl acetate, linalool, nerolidol, sclareol
Clove oil	Eugenia carophylata, flowers, buds and leaves	Steam distillation, solvent extraction	Eugenol, acetyleugenol, methyl salicylate, β-carophyllene, methyl-n-amyl ketone, methyl hetyl ketone
Pepper-mint oil	Mentha pipereta, flowers and leaves	Steam distillation	l-menthol, menthone, isomenthone, 1-8-cineol, β-carophyllene, menthofurane, methyl acetate
Geranium oil	Pelargonium graveolens leaves	Steam distillation, solvent extraction	l-cetronellol, gernisol, menthone, linalool, geranyl formate, geranyl tiglate, citronellyl formate, isomenthone
Patchouli oil	Pogostemon cablin, dried leaves	Steam distillation	Patchouli alcohol, patchoulene, patchoulenone, β-caryophyllene, β-bulnessene, α-guajene

Contd. . .

Name of Essence	Plant and plant part used	Extraction method	Main components of essence
Sandal-wood oil	Santalum album, wood	Steam distillation	α-β-santalol, santene, santenone, santenol, teresantalol, α-β-santalene, santalone
Cinnamon oil	Cinnamomum zeylanicum, bark	Steam distillation	Cinnamic aldehyde, eugenol, l-phellandrene, pinene, 1-8-cineol, pinene, linalool, caryophyllene
Lemon oil	Citrus lemon, fruit peel	Expression	d-limonene, y-terpinene, citral, α-β-pinene, camphene, methyl heptanone, β-phellandrene, α-bergamotene, β-bisabolene
Orange oil	Citrus limon, fruit peel	Expression	d-limonene, n-decyl aldehyde, citral, d-linaloo, n-nonyl alcohol, d-terpinol, nootkatone
Coriander oil	coriandrum sativum, seeds	Steam distillation	d-linalool, α–β–pinene, limonene, terpinene, phellandrene, geraniol l-borneol, n-decyl aldehyde
Nutmeg Oil	Myristica fragrans, seeds	Steam distillation	Sabinene, β-pinene, camphene, limonene, linalool, borneol, terpineol
Pepper oil	piper nigrum fruit	Steam distillation	β-pinene, sabinene, caryophyllene, elemol
Bergamot oil	Citrus aurantium bergamia, fruit peel	Expression	Linalyl acetate, l-linalool, limonene, citral, p-cymene, decanol

It will be relevant to discuss briefly the methods which are commonly used for obtaining natural essences.

Steam Distillation

When steam is passed over fresh or dried plant materials, essential oils which are volatile are carried by the steam. Steam carrying the volatile essential oils is condensed. Condensation results in essential oils and water which are collected. The collected liquid comprises of water, water containing essential oils and a separate layer of essential oils over the water. Rose oil and rose water is obtained using this method. This method is useful for the production of heat resistant essential oils.

Solvent Extraction

This method is used to obtain essential oils which are either thermolabile or have high boiling point. Plant material is extracted with solvents such as hexane, petroleum ether. The plant materials are soaked in the solvent and slightly warmed to extract the oils. The oil thus obtained is referred to as the "concentrate". The concentrate can be used without further processing. However, the concentrate is often re-extracted with cold ethanol. The later extraction produces absolute oil.

Expression

This method is used to obtain essential oils from citrus fruits peel. Citrus fruits peel is expressed in an oil expresser and essential oil present in the peel is expressed out and is collected. Citrus oils are unstable. Therefore, they require processing at low temperature.

Aroma Chemicals

After the middle of the 19th century, when the foundations of terpene chemistry were laid, many synthetic technologies have been developed. Ruzicka won the 1939 Nobel Prize in Chemistry for his work on macrocyclic chemicals. With the development of synthetic chemistry, high cost of natural essential oils and problems of their availability, many aroma chemicals have been synthesizes for use in perfumes. There are now synthesized chemicals which are present in natural essential oils and there are aroma chemicals with good smell which are not found in natural essential oils.

Aroma chemicals belong to different class of chemicals. For example, alcohols, aldehydes, ketones, esters, lactones, phenols, oxides, acetals etc. are based on the functional group. Some typical aroma chemicals with classification are given in Table 2.7.

Table 2.7: Some typical aroma chemicals

Chemical classification	Aroma chemical	Odour
Monoterpenes	Limonene	Orange
Sesquiterpenes	β-caryophyllene	Woody
Fatty alcohols	cis-3-hexanol	fresh green leaves
Monoterpene alcohols	linalool	Lily of the valley
Sesquiterpene alcohols	farnesol	Fresh green and floral
Aromatic alcohol	β-phenyl ethyl alcohol	Rosy
Fatty aldehydes	2, 6 nonadienal	Violet, cucumber

Contd. . .

Chemical classification	Aroma chemical	Odour
Terpene aldehydes	Citral	Lemon
Aromatic aldehydes	α-hexylcinnamic aldehyde	Jasmine
Alicyclic ketones	β-ionone	Violet when diluted
Terpene ketones	l-caryone	Spear mint
Macrocyclic ketones	Cyclopentadecanone	Musky
Terpene esters	Linalyl acetate	Bergamot and lavender
Aromatic esters	benzyl benzoate	Faint balsamic
Lactones	γ-undecalactone	Peach
Phenols	Eugenol	Clove
Oxides	Rose oxide	Green and floral
Nitrogen compounds	Indole	Fecal when strong, jasmine when dilute
Acetals	Phenyl acetaldehyde dimethyl acetal	Faint hyacinth

Base Compounds

Floral base

Floral base perfumes are the most important perfumes. These have been used by people in every culture. Important floral base compounds are rose, jasmine, mugnet, lilacs, cornation, tuberose, hyacinth, orange flower, gardenia, violet, honeysuckle, narcissus, ylang ylang etc. Only two floral bases are given below as illustrative examples.

(i) Rose base

Rose is a popular flower. Its colour and fragrance are very popular. In compounding of perfumes, addition of rose base makes it seem more complete. A rose base can be prepared with the formula.

Rose flower base

	parts
Phenyl ethyl alcohol	26.0
Citronellol	49.0
Geraneol	5.0

Contd. . .

	parts
Linalool	12.0
Eugenol	2.0
Nerol	1.0
Amyl phenyl acetate	5.0
Rose oxide	0.5
Damascone alpha 10%	1.0
Geranyl acetate	2.5

(ii) Jasmine base

While the flower of rose is popular, Jasmine is the flower of kings. Jasmine flower base is an important element of the perfumers' palette. It blends well with other fragrances. A jasmine type flower base can be prepared with the formula.

Jasmine flower base

	parts
benzyl acetate	16.0
Hexyl cinnamic aldehyde	44.0
Indole 10%	2.0
Methyl dihydrojasmonati	11.0
Hexyl salicylate	7.0
Eugenol 10%	3.5
Damascone alpha 1%	3.5
Mayol	9.0
Undecalactone gamma 10%	4.0

Woody base

Typical woody bases include vetiver types, the heavy and sweetly sexy sandalwood types, the strongly exotic patchouli types, as well as the cedarwood types.

Chypre base

Chypre is the arche type perfume. It was developed by Coty in 1917. It has characteristic perfumes of a mixture of berga mot, oak mos, orange, rose, jasmine, musk, amber, etc. and is an important base in blending.

Citrus base

Citrus base is prepared with such perfumes as bergamot, lemon, orange, lime, grape fruit and maudarin. It is mainly used in colognes.

Green base

These bases give an impression of smell of cut grasses and leaves or vegetables like cucumber and tomato.

Oriental base

This name was given to fragrances important from the orient into Europe. These bases have balsamic and vamillier notes with woody and animals notes.

Fruity base

There are bases which are non-citrus fruity bases in nature. These bases are typified by fruits like peach, strawberry, apple, banana, pineapple, raspberry etc.

Spice base

Spicy bases have stimulating nature. These bases are characterized by clove, cinnamon, thyme, pepper, nutmeg etc.

Oriental base

Aldehyde bases have also been popular. These bases usually incorporate C_7-C_{12} elements in fatty aldehyde. These bases form an important group. These have been incorporated in popular perfume, channel no. 5.

Animal base

The bases containing such perfumery chemicals as musk, civet, amber etc. are animal bases. Nowadays, synthetic chemicals having similar aroma that of natural materials are used.

Other base compounds

The base compounds mentioned above from the basic groups for developing perfumes. But there are other fragrances which are used in small quantities to modify fragrances as well as body of the perfume.

Compounding or Blending or Perfume

The expert who compounds or blends perfumes is called a perfumer. The raw materials for blending perfumes comprise of about 500 natural aromatic raw materials and about 1000 aroma chemicals. A simple perfume may contain a blend of 10-30 materials. A complex and sophisticated perfume may contain a blend of 50-100 materials. In the extreme cases the number of raw materials may be as large as 200.

A perfumer blends a number of natural and synthetic materials to make a perfume. This mixture, usually is difficult to describe and it is known as "perfume compound" or "compound". These blends may contain two or three materials which is very rare or may contain many (about a dozen) or very many (a few hundreds) materials. Raw materials perfume compound can be broadly classified into three classes:

- plant oils
- animals secretions
- chemical substances.

Plant oils may be essential oils, flower oils or resins/gums/ exudations. Parry defined essential oils as odoriferous bodies of an oily nature obtained almost exclusively from vegetable sources, generally liquid (sometimes semi-solid or solid) at ordinary temperature and volatile without decomposition. Thousands of essential oils have been screened. Out of these about 150-200 essential oils are usually used in commerce. Essential oils can be obtained from different parts of plant, e.g., flower, seed, twigs, leaves, bark, root. An essential oils is a complex mixture of chemical substances. In a few cases, one chemical substance is present in larger proportion and the fragrance to the plant is imparted by this chemical. For example, methyl salicylate in oil of wintergreen. Many of the chemical substances present in essential oils have been identified and synthesized, e.g., phenyl ethyl alcohol, farnesol. Essential oils are usually prepared by steam distillation.

Flower oil (floral oils) are essence obtained generally from flowers by extraction with volatile or non-volatile solvent. These materials in trade are known as "absolute". The three processes that have been used for production of flower oils are:

- volatile solvent extraction,
- immersion in warm fats (maceration), and
- extraction by cold fats (enfleurage)

Some oils have been produced by expression process also. Oils bearing plant material is pressed mechanically. This process is suitable only for citrus oils, e.g., lemon, orange, bergamot, lime, etc. Expressed oils generally contain terpenes.

The third type of materials gums, resins and exudations are not so well defined. Some such materials which have been used are gum styrax, balsam peru, benzoin, myrrh. These materials are viscous, heavy and odourous.

Animal secretions are valued and precious materials. Many animals secrete odourous materials but about a dozen only have been exploited commercially. Of these four materials are of great importance, namely, castoreum, civet, musk, and ambergris. In India, musk deer is endangered species and musk ordinarily cannot be obtained. Odour of these materials is lingering and long lasting. As such, these contribute a lot of fixation of perfume.

The chemical substances used in perfumery may be isolates from plants. For example, linalool which is usually obtained from Brazilian rosewood, citral which is obtained from lemongrass oil which is turn is obtained from lemongrass. There are certain chemical substances which are derived from either isolates or essential oils by chemical reactions. Examples of such chemical substances are esters (acetates, propionates and other esters) of linalool, geraniol, terpineol. Their other chemical substances are totally synthetic. Totally synthetic materials may be those which occur in nature, e.g. phenyl ethyl alcohol (found in rose and other oils), benzyl acetate (found n jasmine oil) or those which do not occur in nature.

Usually the ingredients of perfume blend are used in the form they are obtained. But there are certain materials which are used advantageously in the form of dilution, tincture etc. For example, tincture of civet improves odour and enables perfumer to standardize his product. Some materials, have better stability in dilution. Phenyl acetaldehyde tends to polymerize but it is quite stable in 50% solution in benzyl alcohol.

Perfumes have been described in different manners. Perfumes which simulate the fragrance of an individual material (usually a flower) are described in terms of that material, e.g., rose, lilac perfume. Perfumes which do not simulate an individual material are referred to as floral bouquet. Such terms as light or heavy floral or oriental are also used. But these terms lack specificity. The other terms which are used include aldehydic, woody, minty, mossy, etc. appear to convey a more uniform concept.

The quality of perfume changes from the moment the bottle is opened and it reaches nose through air and ultimately when the last residual odour has vanished. This is called life cycle of perfume. Ideally, perfume should smell same throughout its life cycle. But practically it is not possible except when a single chemical is used as perfume. Thc first note that volatilizes is known as "topnote". This is usually light and is dominated by quickly volatile substances. The note which is smelt during volatilization of the body of the perfume is its main life. The lingering smell at the end is the end of life cycle of the perfume.

To make the perfume longer lasting, process of fixation is used. More volatile substances are lost quickly. However, rate of volatility is affected by presence of other substances. If the substances of low vapour pressure and of same range could be selected, the perfume is likely to result in longer lasting. The materials which retard volatility act as fixative.

According to Pickthall a fixative material should have two properties besides being oil soluble:

- it should have low vapour pressure,
- it should have low molecular weight.

But these two properties in a chemical substance are, often, not found. Benzyl benzoate was demonstrated having the power of retarding evaporation. Other more volatile substances. According to Poucher, fixative seeks to equalize the different rates of evaporation of various other constituents. Poucher suggests blending of aromatic notes of lasting characters with topnotes to be blended. He further suggests that besides this, for final fixation a blend of animal fixative and sweet notes from natural origin like bergamot may be used. The choice of fixative is still subjective and empirical. Some of the substances which have been used as fixative are benzyl benzoate, diethyphthalate and essential oil-clay sage.

Perfumes for alcoholic fragrances must be sophisticated while the perfumes for creams and toilet waters must match the product image. In case of toothpastes a refreshing flavour must be used. Soaps and shampoos need clean and refreshing perfumes. Thus it may be seen that in each cosmetic product such a perfume should be used which would match the cosmetic usage.

Since cosmetics are blends of different types of materials addition of perfumes have potential of chemical interactions. Interaction may result in changes in colour and odour. Fragrant compounds are affected by oxygen, light, temperature and these factors may cause reactions such as oxidation, polymerization, condensation, hydrolysis etc. Fragrances may also cause physical changes like changes in viscosity of cosmetic preparation. Therefore, cosmetic and perfume compatibility studies should be carried out at the time of development of cosmetics.

COLOURS

Colour has been used in cosmetics from the very beginning. Basically a desire to buy a cosmetic product is controlled by three senses, namely, sight, touch and smell. As such, colour is an important ingredient of cosmetic formulations. This chapter will be incomplete without a brief discussion on colours.

There are many terms which are used by dye stuff and pigment chemist. It will be appropriate to clarify these terms before proceeding further.

By the term, pigment, it is understood that it is a white or coloured chemical compound which is insoluble in a particular solvent. For example, Toluidine Red Toner is not soluble in water and is slightly soluble in mineral oil. But it is soluble in organic solvents like benzene, chloroform, dioxane. Therefore, it can be regarded as pigment in context with water and dye in context with organic solvents.

By the term, dye, it is understood that it is a chemical compound usually of coal-tar origin which is soluble in the vehicle to which reference is made. On the basis of their solubility, these are often termed as water soluble dyes and oil soluble dyes.

The terms, lake and toner have been defined in more than one ways. A lake can be defined as an organic pigment prepared by precipitating a soluble dye on either a reactive or absorptive substratum or diluent (in the composition of pigment, subtratum is an essential part). A toner can be defined as an organic pigment which does not contain a substratum or a diluent. Commercially, a toner is used in full strength form.

Colour can be defined as visual sensation caused by a definite wavelength or a group of wavelengths by an object by one or more phenomena of emission, reflection, refraction or transmission. Visually colour can change in three ways. According to Munsell's nomenclature these are hue, value and chroma. A colour can be distinguished from the other colour by its hue. Hue tells whether a colour is red, yellow, green, etc.

A light colour is distinguished from dark colour by value. Value indicates how much light energy strikes the eye. Chroma tells the intensity of colour. By this attribute, a strong colour can be distinguished from weak colour. A colour can be specified completely in terms of these three attributes.

Another term which is associated with colour is bleed. As mentioned earlier, a pigment is insoluble with reference to particular solvents. Solubilities of the order of 0.0001% are generally regarded as insoluble. But sometimes, a pigment in this order of solubility imparts colour to the solvent. This phenomenon is called bleeding. The degree of this phenomenon can be determined in the following manner.

Pigment is shaken with a particular solvent in a test tube and the solvent is filtered. The colour of the filtrate is compared with the colour of the solvent. If the filtrate has changed noticeably in colour, it is termed as bleed. If the change in colour is slight and can be detected only when compared with control, it is termed as slight bleed. If the filtrate remains unchanged in colour, it is termed as non-bleeding. Sometimes, a pigment does not go into solution but its colloidal particles exhibit colour. This is called pseudo or collodial bleed. True bleed gives a clear transparent solution while colloidal bleed gives a cloudy suspension. Colloidal particles can be removed by mechanical means, e.g. centrifugation.

The terms, masstone, undertone and reduction are used to describe or compare visually the pigments grounded in oil, wax or other suitable grinding medium. To compare colours, the grounded colours are smeared side by side on a piece of white paper by means of a spatula. When spatula is pulled down on a paper, first a thick film is made and then a thin film is made. These films reveal colour differences. Appearance of thick film regardless to background is called masstone or toptone. Appearance of thin film on white paper is called undertone. Sometimes this is also referred to as skintone or print tone. When grounded colour samples are mixed with white pigment such as titanium dioxide, zinc oxide in the same vehicle and are compared on white paper or glass, the results are described as reduction, strength, tint or let down with white.

Colours which can be used in cosmetics can be classified into three classes:

- natural colours,
- inorganic colours,
- coal tar colours.

Natural Colours

Most of the natural colours have been replaced by coal tar colours so far as cosmetics is concerned. A few of the natural colours might still be used. Important one of them are given below:

(i) Cochineal

It is a red dye stuff. It consists of dried bodies of female insects, *coccus cacti,* which lives on a species of cactus. The principal colouring matter of cochineal is carminic acid. Cochineal contains about 10% of this colouring matter. Carminic acid is extracted from ground insect mass. Carminic acid is anthraquinone type of dye. It forms red needles on crystallization. When heated needles darken at 130°C and carbonize at 250°C.

Carmine can be prepared by extracting cochineal with water and precipitating aluminium salt of carminic acid with alum.

(ii) Saffron

It is dried stigma of flowers of the plant, *Cross Sativus Linne.* It is a perennial plant and is grown in Kashmir in India. It is also cultivated in Spain, France, Greece and Iran. The principal colouring agent in saffron is crocin, a glycoside. Crocin is yellow powder easily soluble in water.

(iii) Chlorophyll

Chlorophyll occurs abundantly in nature. Green colour to leaves is imparted by chlorophyll. In plants this green pigment acts as catalyst for photosynthesis. Chlorophyll can be extracted from plant leaves.

Inorganic Colours

A number of inorganic colours (pigments) are used in cosmetics. Some of the most commonly used pigments are:

- iron oxides,
- chromium oxides,
- ultramarines,
- carbon black,
- titanium dioxide,
- zinc oxide,
- aluminium hydrate.

Some of these will be discussed in brief.

(i) Iron Oxides

Though iron oxides are found in abundance on the surface of the earth but natural iron oxides are not used because of difficulty in purification. Iron oxides for use are manufactured under strict control. Iron oxides for commercial use are generally manufactured from iron scrap. But any iron scrap may not be suitable for preparing iron oxides for cosmetic use as usually iron scrap contains prohibitive quantities of arsenic in them. Therefore, iron scrap of controlled purity is used for preparation of iron oxides for cosmetic use. Iron scrap is treated with acid, usually, sulphuric acid is obtain iron salt. Hydrated iron oxide is precipitated from iron salt by adding alkali and is subjected to oxidation. Shades from light lemon yellow to orange may be obtained by this process. Conditions of precipitation and oxidation play an important role. Red iron oxide is usually manufactured by calcining the precipitated yellow iron oxides. Brown red oxide an be manufactured by blending red, yellow and black iron oxides. It may also be prepared by precipitation of iron oxide and partial oxidation. Black iron oxide is a mixture of ferrous and ferric oxides and is manufactured by precipitation of Fe_3O_4 under controlled conditions.

(ii) Chromium Oxide

Chromium oxide green is different from chrome greens which are not suitable for cosmetics. Chromium oxide green, essentially, is pure chromium oxide containing no lead chromate or iron blue. It is purified by washing of acid and alkali. These greens are available either in anhydrous from or in hydrous form. The anhydrous form is dull green and hydrous form has a bluish tint. These pigments are quite stable and are commonly used in eye makeup preparations.

(iii) Ultramarines

The raw materials, sulphur, soda ash, china clay, charcoal pitch or rison are mixed in necessary proportions and are heated in muffle furnace to about 850°C for about 24 hours. The pigment is cooled slowly, washed and purified so that it does not contain lead and arsenic more than 20 and 2 ppm respectively. Depending upon the proportions of raw materials, blue and pink shades are produced. In general, low silica type are blue shades and high silica type are red to pink shades. Ultramarine blue is stable is presence of alkalis and organic solvents but is sensitive to acids. In presence of acids it decolourizes with odour of hydrogen sulphide. In cosmetics it is used in mascara and eye brow pencils.

(iv) Titanium dioxide

Titanium dioxide occurs in nature in three different crystalline forms, i.e., anatose, brookite and rutile. Titanium dioxide of commerce is anatose form. Pure titanium dioxide has high refractive index, fine particle size and has the greatest hiding power. It is used in all type of cosmetics because of its inertness.

(v) Zinc Oxide

Zinc oxide is a white pigment. It varies in particle size from 0.12 to 5 microns. It is high in brightness and low in tinting strength. It finds extensive use in face powders.

For details list of natural, organic and inorganic colouring matter readers are advised to refer to IS:4707 (Part I)–1988.

Coaltar Colours

Every coal tat colour cannot be used in cosmetics. Rule 144 of the Drugs and Cosmetics Rules prohibits use of coal tar colours other than coal tar colours specified under Schedule Q. This rule further prescribes that Schedule Q colours should not contain more than:

- 2 ppm of arsenic calculated as arsenic trioxide.
- 200 ppm of lead calculated as lead,
- 100 ppm of heavy metals other than lead calculated as the total of the respective metals.

Schedule Q has two parts. Part I contains list of coal tar colours which can be used in cosmetics other than soap. Part II of Schedule Q contains list of coal tar colours which can be used in soaps. For the benefit of readers, Schedule Q is reproduced here.

Schedule Q
(See Rules 134 and 144)

Part I–List of Dyes, Colours and Pigments permitted to be used in Cosmetics and Soaps as given under IS: 4707 (Part I)–1988 as amended by the Bureau of Indian Standards

Common name of the colour	Colour Index Number	Chemical name of the colour
1	2	3
Guinea Green B	42085	Monosodium salt of 4-N-ethyl-p- sulfobenzyl-amino) diphenylmetylone- (1-(N-ethyl-N p-sulfoniumbenzyl) Δ2, 5-cyclohexadienimine)
Light Green SF Yellowish	42095	Disodium Salt of 4-[4-(N-ethyl-p-sulfobenzyl-amino)-phenyl)-4 sulfoniumphenyl) methylene]-2-(N-ethyl-N-sulfobenzyl) Δ2, 5-Cyclo-hexa-dienimine.
Tartrazine	19140	Trisodium salt of 3-carboxy-5-hydroxy-1-p-sulfophenyl-4-sulkfophenylazo-pyrazole.
Sunset yellow FCF	15985	Disodium salt of 1-ps-sulfophenylazo-2- naphthol-6-sulfonic acid.
Ponceau 3R	16155	Disodium salts of a mixture of 1-alkyl-phenyl- azo-2-naphthol-3, 6-disulphonic acids.
Amaranth	16185	Trisodium salt of 1-(4slfo-1-napthylazo) 2-naphthol 3, 6-diisulphonic acid.
Erythrosine	45430	Disodium salt of 9-0-carboxyphenyl-6 hydroxy 2, 4, 5, 7-tetraiodo-isoxanthone.
Ponceau SX	14700	Disodium salt of 2-(5-sulfo-2, 4-xylyl-axo)-1-naphthol-4-sulfonic acid.
Brilliant Blue FCF	42090	Disodium salt of 4-(9-4-(N-ethyl-p-sulfo-benzylamino-phenyl)-2-sulfonium-phenyl)-methylene)-(1-N-ethyl-N-p-sulfobenzy(-Δ 2, 5-cyclohexadienimine).
Indigocarmine	73015	Disodium salt of 5, 5'-indigot-indisulfonic acid.
Wool Violet 5BN (Acid violet 6B)	42640	Monosodium salt of 4-(N-ethyl-p-sulfo benzyl amino-phenyl)-4-(N-ethyl-p- (sulfonium-benzyl-amine,-phenyl) methylene)-(N, N-dimethyl-D 2, 5-cyclohexadienimine).

Contd. . .

Schedule Q *(contd...)*

1	2	3
Light Green SF Yellowish	42095	Calciul salt of 4-(4-N-ethyl-p sulfobenzyl) (minophenyl) (4-sulfonium-phenyl)-methyl- lene), (1(N-ethyl-N-p-sulfobenzyl-)D 2, 5- cyclo-hexadienimine)
Alizarin cyannine	61570	Disodium salt of 1, 4-bits (O-sulfo-p-tuluino) Green F. anthraquinone.
Quinazarine Green SS	61565	1, 4-bis-(p-Tuoluino)-anthraquinome.
Fast Green FCF	43053	Disodium salt of 4-)4-(-ethyl-p-sulfobenzyl- amin)-phenyl) (4-hydroxy-2 sulphonium-phenyl) methylene-(1-N-ethyl-N-p-sulfo-benzyl)-Δ 2, 5-cyclohexadienimine.
Acid violet 6B	42640	Monosodium salt of 4-(N-ethyl-p-sulfobenzyl amino-phenyl)-4-(N-ethyl-p-(sulfonium-benzylamine)-phenyl) methylene)-(N,N-dimethyl-Δ 2, 5-cyclohexadieniine).
Pyranine	59040	Trisodium salt of 10-hydroxy-3, 5, 8-pyrene-trisulfonic acid
Quinoline yellow WS	47005	Disodium salt of disulfonic acid of 2-(2 Quinolyl)-1, 3-indandione.
Quinoline Yellow SS	47000	(2-(2-quinolyl)-1, 3-indandione.
Ponecaue 2R	16150	Disodium salt of 1-xylylazo-2-naphthol-3, 6-disulfoniac acid.
Lithol Rubin B	15850	Monosodium salt of 4-(0-sulfo-p-tolylazo) 3-hydroxy-2-naphthoic acid
Lithol Rubin BCA	15850	Calcium salt of 4-(0-sulf-p-tolylazo) 3-hydroxy-2-naphthoic acid
Lake Red D	15500	Monosodium salt of 1-0-carboxyphenylazo 2-naphthol
Lake Red DBA	15500	Barium salt of 1-0-carboxyphenylazo-2-naphthol
Lake Red DCA	15500	Calcium salt of 1-0-carboxyphenylazo-2-naphthol
Toney Red	26100	1-p-phenylazophenylazo-2-naphthoil
Oil Red OS	26125	1-Xtlylazomylylazo-2-naphthol
Tetrabromo-fluorescein	45380	2, 4, 5, 7-Tetrabromo-3, 6-fluorandiol
Eosin TS	45380	Disodium salt of 2, 4, 5, 7-tetrabromo-9-0-carboxyphenyl-6-hydroxy-3-isoxanthone.
Eosiin YSK	45380	Dipotassium salt of 2, 4, 5, 7-tetrabromo-9-0-carboxy-phenyl-6-hydroxy-3-isoxanthone.
Tetrachloroflu-Orescein NA	45366	2, 4, 5, 7-terachloro-S, 6-Fluorandiol.

1	2	3
Tetrachloroflu-orescein K	45366	Disodium salt of 9-0-carboxyphenyl 2, 4, 5, 7-tetra-chloro-6-hydroxy-3-isoxanthone
Tetrachloro-tetra	45410	2, 4, 5, 7-Tetrabromo-12, 13, 14, 15-tetra-chloro-3, 6-fluorandiol-bromofluorescien
Phloxine B	45410	Disodium salt of 2, 4, 5, 7-tetrabromo-9-(3, 4,5, 6-tetrachloro-o-carboxyphenyl)-6-hydroxy-3-isoxanthone.
Bluish Orange TR	45457	1, 4, 5, 8, 15-Pentabromo-2, 7-dicarboxy-3, 6-fluorandiol.
Helindone Pink CN	73360	5, 5-Dichloro-3, 3i-dimethyl-thloindigo
Brilliant Lake R	15800	Calcium salt of 3-hydroxy-4-phenylazo-Red 2-naphthonic acid.
Deep Maroon (Fanchon Maroon)	15880	Calcium salt of 4-(1-sulfo-2-naphthylazo)-3-hydroxy-3-naphthoic acid.
Toluidine Red	12120	1(o-Nitro-p-tolylazo)-2-naphthol.
Flaming Red	12085	1-(o-Chloro-p-nitrophenylazo)-2-naphthol
Deep Red (Maroon)	12350	3-Hydroxy-N-(m-nitrophenyl)-4-(o-nitro-p-tolylazo)-2-naphthanmide
Alba Red	13058	o-(p-β, β'-dihydorxy-diethylamino)-phenyl-azo)-benzoic acid
Orange G	16230	Disodium salt of 1-phenylazo-2-naphthol-6-8-disulfonic acid.
Orange II	15510	Monosodium salt of 1-p-sulfophenylazo-2-naphthol
Dichlorofluo-rescein	45365	4, 5-Dichloro-3, 6-fluorandiol
Dichlorofluo-rescein NA	45365	Disodium salt of 9-o-carboxyphenyl-1-45-dichloro-6-hydroxy-3-isoxanthone
Diiodofluo-rescein	45425	4, 5-Diiodo-3, 6-fluorandiol
Erythrosine Yellowish NA	45425	Disodium salt of 9-o-carboxyphenyl-6-hydroxy-4, 5-diiodo-3-isoxanthone
Erythrosine Yellowish K	45425	Dipotassium salt of 9-o-carboxyphenyl-6-hydroxy-4, 5-diiodo-3-isozanthone
Erythrosine Yellowish K	45425	Dipotassium salt of 9-o-carboxyphenyl-6-hydroxy-4, 5-diiodo-3-isoxanthone
Orange TR	45456	4, 5, 15-Tribromo-2, 7-dicarboxy-3, 6- fluorandiol
Alizarin	58000	1, 2-Anthraquinonediol
Dibromodiiodo-fluorescein	45371	4, 5-Dibromo-2, 7-diiodo-3, 6-fluorandiol
Resorcin Brown	20170	Monosodium salt of 4-p-sulfophenylazo-2-(2, 4, xylylazo)1, 3-rescorcinol

Contd. . .

Schedule Q *(contd...)*

1	2	3
Alphazuirine FG	42090	Diammonium salt of 4-(-N-ethyl-p-sulfo benzyl-amino-(2-sulfoniumphenyl)-methylene)-(1-N-5-cyclohexadienimine).
Alizarin Astrol B	61530	Monosodium salt of 1-methylamino-4-o-sulfo-p-toluino)-anthroquinone
Indigo	73000	Indigotin
Patent Blue NA	4202	Monosodium salt of 4-(4-(N-ethyl-benzyl-amino)-phenyl)-(5-hydroxy-4-sulfo-sulfonium-phenyl-methylene) (N-ethyl-N-benzyl-Δ2-5 Cyclohexa-dienimine)
Patent Blue CA	42052	Calcium salt of 4-(4-(N-ethyl-enzyl-amino-phenyl) (5-hdroxy-4-sulfo-sulfonium-phenyl-methylene) N-ethyl-N-Benzyl-Δ2-5-Cycloh-exadienimine)
Carbanthrene Blue	69725	3, 3-Dichloroindanthrene.
Naphthol Blue Black	20470	Disodium salt of 8-amino-7-p-nitrophenylazo 3-phenylazo-1-naphthol 3,6-disulfonic acid.
Alizurol Purple SS	60725	1-hydroxy-4-p-toluino-anthraquinone
Acid Red 89	23910	..
Acid Red 97	22890	..
Acid Blue 1	42045	..
Food Blue 3	42045	..
Natural Orange 6	75480	..
Solvent Blue 4	44045	..
Solvent Yellow 18	12740	..
Food Yellow 12	12740	..
Solvent Red 1	12150	..
Solvent Yellow 32	48045	..
Fanchon Yellow	11680	(a)-(o-Nitro-p-tolylazo) acetoacetanilide.

Part-II: List of Colours permitted to be used in Soaps

Common name of the colour	Colour Index No.	Chemical name of the colour
1	2	3
Phthalocyanine Blue	74060	Phthalocyninate 2-copper
Iragalite Red CVPB Paste or pigment Orange 5	12075	1-(2, 4-dinitro phenylazo)-2-Naphthalenol

1	2	3
Citrus Red No. 2	12156	1-2(2, 5-dimethoxy phenylazo) 2-naphthol
Rhodamine B 500	45170	3-ethochloride of 9-0 carboxy-thenyl-6-diethylamino-3-ethylamine-3-isoxanthene.
Aqueous Green Paste	74260	Polychloro copper Phthalocyanine
Pigment Yellow 3	11710	2-(4-Chloro-2-nirophenyl)-azo-N-(-2-Chlorophenyl)-3-Oxobutamide
Irgalite Carmine F-P Powder or Pigments Red 5	12490	N05-Chloro-2, 4-dimethoxy-phenyl)4-(CS diethylamine) Sulfonyl-2-methoxyphenyl)-azo-3-hydroxy-2 naphthalene carboxamide
Monolite Red 4R HV Paste or Pigment Red 7	12420	N-(4-Chloro-2-methylphenyl-4-(-4-Chloro-2-methylphenyl) azo 3-hydroxy-2-naphthalenol Carboxamide
Oil red No. 1 or Solvent Red 24 or Oil Red 3R	26105	4-0-Toyalazo-Toluidine azo 2-naphthalenol

Note: Every care has been taken to reproduce the schedule correctly, inadvertent mistakes, if any, are regretted.

The Drugs and Cosmetics Rules also prohibit use of lead and arsenic compounds for the purpose of colouring.

Readers are advised to refer to IS:4707 (Part I)–1988. This standard lists dyes, colours and pigments which are generally recognized safe (GRAS) for use in cosmetics. A list of colours for use in toilet soaps has been given separately. In this standard colours have been classified into four classes, namely:

- status A,
- status B,
- status C,
- status D.

Status A is allotted to those colours which are permitted for use in all cosmetics with restriction in the level of use in any product. Maximum concentration that can be used is also given. Status B is allotted to those colours which are permitted for use in cosmetics except for preparations like eye make-up remover, products which in normal course of use may come into contact with mucous membranes of the eye. Status C is allotted to those colours which are exclusively suitable for use in cosmetics intended not to come in contact with mucus membranes, for example, lipsticks, Status D is allotted to colours which are permitted for use in cosmetics intended exclusively for external use and come into contact only briefly with the skin.

SILICONES

Silicones are polymers. These polymers have alternate atoms of silicon and oxygen (-Si-O_2-SI-O_2--), organic groups such as methyl or phenyl can be attached to Si atoms. Viscosity of silicon polymers increases with increase in molecular weight. Silicon polymers having viscosity ranging from 0.65 centistokes to 3 million centistokes are available. Various grades of silicones are distinguished by numbers. Higher polymers take the form of grease, waxes, and resins.

Silicone fluids are odourless, colourless and tasteless. They are stable to heat and resistant to chemicals. Solubility of silicon polymers in organic solvents decreases with increase in molecular weight. These are insoluble in water. However, polymers adducts provide solubility in water and lower alcohols by producing much more polar silicon product. Amine groups increase the ionic bonding capabilities to the hair and the skin.

Low molecular weight cyclic materials (e.g. tetramer, pentamer) are volatile. These serve transitory emollients and lubricants in antiperspirants, hair care and skin care. Silicone oils with low molecular weight are used as lubricants in the skin and the hair cosmetic products. High molecular weight dimethicones (silicon gums) are also used in hair care cosmetics. Properties of these materials range from excellent residual conditioning on hair to significant water resistance to the skin.

SOME FUNCTIONAL RAW MATERIALS

There are some materials which are incorporated in cosmetics for their specified functions and are used in a variety of cosmetics. Materials which have been discussed briefly in proceeding paragraphs should not be considered as an exclusive list.

Vitamins

Vitamins play an important role in maintaining the physiological function of the whole body. They also help us maintaining physiological function of the skin.

(i) *Amino benzoic acid (para-aminobenzoic acid, vit. H):* Amino benzoic acid is widely distributed in plant and animal tissues e.g. rice polishings, yeast, liver etc. Amino benzoic acid and its esters are used in cosmetics as sunscreening agents. The acid is more efficacious sunscreening agent than its esters.

(ii) *Ascorbic acid (Vitamin C):* Ascorbic acid is essential for human body. It is widely distributed in plants, e.g. citrus fruits, Indian gooseberry etc. It's Importance may be judged from the fact that it is essential for the formation of collagens and inter cellular material and hence is essential for the development of cartilage, bone and teeth. It is also essential for conversion of folic acid to folinic acid and for healing of wounds. It has been used as antioxidant in emulsions of fats and oils. It is a protective and corrective vitamin. It is skin lightener and also helps in protection from UV light. It has been used in cosmetics for there properties.

(iii) *Biotin (Vitamin H, Coenzyme R):* Biotin is widely distributed in plants and animals. The richest sources are liver, kidney, pasture yeast, milk and eggs. It was first recognized as growth factor for yeast. It is a coenzyme for carboxylation during metabolism of proteins and carbohydrates. It enhances flexibility and strength of fingernails. It has positive effects on scalp and hair roots. It has been used in cosmetics for these effects.

(iv) *Calcium Pantothenates and Panthenols:* Calcium pantothenate is calcium salt of pantothenic acid. Pantothenic acid is present in all living tissues, and is considered a member of vitamin B group. It is component of our enzyme system associated with acetylation reaction, in tissues. Its deficiency symptoms in animals include dermatitis, keratitis, adrenal haemorrhage and atrophy, depigmentation of hair and arrest of growth. It is usually used as calcium salt.

Racemic pantothenic acid or panthenol has not been used more in cosmetics than calcium pantothenate and ethyl panthenol. Calcium pantothenate and ethyl panthenol are long lasting moisturizers for the hair, skin and the nails.

They nourish and strengthen hair, prevent hair damage due to over heating or overhanging. They make nails flexible and less brittle. They also promote keratinization. They soothe and help enhance healing of the skin.

(v) *Niacinamide (Nicotinic Acid Amide):* Nicotinic acid is required by the body for the formation of coenzymes which are important in tissue respiration also. Recent studies suggest that it has anti-inflammatory activity on blemished skin. It has been used in cosmetics as skin lightener also.

(vi) *Vitamin A:* Vitamin A is essential for normal vision in dim light and for the integrity of epithelial cells. Vitamin A is closely related to the plant pigment carotene which exists in 3 isomeric forms all of which are converted to some extent into vitamin A in the livers of man and animals. Of three isomers of carotene, the β (beta) compound is more active than the α (alpha) or γ (gama) isomer. Deficiency of vitamin A may give rise to skin changes like dry rough skin. Its use in cosmetics is likely to result in healthy and soft skin.

(vii) *Vitamin E:* Vitamin E occurs in oils such as soybean, what germ, rice germ, cottonseed and in green leaves such as that of lettuce. Chemically, vitamin E is tocopherol. There are different isomers of tocopherol α, β, γ. α–Tocopherol has more activity than other isomers.

A fourth form of tocopherol has been isolated from soybean oil. However, its activity is only one hundredth of natural α-tocopherol.

Vitamin E blocks lipid peroxidation in cells and tissues. It is a very good antioxidant. It helps enhance the performance of UV filters, softens skin and moistures within.

Vitamin E is generally used as acetate or is used in its natural form like wheat germ oil.

Amino Acids

There are several amino acids, but there are certain amino acids with which the body must be supplied such amino acids are called essential amino acids. Essential amino acids include:

- isoleucine;
- leucine;
- lysine;
- methionine;
- phenylalanine;
- threonine;
- tryptophan;
- valine;
- histidine;
- arginine.

Amino acids are effective in helping recovery of dry and rough skin by moisturizing the epidermis system. Cysteine hydrochloride has been used for its healing properties.

Anti-inflammatory Agents

(a) Allantoin

It occurs naturally in comfrey roots but it is prepared synthetically. It has been used to stimulate tissue formation and wound healing. It has also been used in psoriasis and other skin disorders.

It is used in hand creams and lotions, night creams, sun protection formulations, scalp treatment preparations. It can be enhance functional performance and soothing properties of talcum powders, baby care products, foot therapy formulations and lipsticks.

(b) Cade oil

Cade oil is obtained by destructive distillation of the branches and wood of *juniperus Oxycedrus.* It is dark reddish brown or nearly black oil. It contains guaiacol, ethylguaiacl, cresol and cadinene.

It has been used in the treatment of psoriasis and eczema. It has also been used in medicated soaps.

(c) Calamine

Calamine is basic zinc carbonate coloured with ferric oxide. On ignition it yields 68-74% of oxides of zinc and iron. Its colour depends on the variety and amount of ferric oxide present and the process by which it is incorporated. It has mild action on the skin.

It has been used in powders, creams, lotion and ointments.

Miscellaneous Functional Materials

Other functional materials like sunscreening agents, anti-dandruff agents etc. have been dealt in the chapters where cosmetics in which these are used, have been covered.

HERBAL OR PLANT MATERIALS

In good old days many herbal and natural materials used to be employed for beauty treatment. Gradually with the advancement of science, ready made cosmetic preparations came into existence. Today a variety of chemical substances of different origins are used in cosmetics. There is resurgence of use of herbal ingredients in cosmetics. Nowadays, a number of herbal cosmetics are being marketed in the country. It is believed that herbal ingredients in cosmetics make them more useful. Some of the herbal ingredients which are being commonly used in cosmetics are given below.

Commonly Used Materials

(i) Almond

Fixed oil obtained from almonds is emollient in nature. It is extensively used in cosmetics. A white milk used in cleansers and astringents is obtained by soaking ground almonds in milk or water and then by milling. Ground almonds are used in facial and body scrubs.

(ii) Apricot

Apricots contain highly nourishing oil. This oil is rich in vitamin A. It is believed to improve condition and elasticity of the skin. The pulp of both fresh and dry fruit is used in face masks. Finely ground shell and kernel of the stone is used in facial and body scrubs.

(iii) Avocado

Oil of Avocado is rich in vitamin A. It uses are similar to apricot oil.

(iv) Azadirachta (Neem)

Leaves of neem are considered antiseptic. Neem fruits yield an oil called neem oil. Nimbidin is the chief bitter principle of neem oil. Neem oil is used in soaps. Extract of leaves can be used in tooth pastes and skin care products.

(v) Cabbage

It is chiefly valuable for its high mineral and vitamin contents. It has wonderful cleansing and reducing properties. Its juice can be used in skin care products.

(vi) Camomile

Camomile flower contains a dye and therefore, can be used with henna in herbal hair due. Infusion of flowers can also be used for mild astringency in cleansers, conditioners and hair rinses.

(vii) Carrots

Carrots are rich source of vitamin A. These are good for irritated or sunburnt skin. The raw grated vegetables and juice make excellent cleanser. Carrot juice can be used in masks and tonics.

(viii) Comfrey

Decoction of root and infusion of leaves have antiseptic and healing properties. These can be used in creams and lotions.

(ix) Common Basil (Tulsi)

Flowers and leaves yield an essential oil which is considered antiseptic. Juice of its leaves can be used in skin creams and lotions.

(x) Cornflower

Infusion of flowers can be used in skin tonics and fresheners.

(xi) Cucumber

Cucumber juice is used in cosmetics. Cucumber juice is soothing, healing and slightly astringent. It can be used in masks, cleansers and toners.

(xii) Dandelion

Infusion of dandelion flowers can be used in masks, cleansers. Sap from the stem can be used in bleaching creams.

(xiii) E. Alba (Bhringaraja)

It is a source of black stain and is used in hair preparations.

(xiv) Elderflower

Infusion of flowers are mildly bleaching and therefore can be used in skin cleansers, conditioners and creams. Decoction of leaves is healing and can be used for fun-burnt or wind-burnt skin.

(xv) Eucalyptus

Decoction of leaves of eucalyptus is antiseptic and invigorating. Decoction can be used in skin care products.

(xvi) Fennel

Infusion of chopped leaves is soothing and stimulating. Infusion can be used in masks, cleansers and toners.

(xvii) Fenugreek

Fenugreek (Methi) is a traditional component of hair care products. It is used for its cleansing and softening activity. It promotes scalp health. It can be used in hair care, skin care products.

(xviii) Garlic

Carlic juice is considered antiseptic. Its juice can be used in antiseptic and smoothing creams.

(xix) Geranium

Geranium yields an essential oil which is used in perfumery. Geranium leaves and flowers can be used for healing or rejuvenating. Alternatively, geranium oil can be added in healing and cleansing creams.

(xx) Henna

Henna leaves contain a dye. Henna leaves are used in herbal hair dyes. Henna can be used with camomile flowers for dyeing the hair. Leaves and flowers yield an essential oil.

(xxi) Indian Gooseberry (Amla)

Fruits, bark and leaves of Indian Gooseberry are rich in tannins. Fruits are used in herbal hair dyes, particularly with henna. Dried fruits are also used for washing the hair.

(xxii) Indian Nard (Jatamansi)

Indian nard yields an oil, called spikenard oil. Oil is considered to improve hair growth and is also believed to darken hair. Spikenard oil can be used in hair preparations.

(xxiii) Jasmine

Flowers of jasmine yield an essential oil, called jasmine oil. Jasmine oil is used in traditional hair oils.

(xxiv) Lady's Mantle

Juice of leaves of lady's mantle has healing and mild bleaching properties. Its juice can be added to tonics for oily skin or to the creams for dry skin.

(xxv) Lavender

Flowers and leaves of lavender yield an essential oil called lavender oil. Infusion of leaves and flower is considered antiseptic. Infusion can be used in skin creams and toners.

(xxvi) Lemon

Peel of Lemon yields an essential oil which is used in perfumery and soaps. Infusion of leaves of lemon has soothing and mild astringent properties which can be used in skin tonics and cleansers.

(xxvii) Lime

Infusion of flowers and young leaves can be used in healing and moisturizing creams and lotions.

(xxviii) Marigold

Infusion and decoction of flowers and leaves can be used in skin creams and lotions. These can also be used for hair lightening rinses.

(xxix) Marsh Mallow

Infusion of flower of marshmallow and decoction of its roots have antiseptic properties. These can be used in skin creams and cleansers.

(xxx) Nutmeg

Nutmeg butter or fat obtained from nutmegs is used as external stimulant in hair lotions. Nutmeg oil is also used in spicy perfumes in soaps.

(xxxi) Orange blossom

Its essential oil is soothing and can be used in creams to soothe dry skin.

(xxxii) Parsley

Crushed leaves or juice of parsley can be used in poultices. Juice or infusion of leaves can be used in skin creams, lotions or cleansers. It also has anti-dandruff and deodorizing properties. It can therefore be used in hair preparations also.

(xxxiii) Peach

The pulp of fresh peach is used in face masks, cleansers and moisturizers. Peach nut oil is fragrant and rich and is used in nourishing creams.

(xxxiv) Rose

Rose petals yield an essential oil, called rose oil. Infusion of petals can be used in skin toners, cleansers, moisturizers and colognes.

(xxxv) Rosemary

Flowers and leaves of rosemary have antiseptic and anti-dandruff properties. Infusions of flowers and leaves can be used in skin creams and lotions. Herbal oil made from leaves can be used for the hair.

(xxxvi) Safflower

Flower head are a source of red and yellow dye called safflower. This dye is used in rouges.

(xxxvii) Sage

Infusion of flowers and leaves is healing and mild astringent. The infusion can be used in skin tonics and cleansers.

(xxxviii) Sandal

Sandalwood oil is extracted from heartwood of sandal tree. Sandalwood oil is used in perfumes.

(xxxix) S. Racemosa (Lodhra)

Decoction of Lodhra is used to stop bleeding of gums.

(xl) Tea Tree Oil

Tea tree oil is obtained by the steam distillation of leaves and terminal branches of Melaleuca alternifolia, commonly known as Australian tea tree. It is widely recognised as potent natural germicide. It can be incorporated in hair care products in the concentration of 1 to 5%. In skin care products, particularly for problems caused by *propionebacterium acnes* in pimples and other bacteria, it can be used in concentration of 0.5 to 2%. For its anti-erythematous effect it can be used in concentration of 1%.

(xli) Thyme

Leaves of thyme make astringent infusion. Leaves also make strongly perfumed herbal hair oil. Thyme also has deodorizing and anti-dandruff properties.

(xlii) Turmeric

Turmeric has been long used in poultices and scrubs in India. Its water extract has antiseptic properties. It can be used in skin creams.

(xliii) Wheatgerm

It is rich in vitamins and minerals. It is extremely beneficial in face masks and body scrubs. Wheat germ oil is rich in vitamin E which is considered good for the skin.

(xliv) Witch Hazel

Steam distillate of bark is astringent and antiseptic and can be used in skin creams, lotions and toners.

How to Use Herbs

In earlier times, herbs were used for both medicinal purposes as well as for beautification. These had been used in both forms, i.e., fresh form and dried form. These can be used by mashing and directly applying to the body with or without using other ingredients. In fact, in earlier times these were used this way only. But nowadays, their extracts, decoctions, infusions, tinctures, steam distillates etc. are used rather than herbs themselves. There are a many manufacturers of herbal extracts in India. Basic of making plant materials will be given in the proceeding paragraphs for the benefit of readers. Whenever these are prepared, preservatives should be added to them as these are perishable.

(i) Infusions

Infusions are basically strong teas of herb(s) and can be prepared either in china clay pots or stainless steel vessels. Aluminium vessels should not be used as these can taint the infusions.

The following method can be employed for preparing infusions:

Place the herb (coarse powder) in the vessel and pour freshly boiled water. Cover and leave for at least three hours. Strain and filter. The quantity of herb and solvent (water) may vary depending on whether herb is fresh or dried. Usually, for 4 Oz (100 gm) of fresh herb or 2 Oz of dried herb and 1 pint (575 ml) or water can be used.

(ii) Decoctions

Decoctions are prepared by boiling the herb with water. The following method can be adopted for preparing decoctions.

Place the herb (coarse powder) in stainless steel or enamel pan, add sufficient water and cover the pan. Gently boil and continue boiling on gentle heat till the water is reduced to one quarter. This may require boiling for about 2-3 hours. Strain and filter. The same proportions of herb and water can be used as recommended in the case of infusions.

(iii) Extracts and Tinctures

Extracts are generally prepared with hydro-alcoholic solvents and tinctures are prepared with either alcohol or hydro-alcoholic solvent with high percentage of alcohol. The following method can be used for preparing extracts and tinctures:

Crush the herb or flowers and place them in a macerator. Add alcohol or alcohol-water mixture to cover the herb. Close the macerator tightly with lid and leave overnight. Add more solvent and further macerate for 2-3 days. Sometimes maceration may be as long as a week. Strain the mixture firmly with a strainer and filter the extract/tincture. Depending upon the solubility of constituents, this extract/tincture could be used or this could be used as solvent for maceration of fresh herb. The recommended proportions are 4 Oz (100 gm) of fresh herb or flowers and 1 pint (575 ml) of solvent (e.g. water, alcohol-water mixture or alcohol). Extracts/tinctures should be stored in tightly closed containers.

(iv) Flower Waters

Flower waters are made in the same way as infusions. The same proportions of herbs and water can be used. However, the difference in infusion and flower waters is that solvent is allowed to remain in contact with flowers overnight in case of flower waters.

Flower waters can also be prepared by using flower essence (essential oil) and purified water.

(v) Oil Soluble Extracts

Oil soluble extracts can either be prepared by extracting herbs with petroleum ether or by adopting method used for preparing ayurvedic oils. In the latter method, the herb in coarse powder is left in contact with water overnight. More water is added next day. This herb-water mixture is placed with oil in a vessel and the vessel is heated till all the water has been removed. The oil is allowed to cool and is then filtered. Herb soaks water and its cells get swollen, with further soaking of water cells rupture exposing oil soluble principles. In this way oil soluble principle of herb get into oil.

Some herbal extracts are available commercially Balsara Herbal Products (Pvt.) Ltd. are making herbal extracts under the trade name Folicon. Some of the extracts are oil extracts and some are aqueous glycol extracts. A list of these extracts and the products in which these can be used in given below (Table 2.8).

Table 2.8: Folicon Herbal Extracts (Cosmetic Grade)

Application	Type	Code	
Amla	Aquest extract	C 3101	Hair Care
Amla	Oil Extract	C 3101	Hair Care
Aloe	Aqueous Extract	C 3102	Skin and Hair Care
Bhringraj/Maka	Aqueous Extract	C 3103	Hair Care
Bhringraj/Maka	Oil Extract	C 3203	hair Care
Brahmi	Aqueous Extract	C 3104	Hair Care
Brahmi	Oil Extract	C 3204	Hair Care
Henna/Mehendi	Aqueous Extract	C 3105	Hair Care
Haldi/Turmeric	Aqueous Extract	C 3106	Skin Care
Hibiscus	Aqueous Extract	C 3107	Skin and Hair Care
Khus	Aqueous Extract	C 3108	Skin and Hair Care
Lemon Peel	Aqueous Extract	C 3109	Skin and Hair Care
Methi/Fenugreek	Aqueous Extract	C 3110	Skin and Hair Care
Neem	Aqueous Extract	C 3111	Skin and Hair Care
Rose Petal	Aqueous Extract	C 3112	Skin and Hair Care
Shikakai	Aqueous Extract	C 3113	Hair Care
Sandalwood	Aqueous Extract	C 3114	Skin Care
Tulsi	Aqueous Extract	C 3115	Skin Care

These are recommended to be used in a certain concentration in certain type of preparations. Recommended concentrations are shown in Table 2.9.

Table 2.9: Folicon Herbal Extracts Cosmetic Products Guidelines (use levels)

Folicon	Anti-perspitant	Cleansers, fresheners and masks	Lotions, creams	Hair-conditions	Medicated creams	Shampoos	Sunscreens	Hair oil, vitalizer and creams
	%	%	%	%	%	%	%	%
Amla	–	5-10	5-10	5-10	–	1-5	–	5-10*
Aloe	5-10	5-10	5-10	5-10	10-15	1-5	–	–
Bhringraj/Maka	–	–	–	–	–	–	–	5-10*
Brahmi	–	–	–	–	10-15	' 1-5	–	5-10*
Henna/Mehendi	–	–	–	5-10	–	1.5	–	–
Haldi/Turmeric	–	5-10	–	–	5-10	–	–	–
Hibiscus	–	–	–	–	–	1-5	–	–
Khus	5-10	1-5	–	–	–	–	1-5	–
Lomon peel	–	1-5	–	1-5	–	1.5	–	–
Neem	5-10	–	–	–	5-10	–	–	–
Rose petal	5-10	–	1-5	–	–	–	–	–
Shikakai	–	–	–	5-10	–	–	–	–
Sandal wood	5	–	1-5	–	–	–	10	–
Tulsi	1-5	–	–	–	5-10	–	5	

3

Hair Structure and Its Chemistry

A number of products are used on the hair by both men and women. However, there are some products which are used by men only e.g., shaving cream, shaving soap. Products which are used on hair include shampoos, hair oils, hair colourants (dyes), hair waving products, hair straighteners, shaving products and depilatories. Thus it may be observed that hair preparations form a very important class of cosmetics.

For formulation of different products for the hair, knowledge of hair structure and its chemistry will be useful to a cosmetic chemist. Therefore, structure of the hair and its chemistry will be briefly mentioned in succeeding paragraphs.

Hair consist of the central medulla surrounded by the cortex. The central medulla is composed of soft keratin while the cortex is composed of hard keratin. Outer surface of the hair consists of very thin overlapping flat scales which interlock to form cuticle. However, there is no medulla in fine and blonde hair. Hair can be defined as modified epithelial structure formed as a result of keratinization of germinative cells. A hair follicle is formed due to downward growth from the epidermis to dermis tissue. At depth of downward growth a germinal matrix is formed over papilla of connective tissue and is canalized. This acts as a source of tissue fluids to the area. Proliferation at the germinal matrix forces the cells up and as they go farther from the source of nourishment i.e., outside the external root sheath, transition into keratin takes place. Thus growth of hairs is the result of continuous proliferation of epidermal cells of the matrix. During the development of follicle some of the cells which form external root sheath grow out into dermis forming sebaceous glands. The ducts of these sebaceous glands open into follicle. Hair structure is shown in Figure 3.1.

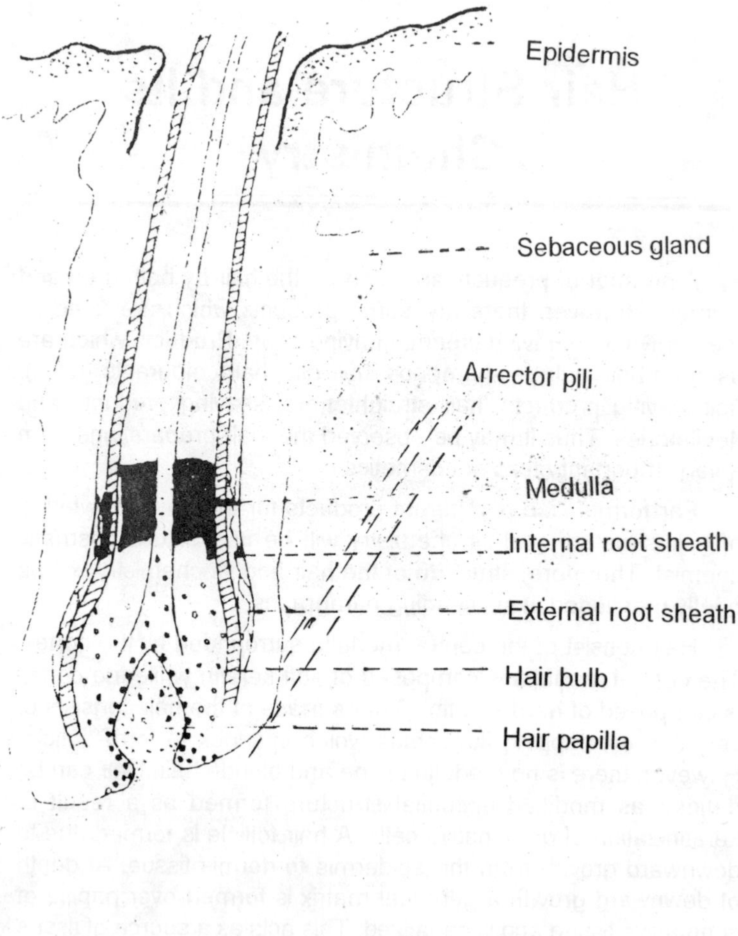

Fig. 3.1 Structure of Hair

The hair follicles, usually, are in slanting position and sebaceous glands, generally, are on the obtuse angle of the follicle. A small bundle of muscle fibres, known as corrector pili extends from the connective tissue sheath of the hair follicle on the obtuse side, upwards towards the dermis at a short distance from the opening of the hair follicle. Contraction of these muscles promotes flow of sebum into the hair follicle and onto the skin.

More or less all hair follicles undergo cyclic activity. An active phase which is called anagen is followed by resting period called telogen. In anagen a hair in produced and in telogen fully formed hair remains anchored in the folicle by its expanded base and the dermal papilla lies free of the epidermal matrix. Between anagen and tolegen there is a relatively short transition phase called catagen in which the newly formed club hair moves towards the skin surface. The folicle becomes active again at the end of telogen by a down growth of the secondary germ, thus matrix becomes reconstituted and a new hair starts to form. As a result, the folicle re-enacts its embryonic development. Ultimately the old club hair is shed. Thus some hair are always shed and new hair grow. Some time, the rate of hair loss becomes more than the growth of hair or new hair do not grow. Such a situation results in hair loss. There could be several factors for the hair loss. Some factors are given below:

Reduced hair follicle function due to male hormones

Thinning of hair in men usually commences at the front of the head on ageing. This is known as male pattern baldness or *androgen alopecia.* This type of alopecia is different form *alopecia aerata* and other medical-related hair conditions. After the hair start thinning there in no change in the number of hair on the total surface area of the head. The hair become more brittle due to reduction in the growth period of the hair cycle.

It was Hamilton who demonstrated in male pattern baldness. He stated that the causes of male pattern baldness were male hormones and genetic factors based on epidemiological finding. The male hormone testosterone is converted to 5α-dehydrote stosterone (DHT) which has higher biological activity at the hair folicles through the action of 5α-reductase. Currently DHT is thought to be the principal cause of the hair loss.

Reduction in metabolic functions of hair follicles and hair bulbs

Three processes of the hair matrix at the hair roots i.e. division, proliferation and differentiation form hair and make it grow up to the dermis. The hair matrix receives the nutrients from the capillaries in the dermal papilla for cell division.

In case, the flow of blood in capillaries surrounding the hair follicles and dermal papilla is reduced, the supply of nutrients to the dermal papilla will not be sufficient and will impair cell metabolism having adverse effect on the hair growth.

Reduction in scalp physiological function

In case of excessive build up of dandruff flakes, pores of the scalp, through which hair exit the epidermis, get blocked. Such a condition adversely affect hair growth. When the dandruff is decomposed by bacteria this may cause irritation of the scalp giving rise to condition, called *pityriasis.* Leaving such a condition untreated may cause the hair loss. This is called *pityriasis* type hair loss.

Excessive secretion of sebum in the upper part of the hair follicles can also cause irritation because of decomposition of sebum and may give rise to seborrhoeic alopecia.

Local impairment of circulation due to tension in the scalp

Loss in flexibility in the scalp may cause reduction in the blood flow in the peripheral blood vessels in the subcutaneous tissue of the scalp. Such a situation will adversely affect hair growth.

Apart from these there could be other factors for hair loss. These include deficient diet, stress, drug side effects, genetic etc.

Various materials have been used as the hair growth promotes. Some materials and their actions are given in Table 3.1

There are three methods for evaluating the hair growth promoters, (i) methods involving use of animals; (ii) methods involving use of humans; (iii) methods involving use of tissue cultures. When animals are used for evaluating the hair growth promoters, growth of their hair is investigated by monitoring the hair weight, hair length and area of hair growth and the time at which the hair started to grow. It is necessary to take into account the species, age, season, feed etc.

Table 3.1

S.No.	Materials	Action
1.	Benzyl nicotinate, vitamin E and its derivatives	blood circulation improvement
2.	Tincture of capsicum, tincture cantharis, camphor	Local stimulation
3.	Placenta extract, pantothenic acid and its derivatives	Hair follicle stimulator
4.	Estradiol, estrone	Anti-male hormone
5.	Sulphur, thioxorone, vitamin B_6	Anti-seborrhea
6.	Salicylic acid, resorcinol	Horny layer dissolution
7.	Glycyrrhetic acid and its derivatives, menthol	Anti-inflammatory
8.	Amino acids, vitamins crude drug extracts	Others

Final evaluation of effectiveness of a hair growth promoter should be made on human beings. Evaluation on human being has many problems. These include individual differences, variation between different locations, difficulty in controlling the people undergoing tests, poor understanding of daily and seasonal fluctuations. Despite this, following evaluations may be made;

- photographic evaluation;
- trichogram method;
- measurement of 5α-reductase;
- hair-wash test;
- measuring blood flow.

Photographic evaluation on growth of hair should be made on a large number of people objectively and quantitatively. Trichogram method is very costly and subject management requires a lot of effort. In this method, the proportion of hair in telogen phase is determined in order to assess the effectiveness of the promotion of the growth of the hair. A random sample of about 100 hairs from different parts of the head is taken. These are categorized into anagen, catagen and telogen by examining the state of their hair follicles under a microscope.

A comparison of 5α-reductase activity is made before and after using a hair growth promoter in order to find out the inhibition of 5α-reductase in the hair root.

In the hair wash test, the number of hairs coming out on washing is determined. In this test, it is very important for persons taking part in the test to control their hair washing routine.

Based on belief that improving the blood circulation in the scalp with promote hair growth, the blood flow is measured after using the hair growth promoter. Devices employing the Doppler effect and those using thermocouples are some of the equipment which have been developed for doing this test.

Wetterings *et al.* have reported success in culturing hair follicle keratinocytes on the membrane covering the crystalline lens of the cow eye. Jahoda and Oliver have studied the culturing of dermal papilla cells, which are considered important for hair growth. Cell cultures could be considered as excellent evaluation tools for evaluation of hair growth promoters.

Brown or black colour of hair is due to a pigment, known as melanin. The colour of hair depends on the amount of melanin present. More the melanin, darker the colour of the hair. Other colours of hair may be due to varying amounts of melanin like pigments. Pigment melanin is formed in epithelial cells of the matrix and is carried with them when these are pushed up and are keratinized. Due to change in the metabolism, pigment, melanin is not formed and therefore is not carried with the cells and pushed up and hair becomes grey.

Colours of human hair are mainly because of two kinds of pigments namely, eumelanin and phaeomelanin. Eumelanin is brown or black and phaeomelanin is yellow or reddish. Eumelanin is formed from tyrosine by oxidation with the help of an enzyme, tyrosinase. Though tyrosine is also a precursor of phaeomelanin but requires presence of an o-amino-phenol derived from tryptophane.

Hair is made up of an insoluble protein material, keratin, vestigial cell membranes, nuclei etc. Proportion of keratin being the highest. Hair, like any other protein, is composed of amino acids, substances of to two general formula:

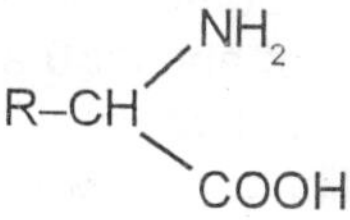

or

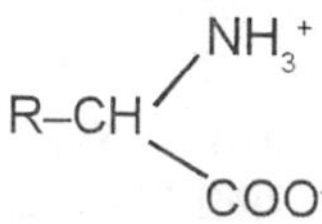

It is because of these substances they give rise to the majority of the most characteristic properties of the proteins. About 25 amino acids are known to occur in proteins. In keratin, out of 25 amino acids 18 are found in measurable amount. These amino acids can form large condensed polymeric structures by formation of amide links between the acid group of one amino acid the amino group of the other amino acid. In this way, a polypeptide is formed. For any protein to have an organized and shaped structure to be hair, peptide chains must be very long and there must be other bonds to keep the chains in fixed relative positions to one another. These additional bonds may be formed in the following manner:

- formation of hydrogen bonds between parallel polypeptide chains;
- formation of sate linkages between acid and basic side chains;
- formation of disulphide linkages

Studies show that hair is intensely cross-linked structure and can be considered as a series of submicroscopic fibrils which have both parallel and linked polypeptide chains. Because of variety of side chain present in polypeptide forming keratin, the reactions are not clear-cut. Hair keratin is not soluble in aqueous salt solutions, weak acids, weak alkalis and saturated neutral urea solution. Acid solutions having pH between 1-2 cause moderate lateral swelling because of hydrogen bonds and salt links are broken. The swelling is more intense at pH around 10 for the same reason. At pH 12, the disulphide bonds begin to break and lateral swelling becomes limitless resulting in solution of hair. All the three types of bonds can be affected by other materials like sulphides, thioglycolates, mercaptoethanol, urea bisulphite, peracetic acid. Understanding of the structure of the hair and its chemistry in brief will help reader in understanding the basis of formulation of different hair cosmetics.

When the hair turns grey, it involves loss of pigment from the hair shaft and progressive loss of tyrosine activity form hair bulbs

It is normal part of aging, white hair first appear at the temples at an average age of about 35 years. By the age of about 50 about 50% hair turn grey. Severe emotional stress can cause greying of hair rapidly. Rapid greying of the hair after fibrile illness is well documented. This is called telogen effluvium. Telogen effluvium causes sudden shedding of dark hair from mixed population leaving grey hair, as such, grey hair become predominant. A traumatic episode can also precipitate loss of the hair and the first hair to grow are grey. There is no known medical treatment for reversing greying of the hair. It is because of this, hair dyes have been developed to colour grey hair.

4

Hair Shampoos

1. GENERAL

Earlier soap cake was used for washing the hair. Today, a large population, both men and women use shampoo for washing the hair. Development of synthetic detergents has revolutionized the shampoo market. Functions of shampoo have been defined by various workers. A good shampoo should be able to perform the following functions.

* It should remove soil, sebum and residues of hair setting lotions/dressings from hair and Scalp.
* It should produce foam of the degree that will satisfy the user.
* It should be easy to remove shampoo by rinsing leaving the hair soft, lustrous and manageable.
* It should impart a pleasant fragrance during use masking the odour of wet hair.

One of the main functions of shampoo is to remove dirt on the hair. The dirt consists of sebum secreted by the scalp, sweat residue, flakes of horny layer, residue from hair care cosmetics, dust and other external matter settled on the hair. Removal of dirt on the hair is achieved by detergents. The mechanism of detergent action involves a number of physical phenomena, wetting, foaming, emulsification and peptization. Removal of dirt, in fact, involves the following process:

– the detergent must wet both dirt as well as the hair i.e. it should lower surface tension;

– the interfacial tension must be reduced so that dirt or oil particles are displaced by detergent solution;

– the dirt particles must be kept dispersed so that these are washed away.

The critical difference between a detergent and a simple emulsifier is that polar group of detergent has the ability to displace oil from a surface. In hair washing this is most important property.

The evaluation of shampoo detergency is difficult process. There are numerous methods. But the method described by Barnett and Powers is typical. It depends on estimating grave-matrically the quantity of soil removed from wool yarn soiled in a standard manner.

Consumers usually believe that more the foam more the detergency. But it is not so. Many very effective detergents do not foam well. However, foaming in shampoo is of psychological importance.

For determination of detergents as shampoo bases, it may be necessary to observe effects on same head. The following points may be looked for in evaluating detergent for shampoo base.

(i) *Ease of spreading:* A shampoo made with a detergent base should be easy to spread i.e. it should be distributed over the hair.

(ii) *Lathering power:* As stated earlier good foaming is necessary for a shampoo base as it has psychological value. Apart from psychological value, foam allows assessment of the amount of shampoo required to ensure that all functions involved in cleansing are performed.

(iii) *Efficient soil removal:* Detergent base for shampoo should remove grime, oil, scalp debris etc. in soft and hard water. *In vitro* study on this aspect may be carried out by hair switches soiled with synthetic sebum.

(iv) *Ease of rinsing:* Some detergent bases can be rinsed easily while other continue lathering and rinsing appears endless. Such detergent base(s) should be used which can be rinsed easily.

(v) *Face of combing wet hair:* Combing of wet hair will evaluate roughness and tangling tendency immediately after treatment with the detergent. The consumer associates this with the cleansing action of shampoo. But simple removal of the oily material is not the whole story. A desirable detergent base should leave the wet hair in a condition where it will be easy to comb wet hair.

(vi) *Lustre of the hair:* Soaps in hard water are likely to leave dull films of insoluble calcium and magnesium soaps on the hair. Some detergents with insufficient suspending power may redeposit dirt or grease on the hair with dulling effect. Detergent base should not leave dulling material on the hair so that the hair after shampooing become lustrous.

(vii) *Speed of drying:* Drying of the hair in shampooing is the most, tedious process. At hairdressers saloon it is costly both in terms of time and equipment. Some detergents have the hair very wet which dry very slowly, others leave behind a hydrophobic surface which can shed water early and thus making drying process faster. However, there is a limit to this as during shampooing water is taken up by the hair and is bound to hydrogen bonds.

(viii) *Ease of combing and setting the dry hair:* If the detergent base during shampooing has induced roughness, the dry hair offers resistance to combing. This resistance has tendency to produce static electricity as the comb is drawn through the hair. The static charge on the hair makes the hairs repel one another making setting difficult. Therefore, detergent base should be such that it does not leave the dry hair rough.

(ix) *Safety;* The detergent base should be non-irritating and non-toxic to the scalp.

2. RAW MATERIALS FOR SHAMPOOS

Originally the shampoos were made from soap or soap mixtures. But today, the shampoos are made from synthetic detergents. Ingredients of present shampoos can be classified as under:

- surfactants,
- foam boosters and stabilizers,
- conditioning agents,
- special additives,
- sequestering agents,
- viscosity modifiers,
- opacifying or clarifying agents,
- fragrances,
- colours,
- preservatives.

2.1 Surfactants

Different types of surfactants are available in the market. According to the most widely used classification these may be:

- non-ionic,
- cationic,
- anionic,
- ampholytics.

Non-ionic detergents have sufficient cleansing power but only a few have sufficient foaming properties. Therefore, these are not used as principal foaming agents. However, these have remarkable foam booster and stabilizing properties and as such, are used as foam boosters and stabilizers. These are mild and non-irritating to the skin. Some newly developed non-ionics possess good foaming power and can be used as principal foaming agents.

Cationic detergents produce form well and have reasonable cleansing power. These also leave hair lustrous and free of electrostatic charge. It would, therefore, appear that cationic detergents are ideal for shampoos. But it is not so. These have two serious disadvantages. One, these have tendency to weigh down hair. Two, these are injurious, particularly to corneal eye tissue.

The remaining two groups of detergents, i.e., anionics and ampholytics are suitable surfactants for shampoo bases. Because of their superior foaming properties and low cost anionics are the most widely used surfactants. Ampholytics are used for their hair conditioning properties.

2.1.1 Anionic Surfactants

Anionic surfactants include a number of class of compounds out of which important ones are mentioned here:

I. Alkyl benzene sulphonates

Alkyl benzene sulphonates are produced in bulk and are used in household washing powder. These have good cleansing properties but leave the hair quite dry and rough causing problem of fly away. These are also irritant to the skin.

II. Alpha olefin sulphonates

Alfa olefin sulphonates (preferred cut C_{14}-C_{16}) have high foaming properties even in the presence of sebum and hard water. These have excellent acid and base pH stability and low cloud point. These can be used in building shampoos of low pH.

III. Alkyl sulfates

Alkyl sulphates are most widely used anionics in shampoos. Lauryl sulphates give greater volume of lather and myristyl sulphates greater richness. Because of this reason a mixture of two is generally used. Cetyl sulphates are not freely soluble and do not produce foaming solution. Octyl and decyl sulphates are foam suppressants. In view of this, fatty alcohols should be distilled before sulphation. Sodium lauryl sulphate is better than all other salts of lauryl sulphate so far as flash foam and foam volume is concerned. Though it has less solubility in cold water but its solubility increases with temperature. At a temperature of about 35-40°C, quite concentrated solutions can be made. Its high cloud point and high viscosity make it suitable ingredient for paste type cream shampoo.

IV. Alkyl polyethylene glycol sulphates (Alkyl ether sulphate)

Sodium salts of polytehoxylated lauryl sulphate are much more hydrophillic and are soluble up to 50% or more. These materials are available as solutions containing about 28% detergent. These have good foaming properties. However, the foam is lighter than alkyl sulphates and collapses in the presence of grease. Therefore, when these are used in shampoos, foam booster and stabilizers are added. These display milder irritancy which decreases with increasing number of ethylene oxide molecules. A condensation product with seven ethylene oxide molecules will be non-irritant.

V. Sulphosuccinates

Though these are average foamers but cause low incidence of irritation to the eye. Therefore, these may be used in mild shampoos such as low pH and baby shampoos.

VI. Acyl lactylates

These are condensation products of a fatty acid and lactic acid. According to the length of fatty acid chain these show foaming, cleansing and thickening properties. They are claimed to improve texture and manageability.

VII. Acylsarcosinates

These surfactants are condensation products of fatty acids with sarcosine. They have some good properties. They foam well and give a good feeling to this skin and the hair. It is because of these properties these are used auxiliaries for lauryl sulphates or amphoterics. Commonly used compounds include sodium myristyl and lauryl sacrosinates. These are quite stable at low pH. However, these lose their foaming characteristics at low pH, but increase viscosity. These can be used with a wide range of cationics also without affecting their conditioning and bactericidal properties.

VIII. Aeylpeptides

These complex mixtures are obtained by reaction of fatty acid chloride with protein hydrolysats. Early products of this group caused dulling of the hair and also produced scum. But the modern products (e.g. Maypons, Lamepons) no longer have these drawbacks. Although these do not foam well but these produce soft, creamy, easily cleanable lather. These are used in combination with alkyl sulphates.

2.1.2 Non-ionic surfactants

As mentioned earlier also non-ionics are not used as principal detergents in shampoos. But these are additives of importance in shampoos. Some of the commonly used non-ionics are mentioned here.

I. Fatty acid alkanolamides

Monoalkanolamides of C_{14}-C_{16} fatty acids are waxy solids insoluble in water. However, they dissolve easily in detergent solution on gentle warming. Properties of some of the monoalkanolamides are given below:

- lauric monoethanolamide improves solubility of sodium lauryl sulphate;
- these increase the viscosity of detergent solutions;
- stearic ethanolamide is a pearlescent thickener;
- these exhibit softening properties on hair after washing, oleic ethanolamides have been recommended as hair conditioning agents;
- volume and richness of the foam are improved.

Use of monoalkanolamides in proportions more than 15 parts for every 100 parts of detergent has not been recomended..

Diethanolamides are available in market either as liquids or low melting point solids. Although their thickening and lather synergist properties are not as powerful as those of monoalkanolamides, but these are used in shampoos as additives because they offer better solubility. Kritchevsky condensation type products should be used with care as these usually have high soap content and free diethanolamine.

II. Polyakoxylated Derivatives

These derivatives are obtained by poly-addition of an alkylene oxide to a hydrophobic compound containing a labile hydrogen atom (e.g., alcoholic or phenolic-OH, thiol), Ethylene oxide or propylene oxide may be used as poly additive agents. Examples of this class of compounds and their useful characteristics are given in Table 4.1.

III. Amine oxides

These are referred to as polar non-ionics as these have highly polarized link N→O. These are used as foam boosters and anti-static agents. Preferred substances are coconut and dodecyl dimethylamine oxides.

2.1.3 Amphoteric Surfactants

Amphoteric surfactants are known for their mildness and are used in mild shampoos. These are compatible with wide range of surfactants. Examples of some commonly used amphoteric surfactants are mentioned here.

Table 4.1: Polyalkoxylated derivatives and their products

S.No.	Name of group of compounds	Properties
1.	Ethoxylated fatty alcohols	Stable in wide range of pH, have stabilizing, emulsifying and oacifying properties.
2.	Ethoxylated alkayl phenols	Very stable, low cost products but irritating to eye mucosa.
3.	Block polymers (pluronics)	Mild detergents imparting a good rinsability, can be used in high percentage in shampoos.
4.	Sorbitol esters polyethoxylated	Solubilizers and emulsifiers, polyethoxylated mono esters (Tweens) are used in non-irritating shampoos.
5.	Polyglyceryl ethers	Foaming properties and non-irritant to eye mucosa.

I. N-alkyl aminoacids

These are mainly of two types, β-amino acid derivatives and asparagine derivatives. Examples of these two groups of compounds and their properties are given in Table 4.2.

Table 4.2: N-alkyl aminoacids and their properties

S.No.	Name of group of compounds	Properties
1.	β-aminoacid derivatives	Foaming properties N-alkyl-β-imino-propionates exhibited in slightly alkaline pH, hair manageability is exhibited in acidic pH.
2.	Asparagine derivatives	Compatible with both anionic and cationic surfactants, exhibit good foaming, cleansing and conditioning properties.

II. Betains

This term refers to zwitterionic compounds derived from trimethyl glycine (betaine). One methyl group of bataine is replaced by a fatty radical (C_{12}-C_{18}) or a fatty amido alkyl radical. These are cationic in acidic pH and anionic in alkaline pH. These are mild, have cleansing and high foaming properties. These are compatible with cationic, anionic and non-ionic surfactants and therefore are widely used. These also exhibit thickening properties.

2.2 Additives

Besides surfactants, many other materials are incorporated in the formulation of shampoos. Some of these may be optional adjuncts but others play an important role. Of these, important additives are given below.

2.2.1 Conditioning Agents

Conditioning agents are intended to improve manageability, feel and lustre of the hair. The materials which have been claimed to have conditioning effect on hair include fatty materials like lanolin, mineral oil; natural products like polypeptides, egg derivatives, herbal extracts; and synthetic products like specifically designed surfactants and resins. Surfactants have already been discussed in foregoing paragraphs.

2.2.2 Viscosity Modifiers

Thickening of shampoo can be achieved by a number of compounds.

Compounds which can be used to modify viscosity of shampoos include:

- Electrolytes:
- Ammonium chloride,
- Sodium chloride,
- Natural gums:
- Gum karaya,
- Gum tragacanth,
- Alginates.
- Cellulose derivatives:
- Hydroxyethyl cellulose
- Hydroxypropyl cellulose
- Carboxymethyl cellulose
- Carboxyvinyl polymers:

- Polymer of acrylic acid cross-linked with poly functioned agent (Carbopol 934)
- Others:
- Ethoxylated fatty acid-diesters
- Phosphate esters
- Amidoamine oxides
- TEA soaps
- Polyvinyl pyrrolidones
- Polyvinyl alcohol
- Alkanolamides

2.2.3 Opacifying and Clarifying Agents

A number of materials can be used for opacifying or giving pearlescent effect. List of these materials is given in table 4.3. Transparency may be improved by solubilizing alcohols, phosphates or non-ionic solubilizers.

These are also shown in Table 4.3.

Table 4.3: Opacifying and Clarifying Agents for Shampoos

Opacifying Agents:
Alkanolamides of higher fatty acids
Glycol mono- and di-stearates, propylene glycol- and glycerol-monostearates and palmitates
Fatty alcohols (cetyl, stearyl)
Milky emulsions of vinyl polymers and latexes
Insoluble salts–magnesium calcium or zinc salt of stearic acid
Finely dispersed zinc oxide or titanium dioxide.
Magnesium aluminium silicate.
Clarifying Agents:
Solubilizing alcohols like ethanol, isopropanol, propylene glycol, hexylene glycol, dimethyl-octyne diol
Phosphates
Non-ionic solubilizers like polyethoxylated alcohols and esters.

2.2.4 Sequesting Agents

These materials are used to prevent deposition of calcium and magnesium salts of soaps on to the hair. EDTA salts (Ethylene diamine tetraacetic salts) and polyphosphates are the most commonly used sequestering agents in shampoos.

2.2.5 Preservatives

Many synthetic products are vulnerable to microbial attack, if not preserved efficiently. Bacterial growth in shampoos can lead to breakdown of detergents in shampoos resulting in discolouration of the product. One important fact to be kept in kind while selecting preservatives for shampoos is that surfactants in shampoos tend to interfere with bactericidal activity of antibacterials. Therefore, higher concentration of preservatives are necessary in shampoos.

The simple and most effective antimicrobial agent is formaldehyde. Formaldehyde remains unaffected by surfactants and can be used in concentration of 0.1-0.15%. But it is not compatible with certain ingredients of shampoos, e.g., protein hydrolysates.

Esters of parahydroxy benzoic acid are quite effective against fungi, but these are inactivated by non-ionics. These are also not effective against Pseudomonas.

5-Bromo-5-nitrodioxan (Bronidox) is not affected by anionic or non-ionic surfactants.

Dimethyloldimethyl hydantoin releases formaldehyde and is compatible with most of the surfactants.

2.2.6 Perfumes

There are two important aspects which should be ascertained before final selection of fragrance of shampoos. One, fragrance must be soluble in shampoo. Two, it must be compatible with shampoo, i.e., it should not affect viscosity and stability. Herbal, fruity or floral fragrances can be used in shampoos.

3. FORMULATION

Shampoo formulations can be classified into the following main groups:

- powder shampoos,
- clear liquid shampoos,
- liquid cream/lotion shampoos,
- cream shampoos,

- jelly shampoos,
- aerosol foam shampoos.

3.1 Powder Shampoos

Earlier powder shampoos were prepared with soap powder and diluents like sodium carbonate, sodium bicarbonate, disodium phosphate or borax or their combination. Formula 1 is an example of such shampoo.

Formula 1

	%
Soap Powder	35.0
Sodium Bi-carbonate	45.0
Di-sodium Phosphate	20.0
Perfume	q.s.

Such formulations were also available with herbal ingredients which were supposed to give slight colouring effect to the hair. Formula 2 and 3 are examples of these.

Formula 2

	%
Henna Powder	5.0
Soap Powder	50.0
Sodium Carbonate	22.5
Potassium Carbonate	7.5
Borax	15.0
Perfume	q.s.

Formula 3

	%
Camomile Flowers Powder	5.0
Soap Powder	55.0
Sodium Carbonate	15.0
Borax	25.0
Perfume	q.s.

With the development of synthetic detergents, soap powder was replaced with detergents. Formula 4 is an example of powder shampoo containing detergent.

Formula 4

	%
Sodium lauryl sulphate	20.0
Sarcoside	5.0

Sodium bicarbonate	10.0
Sodium sulphate	65.0
Perfume	q.s.

Powder shampoo did not remain popular, partly because of trouble involved in using them and partly because these leave the hair in poor condition.

Another type of powder shampoo is dry shampoo. These type of shampoos are used when it is inconvenient to use water. These are effective when the hair is greasy. When these shampoos are used, it should be ensured that all powder is removed by brushing. These are formulated with adsorbent materials like starch, talc, kieselguhr. Formula 5 is an example of dry shampoo.

Formula 5

	%
Starch	15.0
Talc	45.0
Kieselguhr	40.0
Perfume	q.s.

Another approach was tried for dry shampoos i.e., solvents were used to remove grease. Solvents like alcohol, isopropyl alcohol, ethylene di-chloride etc. were used as these are good solvents for grease. But the complete removal of grease solution and hazardous nature of solvent remained problem and therefore, these did not become popular.

3.2 Liquid Shampoos

These are one of the popular types of shampoos. Clear liquid shampoos can be prepared with detergents having lower cloud point. These can also be made with detergents and alkanolamides. Formulae 6, 7 and 8 are typical examples of clear liquid shampoo.

Formula 6

		%
Sodium lauryl ether sulphate		40.0
Sodium chloride (To desired viscosity)		2.0-4.0
Water	to make	100.0
Perfume, Colour and Preservatives		q.s.

Formula 7

	%
Triethanolamine lauryl sulphate	50.0
Lauric isopropanolamide	2.0

Water	to make	100.0
Perfume, Colour and Preservatives		q.s.

Formula 8

		%
Triethanolamine lauryl sulphate		45.0
Coconut monoethanolamide		2.0
Water	to make	100.0
Colour, Perfume and Preservatives		q.s.

Concentrated clear liquid shampoo can be prepared with more soluble monoethanolamine lauryl sulphate. These shampoos may be used by hairdressers by diluting at the time of use. Formula 9 is an example of such a shampoo.

Formula 9

		%
Monoethanolamine lauryl sulphate		70.0
Coconut diethanolamide		2.0
Water	to make	100.0
Colour, Perfume and Preservatives		q.s.

A good mild shampoo can be formulated with detergents having good after-effects. Such detergents includes methyl taurides, amphoterics etc. Formula 10 is an example of such a formulation.

Formula 10

		%
lauryl amino propionic acid		12.0
Triethanolamide lauryl sulphate		24.0
Coconut diethanolamide		2.0
Lactic acid (to adjust pH to 4.5-5.0)		q.s.
Water	to make	100.0
Preservatives, Perfume and Colour		q.s.

Shampoos having higher pH tend to damage the hair and the skin. Mild acidity prevents swelling of the hair and reduce penetration. Lower pH offers favourable conditions for display of conditioning properties, however, it is detrimental to stability of surfactants. These disadvantages can be overcome by either using surfactants not affected by the values between 5.0 and 7.0 (e.g. ammonium lauryl sulphate, ammonium lauryl ether sulphate), or, by development of synergistic combinations (e.g. amphoterics and non-ionics) of by the addition of foam boosters. Formula 11 is an illustrative example of acid-balanced shampoo.

Formula 11

		%
Ammonium lauryl sulphate		38.0
Cocomidopropyl betaine		16.0
Lauric diethanolamide		3.5
P PG 5 ceteth 10 phosphate		3.0
Hydrolyzed protein		2.0
Citric acid (to adjust pH to 5.4)		q.s.
Water	to make	100.0
Perfume, colour and preservatives		q.s.

3.3 Liquid Cream or Lotion Shampoos

Liquid cream or lotion shampoos can be considered as an extension of clear liquid shampoos. These can be prepared by adding opacifier to clear liquid shampoos. Detergent manufacturers also make preformulated concentrated materials which can be diluted, coloured and perfumed. Ethylene glycol monostearate, ethylene glycol distearate can be used as opacifiers. These however, have tendency to redissolve in shampoo in hot weather. Insoluble magnesium stearate can be added to overcome this problem. Formulae 12 and 13 are examples of liquid cream shampoo with pearly sheen.

Formula 12

		%
Monoethanolamine lauryl sulphate		45.0
Ethylene glycol monostearate		5.0
Water	to make	100.0
Perfume, Colour and Preservatives		q.s.

Formula 13

		%
Triethanolamine lauryl sulphate		35.0
Glyceryl monostearate		2.0
Magnesium stearate		1.0
Water	to make	100.0
Colour, Perfume and Preservatives		q.s.

An alkanolamide can be added to such formulation as foam booster as exemplified in formula 14.

Formula 14

	%
Monoethanolamine lauryl sulphate	38.0
Ethylene glycol monostearate	5.0

Lauric isopropanolamide		2.0
Water	to make	100.0
Colour, Perfume and Preservatives		q.s.

De Navarre recommends the use of admixture of mucilaginous thickener like a solution of polyvinyl alcohol, methyl cellulose, alginate, Irish moss and magnesium stearate for opacifying shampoos. He has also mentioned that higher alcohols or alcohol esters can also be used for opacifying effect and their opacifying effect can be improved with lanolin and glycol[1] glyceryl laurate in concentration of 1-2%. Such a formulation is exemplified by Formula 15.

Formula 15

		%
Fatty alcohol sulphate paste		28.0
Magnesium stearate		1.0
Polyvinyl alcohol solution (10%)		20.0
Methyl cellulose solution (3%)		10.0
Lanolin		0.5
Glyceryl monolaurate		1.0
Water	to make	100.0

Shampoos of this class may contain other additives like egg, milk, cream, coconut. The egg is oldest and still popular ingredient. Either dried whole egg or dried egg yolk can be added. The egg powder should be converted into a paste with small quantity of water or glycerine and then should be diluted with some of the detergent solution before adding to the mix. Formula 16 is an example of egg shampoo.

Formula 16

		%
Sodium lauryl sulphate (30%)		25.0
Coconut diethanolamide		2.0
Glycol stearate		1.0
Dried egg powder		2.0
Sodium chloride (to desired viscosity)		q.s.
Phosphoric acid (to adjust pH 7.5-8.0)		q.s.
Water	to make	100.0
Yellow Colour, Perfume and Preservatives		q.s.

3.4 Cream Shampoos

Such type of products are usually demanded by professional hairdresses. These products can be packed in collapsible tubes.

These products are also known as shampoo pastes. Generally, these are based on sodium alkyl sulphates which give products of firm consistency. Cetyl alcohol can be added as builder. Formula 17 is an example of such a product.

Formula 17

		%
Sodium lauryl sulphate		38.0
Cetyl alcohol		7.0
Water	to make	100.0
Colour, Perfume and Preservatives		q.s.

An alkanolamide such as coconut diethanolamide, lauric isopropanolamide can be added in concentration of 1-2% as foam stabilizer.

The major problem with this type of shampoos is that mass of crystals present in shampoo may dissolve in hot weather making the product runny and translucent. On cooling, recrystallization takes place and crystals formed may be large appearing as lumps or fibrous mass. This type of shampoos are not very popular.

3.5 Jelly Shampoos

Jelly shampoos gained some popularity in beauty parlours but did not sustain popularity for long. This type of shampoos can be formulated with detergent alone or in combination with soap. Preparation of different consistency and texture can be prepared by varying the proportions of triethanolamine coconut soap, triethanolamine lauryl sulphate and sodium lauryl sulphate.

Jellies can also be prepared by thickening the conventional clear liquid shampoos with hydroxy-alkyl or methyl cellulose ethers or alkanolamides. Appropriate combination of anionic and amphoteric surfactants can also produce gels. Formula 18 is example where methyl cellulose ether has been used as thickening agent.

Formula 18

		%
Aklyl dimethyl benzalammonium chloride		15.0
Triethanolamine lauryl sulphate (40%)		28.0
Coconut diethanolamide		7.0
Hydroxy propyl methyl cellulose		1.0
Water	to make	100.0
Colour, Perfume and Preservatives		q.s.

3.6 Aerosol Shampoos

Shampoos available in aerosol packing are called aerosol shampoos. Shampoos for aerosol packing are required to be specially formulated. When sprayed, the foam should be manageable and should have enough staying power.

The shampoo foam is sprayed on the palm of the hand and this is thoroughly rubbed into the hair which have been wetted in advance. Thereafter, these may be removed as is done in the case of conventional shampoos. Formula 19 is an example of aerosol shampoo.

Formula 19

	%
Container charge	
shampoo base	90
Propellant	10

Shampoo base may be prepared with the formula:

Ammonium/Triethanolamine lauryl sulphate	60.0
Coconut diethanolamide	2.0
Water, Perfume, Colour and Preservatives	q.s.

3.7 Some Special Shampoos

Some shampoos are formulated for a specific purpose. For example, shampoos for dandruff, shampoos for conditioning effect. These two are, by far the most import groups of shampoos which are marketed for their special effects.

3.7.1 Anti-dandruff Shampoos

It will be appropriate to mention briefly about dandruff. As a result of cell division in deeper layers of epidermis, some cells are being always pushed up towards the surface of the skin. The cells farthest from the dermis are keratinized and subsequently are shed off. This is true of scalp also. For any reason, if normal functions do not synchronize and process of keratinization and shedding off increases to an abnormal rate, cells become visible in the form of flaky scales. Such a condition causes dandruff. In another condition there is abnormal secretion of sebum from sebaceous glands. The former condition is known as seborrhoea sicca and the latter as seborrhoea oleosa. These abnormal conditions of scalp are generally associated with an increase in the growth of bacteria and fungi. This may lead to skin diseases like acne and proriasis. The above-mentioned conditions should, therefore, be treated. One of the approach is, preparation of medicated shampoos for dandruff.

A medicated shampoo is required to have the following functions:

* It should clean both the hair and the scalp and should leave the hair manageable.
* It should not irritate sebaceous glands.
* It should contain an anti-microbial to prevent growth of increased incidence of microbes.
* The active material used should not sensitize the scalp.
* It should reduce the degree of itching and scaling.

Various active materials have been use for treatment of dandruff. These materials are given in Table 4.4.

Table 4.4: Materials used in the Treatment of Dandruff

S.No.	Name of Material	usual Conc. %
1.	Thymol	0.05-0.2
2.	1, 2 Bithionol	0.5-1.0
3.	Pyrithione Zinc	Upto 2.0
4.	Resorcinol	005-1.0
5.	Selenium Sulphide	1.0-2.5
6.	Prepared Coal tar	2.0-2.5
7.	Quaternary Ammonium Compounds when used as shampoo base	15-20

Bithionol because of its adverse effects is no more used in shampoos. Thymol may be mixed with camphor, a counter-irritant. If a cooling effect is desired, menthol may also be added. Pyrithione Zinc can be used in concentration of 2% in anti-dandruff shampoos. Resorcinol is useful material to relieve itching. It is used in concentration of 0.05-1.0%.

Use of thymol, camphor and menthol has been exemplified in Formulae 20 and 21.

Formula 20

	%
Thymol	0.1
Camphor	0.1

Triethanolamine lauryl sulphate		60.0
Water	to make	100.0
Colour, Perfume and Preservatives		q.s.

Formula 21

		%
Thymol		0.05
Camphor		0.1
Menthol		0.1
Triethanolamine lauryl sulphate		55.0
Water	to make	100.0
Colour, Perfume and Preservatives		q.s.

Thymol, menthol and camphor may either be dissolved in alcohol and incorporated in the formulation or should be mixed with the perfume and incorporated in the product.

Cationic surfactants possess varying degree of bactericidal action. Compounds with higher molecular weight have lower bactericidal activity. When these are to be used for a long time, these should be selected carefully as compounds having high bacteriostatic properties may cause defatting of scalp and may give rise to irritation. Of these, quatérnary ammonium compounds are of interest. Cetrimide, a mixture of dodecyl tetradecyl and hexadecyl-trimethyl amonium bromides is non-irrigant and non-toxic in dilutions which are generally used. Other quaternary amonium compounds are benzalkonium chloride and stearyl dimethyl benzyl ammonium chloride. Though stearyl dimethyl benzyl-ammonium chloride is less bacterio-static than cetrimide or benzalkomium chloride, but its use improves appearance of hair. Cetrimide is soluble in two parts of water but alcohol is used so that clarity is maintained during storage. In shampoos based on cetrimide-diethylphthalate is also added to increase the viscosity. Formula 22 is an example of such a formulation. A cream shampoo can be prepared by adding cetyl alcohol (see formula 23).

Formula 22

		%
Cetrimide		15.0
Alcohol		10.0
Diethylphthalate		2.0
Water	to make	100.0

Formula 23

		%
Cetrimide		15.0
Cetyle alcohol		12.0
Water	to make	100.0

Selenium sulphide was developed and patented by Norlander. Treatment with selenium sulphide, sometimes, may cause hair loss. Hairloss, generally, is of temporary nature. However, when persistent hair loss is observed, the treatment with selenium sulphide should be stopped. It is difficult to disperse selenium sulphide as such. Norlander found that if selenium sulphide was heated with bentonite to a temperature where fusion of selenium occurred, the resultant material could be dispersed in water easily.

Formula 24

		%
Selenium sulphide		2.5
Bentonite		5.0
Sodium lauryl sulphate paste		35.0
Water	to make	100.0

Formula 24 is a typical example of shampoo containing selenium sulphide. Selnium sulphide preparations are applied twice a week initially (for two weeks) and once a week subsequently (for two weeks) and occasionally thereafter. While applying selenium shampoos, these should be massaged well on the scalp and the scalp and the hair should be rinsed thoroughly thereafter.

3.7.2 Conditioning Shampoos

The two terms "conditioning shampoos" and "shampoo conditioners" appear to mean the same thing. Though they are similar in application, conditioning shampoos are intended primarily to cleanse and secondarily to improve manageability, feel and appearance of the hair, while the shampoo conditioners are designed to untangle wet hair and to improve manageability of both wet and dry hair.

Quaternary ammonium compounds have conditioning and bactericidal properties. Conditioning properties in quaternary ammonium compounds are imparted by the relatively large complex cation which is substantive to protein. Quaternary ammonium compounds are absorbed on to the hair fibres resulting in removal of static sharge thereby reducing friction between individual hair strands. Thus hair become more manageable. Satisfactory products can be prepared using stearyl dimethyl benzyl ammonium chloride. Formula 25 and 26 illustrate use of stearyl dimethyl benzyl ammonium chloride.

Formula 25

		%
Stearyl dimethyl benzyl ammonium chloride		5.5
Ethylene glycol monostearate		2.0
Cetyl alcohol		2.5
Water	to make	100.0
Perfume and Preservatives		q.s.

Formula 26

		%
Stearyl dimethyl benzyl ammonium chloride		4.0
Cetyl alcohol		3.0
Mineral oil		0.5
Water	to make	100.0
Perfume and Preservatives		q.s.

Dosage for application of shampoos containing quaternary ammonium compounds should be carefully controlled. Directions for use should be given clearly along with the products. High concentration of quaternary ammonium compounds soften hair too much and hair become limp and do not retain a set. Apart from dose, thorough rinsing is also necessary. Otherwise deposition remaining on the scalp has similar effect as overdosing. Cationic polymers can also be used as conditioning agent (see formula 27).

Formula 27

		%
Coconut amidopropyl-3-dimethylamino betaine		5.0
Sodium lauryl sulphate		7.0
Ethoxylated tridecyl alcohol		13.0
cationic cellulose		0.5
Water	to make	100.0
Perfume, Colour and Preservatives		q.s.

In the above formulation, mildness and foaming properties are imparted by combination of ethoxylated non-ionic, amphoteric and anionic surfactants. Thickening and conditioning properties are imparted by cationic cellulose.

Sarcosines have excellent foaming qualities and outstanding conditioning action. A formula based on triethanolamine salt of cocoyl sarcosine is given below.

Formula 28

	%
Triethanolamine salt of cocoyl sarcosine	10.0
Triethanolamine lauryl ether sulphate	5.0
Coco Monoethanolamide	3.0
Coco diethanolamide	2.0
EDTA	0.5
Methyl cellulose	1.0
Phenyl mercuric acetate	0.007
Water	to make 100.0
Perfume	q.s.

4. MANUFACTURE OF SHAMPOOS

4.1 Manufacture of Powder Shampoos

Powder shampoos are manufactured in the same way as bath salts or foam baths.

4.2 Manufacture of Liquid/Cream Shampoos

The basic detergents which are used in the manufacture of liquid/cream shampoos are available from manufacturers as solutions. These solutions either differ in physical characteristics or content of active material. Clear liquid shampoos can be made from preformulated concentrated solutions which are many a time available from detergent manufacturer. These are to be diluted, coloured and perfumed. The dilution can be done in a stainless steel tank with a slow speed stirrer.

There is a general method, if an alkanolamide is being used. Alkanolamide should be dissolved in about half the total amount of the detergent with gentle heating. Then the remaining detergent solution is added slowly. Perfume is dissolved in cold concentrated detergent. Colour and preservative(s) are dissolved separately in water and are added to the mix. The remaining water is added with slow stirring finally to make up the volume. Rapid stirring will cause froth and will incorporate air bubbles. The mixing operations are usually carried out in stainless steel tanks with a stirrer having speed regulator.

Viscosity of solutions of lauryl alcohol ether sulphates is usually controlled by adding electrolytes. This can be done in the following manner:

A solution of sodium chloride (1 part sodium chloride and 3 parts water) is prepared. This solution is added to the shampoo in small proportions. The shampoo is stirred well after each addition. With the addition to salt solution viscosity increases and reaches a maximum. After this stage, if salt solution is added, viscosity decreases.

Many perfumes also affect the viscosity of shampoos. The perfume should be mixed with a small proportion of detergent and added to the mix before final dilution with water. Then viscosity of the final product can be adjusted with sodium chloride as mentioned above.

In case of cream shampoos where glycol stearates are used as opacifiers, glycol stearates are heated gently with a part of detergent to dissolve them. To this solution are then added detergents and other additives. In a cream shampoo where waxes are to be incorporated, the following procedure can be used.

The detergent is heated together with water to about 80°C in a steam or water jacketted vessel. Waxes are separately heated to melt them and to bring to a temperature of about 80°C. Wax(es) are added to detergent solution with slow stirring. The mix is allowed to cool to 40-45°C. Perfume, colour, preservatives are added and stirring is continued. The product is filled into containers while it is still warm.

MAKE YOUR OWN SHAMPOO

Formulation

Ingredients	*Percentage*
Part A	
Sodium Lauryl Ether Sulphate	8-15
Cocodiethanolamide	2-5
Cocobetain	1-5
De mineralised waterto make	100

Ingredients	*Percentage*
Part B	
Propylene Glycol	2
Methyl paraben, sodium	0.25-0.5
Propyl paraben, sodium	0.125-0.5
Part C	
Citric Acid	0.2-0.75
Part D	
Sodium Chloride	0.5-2
Part E	
Colour	q.s.
Part F	
Conditioner (Atlas G1823)	1
Perfume	1

Method of Preparation

Part A

First take out Detergent phase (part A) from set 1. Pour all the ingredients in a 500 ml steel vessel and add to it 70 ml. of demineralised water/battery water. Measure water using measuring cylinder. Stirr with a glass rod to dissolve the ingredients.

Part B

Now take out the preservative phase and pour all the ingredients i.e. methyl paraben sodium and propylene glycol in the the250 ml steel vessel. Heat the vessel to 70-80oC on a gas burner to dissolve the preservatives in propylene glycol. Now mix part B into part A and stirr again.

Part F

Add conditioner to the preparation and mix again.

Part C

Now dissolve Citric Acid in water in a small plastic cup and add drop wise to reduce the pH of the above preparation to near neutral. Check the pH of the preparation by dipping a strip of the pH paper in the preparation andnoting the colour change. Match in with the colour chart given on top of the pH paper strip. The pH of preparation should be between 6-7.

Part E

Now dissolve colour in water in a small plastic up and add drop wise with stirring till the desired blue colour is produced.

Part D

Dissolve Sodium Chloride in water and add drop wise with stirring. The preparation will start to thicken. Add Sodium Chloride solution till you get the desired consistency.

Add perfume and mix again. The Conditioning Shampoo is now ready. Store it in a clean and dry plastic orglass bottle. The bubbles produced in the shampoo will disappear soon.

NATURE SHAMPOO/CLEANSER

For Dry to Normal Hair

Ingredients

Dioscrorea root Power	100 Grams
Water	1 Litre
Methi seed power	2 Table spoon
Horsetail power	2 Table spoon
Rose oil/water	Few drops

Method of Preparation

Boil Dioscrorea root powder, methiseed powder and Horsetail powder for half an hour to reduce the volume to 2-3 cups. Cool and filter through a muslin cloth.

Application of Shampoo

Apply the shampoo on wet hair and scalp with gentle message to enhance foaming and cleansing action of the preparation. Wash the hair with fresh o r luke warm water till the hair is free from cleanser/shampoo residue.

Dioscorea root powder and Methi seed power are good cleansing herb and cleanse the hair from the entire dire, oil pollutants etc. Horsetail is rich source of silica which is one of the major mineral component of the herb. It provides strength and elasticity to the hair.

For Normal to Oily Hair

Ingredients

Reetha Powder	100 Grams

Triphala Powder	3-4T. Spoon
Bay leaf	1 or 2 Leaf
Liquorice Powder	2T. Spoon
Water	1Litre

Method of Preparation

Boil Reetha Powder, Triphala, Bayleaf, Liquorice in water on low flame of a glass burner for half an hour or till the volume is reduced to 3 cups. Cool and filter through a double muslin cloth.

Application of Shampoo

Apply the shampoo on wet hair and scalp with gentle message to produce lather. Apply the preparation thoroughly from scalp to the tips of hair and then wash with luke warm water.

Reetha is traditionally used hair cleanser and a rich source of natural saponins. It has good oil cleansing properties and particularly suitable for washing oily hair. Triphala has good cleansing and astringent properties and improves the scalp condition. Liquorice has good sebum or oil controlling property.

5

Hair Tonics and Conditioners

1. GENERAL

It is unfortunate that the term "hair tonic" has been used for some hair preparations because the term, tonic, even in therapeutics has been viewed with scepticism. However, some products are available in market under the name of hair tonics.

There are two distinct types of products. One, those products which deal with specific problems of the hair and scalp, e.g., greasy hair, dandruff. Two, those products which are intended for improving, restoring and maintaining the condition of the hair. The first type of products can be catagorized as medicated products. The second type of products can be stated as conditioners. Rinses, though are associated preparations to conditioners can be classified as conditioners as many clear rinses with conditioning properties are in vogue in present times.

The main conditions with which medicated products deal with are dandruff, seborrhea and hair loss. Dandruff is caused by excessive scaling of scalp. It occurs more in winter and eases off in summer. Although there may be a relationship between nervous, digestive and metabolic factors, but its causes are not yet clear. It has been observed that proliferation of micro-organisms is associated with dandruff. One of the micro-organism which has been found proliferating is *Pityrosporum ovale,* a sporulating yeast. In fact, earlier this micro-organism was thought to be responsible for dandruff.

Since the cause of dandruff is not known, the product to deal with dandruff is required to have anti-microbial and keratolytic properties.

Seborrhea results from excessive secretion from sebaceous glands. This excessive secretion makes the hair greasy. The sebum is also oxidized by aerial oxidation and by the action of micro-organism present on the scalp. Greasy hair form bunches and catch dust giving unaesthetic look. The products to deal with seborrhea aim at reducing uptake of sebum by the hair.

Conditioners are the result of women's need for attractive and healthy looking hair. Conditioners should give to the hair many characteristics, life, spring, softness, volume, body, sheen, a silky touch, fly-away control and ease of styling. The hair look dull after various treatments like bleaching, permanent waving, frequent shampooing, handling abuse and weathering. The hair may also become porous and brittle. Conditioners take care of such hair. Conditioning is based on the concept of substantivity, i.e., sorption of adequate ingredients to modify the surface properties of the hair. Keratin is anionic in nature and therefore, shows preference for cationic substances. Some treatments like bleaching enhance anionic nature by creating strongly anionic sulphonic acid sites. Though to less extent, long exposure to sun and environmental atmosphere also enhance anionic feature of keratin.

2. FORMULATION

2.1 Medicated Products

As mentioned above, two things are associated with dandruff, one, excessive scaling and two, proliferation of micro-organisms. Therefore, the approach that has been applied to formulate a product for dandruff is to include an anti-microbial agent and a keratolytic agent. Some anti-microbial agents which have been used include:

- Quaternary ammonium compounds;
- chlorophenols;
- PVP-iodine complexes;
- quinolines.

Amongst the keratolytic agents which have been used include:

- colloidal sulphur;

- resorcinol;
- salicylic acid;
- selenium disulphide

Derivatives of 2-yridine-thiol-N-oxide have strong anti-microbial activity. According to Kligman, these derivatives besides anti-microbial activity exert cytostatic activity also. Cytostatic activity results in reduction in turnover rate of epidermal cells and induction of more complete keratinization.

Anti-dandruff formulations can be prepared by incorporating anti-microbial agents in simple aqueous-alcoholic base or in a rinse or setting lotion (see Formula 1 and 2).

Formula 1

		%
Bis (2-pyridyl-1-oxide) disulphide soluble complex		0.15
Camphor		0.75
Menthol		0.05
Isopropyl alcohol		51.0
Water	to make	100.0

Formula 2

		%
Stearyl dimethyl benzyl ammonium chloride		5.0
Cetyl trimethyl ammonium chloride		0.2
Cocopamido propylamine oxide		2.0
Propylene glycol		5.0
Hydroxypropyl methyl cellulose		0.5
Water	to make	100.0

Apart from anti-microbial agents a number of miscellaneous items have been used in medicated hair tonics. Salient of these are given below:

* Stimulating Agents
  - Cantharides,
  - Capsicum tincture,
  - Jaborandi tincture
  - Arnica,
  - Urginea maritima,
  - Rhubarb extract,

  - Camphor,
  - β-naphthol,
  - Quinine salts,
  - Salts and esters of nicotinic acid etc.;
- * Sulphur Derivatives
  - Magnesium cyrsteinate,
  - 4-Thiazolidine carboxylic acid,
  - S-arlkyl and S-carboxymethyl cysteinate;
- * Tars
  - Coal tar,
  - Pine tar oil,
  - Cedar tar oil,
  - Birch tar oil;
- * Vitamins
  - Group B vitamins (vit. B_1, B_2, B_6, B_{12}, panthenol),
  - Vitamin A,
  - Vitamin L,
  - Biotin,
  - P-aminobenzoic acid;

*Miscellaneous

  - Sericine (silk glue),
  - Ginseng,
  - Ferulic acid,
  - Eholic acids.

IS 4707 (Part 2): 1993 has lists of raw materials generally not recognised as safe (GNRAS). Some materials are not permissible to be included in cosmetic formulations, while others can be used in cosmetic formulations in specified concentrations and/or conditions. For example, cantharides appear in the list at Annexure B and are not permissible for use in cosmetic formulations. Therefore, before including any active ingredients, one must go through IS 4707 (Part 2).

Formula 3 to 5 illustrate use of some of various substances which have been used in medicated hair tonics.

Formula 3

		%
Cinchona tincture		2.5
Birch tar oil		0.25
Glycerin		5.0
Resorcinol		0.25
Ethanol		55.0
Water	to make	100.0
Perfume and Colour		q.s.

Formula 4

		%
Jaborandi tincture		0.6
Capsicum tincture		0.4
Panthenol		0.2
Isopropyl alcohol		59.0
Water	to make	100.0

Formula 5

		%
Pyridoxine nicotinate		0.2
Calcium pantothenate		0.05
P-aminobenzoic acid		0.05
Inositol		0.1
Ethanol		60.0
Water	to make	100.0

2.2 Conditioners

As has been mentioned earlier in this chapter conditioning is based on the concept of substantivity to a great extent. Conditioners were first marketed in 1945. These were based on cationic surfactant, cetyl-trimethyl ammonium chloride. Subsequently, other cationics, alkyl dimethyl benzyl ammonium halides, alkyl isoquinolinium and alkyl pyridinium halides were used. Longer chain alkyl compounds exhibited best conditioning properties. Later a wide variety of cationic surfactants were introduced in the conditioners important ones of them being:

- ethoxylated quaternary ammonium phosphates (e.g., Dehyquart SP),
- quaternized fatty acid amino-amides (e.g., noquats),
- N-acyl colaminoformyl-methyl pyridiniumderivatives (e.g., emcol E 6075).

Some cationic polymers have also been used. Due to high substantivity, these polymers lead to problems like excessive build-up.

Another group of compounds that has been used is partially or totally hydrolyzed proteins.

Use of some of the compounds have been illustrated in formula 6 to 8.

Formula 6

		%
Stearyl di-methyl benzyl ammonium chloride		5.0
Cetyl trimethyl ammonium chloride		0.2
Cocoamidoproylamine oxide		2.0
propylene glycol		5.0
Hydroxy propyl methyl cellulose		0.5
Water	to make	100.0

Formula 7

		%
PVP-VA copolymer		1.0
Cetyl dimethyl (hydroxyethyl) ammonium chloride		0.5
Di-methicone		0.2
Ethyl alcohol		23.3
Water	to make	100.0

Formula 8

	%
Stearyl amidopropyl-dimethylamine	1.5
Cetyl alcohol	2.5
Stearyl stearate	0.5
hydrolyzed protein	2.0
Lactic acid	0.5
Sodium chloride	0.5

Water	to make 100.0
Preservatives, Perfume and Colour	q.s.

Lanolin and lanolin derivatives most closely duplicate the action of sebum on hair. Therefore, lanolin and its derivatives are often included in formulae of hair conditioners (see Formula 9 and 10).

Formula 9

		%
Acetylated lanolin		3.0
Glyceryl monostearate (self emulsifying)		14.0
Spermaceti		1.5
Liquid lanolin		5.0
Mineral oil		7.5
Clycerin		5.0
Water	to make	100.0
Preservatives, Perfume and Colour		q.s.

Formula 10

		%
Petroleum jelly		1.0
Glyceryl stearate		0.5
Acetylated lanolin alcohol		2.5
Lanolin alcohol		2.5
Stearyl alcohol		2.0
Cetyl trimethyl-ammonium chloride		1.0
Water	to make	100.0

Still another type of materials that have been used from antiquity are oily and waxy materials like almond oil, castor oil, lanolins, beeswax, spermaceti etc.

Using shampoo and then using conditioner sometimes is time consuming, one step shampoos with conditioner have been developed for convenience in changing life style. For such preparations, amphoteric and anionic surfactants are employed as the major detergents. Conditioning agents in such preparations include cationic surfactants, silicones, and their derivatives and other hydrocarbon oils. Formula 11 is a typical formula for one step shampoo.

Formula 11

	%
Amphoteric surfactant (Imidazolinium betaine type)	15.0
Coconut fatty acid diethanolamide	4.0
Stearyl dimethylammomim chloride	2.0
Sodium N-lauryl-N-methyl-β-alanine	1.0
Silicone derivative	1.0
Polyoxyethylene alkylpolyamine	1.0
Water	to make 100.0
Perfume, Colour and preservative	q.s.

2.3 Anti-seborrheic Preparations

In some persons there is excess secretion of sebum from sebaceous glands. Because of this the hair become greasy quickly after shampooing. Bunches are formed and dust deposits on them. Greasy uptake by the hair can be reduced by applying an oil repellent treatment. Perfluoprinated compounds such as $CF_3(CF_2)X(CH_2)YZ$ (where Z is water- or oil-solubilizing group) have been used. These compounds are used in concentration of about 0.05% to 0.2%. Formula 12 substantially retards the oil uptake by the hair.

Formula 12

		%
Perfluorononanoic acid		0.1
Polyoxyethylene polymethyl siloxane		0.2
Alcohol		30.0
Water	to make	100.0
Perfume		q.s.

Oil adsorbing materials have also been used. These materials have already been discussed under dry shampoos.

In another approach some materials have been applied tropically to reduce secretion of sebum. A number of compounds have been recommended for seborrhea and hair growth. But classes of compounds which seemingly have more selective activity include thio-ether or sulphoxide derivatives of cysteine, cysteamine, glutathione, pyridoxine and hydroxy aminothiols; thiolanediol derivatives; poly-unsaturated acids. But most of these compounds are subject of US patents.

Some lotions based on anti-oxidants like alkyl gallates, t-butyl hydroxy anisole have also been reported. But these do not reduce secretion of sebum. These prevent peroxide transformation of sebum of the scalp and hair.

3. MANUFACTURE OF HAIR TONICS AND CONDITIONERS

Most of the hair tonics are hydroalcoholic solutions and can be manufactured in S.S. mixing vessel with a stirrer. However, commonly used alcohols include ethanol and isopropyl alcohol. These alcohols are inflammable. Therefore, where these alcohols are used, precautions relating to fire safety should be observed.

Hair conditioners are either dispersions or emulsions and can be manufactured according to the processes usually employed for dispersions and emulsions. However, the following manufacturing conditions need specific mention as these will greatly affect the conditioners. These are:

* In case of hair products, if oils or fats are heated to a too high temperature, they tend to form poor film and also lose their sparkle and become dull. Therefore, temperature should be only as high as is consistent with achieving a proper emulsification.
* Better results are obtained if a cream conditioner is to be manufactured with fats like petroleum jelly, lanolin and emulsifying agents like Span 60, Tween 60, by adding water phase to oil phase slowly.
* Viscosity, stability and shelf-life are greatly affected by rate and manner of agitation used. Reader may refer to the reference given in the foot note.
* Where dispersion is of importance, colloid mill should be used because smaller the particle size, better the dispersion. Superior covering film can be achieved with smaller amount of product.
* In case of creams, rate of cooling and length of cooling time are important factors. Sometimes, it may be necessary to bring down the cream to room temperature without using external cooling system. In general, it would be extremely uneconomic production cycle, if no external cooling is employed. Therefore, it has to be decided by actually manufacturing formulation and studying the effect.

6

Hair Wave-Sets, Lacquers and Rinses

1. GENERAL

Though the wave-sets, lacquers and rinses were known long before but their potential was exploited only after the development of newer cosmetic materials by enhancing their effectiveness. There is overlapping of functions of wavesets, lacquers and rinses. The main aims of these preparations are to improve control and manageability of the hair, impart some lustre and to maintain a hair style which will remain unaffected by normal movements of daily activities and by environment. Whatever be the methods, all of them attempt to form a film or coating on the hair. What methods could be used to form and retain the film on hair? The methods that could be used are:

* A solution of water soluble materials can be applied which on evaporation of water will leave the material as a deposit on the hair. This method is applicable to materials like gums, protein derivatives, water soluble synthetic polymers.
* A film/coating of anhydrous materials can be achieved by purely physical means. This method is applicable to fats of vegetable, mineral or animal origin. However, the film/coating is quite greasy. This problem has been overcome by availability of some fatty esters.

* Emulsions can form film or coating with much more ease. Dilution of any phase can be accomplished in a w/o or o/w type emulsion. A wide variety of emulsifying agents offer options also.
* Another method that can be utilized is to make a solution of water insoluble materials in volatile solvents like alcohol and apply to the hair. Volatile solvent(s) evaporate(s) leaving behind a film on the hair.
* Another interesting method of making films on the hair is by adsorption. Properly formed films made by this method resist rinsing, handling and sometimes even washing. Such a phenomenon is exhibited by cationic substances.

All the methods which have been mentioned have their advantages and disadvantages. It may also be noted that sometimes the effect can be achieved with lower concentrations and increase in the concentrations dissipates the effect. The points of concern in such preparations are firmness of dispersion of material(s), freedom from irritation or sensitization.

2. FORMULATION

2.1 Wave-sets

The former formulations of wavesets were based on natural gums like gum karaya, acacia, tragacanth and quince seed. But being natural products, these materials will have varying physical properties according to climate, soil, method of collection. In addition to this, these materials yield dull and brittle films which may crumble and may become sticky in humid weather. In view of this, the products based on natural gums are obsolete. However, for academic interest, formula 1 is given as an example of such products.

Formula 1

		%
Gum karaya		1.5
Sodium alginate		0.5
Glycerin		5.0
Ethanol		5.0
Water	to make	100.0
Perfume, Colour and Preservatives		q.s.

Natural gums have been replaced by synthetic polymers which are soluble in water-alcohol mixture. The first resin which was used for this purpose was polyvinyl pyrrolidone (PVP). Based on this resin, two types of products appeared in the market, clear lotions and aerated gels. These products were certainly an advancement over products prepared with natural gums as, these products formed clear, non-greasy and quite glossy films. These products can be formulated with a film forming material, plasticizer, solvent (water-alcohol), perfume and colour. Formula 2 and 3 are examples of such products.

Formula 2

		%
Polyvinyl pyrrolidone (PVP)		3.5
Propylene glycol		2.5
Ethanol		40.0
Water	to make	100.0
Perfume and Colour		q.s.

Formula 3

		%
Polyvinyl pyrrolidone (PVP)		1.0
Carboxy vinyl polymer		1.5
Prcpylene glycol		2.0
Triethanolamine		1.0
Water	to make	100.0
Perfume and Colour		q.s.

Note: Formula 3 is an aerated gel.

PVP being hygroscopic was subsequently replaced by a vinyl pyrrolidone and vinyl acetate copolymer (PVP: VA). Higher the proportion of vinyl acetate, higher the resistance to water. It was also seen that with increase in the proportion of vinyl acetate, there was increase in the hardness of the films. Plasticizers which can be used include polyethylene glycols, lanolin derivatives, silicones and polysiloxanes. Formula 4 is an example of use of PVP-VA copolymer.

Formula 4

	%
PVP-VA (60:40)	2.0
PEG 40 Castor oil	0.2
Ethanol	50.0

Water	to make	100.0
Perfume		q.s.

A number of patents appeared describing the use of water soluble or alcohol soluble polymers. Their use was recommended in aerosol sprays. These include resins of vinyl acetate and crotonic acid, co-polymers of alkyl vinyl ethers or vinyl esters and maleic acid hemi esters.

Later on hair setting or styling gels became popular. Hair setting lotions have low solid content and therefore, these cannot form gels. Thickening agents are required to be added to the formulation to make gels. Carboxy polymethylene resins (Carbopols-Goodrich) have been extensively used for making gels. Propylene glycol and phthalates (e.g., dimethyl phthalate) are used as plasticizers (see formula 5 and 6).

Formula 5

	%
Carbopol 940	025
PVP	3.00
Di-isopropanolamine	0.25
Di-methyl Phthalate	0.50
Ethyl alcohol	10.00
Water	to make 100.0
Preservatives, Perfume and Colour	q.s.

Formula 6

	%
PVP/VA (50:50)	5.0
Carbopol 940	0.3
Proylene glycol	3.5
Di-isopropanolamine	0.5
Water	to make 100.0
Preservatives, Perfume and Colour	q.s.

2.2 Hair Lacquers

Early hair lacquers were alcoholic solutions of materials like benzoin, styrax or rosin. These were mainly used after styling the hair to maintain the style in place and to impart gloss. But these lacquers were not satisfactory as, these were not removed from the hair easily. This problem was overcome by adding mild alkalis like borax, triethanolamine in the formulation. The film forming material, however, remained shellac. Bleached shellac is used for making hair lacquers. Formula 7 is an example of such a product.

Formula 7

		%
Shellac		80
Triethanolamine		2.0
Ethanol		20.0
Water	to make	100.0
Perfume		q.s.

Method of Preparation: Dissolve perfume in alcohol and add this mixture to shellac. Dissolve triethanolamine in water, add alcohol-shellac mixture to the aqueous triethanolamine solution with slow stirring.

Later, shellac was replaced by PVP, a versatile material.

2.3 Hair Rinses

Hair rinses have long history. Vinegar and lemon juice have been used for centuries to remove lime soap after shampooing. Subsequently, solutions of polybasic acids like citric acid, tartaric acid were used. These were marketed in solid formulations with instructions to make solutions for rinse. Single application package were also available. These also contained colour and were called temporary colour rinses.

The modern hair rinses are made from entirely different materials which were used earlier. Certain cationic substances such as quaternary ammonium compounds form a film on the hair which could be called as monomolecular film. This film imparts smooth and soft feel to the hair and also makes combing easier.

Though clear solutions can be made with quaternary ammonium compounds but usually products made with them are available as emulsions or creams. The earliest quaternary ammonium compounds that were used are alkyldimethyl benzyl ammonium chloride. A simple cream rinse can be prepared with alkyl dimethyl benzyl ammonium chloride and glyceryl monostearate. This cream rinse should be diluted to about 15 times before use. While selecting quaternary ammonium compounds their skin irritancy should be taken into consideration because these are potential irritants. Usually concentrations of 0.1% lose their irritancy and are still effective in their action on hair shaft. Formula 8 is an example of cream rinse.

Formula 8

		%
Alkyl dimethyl benzyl ammonium chloride		2.5
Glyceryl monostearate		2.5
Water	to make	100.0
Colour, Perfume		q.s.

Lauryl isoquinolinium bromide is said to be useful in dandruff. A simple rinse with this compound can be prepared by mixing one ounce of 10% solution of lauryl isoquinolinium bromide with one gallon of water.

Triton X-400 (Rohm and Haas) is trade name for a material which is 20% stearyl dimethyl benzyl ammonium chloride and 5% stearyl alcohol. A dispersion product of Triton X-400 can be prepared as given below (see formula 9).

Formula 9

	%
Triton X-400	12.5
Octyl phenoxy ethanol (OPE)	1.0
Distilled water	86.5
Perfume and Colour	q.s.

Procedure

Add the OPE to the Triton X-400 with slow but thorough stirring until uniform. The total amount of water in formulation is then divided into two equal parts. Heat the first part of the water to 63°C and add this heated water slowly to the previously formed paste, mixing thoroughly but not too rapidly. Cool to room temperature with a very slow, even mix. Chill the remaining portion of water to 2°C and add slowly to the aqueous OPE-Triton solution. Stir until smooth and consistent, add perfume, colour and (if necessary acidifying agents such as citric acid) to bring the finished product to the desired pH.

This product contains about 3% of active material. It should be diluted about 10 times before use.

Other types of materials can also be incorporated into cream rinse and include fatty amides or fatty surface active derivatives.

Hair conditioners are also similar formulations. But the conditioners are used in greater concentrations than hair rinses.

7

Hair-Grooming Preparations

1. GENERAL

Hair dressings have been used from very early times. The tombs of Egyptian kings of the period as early as 3500 B.C. show evidence of perfumed hair oils. Most of the products used in early times were home made and were from plant and animal origin. At the end of 19th Century, attention was paid to the uniformity of the product and cosmetic elegance. Subsequently, with the availability of newer raw materials, quality of the products was considerably improved. Improvements have been made in the past and are being made even now.

The natural function of the hair on the head is protection of the head. But the hair also impart an attractive feature to men and women. The scalp secretes sebum (oily material) which lubricates the hair and prevents loss of moisture from them. If this secretion is below normal, or the hair are exposed to chemical treatments, dehydration of the hair may occur which makes the hair brittle resulting in split and break of the hair.

Animal, vegetable or mineral oils can be used to supplement the natural secretion of the scalp which may provide adequate protective properties and lustre. But these cannot remove brittleness of the hair. Brittleness can be removed with water. But since water evaporates if applied directly, it may not be of help. Therefore, a method should be found out by which water absorbed by the hair is prevented from evaporation. Some of the w/o type emulsions are of benefit in this respect. Aqueous phase which is continuous phase in such emulsions is absorbed by the hair, this causes breaking of the emulsion and the separated oil forms a film on the hair shaft.

Hair dressings which are usually available in the market can be divided in the following groups:

- brilliantines,
- alcoholic solutions,
- two layer systems,
- hair tonics,
- gum-base hair dressings,
- oil-in-water emulsions,
- water-in-oil emulsions.

2. FORMULATION

2.1 Brilliantines

If the secretion of sebum by the scalp is below normal or natural fat of the hair has been removed by soaps or detergents, the hair have dull appearance. This can be overcome by brilliantines. The main function of a brilliantine is to impart a measure of grooming and sheen to the hair. There are two types of brilliantines, liquids and solids.

Formerly, vegetable and animal oils were used to overcome the dullness of the hair. But these oils are vulnerable to rancidity. Mineral oil does not go rancid and it provides a thin protective film to the hair because of its low viscosity and penetrating power. But heavier the viscosity, better the grooming power. Though the grooming of the hair is better with heavier viscosity oils but it is difficult to spread them thinly and uniformly. This can be overcome by using a volatile solvent for heavier oils. This became basis for liquid brilliantines or hair oils. Deodourized kerosene oil can be used as solvent for heavy oils. The product made with it spreads easily and on evaporation of it deposits a thin uniform layer of viscous oil which grooms and imparts a high gloss to the hair. Formula 1 and 2 are examples of simple hair oils.

Formula 1

	%
Mineral oil (light)	100.0
Colour, Perfume	q.s.

Formula 2

	%
Mineral oil (heavy)	75.0
Deodorized kerosene	25.0
Colour, Perfume	q.s.

Because of low solubility of perfume oils in mineral oils, coupling agents may be added to keep the product clear on storage. Materials like vegetable oils, fatty alcohols/esters, non-ionic surfactants can solubilize perfume oils.

Some persons feel that mineral oil being foreign to human body may not be as useful as vegetable or animal oils which are similar to human sebum. Therefore, oils from vegetable or animal origin have also been used in hair oils. However, only non-drying or semi-drying oils can be used for this purpose. Commonly used vegetable oils include castor, almond, olive, sesame, peanut, avocado, peach and soyabean oils. Vegetable oils are liable to become rancid, therefore, use of anti-oxidants in hair oils containing vegetable oils is necessary. Tocopherols are good anti-oxidants and can be used in oils Alkyl gallates like propyl gallate has been found useful in combination with other compounds like butylated hydroxy anisole (BHA) and sequestering agents. Octyl, dodecyl, cetyl and stearyl gallates have also been found effective due to their greater stability. Phenolic derivatives like thymol, pyrogallol, *p*-chloro-*m*-cresol also act as preservatives. Addition of mineral oil to the extent of 10% also retards rancidity of vegetable oils. Formula 3 and 4 are examples of hair oils containing vegetable oils.

Formula 3

	%
Castor oil	20.0
Deodorized kerosene to make	100.0
Colour, Perfume and Preservatives	q.s.

Formula 4

	%
Castor oil	60.0
Almond oil	40.0
Colour, Perfume and Preservatives	q.s.

Hair oils based on mixtures of mineral oil and vegetable oil(s) have also been formulated. Formula 5 is an example of such a product.

Formula 5

	%
Mineral oil	70.0
Peanut oil	30.0
Colour, Perfume and Preservatives	q.s.

Addition of fatty acid esters in hair oils is an agreeable modification as these are completely miscible, resistant to rancidity, absorbed by hair shaft, emollient and glossy. These facilitate incorporation of lanolin also, if it is desired to be incorporated. Use of fatty acid esters has been exemplified in formula 6 and 7.

Formula 6

	%
Mineral oil	70.0
Ethyl myristate	30.0
Colour, Perfume and Preservatives	q.s.

Formula 7

	%
Mineral oil	40.0
Castor oil	40.0
Isopropyl myristate	20.0
Colour, Perfume and Preservatives	q.s.

Solid brilliantines, usually, are mineral oils or vegetable oils which have been stiffened with waxes to desired consistency. The term, "Pomade" which was earlier used for the residual fatty material left from the enfleurage process of extracting floral odours, has become synonymous with solid brilliantine. However, the term, pomade refers to a product of softer consistency.

Solid brilliantines are used for unruly or kinky hair where greater grooming is required. These products are invariably opaque. Opacity of these products increases with increases proportion of waxes. Formula 7I is an example of typical solid brilliantine.

Formula 8

	%
Mineral oil	75.0
Stearic acid	25.0
Colour, Perfume	q.s.

To stiffen mineral oil, paraffin wax appears an obvious choice. But it is not so. It has two drawbacks. One, it crystallizes, two, it permits oil exudation. Due to its shrinkage on cooling, it draws brilliantine mass away from the sides of the container. These problems can be overcome by adding petroleum jelly in formulation. Formula 9 is an example of such product.

Formula 9

	%
Mineral oil	50.0
Paraffin wax	18.0
Petroleum jelly	32.0
Colour, Perfume	q.s.

Oozing out of mineral oil can be better controlled by ozokerite, spermaceti or ceresin wax. Formulation can be modified by the addition of these materials. These modifications have been exemplifie.' in formula 10 and 11.

Formula 10

	%
Mineral oil	40.0
Petroleum jelly	50.0
Ceresin	10.0
Colour, Perfume	q.s.

Formula 11

	%
Mineral oil	70.0
Petroleum jelly	15.0
Ozokerite wax	15.0
Colour, Perfume	q.s.

Vegetable oils have also been used in solid brilliantines. Formula 12 and 13 are examples of solid brilliantines having vegetable oils in them.

Formula 12

	%
Castor oil	40.0
Cocoa butter	10.0
Petroleum jelly	50.0
Colour, Perfume and Preservatives	q.s.

Formula 13

	%
Coconut oil	77.0

Ceresin	23.0
Colour, Perfume and Preservatives	q.s.

Rosin has been used in Europe as an ingredient of solid brilliantines. It is economical and has good fixative action and improves gloss also. Formula 14 is an example of such product.

Formula 14

	%
Mineral oil	15.0
Paraffin wax	13.5
Petroleum jelly	70.0
Rosin	1.5
Colour and Perfume	q.s.

2.2 Alcoholic Solutions

Alcoholic lotions as hair dressing can be prepared diluting viscous oils with alcohol. With such formulations, it is possible to get wetting action first and deposition of thin layer of oil next after evaporation of alcohol. Some persons may like temporary stimulation of scalp by the alcohol. Castor oil is soluble in alcohol in all proportions and therefore, enjoys the unique place amongst fixed oils. Habitual use of concentrated alcohol on scalp may cause dehydration and is not recommended for this reason. Another material which is used in grooming preparation is glycerin. Tincture benzoin is claimed to reduce stickiness of castor oil and hence may be used in the formulation. Formula 15 and 16 are examples of alcoholic lotions.

Formula 15

	%
Castor oil	30.0
Glycerin	10.0
Ethanol	60.0
Colour, Perfume	q.s.

Formula 16

	%
Castor oil	20.0
Tincture benzoin	2.0
Ethanol	78.0
Colour, Perfume	q.s.

Fatty alcohols, fatty acids and synthetic oils have also been used in alcoholic solution as shown in formula 17.

Formula 17

	%
Isopropyl myristate	7.0
Glycerin	3.0
Ethanol	90.0
Colour, Perfume	q.s.

2.3 Two Layer Lotions

Two layer lotions is the result of an attempt to overcome the inherent greasiness of the brilliantines by diluting the brilliantine with water or alcohol. These type of preparations have not been popular. These preparations are required to be shaken vigorously before application to form a temporary emulsion. When the container is allowed to stand for some time, the two phases separate clearly. While formulating such products it should be kept in mind that specific gravities of two phases are sufficiently different to produce two clear-cut layers. A simplest formulation of this type is suitably perfumed and coloured mixture of mineral oil and water. If a faster drying product is desired, water can be replaced partially or completely. Similarly, mineral oil can be replaced partially or completely with vegetable oil according to the degree of grooming desired. Vegetable oils in such preparations are more vulnerable to rancidity. Rancidity is promoted by trace minerals. Therefore, sufficient amount of anti-oxidant should be added and distilled water should be used. Formula 18, 19 and 20 are examples of two layer hair dressings.

Formula 18

	%
Mineral oil	60.0
Ethanol	15.0
Water	25.0
Perfume, Colour	q.s.

Formula 19

	%
Mineral oil	45.0
Castor oil	15.0
Water	40.0
Perfume, Colour	q.s.

Formula 20

	%
Mineral oil	30.0
Sesame oil	10.0
Ethanol	40.0
Colour, Perfume	q.s.

2.4 Oil-in-Water Emulsions

Acceptance of oil-in-water (o/w) emulsion type hair dressings was immediate for their good pouring, spreading and attractive cream like properties. The greasy feeling of brilliantines is not experienced with o/w emulsion hair dressings and these can be easily removed by shampooing. Since emulsions are vulnerable to microbial growth, preservatives soluble in oil phase and soluble in water phase should be added. Desired grooming can be achieved by properly selecting the oily materials. Mineral oil of low or medium viscosity is generally used. Other materials like petroleum jelly, waxes are added to increase the body of the emulsion. Gums have also been used to increase fixative properties, viscosity and stability of emulsions.

A simple formulation of this type comprises of oil and water with a suitable emulsifier. Formula 21 is a typical o/w emulsion.

Formula 21

		%
Mineral oil		45.0
Stearic acid		5.0
Triethanolamine		1.0
Water	to make	100.0
Perfume, Colour and Preservatives		q.s.

Method of Preparation

Heat mineral oil, stearic acid and preservative (oil soluble) to about 70°C. Heat water triethanolamine and preservative (water soluble) separately to about same temperature. Add aqueous solution to oil with slow stirring. Continue stirring and allow to cool to about 45°C. Add perfume and colour and blend thoroughly.

Materials of different kinds can be added to the basic formula mentioned above to give additional attributes to the product. These include lanolin, lanolin esters, fatty acids/esters for emollience, glycerin, propylene glycol for humactancy, gums to increase stability and fixative properties.

Formula 22 and 23 are examples of such modifications.

Formula 22

		%
Mineral oil		10.0
Lanolin (anhydrous)		5.0
Stearic acid		5.0
Triethanolamine		1.5
Propylene glycol		10.0
Sodium alginate (2%)		4.0
Water	to make	100.0
Perfume, Colour and Preservatives		q.s.

Formula 23

		%
Stearyl alcohol		5.0
Mineral oil		35.0
Petroleum jelly		5.0
Sodium lauryl sulphate (15% solution)	to make	100.0
Colour, Perfume and Preservatives		q.s.

O/W emulsions with much less than 50% water can be prepared using fatty acid condensates of sorbitol and mannitol and their polyoxyethylene derivatives (Spans and Tweens). Formula 24 is an example.

Formula 24

	%
Petroleum jelly	10.0
Mineral oil	15.0
Lanolin	10.0
Beeswax	15.0
Span 60	5.0
Tween 60	5.0
Borax	1.0
Water	39.0
Perfume and Preservatives	q.s.

2.5 Water-in-Oil Emulsions

Water-in-oil emulsions are more difficult to prepare and have tendency to separate in layers of water and oil. In spite of this, hair dressings of this type have gained popularity. These products are smooth lustrous creams which give excellent grooming and high sheen to the hair. The film deposited on hair is water resistant and this makes this type of hairdressing useful to swimmers. W/O emulsions have greasier feel but not as pronounced as in the case of brilliantines. These dressings are more popular with men than women.

Several types of emulsifying agents have been used to prepare w/o hair dressings, polyvalent soaps being the oldest of them. Calcium stearate and oleates were used earlier but subsequently it was found out that magnesium is more stable. A combination of emulsifiers has been found more useful than any single emulsifier. Zinc and aluminium stearates have been used in combination with other emulsifiers. Vegetable oils, waxes, lanolin can be added for desired attributes in the product. Formula 25 can be considered as an example of what has been mentioned above.

Formula 25

		%
Mineral oil		38.0
Petroleum jelly		20.0
Beeswax		18.0
Oleic acid		0.6
Lanolin absorption base		1.0
Sodium hydroxide		0.4
Magnesium sulphate		1.0
Borax		0.5
Water	to make	100.0
Perfume and Preservatives		q.s.

Use of sorbitan sesquioleate produces stable emulsions of low viscosity. It can be used with other emulsifiers also. Formula 26 is an example in which sorbitan sesquioleate has been used in combination with beeswax-borax emulsifier system.

Formula 26

	%
Mineral oil	40.0

Petroleum jelly		10.0
Beeswax		2.5
Absorption base		7.5
Sorbitan sesquioleate		4.0
Borax		0.5
Water	to make	100.0
Perfume and Preservatives		q.s.

2.5 Hair Foam

Hair Foam is general name given to hair-styling preparations which consist of styling concentrate and a propellent. Liquefied gas(es) is/are used as propellent. When styling concentrate is sprayed out of the can, liquefied gas vaporizes under atmospheric pressure increasing the volume of styling concentrate and thus converting it into foam. Types of hair foam include those with setting ability, those focussing on hair treatment and those which produce wet gloss. Setting preparations incorporate such ingredients as oils, humectants and activators. Commonly used oils are liquid paraffin and silicones (see Formula 27).

Formula 27

	%
Styling concentrate	90.0
Propellent	10.0

Hair setting formula generally contain a film forming material, solvent, plasticizer and fatty material to impart gloss. Guide formulae for hard set type and treatment type concentrates are given below (See Formula 28 and 29).

Formula 28

Hair foam (hard set type)		%
Acrylic resin alkanolamine solution (50%)		7.5
Ethyl alcohol		15.0
Liquid paraffin		5.0
Glycerin		2.5
Water	to make	100.0
Polyoxyethylene hydrogenated castor oil		q.s.
Preservative and Perfume		q.s.

Formula 29

hair foam (treatment type)		%
Cationic cellulose		2.5
Ethyl alcohol		15.0
Silicone oil		5.0
Dipropylene glycol		7.5
Water	to make	100.0
Polyoxyethylene hydrogenated castor oil		q.s.
Preservative and Perfume		q.s.

Method of Preparation

(i) Add liquid paraffin to a solution of polyoxyethylene hydrogenated castor oil. Emulsify it and pass through homogenizer. Add this emulsion to a solution of other ingredients. Fill cans with styling concentrate, fix valve and fill in gas.

(ii) Add the silicone oil to a solution of the dipropylene glycol and the polyoxyethylene hydrogenated castor oil. Emulsify it and pass through homogenizer. Add this emulsion to a solution of other ingredients. Fill can with styling concentrate, fix valve and fill in gas.

3. MANUFACTURE OF HAIR-GROOMING PREPARATIONS

3.1 Brilliantines

Liquid brilliantines or hair oils are manufactured by mixing of ingredients in suitable mixing tank. Since all the ingredients are miscible, mixing does not offer any problem. However, when liquid brilliantine is based entirely on low viscosity mineral oil, solubility of perfume may be a problem. Therefore, solubility of the perfume should be predetermined. Perfume can be made oil soluble by using deodorized kerosene or isopropyl myristate. Before adding perfume, the perfume is first dissolved in deodorized kerosene or isopropyl myristate and then added to the bulk. Similarly colour (oil soluble colour) is first dissolved in a part of oil and added to the bulk. Perfume and colour are thoroughly blended. For bright and crystal-clear appearance the bulk finished product may be filtered.

When vegetable oils are also ingredients of the formulation, such product should be processed either in stainless steel or high density polymer vessel. Anti-oxidants (oil soluble) should be mixed in a part of oil and should be added to the mix with stirring.

For preparing solid brilliantines and pomades, all the ingredients except perfume, colour and preservatives (anti-oxidants) are heated to the lowest possible temperature to melt all the solid ingredients and are mixed with a stirrer. The heating is carried out in a water jacketted vessel. Colour and anti-oxidants are mixed in warm oil which will not cause solidification of the bulk. This mixture is added to mixing vessel. Perfume is added as the cooling occurs but well before solidification. Materials should not be worked when partially solidified, otherwise, air bubbles will be permanently incorporated. The product, while hot is run into warmed jars and these filled containers are allowed to cool slowly in a warm room.

3.2 Alcoholic Solutions

Alcoholic solutions are solutions of alcohol soluble fatty materials, are manufactured by process of mixing. However, the equipment should be such that would not permit evaporation of significant amount of alcohol. All precautions that are necessary in processing alcoholic preparation should be taken. Since alcohol is inflammable, all facilities and precautions should be such as to take care of fire safety.

3.3 Two Layer Lotions

Two layer solutions are manufactured by dissolving oil soluble materials in oils and alcohol soluble materials in alcohol and the two phases are emulsified in an emulsification tank and the product is filled into containers. The product separates into two clear-cut layers on standing.

3.4 O/W and W/O Emulsions

O/w and w/o emulsions are manufactured according to the general procedure of emulsions described under creams.

8

Permanent Hair Waving Preparations and Hair Straighteners

1. GENERAL

Hair waving has been practised from early periods. Among the countries where it was practised early include Egypt, Italy and Greece. A London hair dresser, Nessler produced hair waves by winding hair on mandrel and moistening it with hot aqueous solution of alkali. It may be said that modern permanent waving began with nessler's method. Improvements in the original process included development of various methods of supplying heat to the hair, use of more volatile alkali and inclusion of sulphite to accelerate waving. Sartory in his equipment utilizer exothermic reaction between calcium oxide and water to generate steam. Winkel patented heating pad which could be applied directly to the hair.

Cold waving began in 1930s. In this process, heat was not required to be applied externally and the process took 6-8 hours for completion.

This was followed by a fast method of waving in 1940 based on bisulphides. However, the waves were shortlived. Almost in the same period, cold wave lotions based on thioglycolates became available and are being used even today.

Because of human's desire to achieve what he does not have and his quest for beautification, individuals who have curly hair want to have straight hair and individuals who have straight hair want to have curly hair. This has led to the development of hair straighteners. Earlier curl hair were plastered down by gums or resinous fatty materials. But later, products based on strong alkali such as sodium hydroxide were used. But these products were risky. After the introduction of thioglycolates based hair waving preparations, hair straighteners based on these chemicals were also introduced.

Human hair is composed almost entirely of keratin. Keratin, chemically, is protein. But has outstanding properties which include:

- it is not soluble in acids;
- it is not soluble in alkalis;
- it is not soluble in solvents that dissolve other proteins;
- it is resistant to enzymatic digestion.

These outstanding properties of Keratin are attributed to the presence of comparatively high percentage of combined cystine (an amino acid). Keratin fibres are composed of long polypeptide chains which are connected laterally by various linkages. The disulphide linkage is of interest in connection with permanent waving or hair straightening process. It is now generally accepted that disulphide cross links are broken and then are re-established during permanent waving and hair straightening processes.

2. HEAT WAVING PREPARATIONS

2.1 General

As the name suggests these preparations are used when waving effect is achieved by heat. The hair are wound, moistened with heat waving preparations and are heated to about 93 to 104°C electrically or by means of heating pads. Scalp is protected from heat by so called "spacers" which are generally made of felt. After completion of heat treatment, the hair is rinsed with water or dilute acid or with solutions of oxidizing agents to remove the residual alkali. Since originally these were used to remove excess alkali, these were termed as "neutralizers". Though the modern rinses generally are oxidizing agents but the name, "neutralizers" originally used has been retained.

2.2 Formulation

Formulations of early heat waving preparations contained non-volatile alkalis like borax, alkali carbonates (e.g., Potassium carbonate, sodium bicarbonate). Since formulations containing these ingredients are no more used, formulae of this type of preparations will not be given.

To protect the hair from drying and damage, non-volatile alkalis were replaced with volatile alkalis like ammonia, ammonium carbonate, morpholine etc. These alkalis initially provide strong alkaline medium (pH 9-11) but being volatile volatilize during heating with drop in pH. Thus the chances of overwaving or partial hydrolysis of hair protein are minimized. However, these have disadvantage of having objectionable odour of ammonia and their premature loss from solution. To minimize premature loss of alkali, alkanolamines can be added in the formulation. The use of sulphites in the heat were preparations occurred about the same time as the use of volatile bases. Addition of a surface active agent helps in wetting of the hair. Formula 1 is an example of such a formulation.

Formula 1

		%
Ammonium Carbonate		3.5
Potassium Carbonate		2.0
Borax		0.5
Potassium sulphate		2.0
Monoethanolamine		5.0
Sulphonated Castor oil		1.0
Water	to make	100.0

A similar formulation can be incorporated in absorption base to make a creamy preparation.

Heat waving process has been largely replaced by cold waving process and therefore, no further discussion on this subject will be useful.

3. COLD WAVING PREPARATIONS

3.1 General

In the cold waving process, external heat is not applied to the hair. The process is performed at room temperature. The hair are shampooed first, divided into sections for ease of application, moistened with waving lotion and then wound on to curlers. After winding, the hair is left to the process for 10-40 minutes. After this processing, the wound curls are rinsed with oxidizing solution (neutralizers). After about 10 minutes the curls are unwound and usually a further rinse with neutralizer is given. The hair is finally rinsed with water and is set into the desired style.

Cold were lotions are mainly based on thioglycollates. Ammonium thioglycollate is generally used. Thioglycollates prepared by neutralization with ethanolamine and isopropanolamine are also used. However, monoethanolamine thioglycollate gives a curl which is more difficult to control. Sodium and Potassium thioglycollates are slower in action than ammonium or amine-thioglycollates, but preparations containing these make the hair very soft to handle. Thioglycollates are prepared by neutralization of thioglycollic acid with selected alkali. Since heat is evolved during neutralization, both materials should be diluted before mixing. For dilution iron free water should be used. All containers and mixing vessels should be made of or should be lined with glass or polythene to avoid contact with iron.

3.2 Formulation

Most of the cold wave preparations are based on thioglycollic acid. Lotions are prepared with different concentrations of thioglycollic acid depending on whether the product is meant for professional use by the hair dresser or for home use by the consumer. Lotions meant for professional use may contain maximum up to 10% thioglycollic acid. Usual concentrations for different types of hair are given below:

Type of the hair	Thioglycolliac acid %
Difficult (hard-to-wave) hair	8-9
Medium and easy natural hair	7
Slightly bleached hair	5
Medium bleached hair	3
Heavily bleached hair	1

pH is a very important factor for these preparations to be effective. The optimum pH range is 9.5-9.7. If the pH of the preparation drops to 9.0-9.2 during storage because of loss of ammonia, it will not give satisfactory result. If the pH of the preparation during its manufacture goes beyond 9.7, it may cause damage to the hair and depilation may occur. Therefore, it is very important to adjust the pH between 9.5-9.7. The final adjustment of pH should be done with ammonia. There are some additives which can be added in the formulation. Surface active agent can be added as a wetting agent (1.0-1.5%). Materials which are used for shampoos can be used (e.g., sod. Lauryl sulphate). Non-ionic surface active agents are compatible with other additives present. Opacifying agents are used to give opaque or milky appearance to the finished product. However, before finalizing the formulation the opacifying agent should be tested for compatibility. Polyvinyl pyrrolidone has been suggested as a useful additive in concentration of 1-3%. A quaternary ammonium compounds is, sometimes, included in the formulation as a conditioning agent. The compounds which can be used are cetyl trimethyl ammonium bromide, stearyl dimethyl benzyl ammonium chloride and dodecyl trimethyl ammonium bromide. Perfumes can be affected. Therefore, these should be tested for stability. Perfumes with strong floral character (e.g., sweet pea, violet or wall flower) can be used. High concentrations (about 1%) provide effective cover.

Neutralizers used are mild oxidizing agents like sodium perborate, sodium or potassium bromate or sodium percarbonate. These are packed in separate sachets and are dissolved in lukewarm water just before use. Solution of neutralizers is poured on curlers for several minutes to saturate the hair. It is advisable to leave the neutralizers on hair for 10-15 minutes because success of the process depends on oxidation. Thereafter, the hair is rinsed with lukewarm water

Thus permanent waving preparations have two parts. Part one contains thioglycollates and other additives. Part two contains oxidizing agents.

Formula 2 is an example of liquid cold waving preparation in the formulation of solid composition patented by Schnell.

Formula 2

	Parts
Calcium thioglycollate	80
Ammonium chloride and/or	47-65
Ammonium formate .	55-77

Creams containing thioglycollates can also be prepared. However, creams have been used for hair straightening rather than hair waving. A typical product patented by Ramsey[2] is shown in formula 3.

Formula 3

		%
Modified and stabilized polyglycerol monostearate emulsifier		21.0
Polyglycerol monostearate		18.0
Stearyl amide		2.1
Thioglycollic acid (38%)		13.0
Ammonia (26%)		1.0-2.0
Ammonium sulphite		1.0
Sodium lauryl sulphate		1.0
Water	to make	100.0

Thioglycollate based waving lotions develop objectionable odour due to formation of hydrogen sulphide. Freud suggested use of zinc tetramine sulphate in the concentration of 90.1-3%).

Waving lotions containing suspensions of poly-acrylates as opacifying agents have been popular. Peterson has described such a formula in a patent and is shown in formula 4.

Formula 4

	fl.oz.
Thioglycollic acid	0.90
Ammonium hydroxide	1.66
Water	13.44
Cream agent	0.7
Acrylic acid derivative (copolymer)	
Rhoplex and Triton dispersing agent, water in equal parts	720

Later on synthetic opacifiers were replaced with emulsions of oily materials. Besides opacity, these materials imparted emollient effect. Mineral oil is the most commonly used oily raw material. A mixture of mineral oil, sulphonated castor oil, lanolin oil (75%, 5%, 10%) and diglycol oleate (10%) forms a good creaming agent.

In a German Patent, an ingenious method to ensure supply of ammonia has been suggested by using urea and urease enzyme. Ammonia is produced in *situ* in presence of water.

In another German Patent, to maintain the reducing activity throughout the curling process, it has been proposed that reducing agents should be supplied in two phases. In the first phase, reducing activity is supplied by urea, ammonia carbonate and bicarbonate and in the second phase reducing activity is supplied by ester of thioglycollic acid (a more potent reducer) and at the same time pH is reduced (see formula 5).

Formula 5

	Parts by weight
Ammonium mercapto-acetate	9.4
Ammonium bi-carbonate	4.2
Ammonium carbonate	0.5
Urea	3.0
Perfume	0.4
Oleic acid pentaerythritol polyglycol ether	0.4
Water	62.1

Procedure for use

40 grams of this lotion is applied to the hair. Another 40 gms is mixed with 4 gm mono-mercapto-acetic glycerol ester and the hair is treated for 10-15 minutes, then washed with water and fixed with hydrogen peroxide.

For improved strength, body or elasticity to the waved hair, cationic compounds, chiefly resins (e.g., PVP-VA polymers, polyamide-epichlorhydrin resins) have been used in formulations of hair waving preparations. For the hair which have been weakened by other treatments like bleaching, less potent reducers such as thiomalic or tiolactic acids can be used. These formulations are called acid permanent waving formulations.

As mentioned earlier, oxidizing agents are used as neutralizers and form the second part of the hair waving preparations. Solutions of hydrogen peroxide in the presence of organic acids like acetic, tartaric or citric acid have been used earlier as neutralizers. Subsequently oxidizing agents like bromates, perborates were used as neutralizers. At the time of application of oxidizing agent, if alkali is present, mild bleaching can occur. To counteract this, a buffer salt with acid reaction can be included in the formulation of neutralizers. Formula 6 is an example of such a neutralizer.

Formula 6

	%
Potassium bromate	50.0
Sodium di-hydrogen phosphate	50.0

Such formulations are usually packed in sachets. Both the chemicals are dried before mixing until the moisture is about 0.01%, because, if moisture is present they react and tend to cake.

Neutralizers are also available in the form of lotion or cream. Such neutralizers do not require preliminary mixing. Formula 7 is an example of such a product.

Formula 7

	%
Cetyl alcohol	10.0
Sodium bromate	10.0
Water	80.0
Perfume and Preservatives	q.s.

Method of Preparation: Warm cetyl alcohol with half of the total quantity of water and warm separately sodium bromate with rest of the water. Add sodium bromate solution thus prepared with stirring. Add perfume and continue stirring. Preservative can be dissolved in water before mixing other ingredients.

A neutralizer having creamy consistency can be prepared from formula 8.

Formula 8

		%
Stearyl dimethyl benzyl ammonium chloride		10.0
Cetyl alcohol		2.5
Non-ionic emulsifier		4.0
Sodium bromate		10.0
Water	to make	100.0
Perfume and Preservatives		q.s.

Foam neutralizers can be prepared by mixing hydrogen peroxide with a detergent base or emulsion base just before use. Detergent base can be prepared with the detergents which are used in shampoos (e.g., sodium lauryl ether sulphate). Formula 9 is an example of foam neutralizer.

Formula 9

Part A		%
Sodium lauryl ether sulphate		10.0
Sodium chloride		10.0
Water	to make	100.0
Part B		
Acid stabilized solution of hydrogen peroxide		20 volume

When required, take equal parts of part A and part B and mix vigorously until a foam like preparation is produced. Detergent present in foam neutralizers helps the neutralizers to penetrate the hair wound on curls. These type of neutralizers can also be prepared with potassium or sodium bromate (see formula 10).

Formula 10

		%
Sodium bromate		10.0
Shampoo base		60.0
Water	to make	100.0
Perfume and Preservatives		q.s.

A waving lotion based on combination of dithio-diglycollic acid (2-3%) and thioglycollic acid (4-7%) is claimed to protect hair against damage during waving and to be safe for use on dyed or bleached hair. The formulations based on these compounds have pH between 9.0 and 9.4.

The fact that commercially available waving lotions are based on thioglycollic or thiolactic acid indicates that other mercaptans are not a match for them in terms of safety, odour and/or cost. For academic interest, the mercaptans other than thioglycollic acid which have been suggested for cold waving include:

- α-thioglycerol;
- β-aminoethyl mercaptan and mercapto ethyl alcohol;
- β–μερχαπτο propionamide;
- thiolactic acid;
- thioparaconic acid and its derivatives;
- N-acetyl cysteine;
- 1, 4-dimercapto-2, 3-butanediol;
- derivatives of thioglycollic acid:

- carbaminyl thioglycollic acid;
- glycollic acid esters of di-and tri-thiocarbonic acids;
- di-thiocarbamyl derivatives;
- 2, 4-thiazoledione;
- di-thiodiglycollic acid salts;
- thioglycollamide.

Some compounds other than mercaptans include reducing agents like organic and inorganic salts of sulphurous acid (bi-sulphites are preferred over sulphites), borohydride and phosphene derivatives. Michaels and Lusting suggested that bi-sulphites of organic nitrogen bases are useful as they cause effective swellong and relaxation of keratinous fibres. They recommended solutions of monoethanolamine and guanidine bi-sulphites at pH of 5-6. Alkyl or aryl substituted guanidium bi-sulphites have also been suggested for cold waving. Though bi-sulphites are free from mercaptan odour but these wave slowly and also have tendency to bleach the hair.

To overcome bleaching effect attempts were made to accelerate the rate of waving by bi-sulphites through chemical additives like quinones, polyphenols, urea, formamide.

Bogaty and Brown patented the use of solution of a borohydride (stabilized solution). To improve stability, dispersion of borohydride in inert but water soluble material such as polyoxyethylene or fatty alcohol ethers thereof has been recommended.

Another group of strong reducing agents that was recommended is phosphine derivatives. Tetrabishydroxy methyl phosphonium chloride can reduce di-sulphide bonds in Keratin, but it has not been used commercially.

Use of glyceryl monomercaptan has been illustrated in formula 11.

Formula 11

Glyceryl monomercaptan	5.0 gm
Ammonium hydroxide	2.5 ml
Water	100.0 ml

Efforts have been made to formulate dry preparations. Dry preparations have less shipping weight and are less bulky than lotions. One dry preparation was patented by Schnell. He used calcium thioglycollate which is produced commercially in dry form. A typical formulation is shown in formula I. Martin has described dry amines or ammonium salts of thioglycollic acid (e.g., monothioglycollate and di-thioglycollate of ethylenediamine, ammonium thioglycollate, guanidinium thioglycollate). Scheweizer has described preparations of di-potassium salt of zinc bis-thioglycollic acid. He has suggested that these dry preparations should be dispensed together with large quantity of sequestering agent and a suitable alkalizing agent (see formula 12).

Formula 12

	%
Di-potassium salt of zinc bis-thioglycollic acid	32.5
Trishydroxy methyl aminomethane	30.5
Sodium hydroxide	2.7
Tetrasodium ethylene diamine tetraacetate	32.5
Perfume	1.8

Dry mixtures of thioglycollic acid such as those mentioned above require dissolution in proper quantity of water prior to use. In order to simplify this process end wraps with dry thioglycollates were suggested. These end wraps made from non-woven fabric, generally, referred to as end papers did not become popular because these primarily yielded end curls.

Salts of dithioglycollic acid can be crystallized readily and relatively are more stable in air. Therefore, attempts have been made to pack dry salts of dithioglycollic acid with materials which can reduce them to thioglycollates on dissolution in water. Brown and Bogaty have recommended mixtures of diammonium dithioglycollate and thiourea dioxide. Other mixture recommended by them include diammonium thiomalate and diammonium α, α'-dimercapto-adipate.

Cysteine has also been used as reducing agent. It has less irritating smell and does not damage the hair much. But its disadvantages is that it does not form strong waves. Cysteine reduces hair bonds and itself is reduced to cystine. So produced cystine crystallizes to form an insoluble white powder. This powder gets on to the hands and the hair. This powder cannot be removed by rinsing alone. Adding ammonium thioglycolate prevents the crystallization of cystine. Therefore, ammonium thioglycolate is also included in cysteine based formulation. Formula 13 is a cysteine based formula.

Formula 13

		%
Cysteine		5.0
Ammonium thioglycolate		0.25
Monoethanol amine		2.0
Water	to make	100.0
EDTA		q.s.
Perfume		q.s.

3.3 Manufacture of Cold Waving Lotions

Cold wave preparations are usually marketed in the formulation of lotions. General process of manufacture of lotions will appear adequate. But manufacture of cold wave lotion require certain precautions. Salient of them are:

* Contamination by metals should be avoided, because thioglycollic acid oxidizes in the presence of heavy metals.
* Contamination by iron in as small quantity as 0.25 ppm can produce purple colouration, therefore, contamination by iron should be totally avoided.
* In view of the above precautions, glass lined container should be used, however, thioglycollic acid salts after these are made alkaline can be processed in stainless steel, polyethylene or teflon containers.
* For preparing thioglycollate solution, either thioglycollic acid can be neutralized with alkali or ammonium salt can be diluted directly with distilled water or deionized water, free alkali is added to adjust the desired pH and then all other ingredients such as perfume, colour, opacifier are incorporated into the lotion and final volume is adjusted with distilled or deionized water.
* Concentration of mercaptan, free alkali and pH should be determined in each batch.

From the foregoing account it may be seen that cleanliness and absence of contamination is of utmost importance in the manufacture of cold waving lotions. Hollenberg has outlined manufacturing procedure for such lotions.

It appears unlikely to get waving effect in one operation. A method has been patented for single operation waving. In this method, the hair are subjected to a mixture of thiol and disulphide for 20-30 minutes. After the treatment, the hair are rinsed and the curlers are removed.

4. HAIR STRAIGHTENERS

4.1 General

As mentioned earlier, the persons who have curly hair want straight hair and the persons who have straight hair want to have curly hair. This led to the need for formulation of the hair straighteners. According to the most accepted theory the straight hair appear to be circular while curly or kinky hair appear to be oblate spheroid. Earlier, materials like gums, resinous fatty materials were used for straightening the hair. Hot comb methods were used subsequently. In these methods substances like petroleum jelly, sodium hydroxide were used as aids for hair straightening. Later, formulations based on thioglycollic acid and its salts were developed.

4.2 Formulation

The earlier method of hair straightening was plastering them down by the use of gums or resinous fatty materials. Formula 14 and 15 are examples of such methods.

Formula 14

		%
Gum Karaya		1.5
Boroglycerine		2.0
Ethyl alcohol		6.5
Water	to make	100.0
Colour, Perfume and Preservatives		q.s.

Method of Preparation

Prepare mucilage of gum karaya with water and alcohol. Add boro-glycerine, colour and perfume. Pass through a colloid mill.

Formula 15

	%
Petroleum jelly	88.0
Paraffin	12.0
Perfume and Colour	q.s.

Method of Preparation

Melt petroleum jelly and paraffin, add colour, allow to cool and mix perfume when the mix is warm enough to be in liquid state. Pour into warmed jars.

In formula 15, paraffin can be replaced with other waxes like beeswax, ozokerite etc. Resins can also be incorporated in the formula 15. If synthetic resins are incorporated, these should be tested for sensitization reactions.

The above-mentioned formulations act only through adhesive qualities. There is not chemical reaction. The curly or kinky hair, if not changed chemically return to their original state as the adhesive is weakened. Moisture accelerates this process.

In the early 1900, Madam C.J. Walker conceived the idea of use of a petroleum jelly product and a hot metal comb. In this method, petroleum jelly product is applied to the hair after washing and drying and then hot comb is applied. Another type of products that were developed for use in the hot comb method were alkali type of straightener. Formula 16 is an example of alkali type hair straightener.

Formula 16

		%
Sodium hydroxide		5.0
Glyceryl monostearate		17.5
Glycerin		7.5
Water	to make	100.0
Perfume		q.s.

Method of Preparation

Heat Glyceryl monostearate, glycerine and a part of water to about 95°C. Dissolve sodium hydroxide in another part of water. Allow to cool the glyceryl monostearate mix to about 60°C, add sodium hydroxide solution and stir. Allow to cool to about 40°C, add perfume and mix. Fill into containers.

This type of preparation had the potential of alkali burns. After the introduction of permanent waving preparations based on thioglycollic acid salts, hair straighteners based on these chemicals were also made available. Originally these products were in the form of paste like creams. In the hair straighteners based on these chemicals, a particular attention has to be paid to the base of these preparations. The bases required for these preparations were required to have viscosity and adhesion which will keep the hair reasonably straight. This is a basic difference between cold waving preparations and the hair straighteners based on thioglycollates. A number of products have been formulated as o/w emulsions. A typical formulation for hair straightening is shown in formula 17.

Formula 17

		%
Glyceryl monostearate		17.5
Stearic acid		2.5
Ceresin		1.0
Paraffin wax		1.0
Thioglycollic aid (26°Be)		6.6
Ammonium hydroxide		20.0
Sodium lauryl sulphate		1.0
Water	to make	100.0
Perfume		q.s.

Method of Preparation

Heat glyceryl monstearate, stearic acid, sodium lauryl sulphate with 40 pars of the water in a jacketted mixer to about 95°C. Allow to cool to 50°C with sterring on. Prepare separately ammonium thioglycollate by adding ammonium hydroxide to a mixture of thioglycollic acid and remaining water (while preparing ammonium thioglycollate the temperature should not be allowed to go above 50°C and this may require cooling). Add thioglycollate solution to the fatty phase slowly and mix thoroughly. Cool the resulting mixture to 40°C rapidly, add perfume, mix and fill into the containers.

Thioglycollate content, free alkali and pH are important in these preparations (like in the cold waving preparations). Thioglycollae content should be 6.4-6.8% and free ammonia between 0.8-0.90%. Like the cold waving preparations, use of neutralizers is recommended in these preparations also. Popular neutralizers include perborates or bromates.

4.3 Manufacture of Hair Straighteners

Manufacture of hair straighteners is carried out according to the type of product. The basic method of manufacture has been described in the formulation section below the formulae printed there. Hair straighteners containing thioglycollates are manufactured in similar manner as the cold wave lotions.

For the formulations based on thioglycollates, packaging materials should also be selected with care. Information on method for use and precautions to be taken should be enclosed along with the containers. Some typical precautions are given below:

* If there are abrasions or cuts on your scalp, do not use hair straightener.
* If you are sick or under medical care, do not apply hair straightener without consulting the physician.
* If warm water is indicated, use warm, do not use hot water.
* Use neutralizer as per directions given.
* After treatment with the hair straightener, do not use hot comb.

9

Hair Bleachers and Hair Colourants

1. GENERAL

Dissatisfaction with the colour of the hair, man has been using different materials to change the colour of the hair from early times. History of social life and customs of various countries like Egypt, Greece, Persia, China, India indicates that coloring materials were being used by old civilizations. Metallic compounds and plant materials have been used for a long time. The discovery of some synthetic organic compounds to dye animal fibres gave impetus to the development of new kind of hair colourants. It was only in the middle of Twentieth Century that the new type of hair colourants were accepted in the society.

Two types of practices are in vogue to change the colour of the hair. One, bleaching of the hair to reduce the original colour. Two, colouring of the grey hair. These products can he classified into the following categories.

- bleaching agents,
- temporary colourants,
- natural organic colourants,
- synthetic organic colourants,
- inorganic colourants.

Each category will be dealt with separately in the proceeding paragraphs.

2. BLEACHING AGENTS

2.1 General

Like hair colourants, hair bleaching agents have been used for a very long time. Roman ladies admired the golden hair of the captives brought from northern regions and tried to imitate it. The materials used by them included minerals like rock alum, quicklime, wood asH and water. Sometimes old wine was also combined with water. The old books on this and related subjects mention the use of alum, ashes, borax, soap, soda etc. With decoction of plants like birch bark, celandine, myrrh, saffron, turmeric.

E.H. Thiellay of London and Leon Hugo of Paris demonstrated the bleaching effect of hydrogen peroxide. This treatment became popular in Europe and America by the turn of the Century and hydrogen peroxide superseded all other materials for bleaching of human hair.

2.2 Formulation

Solutions of hydrogen peroxide have been available under different brand names. Solutions of hydrogen peroxides are stabilized with chemicals such as acetanilide dilute acids, p-hydroxybenzoates, sodium stannate. Peroxides like barium peroxide, sodium peroxide have been used to produce hydrogen peroxide.

Bleaching preparations have been formulated in different forms like pastes, powders, liquids and creams.

Bleaching pastes can be prepared by mixing hydrogen peroxide solution with an absorbent powder, The paste so formed is easier to apply, does not run and acts only where it is applied. Because of the latter reason it can be applied to the roots of the already bleached hair. A powder that could be suitably mixed with hydrogen peroxide was, at one time, sold as 'white henna'. Magnesium carbonate is the most commonly known material for this type of formulations. A solution containing 3-4% of hydrogen peroxide (liberating 10-12 volumes of oxygen) is suitable for use at home. A solution containing 5-6% of hydrogen peroxide (liberating 17-20 volumes of oxygen) is suitable for beauty shops where more rapid action is required.

Bleaching powders which can be converted into paste either with water or hydrogen peroxide are a development over 'white henna'. When these are to be mixed with hydrogen peroxide they are composed of absorbing materials like magnesium carbonate, and mild alkali such as ammonium bicarbonate. Formula 1 is a typical formula of this type of powder bleach.

Formula 1

	%
Magnesium carbonate (light)	55.0
Calcium carbonate (light)	15.0
Ammonium bicarbonate	20.0
Ammonium bi-sulphate	10.0

Since ammonium bicarbonate decomposes slowly during storage, ammonium bi-sulphate has been included in the formula as stabilizer. When the powder is to be mixed with water, these are composed of absorbent like magnesium carbonate, calcium carbonate, peroxides, mild alkali. Formula 2 is a typical formulation of this type.

Formula 2

	%
Magnesium Carbonate (light)	45.0
Calcium Carbonate (light)	15.0
Sodium Peroxide	10.0
Sodium Sulphate (anhydrous)	10.0
Ammonium bicarbonate	10.0
Ammonium bi-sulphate	10.0

Hair bleaches are also prepared as liquids and creams. Liquid bleaches are generally sold as two solutions pack, one pack containing stabilized hydrogen peroxide (20-25 volumes) and the other containing the activator. When these two solutions are mixed, a thin cream is produced which can be applied. The activator in this type of products, generally, is concentrated soap solution. Product based on oleate soap is called oil bleach by professional hairdressers. Formula 3 is an example of an activator based on oleate soap.

Formula 3

	%
Oleic acid	45.0
Triethanolamine	13 .0

Alcohol	20.0
Ammonium hydroxide (0.88)	22.0
Perfume	q.s.

One part of oil bleach is to be mixed with two parts of hydrogen peroxide solution (20 volumes) when required for use.

Cream bleach can be prepared by incorporating a surfactant in the formulation of oil bleach. Formula 4 is an example of cream bleach.

Formula 4

	%
Oleic acid	40.0
Triethanolamine	12.0
Alcohol	18.0
Ammonium hydroxide (0.88)	20.0
Sodium lauryl ether sulphate	10.0

One part of cream bleach prepared according to formula 4 should ne mixed with four parts of hydrogen peroxide when required for use. On mixing, a cream is produced which can be applied to the hair. Since creams are more convenient to use and can be controlled on the hair and degree of bleaching can be regulated, bleaches have been formulated in the form of creams. The cream base is prepared usually with glyceryl monostearate or cetyl alcohol using an emulsifying agent (usually non-ionic). Lanolin derivative can also be included in the formulation. If thickening is required, a thickener can be added (see formula 5).

Formula 5

	%
Carboxy vinyl polymer (carbopol 934)	2.0
Hydrogen peroxide	88.0
Triethanolamine (10% aqueous solution)	10.0

Formula 5 is an example of cream prepared with thickening agent. Carboxy vinyl polymer should be dispersed in hydrogen peroxide solution with a stirrer and should be allowed to stand for 15 minutes. Then solution of triethanolamine should be added to a pH of 5.5.

A liquid preparation can be prepared by mixing a solution of stearyl dimethyl benzyl ammonium chloride and hydrogen peroxide (see formula 4).

Formula 6

		%
Hydrogen Peroxide solution		80.0
Stearyl dimethyl benzyl ammonium chloride		1.0
Water	to make	100.0

The product prepared from formula 6 has a pH between 5.0 and 5.5. This type of lotions are applied to the hair and are allowed to dry. Applications may be repeated, if more bleaching is required.

It will be relevant to mention certain precautions and recommendations while preparing these for use and while applying.

* When two solutions are to be mixed before use, these should be mixed in glass or porcelain containers.
* Metallic containers should not be used for mixing.
* Bleach preparations should be applied with tooth brush or a piece of cotton wool.
* Metallic spoons should not be used for application.
* Bleaching process is affected by temperature. Heat accelerates the process, therefore, head should be wrapped in hot towel. Alternatively, treated hair can be warmed with hair dryer.
* Rinsing with lukewarm water alone is not sufficient to prevent oxidation process especially when peroxide salts have been used. For cleaning the hair more effectively mild acid solution can be used.

2.3 Manufacture of Hair Bleaches

Many bleaching preparations require use of hydrogen peroxide solution. Hydrogen peroxide is commercially available in solution form containing 35-50% of hydrogen peroxide. Solutions containing 3-4% (producing 10-12 volumes of oxygen) and 5-6% (producing 17-20 volumes of oxygen) are required to be made. This can be done by diluting commercial hydrogen peroxide solution. Only de-mineralized or distilled water should be used for dilution as metallic ions cause catalytic decomposition of hydrogen peroxide. Mixing is carried out in stainless steel (316) or glass-lined mixing vessels. Stabilizers should be added to the diluted solutions. Acetanilide (450 ppm) can be used as a stabilizer. Stability is also improved if pH is adjusted to 4.0. pH can be adjusted with phosphoric acid.

Bleach powders are prepared by grinding (if necessary) the ingredients except oxidizing agent and then blending them in mixer. Before blending, oxidizing agent should be mixed with a small portion of the base and then it should be mixed with the bulk. Since inert powders like sodium sulphate (anhydrous), magnesium oxide (light), magnesium silicate which are used as vehicle for bleach powders or alkali, vary in density, it will be necessary to experiment to obtain a product of the correct specific volume.

General methods of manufacture of lotions, creams can be applied for the manufacture of activators in the form of lotion and cream.

3. HAIR COLOURANTS

3.1 General

In general, the reasons for colouring the hair are:

- to change the natural colour of the hair;
- to colour the grey hair;
- to change the colour of the hair temporarily for a particular occasion.

To achieve these objectives, a variety of materials are used. To select a material for hair colouring purpose, one should know the characteristics which should be possessed by a hair colourant. An ideal hair colourant should possess the following characteristics:

* It should colour the hair without reducing natural gloss and without impairing its texture.
* It should not injure the hair shaft.
* It should be non-irrigant and free from sensitizing action.
* It should not have systemic toxicity.
* Colour of the dyed hair should be stable to physical factors like air, sunlight, friction (caused by rubbing or combing) and chemical factors like sweat.
* It should not change colour on application of toilet preparations which are usually applied to the hair (e.g., shampoos, brilliantines, setting lotions etc.).
* It should be stable in the formulation sold in the market.

Depending on their effect as to how long it lasts, hair colourants can be divided into three groups namely:

- temporary hair colourants,
- semi-permanent hair colourants, and
- permanent hair colourants.

3.2 Formulation

3.2.1 Temporary Hair Colourants

Before the introduction of shampoos based on synthetic detergents, soap or shampoos based on soaps were used to wash the hair. Residual soap on hair has dulling effect. Therefore, it was common practice to rinse the hair with materials such as vinegar, lemon juice etc. to give highlighting effect. Similar effect is obtained by rinsing the hair with solutions of citric acid or tartaric acid. Employing this principle temporary colourants are prepared. They are composed of dye stuff and acid. Sometimes, these are referred to as water rinses. These colourants do not penetrate into the cortex or medulla, they are absorbed on to or become substantive to hair cuticle. As such, the dye can be removed easily with a shampoo and hence these are knows as temporary hair colourants.

The dye stuffs which have been used include basic dyes, acid dyes, disperse dyes and metallized dyes (pigments) and belong largely to azo, anthraquinone, triphenyl methane, phenazanic, xanthenic or benzoquinoneimine dyes. Temporary hair colourants have been formulated in different forms i.e., powders, crayons, liquids and shampoos. The use of powder for changing colour of the hair is now very limited and is confined to theatrical make-up and masquerades. These powders usually consist of starch, talcum and pigments.

Coloured crayons have been formulated in handy shapes primarily for retouching new growth of hair between applications of permanent hair dyes. These crayons can be prepared with waxes, soap and dyes/pigments in various shades. The consistency of the crayons should be such that these could be rubbed directly over the hair or material could be transferred from crayon to the hair by moist brush. Formula 7 is a typical formula of crayons.

Formula 7

	%
Stearic acid	15.0
Triethanolamine	7.0
Beeswax	50.0
Carnauba wax	13.0
Ozokerite	7.0
Glyceryl monostearate	6.0
Gum tragacanth	2.0
Colour	q.s.

Method of Preparation

Heat Triethanolamne, Glyceryl monostearate and gum tragacanth to 70°C, add stearic acid and heat further and raise temperature to 75°C. Melt waxes separately at about 75°C-80°C, add molten waxes to the previous mixture and stir well to complete blending. Add colour and mix thoroughly. Pour into moulds for cooling.

Water can also be incorporated in the formulations of soap based crayons. Formula 8 is typical of such crayons.

Formula 8

	%
Sodium stearate	18.0
Gum arabic	25.0
Glycerin	15.0
Water	25.0
Colour	17.0

Method of Preparation

Mix water and glycerine. Divide it into two portions. To one portion, add gum arabic and allow to stand. Add sodium stearate top the remaining portion and warm until it is dissolved. Mix these two and add colour. Mill thoroughly, run the paste so formed into moulds and dry with heat.

Water rinses which have been described in the introductory part of this section are marketed either in powder form or in liquid form. Products in powder form are prepared by mixing dye stuff with citric acid or tartaric acid. The mixture is packed either in sachets or in capsules. A general formula for such products is as shown in Formula 9.

Formula 9

	%
Dye stuff	5.0
Acid (citric or tartaric)	95.0

To prepare rinse for use, content of one sachet or capsule are mixed with warm water and the solution is poured over the wet head just after shampooing. Being acidic in nature, water-rinse is used for giving pastel shades to the bleached hair and to prevent alkali degradation of the hair. Shades like blue, pink, light golden or auburn can be achieved with success. Liquid rinses are aqueousalcoholic solutions of dyes. Formulae 10 and 11 are typical formula of liquid rinses.

Formula 10

		%
Dye stuff (acidic)		6.0
Acetic acid (30%)		10.0
Ethyl alcohol		10.0
Water	to make	100.0

Formula 11

		%
Dye stuff (acidic)		5.0
Citric acid		35.0
Ethyl alcohol		10.0
Water	to make	100.0

De-ionized or distilled water should be used as metallic ions can causae colour change in colourants. It is advisable to add sequestering agent like EDTA in this type of hair colourants. A dye may give satisfactory colour with one acid but may not give satisfactory colour with other acid. Therefore, it should be found out that which acid should be used with which dye.

Sometimes, basic dyes such as methylene blue, rhodamine and gentian violet are used. Solutions of these dyes give pastel shades. On bleaching hair, these dyes produce white or platinum blonde effects and therefore, solutions of these dyes are also mixed with bleaching mixture to reduce harsh red and yellow tones.

Dye stuff incorporated in a detergent base shampoo acts in similar way as water-rinse. To prepare such preparation, dye is dissolved in water (usually 0.5-2%) and is mixed with shampoo detergent base (e.g., Triethanolamine lauryl sulphate) and pH value is adjusted to about 5.0. Like in water-rinses, acid which is used for adjusting pH should be tested with the dye for satisfactory results.

3.2.2 Semi-Permanent Hair Colourants

These products are different than colour shampoos in respect of the duration for which they last. These are designed to give stronger and more permanent colouration to the hair than colour shampoos. Some colour will be removed in each shampooing and will be removed completely in 6-8 shampooings.

The dyes which are used in semi-permanent hair colourants largely belong to nitrophenylenediamines, nitroaminophenols and aminoanthraquinones classes of dyes. Various colour shades can be achieved with these dyes. However, before attempting to prepare colour shades, effect of the dye or mixture of dyes should be studied on white wool or hair. Factors which may be taken into consideration are:

- solubility of the dye in water;
- composition of the vehicle or base of the formulation;
- effect of pH value on the dye;
- effect of solvents which may be added to the formulation.

Solubility in water determines the selection of vehicle. For example, a nitro-amino dye does not give satisfactory results when applied in an ionic surfactant. In such cases, the effect of the dye is increased by alkanolamides in concentrations of 2-5%.

These dyes have cation active properties and are, therefore, absorbed on to the hair fibre to some extent. As such, it is likely that these will be absorbed more from a cation-effective vehicle. But it does happen so in many cases, the dye becomes so finely dispersed in the solution that most of it is rinsed off the hair immediately. Because of this, hair colourant bases are prepared by mixing anionic and/or non-ionic surfactants with cation-active material. The mixtures form anion-cation colour complexes. Formula 12 is a basic formula which may be used for experimentation.

Formula 12

		%
Quaternary ammonium compound		10.12
Anionic surfactant		08.10
Acid		06.08
Alkanolamide		04.06
Dye stuff		01.02
Water	to make	100.0

To prepare colour complex, first dissolve the dye in a mixture of alkanolamide and anionic surfactant. Next dissolve acid and quaternary ammonium compound in water. Add aqueous solution to the dye solution with stirring.

While experimenting, effects of the following may be studied:

- effect of quaternary ammonium compounds;
- effect of the pH;
- effect of addition of solvents like aldehydes and alcohols.

After the best results have been obtained, viscosity of the product can be adjusted by addition of hydrophilic colloids such as methyl cellulose, carboxy vinyl polymer of natural gum.

Basic dyes can also be used in an amphoteric system. Non-ionic thickener may be used to increase the viscosity of the product. Formula 13 is an illustrative example of such a product.

Formula 13

		%
Amphoteric surfactant		10.0
Lauric isopropanolamide		1.0
Non-ionic surfactant		5.0
Oleyl alcohol		1.0
Non-ionic thickener		2.0
Dye(s)		2.0
Water	to make	100.0
Perfume and Preservatives		q.s.

3.2.3 Permanent Hair Colourants

The effect of permanent hair colourants lasts for longer period than semi-permanent hair colourants and, therefore, these are known as permanent hair colourants. The earliest permanent hair dyes were obtained from plants. Infusions, decoctions or packs of plant materials were used. One of the plant material which is still used is henna leaves. Powdered henna leaves are available in market. This powder is made into a paste with boiling hot water. After cooling it is applied to the hair with the help of stiff brush and is allowed to dry. Hot towels can be used to wrap the head for enhancing the effect.

Henna contains an active principle, lawsone (2-hydroxy-1, 4-napthaquinone) which is substantive to Keratin. The main advantages of henna are that it is non-toxic and does not cause sensitization reactions. But preparation of henna paste, its application etc. are laborious processes and repeated use of henna packs may give an unnatural reddish-auburn colour and may cause staining of hands and finger nails. This shade however, can be modified by adding other ingredients like indigo plant leaves or synthetic indigo. Pyrogallic acid and metallic salts (e.g., copper sulphate) are other additives which can be used with henna. Darker shade can be obtained by increasing the proportion of pyrogallic acid. Formula 14 is an example of such a product.

Formula 14

	%
Powdered henna	89.0
Pyrogallic acid	6.0
Copper sulphate	5.0

Camomile is another vegetable dye which has been used. Flowers of camomile contain active principles. Camomile powder can be used similar to henna pack. The colouring effect is due to deep blue volatile oil. Since camomile flowers alone do not form cohesive pack, camomile powder is mixed with either Kaolin (2 parts) or Fuller's earth (1 part).

To modify colours produced by either of them, henna and camomile can be in mixed in different proportions as shown in Formula 15 and 16.

	Formula 15 %	**Formula 16** %
Camomile powder	70.0	30.0
Henna powder	30.0	70.0

Metallic hair colourants, also referred to as 'colour restorers' are compounds of lead, silver, iron, cobalt, cadmium and copper. These compounds act by depositing coloured metallic salt on hair shaft. Lead dyes, usually, are based on lead acetate. It is believed that insoluble salts of lead are produced by the reducing action of Keratin. The reaction takes place slowly and the rate is influenced by content of lead and such factors as air and light. Thus the grey hair are gradually coloured. Because of this reason, these are, sometimes, referred to as 'progressive' hair dyes. The preparations of lead compounds can be made with lead acetate and sodium thiosulphate or precipitated sulphur. Examples of such products are shown in formulae 17 and 18.

Formula 17

		%
Lead acetate		5.5
Sodium thiosulphate		11.0
Glycerin/propylene glycol		8.5
Ethyl alcohol		10.0
Water	to make	100.0
Perfume		q.s.

Formula 18

		%
Lead acetate		12.0
Precipitated sulphur		24.0
Propylene glycol		12.0
Ethyl alcohol		10.0
Water	to make	100.0
Perfume		q.s.

These preparations are packed in amber coloured bottles.

Before the advent of organic chemical dyes, silver dyes were one of the important dyes. The shades could be varied by varying the amount of silver. Preparations containing two separate solutions consisted of silver nitrate solution with ammonium hydroxide/ ammonium nitrate in one container and the 'developer' in the second container which was reducing agent (e.g., a mixture of gallic acid and sodium meta-bi-sulphite). Formula 19 is an example of such a preparation.

Formula 19

Solution A		%
2% solution of silver nitrate in ammonium hydroxide		
Solution B		
Pyrogallic acid		3.0
Sodium meta-bi-sulphite		1.0
Water	to make	100.0

For applying these preparations, the hair are shampooed first and then petroleum jelly/cold cream is applied to forehead, ears, neck and finally the silver dye is applied. These dyes are very slow in action and may require two or three applications.

The first synthetic organic dye used was pyrogallol but its use was discontinued after the reports of irritation on the skin and harmful effects when taken internally.

Another important class of permanent hair colourants is oxidation dyes. These substances are colourless at the time of application to the hair but are transformed into coloured materials on to the hair as a result of chemical reactions. The chemical reactions involved include oxidation reactions and coupling or condensation in alkaline pH. Three reactants are required for these reactions to be complete, namely, bases (primary intermediates), couplers (modifiers) and oxidizing agent. Oxidizing agent almost always is hydrogen peroxide. Most commonly used bases are *p*-phenylene diamine and *p*-tolylenediamine. Like bases, couplers are also aromatic compounds almost invariably benzene derivatives substituted by amino-and hydroxyl groups but in *meta* position. Couplers are not easily oxidized by H_2O_2. The usual couplers include *m*-phenylene-diamine, 2 4-diaminoanisole, resorcinol, *m*-chloro resorcinol etc.

In spite of lot of studies, clear cut mechanism of action of these dyes has not emerged. Therefore, a lot of experimentation is required to achieve the reproducible results. Thee dyes have potential for allergic reactions. Therefore, The Drugs and Cosmetics Rules require that statutory caution in English and local language should appear on both inner and outer label. Statutory caution is reproduced below:

"***Caution:*** *This product contains ingredients which may cause skin irritation in certain cases and so a preliminary test* *according to the accompanying directions should first be made. This product should not be used for dyeing the eyelashes or eyebrows; as such a use maycause blindness."*

It is also required under the said rules that package should contain instructions in English and local languages on the lines given below:

"This preparation may cause serious inflammation of the skin in some cases and so preliminary test should always be carried out to determine whether or not special sensitivity exists. To make the test, clean a small area of skin behind the ear or upon the inner surface of the forearm, either using soap and water or alcohol. Apply a small quantity of the hair dye as prepared for use to the area and allow it to dry. After 24 hour wash the area gently with soap and water. If no irritation or inflammation is apparent, it may be assumed that no hyper sensitivity to the dye exists. The test should, however be carried out before each and every application. This preparation on no account be used for dyeing eyebrows or eyelashes as severe inflammation of the eye or even blindness may result."

Though these dyes are referred to as 'para dyes' but other bases like o-aminophenol, o-phenylene diamine are also used.

While developing formulations of oxidation dyes the following factors should be taken into consideration:

*Formulation base :

- powder;
- shampoo;
- gel;
- emulsion;
- solution.

* Dye components:
  - oxidation base;
  - coupling agent;
  - direct colouring agent.
* Alkali:

- sodium hydroxide;
- sodium carbonate;
- ammonium hydroxide;
- others.

* Oxidizing agent:
- ferric chloride;
- potassium dichromate,
- potassium permanganate;
- hydrogen peroxide;
- others.

* Anti-oxidant:
- nitrogen;
- sodium sulphite.

The dye components include oxidation base and coupling agents. Coupling agents can be replaced with direct colouring agent also. Many oxidation bases have been used (see table at the end of this chapter). But out of these the most commonly used oxidation bases which have been used most commonly are *p*-phenylene diamine and *p*-toluenediamine. Various colour shades can be obtained with these bases. The shades which can be achieved with different concentration of *p*-phenylene diamine or *p*-tolulene diamine are given below:

Shade	**Percentage of base**
Black	1.0
dark Brown	0.9
Brown	0.5
Medium Brown	0.45
Light Brown	0.3

Coupling agents, many of them are related to oxidation bases, are used to modify and stabilize colour shades. Coupling agents which have been found useful are:

- metadiamine;
- pyrocatechol;
- resorcinol;
- pyrogallol.

Some other compounds which have been suggested in patents include α- and β-naphthoils, diaminoansole and phenetole. These modifiers may take different time for colour development. Therefore, while preparing instructions of use, the time required by the modifier to develop colour should also be taken into account. Sometimes, direct colourants are also used to modify colour shades.

Very early, in the development of amino dyes, it was found out that these work efficiently in alkaline medium. Erdamnn's solution which contain *p*-phenylend diamine (2%) and sodium hydroxide (1.4%) though was satisfactory for fur, feather and dead hair, but was risky to use on living hair. Use of sodium carbonate was also investigated. But ammonium hydroxide was found to be the best, because, besides being efficient alkalizer, it leaves no residue on hair. However, the amount to be used should be carefully controlled and should not exceed 1-2% in final mixture that is to be applied to the hair. Ammonia has one disadvantage and that is its odour. Therefore, some effort has been made to replace it partially or totally and the substance tried include ammonium carbonate, mono-, di- or tri-ethanolamine, alkanolamides, guanidine or arginine derivatives etc.

Although amino dyes darken on exposure to air but an oxidizing agent is required to develop the colour of desired shade. Various oxidizing agents like (ferrichloride, potassium di-chromate, potassium permanganate) peroxides have been investigated for use as developer of hair colourants. But out of these, the most commonly used oxidizing agent is hydrogen peroxide. Normally, a 5-6% solution of hydrogen peroxide (generating 20 volumes of oxygen) is used for developing colour of oxidation hair colourants. Many products are packed in twin bottles of dye and developer. Peroxides which liberate hydrogen peroxide can also be supplied along with such colourants. For example, tablets of urea peroxide can be wrapped in plastic or metallic foil and can be packed with the product.

As mentioned earlier, amino dyes oxidize easily and darken on exposure to air, manufacturing processes are required to be guarded against access of air. This may be achieved by maintaining atmosphere of nitrogen during compounding and filling. But this is cumbersome. The most practical approach is addition of chemical anti-oxidant. Sodium sulphite has been used successfully as an anti-oxidant. The amount of sodium sulphite is calculated on the basis of total amount of oxidizable base and coupling agent used. More sodium sulphite should be used for darker shades.

Different formulation bases can be used as vehicles for amino dyes and modifiers. Distilled water can be used as a vehicle for amino dyes but these have low solubility in water, as such, a mixture of water, ethyl alcohol and glycerine (20-50% ethyl alcohol, 0.5-2.0% glycerine in water) is generally used in liquid type of preparations.

The main purpose of vehicle is to distribute the colourant mixture evenly throughout the hair. Better distribution can be achieved if the preparation is transformed to cream or lotion by using suitable surfactant. These may be either foaming type or non-foaming type. A foaming type cream can be prepared with mono-ethanolamine lauryl sulphate and ethylene glycol monostearate. A non-foaming type cream base can be prepared with mineral oil, cetyl alcohol and non-ionic emulsifier. Formula 20 and 21 are examples of foaming and non-foaming type cream bases respectively.

Formula 20

		%
Monoethanolamine lauryl sulphate		28.0
Ethylene glycol monostearate		1.0
Water	to make	100.0
Preservative		q.s.

Formula 21

		%
Mineral oil		1.5
Cetyl alcohol		5.0
Non-ionic emulsifier		3.0-5.0
Water	to make	100.0
Preservative		q.s.

The base can be improved by adding other additives like lanolin (hydrous), lecithin, sequestering agents etc. (see Formula 22).

Formula 22

Solvent for dye intermediates		%
Ammonium hydroxide (0.88)		10.0
Isopropyl alcohol		3.0
Perfume		q.s.
Base		
Oleic acid		33.0
Polyoxyethylene sorbitan monstearate		12.0
Non-ionic surfactant		4.0
Lanolin (hydrous)		1.5
Lecithin		1.0
Sequestering agent		1.0
Water	to make	100.0

Bleach-dye combination products have also been developed. The double action of bleaching and colouring was first accomplished by an excessive amount of ammonium hydroxide and proportionately more amount of hydrogen peroxide.

Products have also been prepared in powder form. The base formulation contains a solid oxidizing agent like sodium peroxide and an alkali. Such preparations are mixed with water to a paste when required for use.

Colour shampoos impart colour tinge temporarily and usually are prepared in only a few shades. The base for these shampoos may be sulphonated oils, anionic or non-ionic surface active agents. Formula 23 is an example, of typical base for colour shampoo.

Formula 23

	%
Ammonium lauryl alcohol sulphate	30.0
Cocodiethanolamide	2.0
Water	q.s.

Formulation of amino dyes has been subject of patents and therefore, only limited information is available. It will be useful to give the names of various dye intermediates which have been used in semi-permanent and permanent hair colourants. These are given in Table 9.1.

Table 9.1: Dye Intermediates used as semi-permanent and permanent hair dyes

Shades	Names of dye intermediate
	Dyes used in semi-permanent hair colourants
Yellow	4-nitro-*m*-phenylene diamine
	2-(2-hydroxy ethyl) amino-5-nitrophenol methyl ether
	2-(2-hydroxy ethyl) amino-5-nitrophenol-2-hydroxyethyl ether
Orange-yellow	2-amino-4-nitro-N-(2-hydroxy ethyl) aniline
	2-amino-5-nitrophenol
Orange	4-(2-hydroxy ethyl) amino-3-nitrophenol methyl ether
	4-amino-3-nitrophenol-2-hydroxy ethyl ether
	2-amino-4-nitrophenol
	2-amino-4-nitro-N-(2-hydroxy ethyl) aniline
	2-(2-hydroxy ethyl) amino-4-nitro-N-(2-hydroxy ethyl) aniline
	2-amino-4-nitro-N-[tris (hdroxy methyl)] methyl aniline
Deep Orange	4-amino-3-nitrophenol
	2-amino-4], 6-di-nitrophenol
Orange Red	nitro-*p*-phenylene diamine
Red	4-(2-hydroxy ethyl) amino-3-nitrophenol
Rose	4-methyl amino-2-nitrophenol
	4-methyl amino-2-, 6-di-nitrophenol
Violet Red	4-amino-3-nitro-N-(2-hydroxy ethyl) aniline
	4-(2-hydroxy ethyl) amino-3-nitro aniline
Violet	4-(2-hydroxy ethyl) amino-3-nitro-N-(2-hydroxy ethyl) aniline
	1-4-diamino-5-nitro-anthraquinone
Blue Violet	4-(2-hydroxy ethyl) amino-3-nitro-N, N-[bis-(2-hydroxy ethyl)] aniline
	Dye intermediates used in permanent hair colourants
Various shades	Oxidation bases
can be achieved	*p*-phenylene diamine
by varying	*p*-toluenediamine
proportions of	*p*-amino diphenylamine

Contd. .

Shades	Names of dye intermediate
oxidation bases	*p*-aminophenol
and couplers.	*p*-diamino anisole
	o-phenylene diamine
	o-aminophenol
Shades	Names of dye intermediate
	Couplers or Modifiers
	m-phenylene diamine
	2, 4-diamino anisole
	resorcinol
	m-chloro resorcinol
	m-aminophenol
	1, 5-dihydroxy naphthalene
	6-methyl-3-aminophenol
	2-methyl resorcinol

10

Depilatories

1. GENERAL

Men and women, from ancient times, have been removing unwanted hair, references of recipes for removal of hair can be traced to the Papyrus Ebers (about 1500 B.C.). A mixture of quicklime and arsenic pyrites has been used in ancient times by the dancing girls of the East. Not much development work was carried out in subsequent centuries for the removal of hair until changes in attitude and women's apparel occurred. Today, there is large demand for depilatories.

The process, in which the hair are removed by uprooting, is called epilation and the products used for epilation are called epilatories. The process, in which the hair are removed by chemical degradation is called depilation and the products used for depilation are called depilatories. Both types of products will be discussed in this chapter.

2. EPILATORIES

2.1 General

In the present times, the methods which are employed for removing the hair mechanically include shaving, electrolysis, pulling out each hair with tweezers etc. Although elegantly designed razors and good shaving creams are available, but shaving is considered tedious and also has potential for cuts. It is painful to pull out each hair with tweezers. Electrolysis is costly as well as time consuming. Besides this, it requires an experienced operator. In comparison to these methods, epilation with epilating waxes or other epilating compositions appears to be more convenient method.

Epilatories are adhesive compositions to which the hair stick when these are applied to them, the so stuck hair are then pulled mechanically. Thus the epilatories can cause damage to the skin which may catch infection. In spite of this, epilatories are used by women.

2.2 Formulation

For many years epilatories have been prepared with rosin and waxes. Mineral or vegetable oils can be incorporated in such formulations. Other ingredients which have been added include camphor to give cooling effect as well as to reduce discomfort when the hair are pulled. The discomfort can be further reduced by addition of benzocaine, a local anaesthetic. Addition of an anti-bacterial will prevent infection of the damaged skin. Formula 1 is an example of typical product based on rosin and waxes.

Formula 1

	%
Rosin	50.0
Beeswax (yellow)	25.0
Paraffin wax	20.0
Petroleum jelly	5.0
Perfume	q.s.

Formula 2 is an example of the product in which an oil, camphor and benzocaine have been incorporated.

Formula 2

	%
Rosin	62.0
Beeswax	10.0
Linseed oil	25.0
Camphor	1.0
Benzocaine	2.0

When required for use, these waxes are first softened by heating and are spread evenly over the selected area by painting with a suitable brush. When the applied mixture is cooled, it is removed quickly.

There has been no dramatic development in this type of formulations. However, there have been developments regarding modification in the method of application (e.g., flexible backing strip which can be applied and removed easily). A preparation based on liquid glucose and zinc oxide does not require melting before use. Use of rubber solution has been suggested in a U.S. patent. Use of fresh lemon juice in syrup type epilatory has been also suggested.

2.3 Manufacture of Epilatories

The general method of manufacture of rosin wax based epilatories consists of melting of rosin and high melting point waxes first in jacketted vessel and then adding ingredients like petroleum jelly, oil with stirring. If the formulation contains, camphor, benzocaine etc., these are dissolved in a part of oil and are added when the temperature drops to around 45°C. Stirring is continued and the product is filled into the jars.

3. DEPILATORIES

3.1 General

As mentioned earlier, the products which remove hair by chemical breakdown are known as depilatories.

The disadvantages of skin damage and pain of epilatories can be overcome by use os depilatories. However, since the hair shaft and upper layer of the skin have similar composition, a small degree of local damage may occur to the horney layer of the skin. If the skin is healthy, time of application of depilatory is not too long and the product is correctly formulated, damage to the skin can be minimized to a great extent.

A depilatory is expected to have the following properties.

* It should be non-toxic and non-irritant to the skin.
* It should be efficient in action so that the hair are removed rapidly.
* It should not have unpleasant odour.
* It should be stable on storage.
* It should not affect the clothes adversely.
* It should be elegant in appearance.

Depilatories usually contain alkaline reducing agents which cause the hair fibre to swell and produce a cleavage of cystine bridges between adjacent polypeptide chains, a step in the complete degradation of the hair.

3.2 Formulation

The use of sulphides for removing hair is known for a very long time. Sulphides of metals like sodium, potassium, magnesium, calcium, strontium, barium, aluminium, arsenic produce depilation which is accelerated in the presence of calcium hydroxide suspension. The alkali sulphides like sodium sulphide are too drastic (even a 2% solution of sodium hydroxide has pH of 12.0). Sulphides of Barium being milder and strontium have been used in depilatories. The use of barium sulphide has been discontinued abroad as it is poisonous. Strontium sulphide is much milder than sodium sulphide but requires higher concentration. Formula 3 and 4 are examples of powder depilatories based on barium sulphide and strontium sulphide.

Formula 3

	%
Barium sulphide	30.0
Titanium dioxide	20.0
Corn starch	49.5
Menthol	0.25
Perfume	0.25

Formula 4

	%
Strontium sulphide	34.0
Powdered soap	5.0
Corn starch	37.0
Zinc oxide	22.0
Benzocaine	0.4
Perfume	1.6

The powder can be converted into tablets or 'soaps' by using non-aqueous vehicle for making dough and then compressing into tablets/soaps.

These depilatories can be formulated in the form of paste by using water and glycerine as vesicle. Formula 5 is an example of depilatory paste based on strontium sulphide.

Formula 5

		%
Strontium sulphide		22.0
Talc		18.0
Methyl cellulose		2.5
Glycerin		15.0
Water	to make	100.0

Depilatories based on sulphides have also been formulated in cream formulation. But these produce odour on storage. Hydrolysis of sulphides takes place and hydrogen sulphide gas in produced. The odour is due to this gas. This hydrolysis can be controlled by adding alkali and adjusting the pH to about 11.0. Strontium hydroxide crystallizes in the preparations made with strontium sulphide. Milling may control this problem at the time of manufacture, but on storage, due to fluctuation of temperature crystals reappear. Because of these disadvantages these preparations have been largely replaced by thioglycollate preparations which will be discussed in the following paragraphs.

Since stannates have no appreciable odour, attempts were made to overcome the disadvantage of sulphides which have strong foul odour by using sodium stannite. Rochelle salt was used as stabilizer with sodium stannite in a U.S. Patent.

In another patent use of water soluble organic compounds having three or more carbinol hydroxy group or three hydroxyl groups other than those in a carboxyl group was suggested. Soluble silicates could also be used. Examples of such compounds are triethanolamine, dextrine, sugars and potassium/sodium metasilicate. However, in practice, these stabilizers were not found so effective and soluble stannites being unstable did not become popular.

Majority of the depilatories available today are based on substituted mercaptans which act in alkaline pH (e.g., calcium thioglycollate in the presence of calcium hydroxide). Mercaptans have less odour but take more time for depilation. The preparations based on mercaptans are safer than sulphides on the skin and therefore, can be used on even face where women have an aversion to using razor.

Thioglycollate based preparations are non-toxic in the concentrations at which these are usually used (2.5-4.0%). At this concentration, these preparations produce depilation between 5-15 minutes depending upon the pH of the preparation. Higher the pH, faster the depilation. The pH should not be less than 10. It should be around 12.5. At the latter pH, depilation is achieved within fairly short time.

The following general rules will be useful in the formulation of depilatories based on thioglycollates.

* The pH value of the preparation should be between 9 and 12.5.
* Concentration of mercaptans in the preparations should be between 0.1-1.5 mol per litre.
* Alkaline ingredient used in the preparations should have an ionization constant more than 2×10^{-5}.
* To reduce damage to the skin the concentration of alkaline ingredient should not be more than twice the equivalent concentration of the mercaptan.
* Paste form is the most satisfactory form of cosmetic for depilatories based on mercaptans.
* Natural gums give stable formulations.

Trihydrate form of calcium thioglycollate is used in depilatories. This is available in white powder.

The depilatories based on thioglycolate can be prepared in the powder form, semi-fluid and cream formulation. Formula 6 is an example of powder depilatory based on thioglycollate.

Formula 6

	%
Calcium thioglycollate	15.0
Calcium hydroxide	22.0
Strontium hydroxide	10.0
Sodium lauryl sulphate	1.5
Hydroxy methyl cellulose	1.0
Magnesium carbonate	51.0
Perfume	q.s.

Method of Preparation

Mix thioglycollate, hydroxides, sodium lauryl sulphate and hydroxy methyl cellulose in a blender. Blend perfume separately with magnesium carbonate. Add perfumed magnesium carbonate to the former mix and blend thoroughly.

Formula 7 is an example of semi-solid depilatory based on thioglycollate.

Formula 7

A	%
Cetyl alcohol	5.5
Polyoxyethylene lauryl ether	1.5
Water	60.0
B	
Calcium thioglycollate	5.0
Calcium hydroxide	5.5
Strontium hydroxide	3.5
Water	19.0

Method of Preparation

Prepare cream base with A at 70°V and allow to cool. Add calcium thioglycollate to water separately and mix well, add calcium hydroxide slowly with stirring. Then add strontium hydroxide and continue stirring. Combine the two (A and B) and stir well, add perfume.

Formulae 8 and 9 are the examples of cream depilatories. It is believed that tendency for irritation is reduced by addition of an antiseptic.

Formula 8

		%
Calcium thioglycollate		5.5
Calcium carbonate light		21.5
Calcium hydroxide		1.5
Cetyl alcohol		4.5
Sodium lauryl sulphate		0.5
Sodium silicate solution (42.5°Be)		4.0
Water	to make	100.0
Perfume		q.s.

Method of Preparation

Leaving a small quantity of sodium lauryl sulphate, dissolve it in a part of hot water (60°C), add sodium silicate to this solution and mix. Melt separately cetyl alcohol and add to this solution, add to the aqueous solution and stir well while allowing to cool (an emulsion will be formed). Prepare a slurry of calcium carbonate with water. Add the previously prepared emulsion to this slurry and stir for 30 minutes maintaining the temperature at about 40°C. Prepare separately a suspension of calcium thioglycollate and calcium hydroxide with the help of remaining sodium lauryl sulphate. Add this suspension to the mix and stir at about 40°C. Add perfume and blend it thoroughly. Add calcium hydroxide solution to adjust pH and water, if necessary to make up weight. Pass the product through triple roller mill and fill into the containers.

Formula 9

		%
Calcium thioglycollate trihydrate		5.5
Calcium carbonate		20.0
Titanium dioxide		2.5
Cetyl alcohol		4.5
Sodium lauryl sulphate		1.0
Glycerin		5.0
Water	to make	100.0
Perfume		q.s.

Method of Preparation: Prepare a trituration of titanium dioxide and glycerine. Melt cetyl alcohol and add to the glycerine triturate along with little water to form a paste. Dissolve sodium lauryl sulphate in the water, add calcium thioglycollate and calcium hydroxide and mix. Prepare separately a paste of calcium carbonate with water. Add thioglycollate and alkali mixture of calcium carbonate paste. Add this mixture to cetyl alcohol mixture and stir well. Adjust pH and make final volume with calcium hydroxide and water. Before filling the product into container, pass it through triple roller mill.

However, addition of an antiseptic does not prevent allergic reactions. Oxyquinoline sulphate has been suggested in a German Patent. It has also been suggested that higher percentage of thioglycollates can be used by adding 0.25% azulene.

Azulene has antiphlogistic and protective action. With higher percentage of thioglycollates, contact time with skin is reduced because of quicker depilatory action. A humectant is added in the preparation to prevent drying out of the preparation during application and also during storage. However, higher concentrations of glycerine and propylene glycol should not be used as the product may develop colour and odour. A small amount of mineral oil helps in stability. Formula 10 is an example of such product.

Formula 10

		%
Calcium thioglycollate		6.0
Calcium carbonate		18.5
Mineral oil		5.0
Cetyl alcohol		5.5
Sodium lauryl sulphate		1.0
Glycerin		4.0
Water	to make	100.0
Perfume		q.s.

All depilatories should be subjected to storage tests and exhaustive user test to find out stability and the safe period for which the product may be allowed to remain in contact with the skin.

It is difficult to perfume depilatories satisfactorily. Products based on sulphide produce hydrogen sulphide gas on hydrolysis. Strong floral type perfumes like rose, violet type excluding ingredients which are prone to hydrolysis themselves (e.g., esters, aldehydes, alcohols) are suitable for such products. Thioglycollates manufactured employing improved techniques have much less odour than the material available earlier. Perfume used should be stable at high pH and should have strong odour. Camphor can be used to cover the basic odour of sulphides and thioglycollates. Rose alcohols, ionones and diphenyl oxide have been found useful in perfuming these preparations.

A thioglycollate depilatory in anhydrous stick form has been patented in U.S.A. It is applied to moist skin. On application it produces a cream which can depilate in about 10 minutes time. Depilating agent, calcium thioglycollate with alkali like calcium hydroxide are incorporated in anhydrous base.

In some French patents, use of salts of lithium of thioglycollic acid, β-mercapto propionic acid and thiolactic acid has been advocated. Since lithium salts have greater solubility, accelerated depilatory action is expected. It is also claimed that lithium salt of thioglycollic acid is effective at slightly lower pH than its calcium salt. With lithium salts, clear solutions or gels can be made.

Keratinase from *streptomyces fradiae* can degrade Keratin. Depilatory formulation containing keratinase contain 2,00,000-1,000,000 k units/100 gms of product. The formula is required to be buffered between pH 7 and 8. Keratinase preparations act slowly than thioglycollates. They are reported to be non-toxic to skin. However, there are no products in the market containing keratinase.

2.2 MANUFACTURE OF DEPILATORIES

Method of preparation has been generally given where the formula has been mentioned. Depilatories require the same precautions which are required in the manufacture of cold wave lotions based on thioglycollates. Lotion depilatories are generally packed in jars and creams are packed in collapsible tubes. Air spaces between the cap and product surface should be reduce to the minium. Distortion has been observed in polyethylene bottles.

11

Shaving Soaps and Creams

1. GENERAL

Many preparations have been used to render shaving with razor more tolerable. One of the earliest preparation used for this purpose was shaving soap prepared with saponification of potash and caustic soda. Over the years, many developments have taken place and shaving preparations have been presented in various physical forms. These include soap stick, bar and cup; flaked or powdered soap; liquid; lather cream and aerosol foam cream. Of these powdered or flaked soap and liquid preparations are seldom used. Therefore, these preparations will not be discussed in this chapter.

A shaving preparation irrespective of its physical form must have the following properties.

* It must be non-irritating to the skin.
* It must retain moisture during the period it remains on the face.
* It must soften the beard so that the hair are cut easily.
* It should provide sufficient lubricity so that razor glides along the face.
* It should have sufficient viscosity to hold individual hair erect so that it could be cut close to the surface of the skin.

* It should be stable over a wide range of temperature.
* It should be non-corrosive to the containers in which it is packed.
* It should be able to be washed down the drain without creating clogging problems.
* If it is to be used with a brush, it should be able to develop high lather rapidly.

The outer layer of the hair is known as cuticle. The cuticle is a hard surface and offers resistance to the razor blade and makes it dull. The cutting of the hair becomes easy, if this hardness is reduced by a hair-softening agent. Thus hair softening becomes the primary aim of the shaving preparations. Hollander and Casselman reported studied on various aspects of shaving. It was found that water was softening agent and the soap hastened this softening action.

2. SHAVING SOAPS

2.1. General

Ordinarily it will be thought that bar shaving soaps and bar toilet soap will resemble closely. But it is not so. There are significant differences in two soaps, the main difference being saponification mainly by potassium hydroxide in case of shaving soap. Potassium stearate gives quicker and stable lather than sodium stearate. However, potassium soaps alone are usually softer. Therefore, a certain proportion of sodium soap is present in shaving soaps. Shaving soaps can be presented in bar, stick or cup formulation.

2.2 Formulation

For making stick or bowl shaving soap, stearic acid and coconut fatty acids may be saponified with Potassium hydroxide and sodium hydroxide (usually in the ratio of 5:1). Formula 1 is an illustrative example.

Formula 1

	%
Stearic acid	48.0
Coconut fatty acids	15.0

Caustic potash soln. (Sp. Gr. 1.5)		20.0
Caustic soda soln. (Sp. Gr. 1.5)		4.0
Water	to make	100.0

For preparing bar or cake shaving soap, a mixture of toilet soap and fatty acids or fats saponified with potassium hydroxide and sodium hydroxide can be used. Formula 2 is a typical example of such formulations.

Formula 2

		%
Toilet soap		45.0
Coconut oil		7.0
Stearic acid		12.0
Fat (tallow)		20.0
Caustic potash solution (sp. gr. 1.5)		10.0
Caustic soda solution (sp. gr. 1.5)		2.5
Water	to make	100.0
Anti-oxidant		q.s.

Many additives have been suggested to improve upon the soap system. In a German patent use of super fatting agents like monodecyl, doddecyl, tetradecyl ethers of di-glycerol amines have been recommended. Addition of talc (10-15%) is reported to increase persistence of lather. It also helps razor to glide over face more smoothly. Pilomotor agents have been suggested as these cause contraction of hair follicle muscle projecting hair fibre out.

2.3 Manufacture of Shaving Soaps

The solid shaving soap can be made in crutcher using a mixture of sodium and potassium hydroxide. In this method, all glycerin that is produced from fats is used in the finished cake. Thus the product has shiny or sticky feel. It should, however, be seen that glycerin more than 10% is not produced in the soap formed. The other method, that can be used for preparing cake shaving soap is to use a kettle-made boiled soda soap. Soda soap and potassium stearate are added to a crutcher. In this method glycerin is avoided. In yet another method, requisite amount of tallow is saponified with potassium hydroxide in the crutcher. To this is added soda soap. Any excess alkali is neutralized with stearic acid. For shaving stick or shaving bowl soap, it is advantageous to use plodder of great packing power.

3. LATHER SHAVING CREAM

3.1 General

Lather cream has also been used for a long time for shaving. A lather cream may be described as a mixture of soap in glycerin and water. A good lather cream should have the following characteristics:

* It should produce rich and copious lather.
* It should be non-irritant to the skin and should not be astringent.
* It should have good wetting properties.
* It should be smooth, soft and free from lumps.
* It should be sufficiently tacky to adhere to both face and brush and yet be easily removed on rinsing.
* It should retain its consistency over a range of temperature which is likely to be encountered during storage and use.

From the manufacturing point of view, lather cream is one of the difficult formulation particularly in respect of its stability in hot and cold weather. In evaluating a lather shaving cream, points that need attention are:

* Ease of transfer of the cream to the face.
* Ease of its spreading on the face.
* Wetting properties of foam, its texture, rigidity, rheology and stability.
* Closeness of shave.
* Gliding properties for ease of shaving.
* Ease with which lather and shaving debris can be removed from razor and basin.
* Compatibility and acceptance of perfume.
* Compatibility with container.
* Effect of cream on the life of razor blade.

3.2 Formulation

As mentioned above, lather shaving creams are dispersions of soaps in glycerin and water. These creams normally contain 30-50% soaps. Formulations prepared with stearic acid alone do not produce voluminous lather. For improving lather, usually coconut fatty acids are added. Ratio of stearic acid to coconut fatty acids varies widely in different products. Products based on 75% stearic acid and 25% coconut oil are expected to result in satisfactory products. Usually a mixture of potassium hydroxide and sodium hydroxide is used to saponify oil. It has been observed that potassium hydroxide and sodium hydroxide in ratio of 5:1 with 3-5% free acid give good plasticity to the product. Lather creams made with potassium soaps only tend to be less stable. Therefore, a small amount of sodium soaps are required to be included in the formulation. However, lather creams with high level of sodium soaps tend to be thick and stringy.

Usually a humectant is included in the formulation. Commonly used humectant include glycerin, propylene glycol, sorbitol solution. Humenctants prevent premature drying of the cream and make them softer. Propylene glycol influences texture also.

Emollients like lanolin, cetyl alcohol, mineral oil, fatty acid esters should be kept at low level (around 1%) as higher percentage will interfere with lathering. Other additives like synthetic surfactants (as foam stabilizers), cooling agents, anti-bacterials may also be added to the cream. Small amount of borax has significant effect on viscosity of the product. It is used in amounts of 0.1 to 1.0%. Most shaving creams contain superfatting agents. Superfatting agents neutralize any excess alkali and stabilize creams and lather.

The most commonly used superfatting agents are stearic acid, coconut oil, vegetable oils, mineral oil, lanolin. Triethanolamine is avoided in shaving creams as it may discolour creams and produce odour. Some examples of shaving creams are shown in formulae 3 to 5.

Formula 3

	%
Stearic acid	28.0
Coconut oil	12.0

Palm oil		5.0
Potassium hydroxide		6.5
Sodium hydroxide		1.5
Glycerin		10.0
Water	to make	100.0
Perfume and Preservatives		q.s.

Formula 4

		%
Stearic acid		25.0
Coconut oil		10.0
Myristic acid		10.0
Glycerin		5.0
Sodium hydroxide		0.5
Potassium hydroxide		2.5
Water	to make	100.0
Perfume and Preservatives		q.s.

Formula 5

		%
Stearic acid		30.0
Coconut oil		5.0
Palm oil		5.0
Potash lye (200 Baume)		30.0
Soda lye (200 Baume)		5.0
Sorbitol (70% solution)		3.0
Sodium alkyl sulphate		2.0
Boric acid		1.0
Water	to make	100.0
Perfume and Preservatives		q.s.

Although a small percentage of free fatty acid is available in the lather shaving creams but the pH is around 10. This is because of pockets of un-neutralized pockets of free alkali which are formed due to high viscosity of the product. As a part of quality control during manufacture of lather shaving cream, content of free fatty acid should be determined as free fatty acid level influences the stability of the cream at high temperature. Free fatty acids along with less water soluble stearate soaps also give pearliness.

Pearlescence results because of formation of liquid crystalline phases within the cream. These liquid crystalline phases, besides improving appearance, can also stabilize foam generated.

Stearic acid of good quality should be used in lather shaving cream as it is one of the important ingredients. A simple test to judge the suitability of stearic acid is to add an excess of strong potassium hydroxide solution to stearic acid, if the resulting soap is coloured (brown to yellow), it is not suitable for use in lather shaving cream. Coconut oil or coco fatty acids are other important ingredients of lather shaving cream. Sodium and potassium salts of coconut oil/coco fatty acids are very soluble in water and lather freely. However, higher percentage of oil in formulation may be irritating to the sensitive skin. Therefore, only a limited proportion of coconut oil/fatty acids should be used.

Changes in the texture of lather creams occur with the change in temperature during storage. An increase in temperature causes increase in viscosity or makes the cream gel-like. Decrease in temperature (due to cold weather) makes the cream hard and difficult to apply. These variations can be reduced by adding 0.5% borax. Corrosion of metallic tubes by the cream can be reduced by adding 1.0 to 1.5 of sodium silicate.

Substances which reduce surface tension and produce a fine bubble leather include saponins, sodium chlorate and lecithin. Of these only lecithin appears to be used commercially.

Formula 6

		%
Stearic acid		38.0
Coconut oil		5.0
Olive oil/vegetable oil		2.0
Propylene glycol		10.0
Lecithin		2.0
Potassium Hydroxide (80%)		1.5
Sodium hydroxide (90%)		0.3
Borax		1.0
Water	to make	100.0
Perfume and Preservatives		q.s.

3.3 Manufacture of Lather Shaving Creams

Oil/fats are melted and filtered and are saponified with soda lye and part of potash lye in the presence of glycerin. The remainder of potash lye with some water is now run into the mix maintaining the heat. Next, melted stearic acid is added in continuous stream with slow stirring. Samples are tested and acid or alkali is added as the case may be. The cream is then superfatted with one of the superfatting agents (e.g. boric acid, additional stearic acid, lanolin) and heating is continued. Free fatty acids is also determined and is adjusted to standard percentage. Heating is discontinued and stirring is continued, while the cream cools. When the temperature drops at 40-45°C, perfume is mixed and is blended. The cream is allowed to stand for 3-4 weeks before packaging. This is called "curing" process. Crystal formation takes place during this process.

In the manufacture of lather shaving creams one of the important problems is entrapment of air. To prevent entrapment of air, after cream has been made, it can be transferred to a large tank and allowed to cool or the cream can be run over cold rolls fitted with a scrapper. Lather cream can also be cooled under vacuum. But this requires an elaborate equipment.

4. BRUSHLESS SHAVING CREAMS

4.1 General

Brushless shaving cream, as the name suggests does not require brush for applying. The cream is applied and spread with fingers. This method was popularized in the United States after the First World War.

When using brushless shaving cream, the face should be prepared for use by washing it with soap and water (preferably hot) and the brushless cream should be applied. Brushless cream retains the moisture on the face and preserves the beard in soft state already made by soap and water.

4.2 Formulation

A brushless shaving cream is an oil-in-water emulsion. Ingredients that can be used for preparation of brushless shaving cream exceed in number than used in lather shaving creams. Stearic acid is used in brushless shaving creams but coconut oil or other oils containing fatty acids are not used. Triethanolamine is used in brushless creams but it is not absolutely necessary. Lanolin can be used in brushless creams in higher proportions than lather creams. Gums like karaya and Irish moss have been used in these creams and synthetic mucilaginous materials like methyl cellulose, polyvinyl pyrrolidone, sodium carboxy methyl cellulose can be used. These materials provide body to the cream and slip to the face. Preservatives are added to save the cream from microbial attack. Esters of *p*-hydroxy benzoates can be used.

Brushless shaving creams can be prepared according to the general formula given below:

Formula 7

	%
Stearic acid	10.0-20.0
Mineral oil and/or petroleum jelly	2.0-12.0
Alkali	0.5-2.0
Lanolin	0.0-5.0
Gums or thickeners	0.0-0.5
Water	60.0-75.0
Preservatives	q.s.

Examples of some specific formulae are given below (Formula 8 and 9).

Formula 8

		%
Stearic acid		15.0
Mineral oil		15.0
Spermaceti		2.0
Glycerin		5.0
Dilute solution of ammonia		2.0
Water	to make	100.0
Perfume and Preservatives		q.s.

Formula 9

	%
Glyceryl monostearate (self-emulsifying)	10.0
Stearic acid	6.0
Glycerin	4.0
Mineral oil	1.0

Water	to make	100.0
Perfume and Preservatives		q.s.

Silicone oil in a brushless shaving cream is claimed to impart a pleasant feel. It can be incorporated in the cream base (see Formula 10).

Formula 10

		%
Stearic acid		16.0
Mineral oil		4.0
Silicone fluid (viscosity 1000cs)		1.0
Polyoxyethylene sorbitan monostearate		5.0
Sorbitol (70% solution)		4.0
Borax		2.0
Triethanolamine		1.0
Water	to make	100.0
Perfume and Preservatives		q.s.

Different variations have been made in these formulations. But the Formula 11 patented by Bird[1] is entirely on different lines.

Formula 11

	%
Sodium lauryl sulphate	1.0
Glycerol	5.0
Mineral oil	15.0
Water	5.0
Menthol and perfume	0.3
Methyl cellulose aqueous solution to make	100.0

4.3 Manufacture of Brushless Shaving Creams

The standard method of manufacture of brushless shaving cream is to heat water and water-soluble ingredients to 65-70°C and add to the molten oil and fats heated to the same temperature with stirring. Stirring is continued till emulsification is complete. Cream is cooled to about 45°C and perfume is added and blended. Stirring is then discontinued. The cream is then allowed to mature.

This period varies from 24 hours to a weak. After maturing, before filling, the cream is gently stirred and is filled in tubes or jars.

5. OTHER SHAVING PREPARATIONS

5.1 Aerosol Shaving Lathers

Aerosol shaving foams are o/w emulsions. Propellant droplets liquefied under pressure form a substantial part of the oil phase in such preparations. When the preparation is discharged to the atmosphere, droplets of propellant vapourise producing vapour bubbles surrounded by aqueous surfactant phase.

Formulation of aerosol shaving foams may require several experimentation before a product of desired characteristics can be prepared. Following guidelines will be helpful.

* Saturated fatty acids (C_{12}-C_{18}) are main components of aerosol shaving foams. These may be used in proportion of 7-9%. Presence of stearic acid is not essential in shaving foams. In fact, higher proportions of stearic acid give stiffer foams.
* Alkalies like triethanolamine, potassium hydroxide may be used. A mixture of these two is preferred. Sodium hydroxide is rarely used. Mono- and die-ethanolamines may cause skin irritation and therefore, are used occasionally. Quantity of alkali is so adjusted that the formulation contains 1-3% of free fatty acid.
* A variety of surfactants can be used in shaving foams for improving the properties, such as, emulsion stability (e.g., glyceryl monostearate), wetting properties of foam (e.g., sodium lauryl sulphate), water dispensability of foam (e.g., polyethoxylated fatty alcohols), emolliency (e.g., ethoxylated lanolins).
* Humectants such as glycerol, sorbitol and propylene glycol are usually added so that foam does not dry out on the face. Usual concentrations are 3-10%.
* Lubricants can be added to the formulation to make passage of the razor over the face easy. Lanolin, silicone fluid or isopropyl myristate can be added in proportions of 1-2%.
* Commonly used propellants are fluorocarbons (7-10%), hydrocarbons (2.8-3.5%) the higher the concentration of propellants, the lower the foam density. Foam having density less than 65 gl^{-1} may be difficult to spread and

may have little beard softening capability. Though costly, but fluorocarbon propelled shaving foam are popular.

* Soap compatible perfumes are used (0.15-0.65%).
* Other additives like cooling agent (menthol in concentration of 0.05-0.2%), colours and preservatives, if necessary may be used. Bacteriostats (e.g., trichloro hydroxy diphenyl ether-0.05%) may also be added.

A lot of experimentation will be required to obtain product of desired characteristics. Container charge may have 5-13% propellants and the rest shaving cream base. Formula 12 and 13 are examples of shaving cream bases.

Formula 12

		%
Myristic acid		3.0
Stearic acid		5.0
Ethanol		0.5
Glyceryl monostearate (self-emulsifying)		2.5
Lanolin		1.0
Mineral oil		2.0
Triethanolamine lauryl sulphate		1.0
Glycerin		5.0
Triethanolamine		4.0
Water	to make	100.0
Perfume and Preservatives		q.s.

Formula 13

		%
Stearic acid		5.5
Palmitic acid		2.5
Isopropyl myristate		1.0
Coco monoethanolamide		0.2
Sodium lauryl ether sulphate (40% solution)		3.8
Triethanolamine		4.0
Glycerin		5.0
Water	to make	100.0
Perfume		q.s.

5.2 Pre-electric Shave Preparations

Pre-electric shave preparations are designed to dry the skin. In liquid form, these are based on alcohol as it takes up moisture and it dries up quickly. In powder form, these are based on talc. Pre-electric shave preparations are also available in aerosol form.

Pre-electric shave lotions contain comparatively high percentage of alcohol. Alcohol, besides drying up quickly also causes contraction of erector pili muscles. This action can further be augmented by adding an astringent. This action causes the hair to stand out more and thus facilitate cutting. Antibacterials can also be added to the lotion to prevent infection in case of cuts by electric razor. The lotion also contains an oily material to lubricate the hair with thin film oil which acts as cutting lubricant. However, the concentration of oily material is important. If there is too much oil, a pasty mass will be formed with cut hair which may clog the cutting edges of the razor.

A simple pre-electric shave lotion can be prepared with alcohol and isopropyl myristate (see Formula 14).

Formula 14

	%
Alcohol	90.0
Isopropyl myristate	10.0
Perfume	q.s.

Formula 15 and 16 are example so formulations in which other additives have been added.

Formula 15

		%
Isopropyl myristate		10.0
Menthol		0.5
Zinc phenol sulphonate		1.0
Alcohol	to make	100.0
Perfume		q.s.

Liquid acetoglycerides have also been used as lubricant in pre-electric shave lotions. Formula 16 is an example of formulation containing acetoglyceride.

Formula 16

	%
Liquid acetoglyceride	10.0
Menthol	0.5

Boric acid		1.0
Alcohol	to make	100.0
Perfume		q.s.

Vasoconstrictors like adrenaline, epinephrine have also been used in such lotions. In a German Patent, 0.5% adrenaline hydrochloride has been used. The lotion is adjusted to acidic pH.

Pre-electric shave preparation can also be prepared in aerosol form. An example is shown in Formula 17.

Formula 17

		%
Pre-shave base		50.0
Propellant		50.0
Pre-shave base:		
Isopropyl myristate		12.0
Menthol		0.5
Boric acid		1.5
Alcohol	to make	100.00
Perfume		q.s.

Electric shave powders consist mainly of talc and metallic stearates. An absorbent powder like magnesium carbonate, kaolin can also be included. It may be kept in mind while formulating this type of products that abrasive materials are used to the bare minimum as these may damage the cutting edge of the razor. Formula 18 is a typical example of electric shave powder.

Formula 18

	%
Magnesium stearate	7.0
Kaolin	3.0
Talc	90.0
Perfume	q.s.

Other ingredients like etherified starch, glyceryl monstearate, cetyl alcohol can also be added (see Formula 19).

Formula 19

	%
Kaolin	10.0
Magnesium carbonate	12.0

Etherified starch		12.0
Cetyl alcohol		2.0
Glyceryl monostearate		2.0
Zinc stearate		5.0
Zinc oxide		5.0
Talc	to make	100.0
Perfume		q.s.

Pre-electric shave powders can also be packed into aerosol containers. However, ingredients like kaolin, calcium carbonate, zinc oxide which tend to agglomerate are deleted from the formulation. A powder base for aerosol formulation can be prepared from Formula 20.

Formula 20

		%
Aerosil		4.5
Starch		4.5
Magnesium stearate		5.5
Light magnesium carbonate		5.5
Talc	to make	100.0
Perfume		q.s.
Container charge:		%
Powder base		15.0
Propellent		85.0

The powder base is passed through 200 mesh sieve before filling into aerosol containers.

Pre-shave powder can also be converted into a stick. An aqueous dispersion of the powder using colloidal magnesium aluminium silicate (veegum) as the binder can be moulded into sticks. An illustrative formulation is shown in Formula 21.

Formula 21

Part A		%
Zinc stearate		5.0
Light magnesium carbonate		3.0
Talc	to make	100.0
Perfume		q.s.

Part B

Colloidal magnesium aluminium silicate		16.5
Water	to make	100.0

Method of Preparation

Add colloidal magnesium aluminium silicate to water and stir to form an uniform dispersion. Absorb perfume into magnesium carbonate, mix it with zinc and then blend with talc. Make a paste of the powder with aqueous dispersion of magnesium aluminium silicate (Part A) and pour into moulds. Allow to dry till sticks are hard and finally dry the sticks in an oven.

12

Skin Creams and Lotions

1. GENERAL

The word 'cream' is so extensively used that it is difficult to define it. However, it usually signifies a solid or semi-solid emulsion. If an emulsion is of much low viscosity that it can be poured under influence of gravity alone, it is termed as lotion. An emulsion is dispersion of one immiscible liquid in the other. Water is an important ingredient of skin creams and lotions as moisture content of the skin controls the appearance of the skin. Therefore, in skin creams or lotions, either fatty phase (oil) can be dispersed in aqueous phase (water) or aqueous phase can be dispersed in fatty phase. If oil droplets are dispersed in aqueous phase (water), emulsion is termed as oil-in-water (o/w) and if water is dispersed in fatty phase (oil) emulsion is termed as water-in-oil (w/o). It has been observed that o/w emulsions occasionally change into w/o emulsions and vice versa. To make dispersion of one phase into the other suitable emulsifying agents are used. A variety of substances are used as emulsifying agents and most of them belong to the group known as surface active agents. These substances possess both hydrophilic (affinity for water) and lipophilic (affinity for lipids) properties. It is because of this property that these can be held at an oil-water interface, lipophilic portion oriented towards the oil and hydrophilic portion oriented towards the water. A large number of surface active agents are available. It is often difficult to select a most suitable emulsifier. William C. Griffin, in 1947, devised the HLB (Hydrophilic-Lipophilic Balance) system. This system is used to indicate the behaviour of an emulsifying agent depending upon the proportion of hydrophilic and lipophilic groups present in the molecule of the emulsifying agent. An emulsifying agent with low HLB value tends to be lipophilic in character and forms water in oil emulsions and an emulsifying agent of high HLB value tends to be hydrophilic in character and forms oil in water emulsions. HLB values, however, give indication only of the behaviour characteristics of the materials and do not indicate emulsion stability. HLB values of some selected emulsifying agents are given in Table 12.1.

Table 12.1: HLB Values of some Surfactants

HLB Value	Name of emulsifying agent
1.5	Ethylene glycol distearate
2.1	Sorbitan tristearate
3.4	Propylene glycol monostearate
3.7	Sorbitan sesquioleate
3.8	Glyceryl monostearate (non-self emulsifying)
4.5	Propylene glycol monolaurate
4.7	Sorbitan monostearate
4.7	Diethylene glycol monostearate
5.5	Glycsyl monostearate (self emulsifying)
6.1	Diethylene glycol monolaurate
6.7	Sorbitan monopalmitate
7.1	Sucrose dioleate
8.0	Polyethylene glycol (200) monoleate
8.6	Sorbitan monolaurate
9.5	Polyoxyethylene (4) lauryl ether
9.6	Polyoxyethylene (4) sorbitan monostearate
10.3	Polyoxyethylene (6) cetyl ether
10.5	Polyoxyethylene (20) sorbitan tristearate
11.4	Polyoxyethylene glycol (400) monoleate
11.6	Polyoxyethylene glycol (400) monostearate
13.0	Polyoxyethylene (9) monyl phenol
13.1	Pólyethylene glycol (400) monolaurate
13.3	Polyoxyethylene (4) sorbitan monolaurate
15.0	Polyoxyethylene (20) sorbitan monolature
15.4	Polyoxyethylene (20) oleyl ether

Contd. . .

Table 12.1: *Contd. . .*

HLB Value	Name of emulsifying agent
15.6	Polyoxyethylene (20) sorbitan monopalmitate
15.7	Polyoxyethylene (20) cetyl ether
16.9	Polyoxyethylene (40) stearate
18.0	Sodium oleate
18.8	Polyoxyethylene (100) stearate
20.0	Potassium oleate
40.0	Sodium lauryl sulphate

For comprehensive list of HLB values of different emulsifying agents the readers may refers to Cosmetic Emulsions by C. Fox in Emulsions and Emulsion Technology, Part II, Edited by K.J. Lissant, Marcel Dekker, New York, 1974.

The HLB required for emulsifying a particular fatty phase in water can be determined by trial and error. A combination of lipophilic and hydrophilic surfactant, often, is found more useful than a single surfactant. HLB values of combinations an be calculated by taking weighted averages of the individual HLB value of surfactants. For example a combination of sorbitan monostearate (HLB 4.7) and Polyoxyethylene (20) sorbitan mono oleate (HLB 15.0) in ratio of 68:32 will exhibit an average HLB value of 8.0 ($0.68 \times 4.7 + 0.32 \times 15 = 8.0$).

Water sensitive polymers (polymers which either swell or are soluble) are useful as auxiliary emulsifying and thickening agents. Natural or synthetic clays are commonly used for building viscosity of emulsion or for suspending solids such a pigments (e.g., bentonites, attapulgite).

Some naturally occurring gums and synthetic hydrophilic polymers (e.g., gum arabic, gum tragacanth-natural gums and polyoxyethylene polymers, carboxyvinyl polymers/synthetic hydrophilic polymers) are useful as emulsifiers as well as emulsion stabilizers.

There is direct relationship between emulsion viscosity and the viscosity of continuous phase. The use of gums and clays has already been mentioned. In case of w/o emulsions, addition of polyvalent metal soaps or use of high melting waxes and resins in the oil phase results in increase of viscosity. Viscosity changes of internal phase do not appreciably affect the emulsion viscosity. Three interacting effects must be balanced by an emulsion formulator to control emulsion viscosity. These are:

* The viscosity of both o/w and w/o emulsions can be increased by reducing the particle size of dispersed phase.
* Reduction in particle size results in improvement in emulsion stability.
* Flocculation or clumping which tends to structure the internal phase can have stabilizing effect.

As a general use, the viscosity of emulsions increases upon ageing.

Cosmetic emulsions contain a number of ingredients such as carbohydrates, proteins, sterols etc. which support growth of micro-organisms. Contamination may be introduced by contaminated raw materials or poor sanitation during processing. Contamination can also be introduced by the consumer during its use. Therefore, it is necessary to include preservative in cosmetic emulsions. As is true of other ingredients of formulation, preservative(s) too should first meet the general criteria of low toxicity, stability to heat and storage, chemical compatibility, acceptable odour and colour and reasonable cost. Preservative should be effective against a variety of micro-organisms. Preservatives which can be used in cosmetic emulsions are given in Table 12.2.

Concentration of preservatives will depend on its extent to which it is available to interact with micro-organism. Micro-organism can reside in both phases i.e., aqueous phase and fatty phase. Therefore, preservative should be available in effective concentration in both the phases. It is almost impossible for a single preservative to distribute itself in effective concentrative is used. Problems may arise when one of the ingredients interact with preservative thereby rendering the preservative ineffective. Phenolic preservatives are susceptible to interaction with polyoxyethylene compounds. To compensate the loss due to interaction, an extra amount of preservative equal to the complex material should be added. It has been found out that addition of alcohol may activate p-hydroxy-benzoate esters in the presence of non-ionics (e.g., propylene glycol). For more details on preservatives refer to section 2 of Chapter 2.

Table 12.2: Preservatives which can be used in cosmetic emulsions

Group	Representative	Activity
	Preservatives	
Acids and acid salts	Benzoic acid	
	Sorbic acid and salts	Antigungal
	Propionic acid and salts	agents
	Dehydroacetic acid	
Aldehydes	Formaldehyde	Broad spectrum
	Glutaraldehyde	preservatives
Phenolics	Phenol	
	Cresol	
	Chlorothymol	
	O-phenylphenol	
	p-chlorometaxylenol	
	Methyl p-hydroxybenzoate	
	Propyl p-hydroxybenzoate	
	Benzyl p-hydroxybenzoate	Broad spectrum
	Butyl p-hydroxybenzoate	preservatives
Quaternaries	Benzethonium chloride	
	Benzalkonium chloride	Broad spectrum
	Cetyl trimethyl ammonium bromide	preservatives
	Cetyl pyridinium chloride	
Mercurials	Phenyl mercuric acetate	Broad spectrum
	Sodium ethyl mercurithiosalicylate	preservatives
Miscellaneous	2, 4, 4-Trichloro-2'-hydroxydiphenyl ether	Primarily active against gram positive bacteria
	Imidizolidinyl urea compound	Synergist
	Bromo-2-nitropropanediol 1, 3	Broad spectrum
	5-Bromo-5-nitro-1, 3-dioxane	preservatives
	2-Thiopyridine N-oxide and salts	
	2-Methyl-4-isotiazolin-3-one and 5-chloro derivative	

Cosmetic creams are usually marketed on the basis of the their broad claims (e.g., cleansing cream, massage cream etc.) made on their packaging. This is not a very good classification because number of variations in appearance, texture, subjective feel, ease of spreading etc. far outstrip the number of functional categories and therefore, a considerable amount of overlap is inevitable.

Most commonly available creams classified on the basis of their functions are:

- cleansing creams,
- cold creams,
- massage creams,
- night creams
- moisturizing creams,
- foundation creams
- vanishing creams,
- hand and body protective creams,
- all purpose creams.

2. FORMULATION

In the formulation of skin creams and lotions, ingredients of two phases are selected to perform a predetermined function majority of these have been mentioned in Section 1. Formulation consideration of these various creams will be discussed under this Section.

2.1 Cleansing Creams and Lotions

Functions of cleansing cream/lotion are, removal of facial make-up, surface grime, oil, dead cells and crusts. Although water is good and cheap cleansing agent but it is ineffective on its own against oils. Soaps can emulsify oils and therefore, soap and water can effectively remove oils. But disadvantages of this combination are:

- it is inconvenient outside the bath room;
- it may remove too much oil from skin surface leaving it rough and dry;

– residual alkalinity of soap may cause outermost cells to lift and separate from neighbouring cells.

These disadvantages can be overcome by properly formulated cleansing cream or lotion. A cleansing cream should have the following properties:

- * It should be stable and should have a good appearance.
- * It should soften on application to the skin.
- * It should spread easily without dragging.
- * During application it should not have oily or greasy feel.
- * After evaporation of water, the cream residue should not become viscous.
- * Its physical action should be that of flushing on the skin and pore opening rather than absorption.
- * A thin emollient film should remain on the skin after its us.

Though beeswax-borax emulsions were developed very early and now a number of other materials are available for formulation of creams, but these emulsions still occupy an important place in cleansing creams. A soft cream can be prepared from formula 2.

		Formula 1	**Formula 2**
		per cent	per cent
Beeswax		8.0	10.0
Mineral oil		50.0	40.0
Microcrystalline wax		5.0	–
Borax		0.4	0.5
Paraffin		–	12.0
Ozokerite		–	10.0
Water	to make	100.0	100.0
Perfume and preservatives		q.s.	q.s.

These can be stiffened either by increasing the quantity of beeswax or by incorporating other waxes. See formula 2. Non-ionic emulsifying agents like sorbitan fatty a acid ester can be used to supplement beeswax-borax emulsions. These add increased flexibility and stability to the emulsions. Examples of such formulations may be represented by formula 3 and 4.

		Formula 3	Formula 4
		per cent	per cent
Beeswax		10.0	8.0
Mineral oil		48.0	20.0
Lanolin		4.0	3.0
Borax		0.7	0.5
Hydrogenated vegetable oil		–	27.0
Anti-oxidant		–	0.5
Sorbitan sesquioleate		1.0	–
Sorbitan stearate		–	5.0
Polysorbate 60		–	2.0
Water	to make	100.0	100.0
Perfume and preservatives		q.s.	q.s.

Cleansing creams and be formulated using other than beeswax-borax system. Non-ionic emulsifying agents are commonly used and both w/o and o/w emulsions are formed. Formulae 5 and 6 are examples of w/o and formulae 7 and 8 are examples of o/w type.

	5	6	7	8
	per cent	per cent	per cent	per cent
Petroleum jelly	30.0	34.0	5.0	–
Mineral oil	20.0	16.0	50.0	30.0
Paraffin wax	8.0	5.0	–	–
sorbitan sesquioleate	4.0	4.0	1.0	–
Sorbitol solution (70%)	3.0	3.0	–	10.0
PEG-40 Sorbitan lanolate	–	–	4.0	–
Stearic acid	–	–	12.5	15.0
Lanolin	3.0	3.0	2.5	4.0
Sorbitan trioleate	–	–	–	1.0
Sorbitan stearate	–	–	4.0	–
Polysorbate 85	–	–	–	1.0
Water to make	100.0	100.0	100.0	100.0
Perfume and preservatives	q.s.	q.s.	q.s.	q.s.

Though less popular, translucent liquefying cream can be formulated by mixing oils and waxes. These are called liquefying because they liquefy when gently massaged. A mixture of oils and waxes is melted and poured while warm. A common difficulty that is encountered in such creams is crusty surface. This difficulty can be resolved by adding amorphous materials such as ozokerite and petrolatum. Emollient ingredients like lanolin, cetyl alcohol are added to the formulation which leave a thin oily film. The melted product should be filtered through a filter. Liquefying creams are used by women with dry skin. See formulae 9 to 12.

	9	**10**	**11**	**12**
	per cent	per cent	per cent	per cent
Mineral oil	63.0	64.0	65.0	64.0
Paraffin	20.0	17.0	10.0	–
Petrolatum	17.0	18.0	15.0	11.0
Ozokerite	–	–	10.0	10.0
Lanolin (hydrous)	–	–	–	15.0
Cetyl alcohol	–	1.0	–	–

Modern cleansing creams contain sorbitan fatty acid esters and their polyoxyethflene derivatives. These can be used in both beeswax-borax emulsion system or without it. Examples of both types of emulsion systems are exemplified in formulae 13 and 14.

Formula 13

		%
Beeswax		10.0
Mineral oil		20.0
Lanolin (anhydrous)		2.0
Hydrogenated vegetable oil		23.0
*Arlacel 60		5.0
*Tween 60		2.0
Borax		0.5
Water	to make	100.0
Antioxidant		q.s.
Perfume and preservatives		q.s.

Formula 14

	%
Stearic Acid	10.0
Mineral Oil	8.0

Petrolatum		2.0
Cetostearyl alcohol		2.0
Isopropyl myristate		3.0
Sorbitan monolaurate		3.0
Glycerin		5.0
Triethanolamine		1.5
Polyoxyethylene sorbitan monolaurate		2.0
Water	to make	100.0
Perfume and preservatives		q.s.

Skin has a protective sebum layer which is buffered on acid side. Skin returns to normal PH quicker if acid cleansing creams are used. However, there is limitation of emulsifying agents which will make stable acid cleansing creams. Emulsifying agents that can be used in formulation of acid cleansing creams are glyceryl stearate, cetyl or stearyl alcohols, phosphated fatty alcohols. Citric acid, lactic acid and lemon juice are some of the acidic substances that may be used in acid cleaning creams.

Representative formulae of acid cleansing cream are given below:–

Formula 15

		%
Wool wax		4.0
Lanolin		7.0
Stearyl alcohol		2.0
Petrolatum		35.0
Glcyerin		5.0
Lactic acid		1.5
Water	to make	100.0

Formula 16

		%
Sorbitan sesquioleate		4.0
Ozokerite		5.0
Petrolatum		35.0
Mineral oil		8.0
Lanolin		12.0
Lemon juice		5.0
Water	to make	100.0

Beeswax-borax type cleansing creams are difficult to remove with water alone. In contrast with such creams washable cleaning creams can be prepared with detergents as part of emulsifying system. Formula 17 is illustrative of this type of cream in which sodium cetyl sulphate has been used as emulsifying agent.

Formula 17

		%
Mineral oil		38.0
Ozokerite		2.0
Cetyl alcohol		2.0
Sodium cetyl sulphate		1.0
Water	to make	100.0
Perfume and preservatives		q.s.

A cream having gel like texture can be prepared from Formula 18. This gel will cleanse will and can be rinsed off the face witn water.

Formula 18

		%
Stearic acid		10.0
Mineral oil		25.0
Triethanoilamine lanolate		5.0
Terpineol		0.05
Lanolin (anhydrous)		3.0
Propylene glycol		6.0
Water	to make	100.0
Perfume and preservatives		q.s.

The principle of wash off has been extended to such an extent that some creams containing surface active agents will actually lather on skin during use if little extra water is used. Formula 10IX is example of this type of product.

Formula 19

	%
Stearic acid	10.0
Petroleum jelly	1.5
Mineral oil	5.5
Cetostearyl alcohol	10
Isopropyl myristate	3.0

Sorbitan monolaurate		2.0
Sodium lauryl sulphate		4.5
Polyoxyethylene sorbitan monolaurate		1.5
Triethanolamine		1.5
Glycerin		5.0
Water	to make	100.0
Perfume and preservatives		q.s.

Cleansing lotions have been more popular after the introduction of polyethylene plastic containers. Lotions spread in thin layers and because of this sometimes are more economical. Lotions have stability problems. There are two basic types of cleansing lotions. The simplest type of lotion is a solution or emulsion of a detergent in water. For example, a 5% solution of Triethanolamine lauryl sulphate in water or 10% emulsion of sulphonated olive oil in water. The other type is o/w emulsion. To stabilize the formulation besides emulsifying agent, auxiliary emulsifying agents like glyceryl monostearate, fatty alcohols, beeswax etc. are used. See Formula 20.

Formula 20

		%
Mineral oil		38.0
Beeswax		2.0
Triethanolamine stearate		8.0
Water	to make	100.0
Perfume and preservatives		q.s.

Since triethanolamine stearate discolour on standing, it is advisable to make triethanolamine stearate *in situ* by using calculated amounts of triethanolamine and stearic acid. For one part of triethanolamine approximately two parts of stearic acid are used.

Another problem with lotions is viscosity. Viscosity during preparation can be adjusted with water if more viscous lotion has resulted. If the resultant product has low viscosity, viscosity can be improved with materials like triethanolamine stearate.

Oil-in-water (o/w) type of cleansing lotions have tendency to increase in viscosity with ageing. Ethoxylated cholesterol can be used to retard this problem. Use of ethoxylated cholesterol has been illustrated in Formula 21.

Formula 21

		%
Stearic acid		3.5
Cholesterol		0.5
Ethoxylated cholesterol		0.3
Glycyl monostearate (neutral)		2.0
Mineral oil, light		27.0
Triethanolamine		1.5
Propylene glycol		5.0
Water	to make	100.0
Perfume and preservatives		q.s.

A new type of preparations have been developed for oily skin. Majority of women with oily skin cleanse their skin with soap and water. Cleansing products for oily skin are based on synthetic detergents. These products may be in bar, cream or lotion form. If the product is meant for oily skin with acne, substances like salicylic acid, resorcinol and sulphur may be added. Another approach for preparing cleansing products for oily skin is to use solvents like ethyl or isopropyl alcohol in concentrations upto 60%. Presaturated pads of these solvents are also available. Concentration of alcohols should not be more than 60% or else it will cause excessive drying and irritation. Harsh effect of alcohol should be modified with ingredients. See Formula 22.

Formula 22

		%
Alcohol (Ethyl alcohol)		12.0
Menthol		0.05
Camphor		0.1
Cetyl dimethyl benzyl ammonium chloride		0.2
Ethoxylated cetyl alcohol		2.0
Stearylamine		1.0
Water	to make	100.0
Perfume and preservatives		q.s.

A transparent-weekly acidic lotion containing alcohol can be prepared with polyoxyethylene esters and ethers. Formula 23 is an example of such a product.

Formula 23

		%
Polyoxyethylene (20) sorbitan monolaurate		0.5
polyoxyethylene (15) lauryl alcohol ether		0.5
1,3-Butylene glycol		5.0
Glycerin		5.0
Oleyl alcohol		0.5
Ethyl alcohol		10.0
Water	to make	100.0
Preservative		q.s.
Colour		q.s.
Perfume		q.s.

A gel can be prepared with carboxy polymethylene resines (carbopol) and diethylene glycol monoethyl ether where the latter has the solvent effect. Formula 24 is an example of this type of product.

Formula 24

		%
Carbopol 934		1.5
Di isopropanolamine		1.5
Diethylene glycol monoethyl enter		42.0
Water	to make	100.0
perfume and preservatives		q.s.

2.2 Night and Massage Creams

There are certain creams which are applied at night and are removed in morning. There are other creams which are gently rubbed on thee skin with massage like action. These creams are known as 'night creams' and 'massage creams' respectively. These creams should therefore, be formulated with substantial fatty phase having easy spread. These creams provide occlusive layer on the skin which slows the rate of transepidermal water loss. It is because of this reason that these are also claimed to have moisturizing effect. These creams are also known as emollient creams. So far as the skin is concerned, water is the effective emollient, the plasticizer of the stratum corneum. Many factors contribute to the dryness of the skin the salient of them being:

- excessive loss of water from stratum corneum when exposed to low humidities;
- insufficient hydration from the lower epidermal layers;
- prolong contact with soap or detergent solution.

Stratum corneum has water building capacity. Much of the water-binding capacity of the stratum corneum is due to presence of hygrocopic substances. These hygroscopic water soluble substance in some way are protected by fatty material. Therefore, these are not removed by water alone. However, when fatty material is removed either with a solvent or by detergent solution, these substances can be removed with water. Once this happens, skin becomes dry. The dry skin may be made smooth by introducing water into the horney layer. This may be achieved by one or more of three ways:

– by increasing diffusion from living epidermal cells;
– by introducing water to the horney layer from outside;
– by occluding the skin surface to prevent evaporation of water from it.

Emollient materials may be either water soluble or fat soluble. Polyhydric alcohols such as propylene glycol, glycerol, sorbitol are water soluble substances. These are used as humetants. These materials retard evaporation of water in o/w emulsions. This conservation of water in external phase of o/w cream or lotion is related to emollient activity. This can be assumed that humectants hold water in close contact with the skin and thereby introduce water into the stratum corneum (horney layer). Fatty emollients act by forming a thin film over the skin and thereby reduce evaporation from the skin surface. There is long list of fatty emollient materials salient of these are:

– hydrocarbon oils and waxes (e.g., mineral oil, petroleum jelly, paraffin, ceresin etc.);
– silicone oils (e.g., dimethyl polysiloxans, methyl phenyl polysioloxanes etc.);
– triglyceride esters (e.g., vegetable and animal oils and fats);
– alkyl esters (e.g., methyl, isopropyl and butyl esters of fatty acids);

– fatty acids (e.g., lauric acid, palmitic acid, stearic acid etc.);
– lanolin and derivatives (e.g., lanolin, lanolin oil, lanolin wax).

The earlier formulae of emollient creams had a large percentage of mineral oil in borax-beeswax cream base as is shown in Formula 25.

Formula 25

		%
Beeswax		10.0
Spermaceti		12.0
Mineral oil		53.0
Borax		0.5
Rose water	to make	100.0
Preservative		q.s.

But such creams were very greasy and practically had no penetration. For a satisfactory emollient cream, moderate penetration, slip and milder occlusive action are required. This can be achieved by partially replacing mineral oil with vegetable oils like almond oil, peach kernel oil, apricot oil. To reduce drag, quantity of wax(es) should be reduced. Formula 26 is an example of such a modified formula.

Formula 26

		%
Beeswax		9.5
Spermaceti		4.5
Mineral oil		35.5
Almond oil		15.0
Borax		0.5
Water	to make	100.0
Anti-oxidant		q.s.
Perfume and preservatives		q.s.

When vegetable oils are used in the formulation, anti-oxidants are invariably used to retard rancidity of vegetable oils. Anti-oxidant like BHA, BHT or propyl gallate can be used. When more penetration is required lanolin can be added to the formulation. See Formula 27. Lanolin alcohols can also be used in a percentage upto 10% in such creams.

Formula 27

		%
Beeswax		12.0
Mineral oil		30.0
Palm oil		15.0
Lanolin		10.0
Water	to make	100.0
Anti-oxidants		q.s.
Preservatives and perfume		q.s.

Introduction of surface active agents as emulsifying agents has revolutionized cream formulations. Every type of emulsion can be prepared with these emulsifiers. Most commonly used emulsifying agents include glyceryl monostearate, cetyl and stearyl alcohol, diethylene glycol monostearate, propylene glycol monolaurate, polyethylene glycol esters of fatty acids, polyethylene glycol ether of fatty acids. These surfactants can be used in combination. A cream may contain only a non-ionic, anionic or cationic or a combination of nonionic and cationic or non-ionic-anionic surfactants.

A cream made with anionic soap emulsifier is not stable in acidic pH. But a cream prepared with non-ionic emulsifier is stable in acidic pH. Creams prepared with fatty acid esters of polyhydric alcohols are stable in a wide range of pH (4 to 9). Creams prepared with non-ionic ethers are stable in more wider range. Formula 28 is an example of cream where non-ionic emulsifier (glyceryl monostearate) has been used.

Formula 28

	%
Beeswax	4.0
Spermaceti	2.0
Mineral oil	32.0
Glyceryl monostearate	12.5
Glycerin	7.5
Water to make	100.0
Preservative and perfume	q.s.

Formula 29 is an example of emollient cream having more penetration.

Formula 29

	%
Petroleum jelly	12.0
Mineral oil	12.0
Micro-crystalline wax	10.5
Beeswax	4.5
Lanolin absorption base	25.0
Water to make	100.0
Preservative and perfume	q.s.

Use of cationic surfactants is limited as emulsifiers. Cationic surfactants which are commonly used include quaternary compounds of ammonium, pyridinium and imidazolinium salts. These compounds have conditioning effect on the skin and also have antiseptic value. However, antiseptic properties of cationic surfactants are affected by free fatty acids which are usually available in emollient creams. Usually non-ionics are added to the formulations containing anionics to increase stability. See Formula 30 and 31.

Formula 30

		%
Beeswax		12.0
Mineral oil		22.0
Hydrogenated vegetable oil		22.0
*Tween 60		2.0
*Arlacel 60		5.0
Borax		0.6
Water	to make	100.0
Antioxidant		q.s.
Perfume and preservatives		q.s.

Formula 31

	%
Cetyl alcohol	2.0
Beeswax	6.0
Mineral oil	12.0
Liquid lanolin	18.0
Petroleum jelly	22.0
*Arlacel 83	5.0

*Tween 40		1.0
Water	to make	100.0
Perfume and preservatives		q.s.

Emollient preparations can also be prepared in lotion form. Stability of emulsion is problem in lotion form. Emulsion should be stable at room temperature for at least one year. The characteristics which will make an emollient lotion aesthetically acceptable include texture (creamy), feel (smooth), performance (emollient). Materials which are use in the preparation of emollient creams are used in the preparation of lotions. Some thickening agents like cetyl and stearyl alcohol, glyceryl monostearate, sorbitan monostearate, ethylene glycol monostearate, polyethylene glycol distearate are used in the lotions. These materials besides thickening agent act as emulsion stabilizer also. However, these materials should be used in now concentrations only, higher concentration may cause thixotropic gel formation in lotions. Other materials which can be used as thickening agents are:

- plant hydrocolloids e.g., gum arabic/Irish moss, tragacanth,
- cellulose derivatives e.g., methyl cellulose, hydroxy propyl methyl cellulose, sodium carboxy methyl-cellulose, hydroxy ethyl cellulose,
- synthetic high polymers e.g., carboxy vinyl polymer, poly vinyl alcohol.

Humectants like propylene glycol and glycerin exert profound effect on viscosity and stability of lotions. Therefore, their effect must be evaluated on viscosity and stability of emulsion.

Clays e.g., colloidal magnesium aluminium silicate, magnesium aluminium silicate can also be used as thickening agent.

Some basic formulae for emollient lotions are given below:

Formula 32

	%
Cetyl alcohol	1.0
Lanolion	1.5
Mineral oil	36.0
Silicon oil	4.0
*Arlacel 80	2.0
*Tween 80	5.0

Water	to make	100.0
Preservatives and perfume		q.s.

Formula 33

		%
Oleic acid		1.0
Stearic acid		4.0
Lanolin		3.5
Mineral oil		7.5
Triethanolamine		1.5
Water	to make	100.0
Perfume and Preservatives		q.s.

Formula 34

		%
Mineral oil		14.0
Lanolin		1.0
Boric acid		1.0
Pectin		1.0
Cetyl trimethyl ammonium bromide		0.15
Water	to make	100.0
Perfume and preservatives		q.s.

Formula 35

		%
Isopropyl myristate		1.5
Beeswax		7.5
Polyethylene glycol 400 monostearate		10.0
Lanolin		5.5
Stearic acid		1.5
Mineral oil		14.0
Triethanolamine		0.75
Propylene glycol		5.0
Water	to make	100.0
Perfume and preservatives		q.s.

Formula 36

		%
Beeswax		2.0
Mineral oil		32.0

Lanolin		3.5
Petroleum jelly		4.75
Borax		0.5
*Arlacel 83		30
*Veergum		0.25
Water	to make	100.0
Perfume and preservatives		q.s.

Some formulations also include vitamins in such creams claiming beneficial effects. Vitamins that have been included most commonly from time to time are vitamin A, D and E (fat soluble vitamins) and vitamin B_6, pantothenic acid (water soluble vitamins).

2.3 Vanishing and Foundation Creams

Creams which spread easily and seem to disappear rapidly when rubbed on the skin are termed as vanishing creams. These creams are composed of emollient esters which leave little apparent film on the skin. Low percentage of oil phase is also chosen for the above mentioned reason. Traditional formulae of vanishing creams are based on stearic acid. Stearic acid melts above body temperature and crystallizes in a form so as to be invisible providing a non-greasy film. Stearic acid also imparts attractive appearance to the cream. With stearic acid white creams are produced and sometimes because of this whiteness these creams are called 'snow'. An example of simple and typical formula of vanishing cream is given below.

Formula 37

		%
Stearic acid		17.0
Potassium hydroxide		0.7
Glycerin		5.0
Water	to make	100.0
Perfume and preservatives		q.s.

Creams prepared with such formulae contain partly saponified stearic acid, free stearic acid and water. These creams leave a dry, tacky residual film. This film also has a drying effect on skin. Such creams are suitable for hot climates which cause perspiration on the face. Stearic acid of fine quality (triple pressed) should be used in these creams and total proportion should to exceed 25%. Best results are obtained from use of 16-20% of stearic acid. The texture of cream also depends on amount of stearic acid saponified and alkali used. Creams made with sodium hydroxide are harder than those made with potassium hydroxide. Borax is another alkali that can be used to make cream. Creams produced with borax are very white in colour. But the product has tendency to become grainy. Triethanolamine is an excellent alkali. Balancing this and fatty acid variation can be made and other emollients can be added easily. Glycerine when used in soap creams should not exceed 10%. Since soap creams contain a large amount of water these are liable to lose water by evaporation and therefore, should be packed in airtight containers.

In Formula 38, use of triethanolamine and emollient isopropyl myristate has been shown:

Formula 38

		%
Stearic acid		20.0
Isopropyl myristate		2.0
Triethanolamine		1.2
Glycerin		5.0
Water	to make	100.0
Perfume and preservatives		q.s.

Curd soap (soap powder) can be used to obtain pearliness. Pearliness develops gradually and it may take about 10 days for maximum effect to develop. Soap can either be dissolved in the total water required or can be dissolved in a part of it and added after saponification. See Formula 39.

Formula 39

		%
Stearic Acid		20.0
Cetyl alcohol		1.0
Soft soap		0.5
Potassium hydroxide		1.0
Glycerin		6.0
Water	to make	100.0
Perfume and preservatives		q.s.

Self emulsifying glyceryl monostearate can also be used as emulsifying agent in preparation of vanishing creams. The advantage of using self emulsifying glyceryl monostearate is that it does not have drying effect on skin as is the case with creams prepared with alkali stearates. Formula 40 is typical of such formulations.

Formula 40

		%
Mineral oil		2.0
Cetyl alcohol		3.0
Glyceryl monostearate (self emulsifying)		15.0
Glycerin		10.0
Water	to make	100.0
Perfume and preservatives		q.s.

For dry and flaky skin some special oily materials like lanolin, lanolin derivatives are used in vanishing creams. Formula 41 is an example of such formulations.

Formula 41

		%
Glyceryl monostearate (self emulsifying)		12.0
Mineral oil		4.0
Cetyl alcohol		2.0
Lanolin		1.0
Glycerin		6.0
Water	to make	100.0
Perfume and preservatives		q.s.

Foundation creams vary widely in viscosity and are available in the form of pourable lotions to thicker creams. These creams are prepared by incorporating powders like titanium dioxide, kaolin, bentonite and pigments. The desired shade and spreading properties can be obtained by varying the amount of pigments and titanium dioxide and/or other fillers.

Formula 42 is an example of pourable foundation cream and Formula 43 is an example of cream foundation.

Formula 42

	%
Cetomacrogol emulsifying wax	25.0
Mineral oil	5.0

Titanium dioxide		10.0
Pigments		0.5
Glycerine		8.0
Water	to make	100.0
Perfume and preservatives		q.s.

Formula 43

		%
Stearic acid		3.0
Propylene glycol monostearate		8.0
Mineral oil		15.0
Triethanolamine		1.0
Sodium lauryl sulphate		1.0
Bentonite		5.0
Kaolin		5.0
Titanium dioxide and pigments		10.0
Water	to make	100.0
Perfume and preservatives		q.s.

Some materials give porosity to film building materials. These are called porositones. These are ideal for liquid make-up as they do not interfere with insensible respiration of the skin. A formulation of this type is exemplified in Formula 44.

Formula 44

		%
Monoglyceride of poly unsaturated acids		0.5
Glyceryl stearate		3.0
Triethanolamine stearate		2.5
Isopropyl myristate		2.0
Propylene glycol		6.0
Talc		3.0
Titanium dioxide and pigments		5.0
Cellulose gum		0.8
Isopropyl lanolate		2.0
Hydrated magnesium silicate		0.8
Branched chain fatty acid/esters		5.0
Water	to make	100.0
Preservatives and perfume		q.s.

Non-aqueous formulations are used for heavy make-up and are referred to as cream-cake foundation. Formula 45 is a typical example of such formulation.

Formula 45

	%
Petroleum Jelly	75.0
Lanolin	5.0
Isopropyl myristate	2.5
Titanium dioxide and pigments	7.5
Perfume and preservatives	q.s.

Such preparations can also be prepared using vegetable oil and waxes. Formula 46 is an example of such a formulation.

Formula 46

	%
Sesame oil	65.0
Zinc oxide	10.0
Oxycholestrol	2.0
Triglyceryl stearate	1.0
Titanium dioxide and pigments	22.0
Perfume and preservatives	q.s.

By incorporating high melting point waxes this preparation can be made in the form of stick. Formula 47 is an example of this type of formulation.

Formula 47

	%
Mineral oil	24.0
Isopropyl myristate	20.0
Petroleum Jelly	3.0
Beeswax	10.0
Ozokerite	3.0
Kaolin	25.0
Titanium dioxide and pigments	15.0
Perfume and preservatives	q.s.

2.4 Hand Creams and Lotions

Hands may be exposed to water, water-soap, water-detergent contact several times in a day. This results in removal of lipids and other secretions from the skin. Excessive contact of detergent and water may even damage cell walls. Cold and dry winds take out moisture from the skin resulting in chapping of the skin. The chapping sometimes may be associated with cracking of the skin. From this it can be made out that moisture is important for maintenance of normal skin (soft and flexible). Though the water alone would have been sufficient for treatment of dry skin but water evaporates rapidly leaving behind the skin dry without providing emolliency. However, if the hands are immersed in water for a longer period to prevent evaporation there will be danger of abnormal degree of hydration. This may result in swelling of stratum corneum having possibility of cell rupture. Therefore, an ideal emollient will be a substance which will not only make water available to the stratum corneum but will also regulate water take up of the stratum corneum. Because of this, formulations of creams and lotions meant for hands centre around emollients. The most commonly used emollients are lanolin and its derivatives, sterols, phospholipids, fatty acids/esters and hydrocarbons. The following are the desirable qualities in a hand cream:

- it should soften the hands;
- it should apply easily;
- it should not leave a tacky film;
- it should not interfere with normal perspiration of the skin;
- it should have a pleasant smell;
- it should have an appealing colour.

Development of formulations of hand creams will, therefore, require inclusion of emollients, vanishing cream base, a combination of waxes, oils and humectants (to prevent excessive occlusion), pleasing perfume and stable colour. Formula 48 to 50 are example of hand creams.

Formula 48

	%
Cetyl alcohol	2.0
Lanolin	1.0
Mineral oil	2.0
Stearic acid	15.0
Glycerin	10.0

Potassium hydroxide		1.0
Water	to make	100.0
Perfume, preservative and colour		q.s.

Formula 49

		%
Cetyl alcohol		10.0
Sod. Cetyl sulphate		2.0
Stearic acid		10.0
Stearyl alcohol		2.0
Glycerin		8.0
Sod. lauryl sulphate		1.0
Water	to make	100.0
Perfume, preservative and colour		q.s.

Formula 50

		%
Isopropyl palmitate		1.0
Polyethylene sorbitan monostearate		1.5
Sorbitan monostearate		2.0
Stearic acid		17.0
Water	to make	100.0
Perfume, colour and preservatives		q.s.

In some hand creams, dimethicone along with other barrier agents is used to protect skin from irritants. Formula 51 is an example of this type of formulation.

Formula 51

		%
Glyceryl stearate (self emulsifying)		2.5
Cetyl alcohol		3.0
Dimethicone		1.5
Lanolin oil		2.0
Petrolatum		2.0
Sodium lauryl sulphate		0.3
Water	to make	100.0
Perfume and preservatives		q.s.

Hand lotions are not different than hand creams except these differ in total solids. Formulae 52 to 55 are some typical hand lotions.

		Formula 52	Formula 53
		per cent	per cent
Cetyl alcohol		0.5	0.75
Lanolion		1.0	–
Stearic acid		5.0	6.0
Glycerin		2.0	2.0
Triethanolamine		0.75	0.5
Water	to make	100.0	100.0
Perfume and preservatives		q.s.	q.s.

Formula 54

		%
Glyceryl monostearate		1.0
Isopropyl palmitate		5.0
Polyethylene glycol (4000) distearate		2.0
Glycerin		8.0
Sodium cetyl sulphate		4.0
Water	to make	100.0
Perfume and preservatives		q.s.

Formula 55

		%
Glyceryl monostearate		5.0
Lanolin		1.0
Stearic acid		2.0
Glycerin		5.0
Sodium lauryl sulphate		1.0
Water	to make	100.0
Perfume and preservatives		q.s.

Formulation of Hand lotions offer two problems: one, lotion may exhibit gelling tendencies which make it difficult to pour; two, viscosity of lotion may be so low that it may literally run out of the container. The lotion should also retain its viscosity during shelf life period. Lotions of stearate type are more susceptible to gelation. They are also vulnerable to shear action. Excessive mechanical agitation can make these lotions of very low viscosity. The following precautions will retard gelation in lotions:

* Excessive amounts of polyol fatty acid esters (e.g., glyceryl monostearate) or fatty alcohol (e.g., cetyl alcohol) should not be used in the formulations of hand lotions.

* Dispersed wax phase should be plasticized with mineral oils. The concentration of mineral oil that can be used could be as high as 10%.
* Small amounts of alkyl sulphates (0.1-0.5% e.g., sodium lauryl sulphate) should be incorporated in the formulations.

Change in viscosity due to shear action happens due to thixotropic properties of lotion. To reduce the changes in viscosity of lotion such materials should be included in the formulation which will make it less thixotropic.

2.5 All Purpose Creams

The term, "all-purpose" is very popular, but it is misnomer. No cream can have the properties which should be possessed by a foundation cream, cleansing cream, hand cream and protective cream. Any attempted formulation to serve all the functions which the specialized creams have, will be a compromise formulation excelling in none of the functions. Formerly these were also known as sports creams. These are somewhat oily, but non-greasy in use. Being water in oil type emulsion these spread readily on skin and make a protective film. Experiments can be started with the following formulations.

		Formula 56	**Formula 57**
		per cent	per cent
Wool alcohols		2.0	1.0
Microcrystalline wax		5.0	–
Mineral oil		25.0	20.0
Petroleum Jelly		7.0	7.5
Glycerin		5.0	5.0
Magnesium sulphate		0.5	0.5
Cholesterol		–	1.0
Paraffin wax		–	5.0
Sorbitan sesquioleate		–	1.0
Butylated hydroxyanisole		0.002	0.002
Water	to make	100.0	100.0
Perfume and preservatives		q.s.	q.s.

Note: Stability of the cream is increased by the addition of magnesium ion to water phase.

		Formula 58	Formula 59
		per cent	per cent
Stearic Acid		14.0	15.0
Mineral oil		25.0	25.0
Beeswax		2.0	2.0
Lanolin		3.0	2.0
Polysorbate (80)		1.0	–
Sorbitan trioleate		1.0	–
PEG-4-0 stearate		–	5.0
Sorbitol		10.0	8.0
Butylated hydroxyanisole		0.002	–
Water	to make	100.0	100.0
Perfume and preservatives		q.s.	q.s.

2.6 Moisturizing Creams and Lotions

When water is lost form stratum corneum more rapidy than it is received from lower layers of the skin, the skin becomes dehydrated. The dehydrated skin loses its flexibility and appears rough. Water (moisture) plasticizes stratum corneum, provides it flexibility and makes it soft. Soft skin appears smooth. Those creams which restore water (moisture) to the stratum corneum are called moisturizing creams. Water contained in the cream is lost by evaporation when the cream is applied to the body. Therefore, a moisturizing cream must provide a non-volatile residual film capable of retaining the moisture of the skin as well as the moisture which is applied directly by the cream. This may be achieved by including humectants in the aqueous phase of the cream. Commonly used humectants are glycerin, propylene glycol and sorbitol (70% solution).

Formulations which may be used for starting experiments on moisturizing creams are given below:

Formula 60

	%
Stearic Acid	4.0
Mineral oil	8.0
Lanolin	1.0
Glyceryl monostearate (self emulsifying)	3.0
Isopropyl myristate	2.0

Glycerin		4.0
Propylene glycol		4.0
Triethanolamine		0.2
Water	to make	100.0
Perfume and preservatives		q.s.

Formula 61

		%
Cetyl alcohol		2.0
Glyceryl monostearate (self emulsifying)		7.5
Mineral oil		8.0
Isopropyl myristate		1.0
PEG-400 monostearate		10.0
Sodium lauryl sulphate		0.2
Glycerin		5.0
Propylene glycol		3.5
Water	to make	100.0
Perfume and preservatives		q.s.

Formula 62

		%
Cetyl alcohol		2.0
Glyceryl monostearate		5.0
Mineral oil		7.0
Isopropyl myristate		1.0
Polyethylene glycol (400) monostearate		12.0
Laolin		2.0
Sodium lauryl sulphate		0.2
Glycerin		3.0
Propylene glycol		4.0
Sorbitol (70% solution)		2.0
Water	to make	100.0
Perfume and preservatives		q.s.

2.7 Skin Creams with Some Special Ingredients

De Ritter *et al* consider that local vitamin deficiencies may be alleviated by topical application of vitamins. Ellot claims that fat soluble as well as water soluble vitamins are capable of being absorbed through skin. These claims justify in use of vitamins in skin creams. However, these creams should contain sufficient-quantities of vitamins in stabilized form.

Pantothenic acid and its precursor and related materials panthenol, have been quoted as having beneficial effect on the skin. These are usually used with vitamin B_6 (pyridoxine) Ascorbic acid and its isomer, iso-ascorbic acid have been reported to have been used in toilet preparations. Fat soluble vitamins, A, D and E have also been used in cosmetic. Vitamin E is said to enhance percutaneous resorption. Emollient cream bases can be used for incorporation of vitamins. Formulae 29 and 30can be tried for incorporation of vitamins.

In moisturizing creams, film forming materials which approximate in composition or are of allied composition to natural skin secretions can be considered in their formulation. Based on this concept materials like albumin, amino acids, mucopolysaccharide hydrolyzed protein can be included in moisturizing creams. An illustrative example of such type of formulation is shown in formula 63.

Formula 63

		%
Spermaceti		3.0
Lanolin		10.0
Beeswax		10.0
Vegetable oil		20.0
Light mineral oil		5.0
Absorption base		5.0
Cholesterol		2.0
Paraffin		2.0
Petroleum jelly		5.0
Lecithin		1.0
Borax		0.5
Water	to make	100.0
Antioxidants		q.s.
Preservatives and perfume		q.s.

Another type of creams in which special ingredients are used are barrier hand creams. There is growing awareness about skin irritants amongst from housewives to garage mechanics. As such, demand is growing forbarrier creams. Peel has laid down certain basic requirements for a barrier cream and these are:

* It should have good consistency and ease of application.
* It should adhere to the skin reasonably and persistently.
* It should have ability of form a coherent, impervious flexible and non-cracking film.
* It should be free from any tendency to irritate the skin.
* It should be easy to remove when desired.
* It should have aesthetic acceptability.

Barrier creams fall into two main groups water-repellent and oil-repellent. Water-repellent creams from a thin film that acts as barrier to water and water soluble agents having skin irritating properties. Similarly, oil repellent-creams form thin film which acts as barrier to oil and oil soluble irritants These are but only a few products which form film which is water repellent as well as oil repellent.

With the advent of silicones a number of protective cream products can be formulated. Combination of silicones with other barrier agents e.g. petroleum jelly, bees wax, paraffin, etc. can produce excellent barrier creams.

Use of healing agents has also been advocated in hand creams and lotions. Constant use of hands in daily tasks may result in bruises and cracks. Healing agents have ability to stimulate the growth of healthy granulation tissue. Two basic substances have been recommended as healing agents viz. allantoin and urea. Allantoin can be used in the concentration of 0.01 to 0.1% and urea can be used in the concentration of 3-5%. use of barrier agents has been illustrated in formula 64.

Formula 64

	%
Lanolin	1.0
Glyceryl Monostearate	5.0
Isopropyl myristate	4.0
PEG-400 Monostearate	5.0
Stearic acid	7.0
Dimethicone	10.0

Petroleum Jelly		5.0
Water	to make	100.0
Preservatives and perfume		q.s.

2.8 Gels

Gels and jellies are a type of base which produces a uniform external appearance and give a moist feeling. Aqúeous gels have been used as under make up creams particularly in summers. With the development of new materials and technologies aqueous and oils gels having more functions than providing moisture have been developed.

As aqueous gels contain a lot of moisture they are used for supplying moisture and for cooling effects. They may also be used as the base of a cleanser for light make up. They are generally used in summer and are good for oily skin.

Oily gels are used for supplying oil to the skin and are usually applied together with lotion. These are used in winters or for dry skin because of their moisturizing properties. Because of their great affinity for thick make up, they are made into cleansers for removing make up by combining them with suitable surfactants.

Water soluble polymeric substances having gelling abilities are used in the manufacture of aqueous gels. Example of such substances are carboxy vinyl polymer and methyl cellulose. Besides the gelling agent, other ingredients include humectants, surfactants, preservatives, colour etc. As gels are usually transparent, care should be taken to uniformly dissolve or disperse other additives in moisturizing gels.

These gels contain water soluble polymers, humectants, surfactants, perfumes, colour and preservatives. A typical formula of moisturizing gel is given below (See Formula 65).

Formula 65

	%
Carboxy vinyl polymer	0.5
Methyl cellulose	0.2
Dipropylene glycol	8.0
Polyethylen glycol (PEG) 1500	7.0
Polyoxyethylene POE (15) Oleyl alcohol ether	1.0
Calcium hydroxide	0.1

Water	to make	100.0
Preservatives, perfume and odour		q.s.

2.9 Oily Gels

Oily gels an be used for the removal of make up. These can be rinsed off easily after rubbing thoroughly into the make up. Because of their moist feeling these gels are liked very much and are becoming popular. They give light-feeling after use.

A typical formula of oily gel, emulsion type is given hereunder (See Formula 66):

Formula 66

		%
Liquid paraffin		10.0
Glycerol tri-2-ethyl hexanoate		50.0
Sorbitol		10.0
PEG 400		5.0
Acyl methyl taurate		5.0
POE Octyl dodecyl alcohol ether		8.0
Water	to make	100.0
Perfume and preservative		q.s.

To manufacture this gel, add sorbitol, PEG 400 and acyl methyl taurate to purified water and heat to 70°C. Add POE octyl dodecyl alcohol ether to oily phase (liquid paraffing and glycerol tri-2-ethyl hexanoate) and heat to 70°C. Add oily phase to aqueous phase. After emulsification, pass through homogenizer and de-air before filling into containers.

3. MANUFACTURE OF CREAMS AND LOTIONS

The general procedures of manufacture of creams is to heat two phases i.e., oil phase (oil, waxes and other oil soluble ingredients) and aqueous or water phase (water and water soluble ingredients) to 75°C in separate vessels. Usually steam jacketed kettles are used for this purpose. In aqueous phase about 3-5% excess of water is used to compensate the loss of water due to evaporation during manufacture. The exact amount which is lost during the process can be found out by carrying out water analysis of the finished product. Next, the inner phase is added to the outer phase very slowly stirring constantly and homogenizing to ensure efficient emulsion. Sometimes, for preparing w/o emulsion, aqueous phase is added to molten oily phase. Initially when the water is in low concentration a w/o is formed. Slow addition of aqueous phase increases the viscosity of the system while oil phase expands to the maximum. At this point, oil phase breaks up into minute droplets and emulsion inversion occurs forming o/w emulsion. When this happens viscosity suddenly decreases. This process of manufacture proceeds well in well balanced low oil-wax system but coagulation occurs in high oil-wax system. The conventional procedure of adding inner phase to outer phase can be successfully used for manufacture of creams and lotions.

The rates of addition and mechanical agitation of the inner phase are critically important for manufacture of good emulsion. In laboratory work, usually a flow rate of about 175-200 g/min. is employed. But this rate is too slow for large scale production. A practical rate of addition should be determined. It will be a multiple of the rate employed in laboratory. However, too rapid rate makes difficult dispersion of inner phase.

Other important factors in manufacture of creams and lotions are total stirring time and cooling rate. These factors affect lotion viscosity, cream consistency and emulsion stability. If cooling is started too soon after emulsification, crystallization of higher melting waxes may occur. A gradual cooling assures homogeneous dispersion of waxes.

Temperature at which perfume oil is added is also important in the manufacture of creams and lotions. Addition of perfume oil to w/o type emulsion proceeds smoothly due to its solubility in the outer phase. But in case of o/w type emulsion, perfume oil must break through aqueous phase to reach oily phase. It becomes more difficult at room temperatures particularly when emulsion is having high water content. Therefore, perfume oil is added very slowly to the cream or lotion when it is between 45°C and 50°C.

If a cream is to be hot poured, it is stirred to about 5°C above congealing point. Colour solutions are added, if coloured cream is to be prepared. Cream is maintained at that temperature throughout filling operation with occasional stirring. If cold filling is to be carried out, the cream is stirred to 35°C and colour solution is added, if coloured cream is to be prepared. Cream is then filled into the containers.

A schematic presentation of manufacturing of cream and lotions can be made as shown in Figure 12.1.

Equipment made of stainless steel should be used for manufacture of creams and lotions. Where head-room is available, jacketed feeding kettles can be placed above batch mixing kettle. In one kettle, oils, waxes and other oil soluble materials are heated with the help of steam. Cutting waxes into small pieces makes melting easier. The molten oily phase is strained by gravity through unbleached muslin or an edge filter into the mixing kettle. Water and water soluble ingredients are heated in the other feeding kettle and are strained through filter into the mixing kettle. Which phase should be transferred to mixing kettle will depend on the emulsion type. Where head-room is not available, the feeding kettles may be installed on ground and materials after heating may be transferred with the help of pumps.

Use of colloid mill or homogenizer improves the appearance and stability of some creams. Where such advantage is available, colloid mill or homogenizer should be used. The practice that is often used during filling of the creams is to fill three quarter of the cream into the jar, swirl it to leave a continuous film upto the rim and then to fill the jar completely. Filled jars are set aside for cooling before capping. This practice results in smooth and even top.

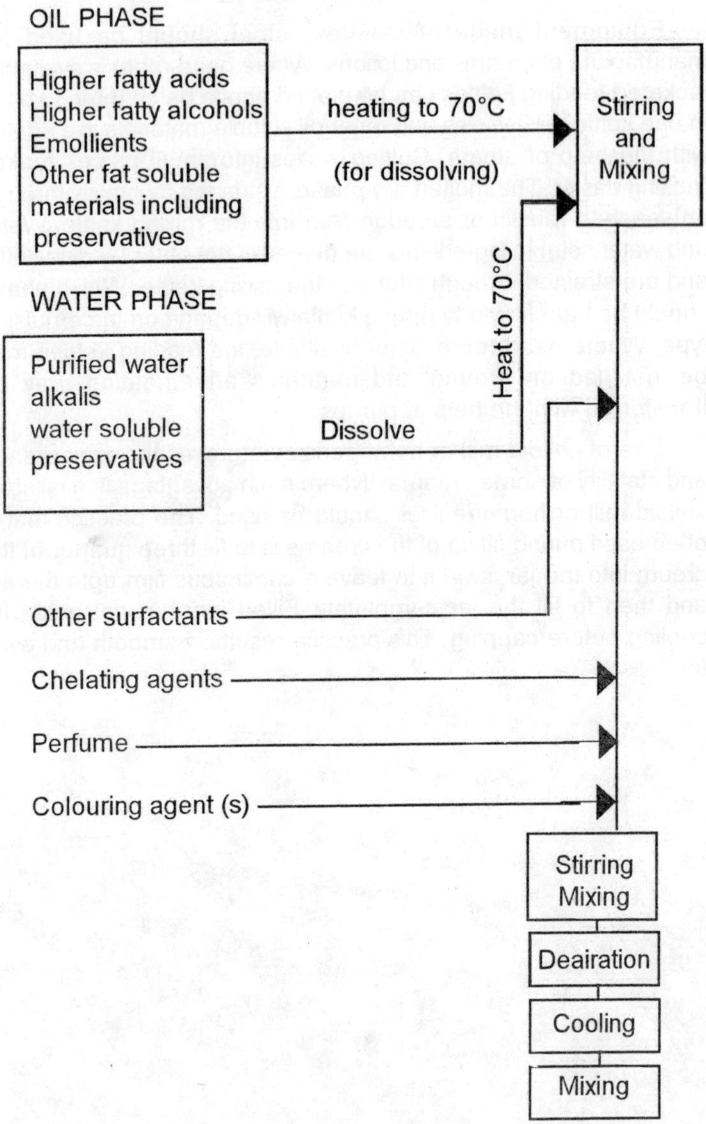
OIL PHASE
Higher fatty acids
Higher fatty alcohols
Emollients
Other fat soluble materials including preservatives
heating to 70°C
(for dissolving)
Stirring and Mixing
WATER PHASE
Purified water
alkalis
water soluble preservatives
Heat to 70°C
Dissolve
Other surfactants
Chelating agents
Perfume
Colouring agent (s)
Stirring Mixing
Deairation
Cooling
Mixing

Figure 12.1

13

Suntan and Anti-Sunburn Preparations

1. GENERAL

Depending upon length and frequency of exposure to sun light, the human body may exhibit beneficial or harmful effects. A moderate exposure to sun light particularly in winter pleases human beings, stimulates blood circulation and increases the formation of haemoglobin. Sun light also activates 7-dehydrocholesterol (pro vitamin D_3) present in the epidermis to form vitamin D which is important for absorption of calcium from intestines.

Prolonged exposures or repeated exposure to sun light affect human beings adversely. Sunlight is composed of radiations of different wavelengths. Radiations of different wavelengths have different penetration power. Radiations of wavelengths 2000-2500 Å penetrate also the network of blood vessels reaching the papillary layer. Radiations of wavelengths 3200-3900 Å reach the derma. Radiations of wavelengths between 2800-3900 Å are both erythemogenic (capable of producing redness) and pigmentogenic. Radiations of wavelengths of 3200-3900 Å are pigmentogenic but produce only a little erythema. Radiations of more than 3900 Å (3900-14000 Å) have heating action.

The first effect of sun light is the erythema (redness) of the skin followed by formation of a tan. Intensity of erythema depends on absorption of ultra violet radiation and usually starts to develop after a latent period of 2 to 3 hours. The maximum intensity is reached within 10 to 24 hours.

The sun tanning depends on one's capacity to produce pigment, melanin. This capacity is genetically predetermined. There are three types of skin tanning:

- immediate tanning,
- delayed tanning,
- true tanning.

Immediate tanning response is elicited by radiations of wavelengths of 3000-6600 Å, the maximum efficacious being 3400-3600 Å. In this response, immediate darkening of un-oxidized melanin granules present in epidermal layer near the surface of the skin starts and reaches its maximum within about one hour. In the delayed tanning melanin granules present in the basal cells layer of epidermis get oxidized and migrate towards surface of the skin. This type of tanning may start one hour after the exposure and may reach maxima within about 10 hours. The delayed tanning is stimulated primarily by radiations of wavelengths of 2900-3200 Å. True tanning or melanogenesis starts about two days after exposure and reaches maxima in about 2-3 weeks. Immediate tanning begins to fade within 2-3 hours of exposure. Delayed tanning starts fading after 100-200 hours.

Symptoms of sun burn are the result of damage or destruction of cells in the prickle cell layer of epidermis. Histamine like substances released by the damaged or destructed cells cause dilation of blood vessels and erythema. These substances also cause swelling of the skin and stimulate basal cells to proliferate. Based on symptoms, the sun burns can be classified into four degrees.

Degree 1 – Minium erythema

Degree 2 – Vivid erythema

Degree 3 – Painful burn

Degree 4 – Blistering burn

Sunburn does not leave scars. However, disappearance of symptoms may take varying time. A slight burn, if not exposed further to sun light may disappear within 24-36 hours. Severe burns may heal within 4-8 days and may be associated with peeling of the skin.

Chronic exposure to sun light produces more serious adverse effects and includes thickening of skin, loss of natural elasticity, appearance of wrinkles, transient dermatitis and even cancer.

Thickness of the stratum corneum and pigmentation of skin are two natural protections against sunburn. Solar radiations increase the mitotic (division) rate of epidermal cells which causes thickening of stratum corneum making it more impervious to solar radiations. Melanin granules in basal cell layer of skin after being exposed to sunlight migrate towards the stratum corneum to be affected first in case of subsequent exposure. Painful effects of sunburn can be prevented by gradual exposure.

1.1 Sunscreens

The purpose of suntan preparations is to assist the skin in tanning without painful effects and the purpose of anti-burn preparations is to minimize the harmful effects of sunburn. The materials which are used for the above purpose are known as suntanning agents and sunburn preventive agents respectively. Combinedly these are known as sunscreens. Suntanning agents are those sunscreens which absorb a minimum of 85% ultra-violet radiations of the wavelengths of 2900-3200 Å, but which transmit ultra-violet radiations of wavelengths of longer than 3200 Å and produce a light transient tan. Sunburn preventive agents are those sunscreens which absorb more than 95% or more of ultra-violet radiations of the wavelengths of 2900-3200 Å. There are another type of sunburn preventive agents which scatter the sunlight. These include titanium dioxide, kaolin, talc, zinc oxide, calcium carbonate and magnesium oxide.

A number of organic compounds have been screened for sunscreening properties. An extensive list of sunscreens was compiled by Klarmann which included the following:

- Anthranilates (0-aminobenzoatse, methyl menthyl, phenyl, benzyl, phenylethyl, linalyl, terpenyl and cyclohexenyl esters)
- *p*-Aminobenzoic acid and its derivatives (ethyl, isobutyl, glyceryl esters, *p*-dimethylamino benzoic acid);

- Azoles (2-acetyl-3-bromoindazole, phenylbenzoxazole, methyl naphthoxazole, various aryl benzo-thiazoles);
- Cinnamic acid dervivatives (menthyl and benzyl esters, phenyl cinnamonitrile, butyl cinnamoyl pyruvate);
- Coumarin derivatives (7-hydroxy-7-methyl, 3-phenyl);
- Dibenzalacetone and benzal-acetophenone;
- Dihydroxy cinnamic acid derivatives (umbellifereone, methyl umbelliferone, methylaceto-umbelliferone);
- Dihydroxy-naphthoic acid and its salts *o*-and-*p*-hydroxy biphenyl disulphonates;
- Hydrocarbons (diphenyl butadiene, stibine);
- Hydroquinone;
- Naphthosulphonates (sodium salts of 2-naphthol-3, 6-disulphonic and of 2-naphthol-6, 8-disulphonic acids);
- Quinine salts (bisulphate, sulphate, chloride, oleate and tannate);
- Quinoline derivatives (8-hydroxy quinoline salts, 2-phenyl quinoline);
- Salicylates (amyl, phenyl, benzyl, methyl, glyceryl and dipropylene glycol esters);
- Tannic acid and its derivatives (e.g., hexaethyl ether);
- Uric and violuric acids.

Non-toxicity and dermatological acceptability are important factors which should be considered. In the Annex. D of IS:4707 (Part 2)-1993 (classification of Cosmetic Raw Materials and Adjuncts) two lists of sunscreens are given. In the first list appears the sunscreens which may be contained in a cosmetic. In the second list appear the sunscreens which may be provisionally contained in a cosmetic.

Usually esters of p-dimethylaminobenzoic acid are more effective sunscreens than esters of p-aminobenzoic acid. The former are superior than the latter in respect of stability, storage and use. Lower esters of p-dimethylbenzoic acid are appreciably soluble in water and as such, are easily removed from the skin by perspiration or by water during bath. This is not a desirable property. But higher alkyl esters like amyl, hexyl, heptyl of p-dimethyl benzoic acid are oily liquids. These sunscreens form a continuous film which is not easily removed by water or perspiration. The same object has been achieved by some polymeric sunscreen materials and most of them have been patented.

An ideal sunscreening agent should have the following properties:

* It should absorb erythmogenic radiations in the range of 290-320 nm without its break down.
* It should allow full transmission of radiations in the range of 300-400 nm for tanning effect.
* It should be resistant to water and perspiration and should also be non-volatile.
* It should have suitable solubility characteristics so that requisite amount of it is included in a cosmetic formulation.
* Preferably it should be odourless or should have only mild odour acceptable to user.
* It should be non-toxic, non-irritant and non-sensitizing.
* It should be capable of retaining its sunscreening property for several hours.
* It should be stable under conditions of use.
* It should not stain.

However, it is almost impossible to find a sun-screen agent which will have all these properties. The one which have majority of these properties should be used in cosmetic formulation.

Pernich and Gallagher examined transmission spectra of various sun-screens and found the following to be effective sunscreens:

- ethyl p-dimethyl amino benzoate
- isobutyl p-amino benzoate
- coumarin
- 8-methoxy coumarin
- 5, 7-dihydroxy-4-methyl coumarin
- 6-amino coumarin

– benzyl-β-methyl umbelliforum
– benzyl acetophenone

The following five sunscreen agents were recommended by the US Deptt. of Health:

– Cycloform (isobutyl p-amino benzoate)
– Propylene glycol p-amino benzoate
– Monoglyceryl p-amino benzoate
– Digalloyl trioleate
– Benzyl salicylate and Benzyl cinnamate (2% each)

All compounds conventionally used as sunscreening agents have relatively low molecular weight, as such, many of them are easily removed from the skin on contact with water. If it happens so, there will be necessity for further application of the product. The higher alkyl esters of p-dimethyl amino benzoic acid are oily liquids which form continuous and adherent films which are not removed easily with water (e.g. amyl, hexyl, heptyl and Octyl esters).

Some water insoluble but alkali soluble polymeric sunscreening agents have also been developed. Formulations described in a patent of National Starch and Chemical Corporation contains about 1% of alkali soluble polymeric sunscreening agents.

There are some patents which suggest use of sunscreening agents which are substantive to the skin and resistant to water and perspiration. In one of the patents, use of highly substantive sulphonium salts, such as p-nitrobenzamide, propyl dodecyl methyl sulphonium bromide, has been disclosed.

2. FORMULATION

Sunscreens can be present in almost in all those cosmetic forms in which these can be applied to the skin. The most important factor in sunscreens is choice of sunscreen and the vehicle. However, the points that should be kept in mind while trying sunscreen formulations are:

* Product, package and closure should be such that it is convenient for use even if it is to be used outdoor.
* Sunscreen should be present in such concentration as is effective.

* Sunscreen and vehicle should be compatible.
* Choice of lipids and hydrophillic materials may be made on the basis of requirement of degree of greasiness or wetness.

The cosmetic forms in which sunscreening agents have been commonly marketed include hydroalcoholic lotions, aqueous suntan lotion with thickening agent, suntan cream (vanishing and cold cream type), sunscreen ointment, suntan oil etc. Some basic formulae for the development of sunscreen preparations are given below:

Formula 1

Alcoholic Suntan Lotion

		%
Glyceryl p-aminobenzoate		3.0
Propylene glycol ricinoleate		8.0
Glycerin		10.0
Alcohol		60.0
Water	to make	100.0
Perfume and colour		q.s.

Formula 2

Aqueous Suntan Lotion with Thickener

		%
Glyceryl p-aminobenzoate		3.0
Glycerin		5.0
Alcohol		10.0
Methyl cellulose		0.5
Water	to make	100.0
Perfume		q.s.

Formula 3

Clear Suntan Lotion

		%
Isobutyl p-aminobenzoate		5.0
Tween-20		10.0
Alcohol		45.0
Water	to make	100.0
Perfume		q.s.

Formula 4

Suntan Cream (Vanishing cream base)

		%
Stearic acid		18.0
Cetyl alcohol		0.5
Menthyl anthranilate		5.0
Sodium hydroxide		0.5
Glycerin		10.0
Water	to make	100.0
Perfume		q.s.

Formula 5

Suntan Cream (Cold cream base)

		%
2-Ethyl hexyl salicylate		5.0
Mineral oil		35.0
Polyoxyethylene sorbitol lanolin derivative		2.0
Cetyl pyridinium chloride		4.0
Beeswax		2.0
Cetyl alcohol		0.5
Isopropyl myristate		0.5
Petroleum jelly		7.0
Water	to make	100.0
Perfume		q.s.

Formula 6

Sunscreen ointment

	%
Homomenthyl salicylate	5.0
Ceresin	14.0
Groundnut oil	81.0
Perfume, colour and antioxidant	q.s.

Formula 7

Suntan Oil

	%
2-Ethyl hexyl salicylate	5.0
Groundnut oil	40.0
Mineral oil	55.0
Perfume, colour, antioxidant	q.s.

Formula 8 is an example of formula which contains light scattering sunscreen and Formula 9 is an example which contains both types of sunscreen agents (i.e., light scattering and light absorbing).

Formula 8

		%
Calamine		15.0
Petroleum jelly, yellow		38.0
Lanolin		12.0
Water	to make	100.0
Perfume and colour		q.s.

Formula 9

		%
Glyceryl monostearate		15.0
Lanolin		4.5
Propylene glycol		4.5
Titanium dioxide		3.0
Sodium lauryl sulphate		0.05
Isobutyl p-aminobenzoate		2.0
Isopropyl myristate/palmitate		17.0
Water	to make	100.0
Perfume and colour		q.s.

A lotion type sunscreening preparation can be prepared with the Formula 10.

Formula 10

		%
Sunscreening agent (Homomenthyl salicylate)		8.0
Mineral oil		12.0
Stearic acid		3.0
Paraffin wax		1.0
Bees wax		2.0
Petroleum Jelly		4.5
Silicone fluid		4.5
Polyethylene glycol monostearate		5.0
Triethanolamine		2.0
Water	to make	100.0

Preservatives	q.s.
Perfume	q.s.

A sunscreen preparation in the form of gel is applied on certain occasions. The amount of the residual film on the skin is negligible with such preparations. A water soluble sunscreening agent will be required for such formulation. Formula 11 is an illustrative example.

Formula 11

		%
Carboxy vinyl polymer (Carbopol)		2.0
Propylene glycol		8.5
Triethanolamine		1.5
Glyceryl p-amino benzoate		3.0
Water	to make	100.0
Preservatives		q.s.
Perfume		q.s.

Method of Preparation

Dissolve the sunscreening agent in a small portion of the water. Dissolve the carbopol in triethanolamine and gradually add major portion of water Dissolve the preservatives in the propylene glycol and add to the mix. Finally add the sunscreening agent dissolved in water. When the gel is uniform, add perfume.

Some persons experience discomfort even with short exposure to the sun. This can be attributed to an allergic reaction caused by some earlier exposure to the sun which might have caused photosensitivity. Such persons should coat lips and skin with a thick layer of suitable sunscreen cream. A suitable product for this purpose can be prepared with Formula 12.

Formula 12

	%
2-Ethyl-2-cyano-3, 3-diphenyl acrylate	10.0
Mineral oil	10.0
Polyethylene glycol monostearate	3.0
Cetyl alcohol	1.5
Titanium dioxide	10.0
Pigments	5.0
Glycerin	5.0

Water	to make	100.0
Preservatives		q.s.

The addition of titanium dioxide in such formulation gives greater degree of protection. Use of 5% titanium is recommended. By adding pigments, it can be tinted and can be used as tinted foundation for protection of sensitive skin. Use of perfume in such formulation should either be avoided or only such perfume should be used which has been tested and has been found non-sensitizing.

The above-mentioned formulae are used to prevent sunburn. Palliative preparations of low viscosity can be used, if there have been sun burns. However, for serious sun burns a physician should be consulted. Formulations of palliative preparations are given below.

Formula 13

		%
Zinc oxide		15.0
Talc		12.0
Bentonite		7.0
Propylene glycol		6.0
Water (distilled)	to make	100.0

Formula 14

		%
Zinc sulfocarbonate		3.0
Propylene glycol		7.0
Camphor water	to make	100.0

Formula 15

		%
Mineral oil		10.0
Lanolin		2.0
Triethanolamine oleate		4.0
Propylene glycol		3.0
Water (distilled)	to make	100.0

In case of mild sunburns, addition of mild antiseptic will minimize the risk of infection.

Enhanced colour of suntan may be considered either as functional (e.g. to prevent damage of the skin by absorption of erythemal radiations) or as cosmetic indicating health and well-being of the user. This effect may be obtained by the use of staining material.

In ancient times, plant materials like walnut were used. A vegetable product can be prepared with cudbear and henna by extracting these with deodorized olive oil.

Based on Egyptian folk medicine, Fahmy and Abu-Shady isolated active principles from the plant, Ammi Majus (Linn.). Folk medicine was practiced in Egypt for restoring pigmentation in vitiliginous skin. These workers demonstrated that extracts from this plant could bring about repigmentation, if taken orally or applied tropically and exposure of the skin to the sun.

Alkoxy porslens and methoxalen have been investigated extensively for treatment of vitiligo. However, this will fall within the definition of drug. As such, these will not be discussed here.

In 1959, a colourless after-shave lotion appeared in the US market which claimed to produce gradual tanning of the skin. Studies indicated that colouring of the skin was confined to the upper cell layers of the skin. The active material used was dihydroxyacetone (DHA). Aqueous solutions of DHA do not spread well and produce relatively little tanning. Increase in pH reduces the reaction and at pH over 8.0, no colour reaction takes place. Fuhrer suggested the following DHA Suntan lotion.

Formula 16

	%
DHA	4.0
Ethanol	28.0
Methyl p-hydroxy benzoate	1.0
Sorbitol Syrup (70%)	3.0
Boric acid powder	1.0
Allantoin	0.3
Perfume	2.0
Distilled water	60.7

Fusaro and Runge described a mixture which stains the skin and then protects it against excessive sunbrun. It consists of a mixture of 3% solution of DHA in 50% isopropanol containing 0.035% of juglone or lawsone. Juglone, chemically is 5-hydroxy-1, 4-naphthaquinone. Juglone is obtained from walnut shells.

Lawsone, chemically is 2-hydroxy-1, 4-naphthaquinone. After repeated applications of this mixture and after washing the skin with soap and water, brownish tan colour is produced on the skin.

Another compound which has been mentioned in the literature for artificial tanning is butane-1, 3, 4-triol-2-one. It is also referred to as erythrulose. A L'oreal patent suggests its use in concentration of 05 to 10% depending on the browning of the skin desired. The patent also suggests that it may be used in combination of an UV absorber, alcohol and surface active agent. Erythrulose can be formulated in the form of a lotion, cream, gel or as an aerosol.

3. MANUFACTURE

As mentioned in section 3 of this chapter, sunscreening agents can be incorporated in a variety of cosmetics e.g., lotions, cream, ointment etc. General methods of manufacture of these cosmetics are applied to manufacture of cosmetics containing sunscreening agents.

4. Skin Types and Choice of Sunscreens

A sunscreen product protects different individuals to the different extent. This depends on individual skin type. US FDA classification system for sunscreens products comprises of five product category designations (PCD) to meet requirements of consumes with different types of skin.

Depending upon skin type and tanning history individuals can be classified into six groups.

- always burns easily and never tans (i.e. sensitive)
- always burns and tans minimally (i.e. sensitive)
- burns moderately and tans gradually to a shade of light brown (i.e. normal)
- burns minimally and always tans well (i.e. normal)
- barely burns and tans profusely – skin becomes dark brown (i.e. insensitive)
- never burns and skin becomes deeply pigmented (i.e. insensitive)

Plough Corporation developed the sun protection factor (SPF) system to define the relative effectiveness of sunscreen agents to protect the skin. Later on US FDA recommended SPF as a means of numerically identifying the efficacy of various sunscreen products and to provide for consumers a guide to the products suitable for particular types of skin. The SPF has been defined as the ratio between the UV exposure required to produce a minimally perceptible erythema on protected skin and the exposure that will produce the same erythema on unprotected skin. The formal definition of SPF by the OTC Panel of the US FDA was

$$\text{SPF Value} = \frac{\text{WMED (PS)}}{\text{MED (US)}}$$

where,

MED (PS) = minimum erythemal dose for protected skin after the application of 2 mg/cm or 2 μl/cm^2 of the final formulation of the sunscreen product.

MED (US) = minimum erythemal dose for unprotected skin, i.e. skin to which no sunscreen product has been applied.

The larger the SPF, the greater the sun protection. The OTC Panel also proposed that all sunscreen products should be rated for the consumer depending on the degree of protection they can provide (the rating numbers to range from (2-8). A product having a rating of 8 would thus provide the maximum protection to individuals who always burn easily and never tan (i.e. sensitive). On the other hand a product having a rating of 2 would be suitable for those individuals who rarely burn but tan profusely (i.e. in sensitive). For skin types mentioned above, sunscreening products with the following SPF are recommended:

Skin Type	SPF
I	8 or more
II	6-7
III	4-5
IV	2-3
V	2
VI	Non indicated

As mentioned above, a classification system for sunscreening products comprises of 5 product category designations (PCD). These are:

PCD 1 – Minimal sun Protection Product	– Such product provides an SPF value of 2-4. It provides least protection but permits sun tanning.
PCD 2 – Moderate sun Protection Product	– Such product provides an SPF value of 4-6. It provides moderate protection from sun-burning but permits some tanning.
PCD 3 – Extra sun Protection Product	– Such product provides an SPF value of 6-8. If provides extra protection from sun-burning but permits some tanning.
PCD 4 – Maximal sun Protection Product	– Such product provides an SPF value of 8-15. It provides maximal protection from sun burn and permits little or no sun tanning.
PCD 5 – Ultra sun Protection Product	– Such product provides an SPF value of 15 or more. It provides greater protection from sun burn and permits no sun tanning.

Conditions like elevated heat and humidity, sweating, swimming may lower SPF value. Practically a person who gets red in the sun after 20 min. would be able to stay in the sun for 120 min., if he applies a sunscreen product of SPF6. Similarly with a product of SPF value of 8 an individual would be able to stay in the sun for 8 times the time he can withstand the sun without sunscreening product. However when the skin becomes accustomed to the sun that is when the skin has developed pigmentation, self protection period is longer such an individual may require product of lower PCD. Sensitive individuals should use products in ultra protection category i.e. products having SPF value of 15 or more.

14

Skin Bleach Creams

1. GENERAL

In imparting colour to the skin, the most important role is played by pigments, carotenes and melanins. Melanins are responsible for racial colour difference. Pigment, melanin is synthesized in dendritic cells (melanocytes) normally present in epidermal basal layer. Melanin binding with protein matrix form melanosomes. Melanocytes transfer their melanosomes to surrounding keratinocytes. Presumably, melanocytes after losing melanosomes migrate upwards through epidermis. Product of pigment, melanin, is stimulated by both ultraviolet light and a hormone, melanocyte stimulatory hormone (MSH). This hormone is secreted by anterior pituitary gland. Black skin is produced by increased melanocytes activity (i.e. formation of melanosomes and their transfer).

The melanins are quinonoid polymers and can be divided into two main groups – one, phaeomelanins; two, eumelanins. Phaeomelanins are yellowish and reddish-brown pigments containing sulphur. Eumelanins are black or brown insoluble pigments. Metabolic pathways of the production of melanin have been described by Riley and are outside the scope of this book. This may be understood that these pigments are derived from the polymerization of tyrosine oxidation products.

Skin bleach effect could be achieved, if the processes involved in production and transfer of pigment are interfered. Bleehen has suggested modes of action of compounds which can interfere with these processes. The compounds may:

- selectively destroy the melanocytes;
- inhibit the formation of melanosomes and alter their structure;
- inhibit the bio-synthesis of tyrosinase;
- inhibit the formation of melanin;
- interfere with the transfer of melanosomes;
- have a chemical effect on melanin or enhance the degradation of melanosomes in keratinocytes.

The other method for skin bleaching effect could be decolourization of melanin already present.

1.1 Skin Bleaching Agents

Most commonly used skin bleaching agents are:

(i) *Mercury compounds*—Mercury compounds such as mercury chloride, red mercuric oxide and ammoniated mercury have been used for their skin bleaching effect. Out of these ammoniated mercury was extensively used. But now, the mercury compounds are prohibited for use in cosmetics.

(ii) *Hydroquinones*—Hydroquinone is the most favourite material which is currently in use. A concentration of 1.5-2.0% produces temporary lightening of the skin. A concentration of 5% can produce redness and burning. The skin lightening effect of hydroquinone can be reversed by exposure to sunlight. The effect is also reversed if the cosmetic containing hydroquinone is discontinued.

Monobenzyl ether of hydroquinone interferes with formation of pigment and also causes bleaching of the skin. But a large number of people are sensitive to it.

It is effective in both low concentrations as well as high concentrations. The reported concentrations vary from less than 1% to 33%. Prolonged used of monobenzyl ether of hydroquinone leads to leucoderma. In view of this, use of this material has been banned in some countries.

Monomethyl and monoethyl ether or hydroquinones are also potent depigmenting agents but have disadvantages similar to that of monobenzyl ether of hydroquinone and therefore did not become popular.

(iii) *Catechol and its derivatives*—Some catechols exhibited skin lightening effect but these were less effective than hydroquinone. Out of these 4-isopropyl catechol is the most potent depigmenting agent. However, concentrations of 3% or more caused irritation and sensitizing reactions.

(iv) *Ascorbic Acid and its Derivatives*—Ascorbic acid, though very safe, do not seem to be very effective as depigmenting agent. Ascorbic acid, however, has been used in skin bleaching cream containing hydroquinone as stabilizer (anti-oxidant). Use of ascorbyl oleate has been reported in concentration of 3% and 5% in creams for bleaching freckles in human skin.

(v) *Oxidizing Agents*—Hydrogen peroxide has been used in skin bleach creams. Zinc peroxide has been used in anhydrous ointments as bleaching agents but its properties have not been proved.

(vi) *Opaque covering Agents*—Make-up products containing white or pale pigments such as titanium dioxide, zinc oxide, talc, kaolin, bismuth pigments can achieve remarkable temporary change in the colour of skin and hence these materials have been mentioned here.

2. FORMULATION

From the foregoing account it may be seen that only hydroquinone and pigments like titanium dioxide, zinc oxide, talc etc. are safe and effective skin bleaching agents. A formulation based on opaque covering agents (pigments) is given below:

Formula 1

		%
Stearic acid		2.0
Lanolin alcohols		5.0
Glcyeryl monostearate		5.0
Oleyl alcohol		2.0
Triethanolamine		0.5
Propylene glycol		5.0
Titanium dioxide		7.0
Pigments		5.0
Water	to make	100.0
Preservatives and perfume		q.s.

Hydrogen peroxide emulsions are used for bleaching action. Emulsions containing hydrogen peroxide are acidic. A surfactant which is acid stable should be used as emulsifier in hydrogen peroxide bleach cream. Use of hydrogen peroxide has been illustrated in formula 2.

Formula 2

		%
Stearyl alcohol		6.0
Cetyl alcohol		4.0
Acid stabilized glyceryl monostearate		3.0
Hydrogen peroxide (35%)		15.0
Water	to make	100.0
Phosphoric acid (10%) (to adjust PH 3.5 to 4.0)		q.s.

Hydrogen peroxide should be added after cooling the cream to 45°C and then PH should be adjusted to 3.5 to 4.0 with phosphoric acid sodium phosphate.

Since the cream will not liberate hydrogen peroxide at pH 3.5 to 4.0, usually an activator is provided with such creams. Most commonly used activator is ammonium bicarbonate. It reacts with the phosphoric acid and causes increase in pH thereby releases hydrogen peroxide. Hydrogen peroxide being strong oxidizing agent causes bleaching. It is advisable to use phosphoric acid-phosphate buffer in creams if glass containers are used as alkalinity of glass can affect stability of hydrogen peroxide in creams.

A hydrogen peroxide lotion can be prepared in a mixture of alcohol and propylene glycol and water (See Formula 3).

Formula 3

		%
Hydrogen peroxide solution		8.0
EDTA		0.5
Hydrogen quinoline		0.1
Ethanol		3.0
Propylene glycol		5.0
Water	to make	100.0
Preservatives		q.s.

A cream containing benzoyl peroxide has bleaching effect as well as bactericidal properties. This cream is used to improve the condition of the skin and to treat minor skin blemishes. This is also used when pustules are present. Formula 4 illustrates the use of benzoyl peroxide.

Formula 4

		%
Mineral oil		5.0
Petroleum jelly		5.0
Polyethylene glycol monostearate		6.0
Benzoyl peroxide		2.5
Potassium hydroxyquinoline sulphate		0.5
Glycerin		3.0
Water	to make	100.0

Method of preparation

Heat the mineral oil, petroleum jelly and PEG monostearate to 75°C. Heat the water also to 75°C. Add the hot water to oily phase with stirring. Continue stirring until cool. Add mixture of benzoyl peroxide, glycerine and potassium hydroxyquinoline sulphate and mix well.

This cream may produce a slight burning effect on severely scarred tissue. However, this should not be taken as alarming. Burning sensation disappears rapidly after the initial application.

Hydroquinone is white crystalline material having melting point, 170-171°C. It is soluble in water in the ratio of 1:14 but freely soluble in alcohol and ether. Its solutions become brown on exposure to air. Oxidation is much faster in alkaline solutions. Therefore, it is necessary to stabilize. It may be stabilized with anti-oxidants like ascorbic acid and potassium metabisulphite. Formula 5 is a typical example.

Formula 5

	%
Cetyl alcohol	10.0
Mineral oil	3.5
Sodium lauryl sulphate	1.5
Hydroquinone	2.0
Potassium metabisulphite	0.1
Glycerin	6.0
Ascorbic acid	0.5

Water	to make	100.0
Perfume and preservatives		q.s.

Formula 6 is another formula for skin bleach cream.

Formula 6

		%
Glyceryl monostearate		14.5
Glyceryl monostearate (self emulsifying)		6.5
Silicone fluid		1.5
Propylene glycol		5.0
Hydroquinone		1.5
Sod. bisulphite		0.05
Water	to make	100.0
Perfume and preservatives		q.s.

Oxidation of hydroquinone is affected by the pH of the product, heavy metals and oxygen. pH of aqueous solution of hydroquinone is 4.5. Oxidation increases with increases in pH. pH of hydroquinone preparations should be between 3.0 and 5.5. Heavy metals, if present, catalyze oxidation process. Oxygen available from entrapped air during manufacturing process will add to the oxidation process.

Hydroquinone solutions darken on exposure to light. Therefore, manufacture of hydroquinone containing creams should be carried out under subdued light.

Every ingredient of hydroquinone preparation should be tested for compatibility with hydroquinone. This may be conducted in the following manner:

* Prepare an aqueous solution of same concentration as that of formulation.
* Subdivide so prepared hydroquinone solution into the number of aliquotes equal to the number of ingredients to be used plus one.
* Add one ingredient in one aliquote. One aliquote will remain extra. Do not add anything to this. Use this as control.
* Expose all the aliquotes (in tightly sealed bottle) to 60°C for 24 hours.

* Compare the darkening in each bottle with the control.

Darkening more than present in control indicates decomposition of hydroquinone due to presence by the ingredient.

3. MANUFACTURE

Skin lightening creams using covering agents are made using a vanishing type cream base. These creams are manufactured according to the general method of manufacture of creams.

Creams containing hydrogen peroxide are generally manufactured by adding oily phase to aqueous phase with stirring, cooling the cream to 45°C and then adding hydrogen peroxide with slow stirring. After addition to hydrogen peroxide pH of the cream is adjusted to 3.5-4.0 with the help of phosphoric acid. A high grade stainless steel equipment should be used when manufacturing hydrogen peroxide cream.

Choice of equipment in the manufacture of hydroquinone creams is also important. Only stainless or glass lined vessels should be used in the manufacture of hydroquinone creams. If possible, the equipment used for hydroquinone cream should not be used for manufacture of other products. Use of alkaline soaps for cleaning the equipment should be discouraged. The mixing equipment preferably should have paddle-type stirrer and should have a cover. Though not mandatory, bubbling of carbon dioxide gas through the batch would be advantageous. The mixing tank should be jacketed also so that the temperature can be controlled.

Some persons may be sensitive to hydroquinone, precautions must be taken in handling hydroquinone. Bright light can darken hydroquinone. Therefore, creams containing hydroquinone should be manufactured under subdued light.

15

Astringents and Skin Tonics

1. GENERAL

Astringents exhibit various effects like erection of hair, sensation of tightening of the skin, temporary reduction of pore size, antiperspirancy, rapid coagulation of blood from fresh wound etc. There are some subjective effects such as refreshing sensation, invigorating feeling which are associated with astringents. But every astringent may not exhibit all these effects. Because of the above mentioned effects, a number of cosmetics products are formulated based on astringents and these products can be grouped in the following categories:

- antiperspirants;
- astringent lotions
- pre-shave and after-shave lotions,
- skin tonics,
- toners,
- colognes;
- astringent emulsions
- antiperspirant creams
- astringent creams and lotions;
- astringent gels.

Antiperspirants, pre-shave and after-shave lotions and colognes will be discussed in other chapters. In this chapter, only skin toners and skin tonics will be discussed.

1.1 Astringent Materials

With a few exceptions, chemically, the astringents can be divided into three categories:

- metal salts of inorganic and organic acids;
- low molecular weight organic acids;
- low molecular weight alcohols.

1.1.1 Metal salts of inorganic/organic acids

Although many metallic ions such as iron, chromium, zinc, lead, mercury, tin are known for their astringent properties, but all of them are not suitable for use in cosmetics because of their toxicity or adverse effects like irritation or discolouration. The metals, salts of which can be used in cosmetics, are zinc, aluminium and zirconium. In metallic salts astringents, the effect is not entirely due to cations, anions also play a part. Further, the solubility of metallic salts will also depend on anions. The list of possible anions is very large. Some important anions are:

- acetate,
- chloride,
- sulphate,
- chlorohydroxide,
- phenosulphonate,
- lactate,
- glycolate,
- formate,
- gluconate,
- alums.

Acetates, usually are not used because of their disagreeable odour.

1.1.2 Organic acids

Low molecular weight organic acids show astringent properties. Of these, formic acid is irritant and is therefore not used in cosmetics. Acetic acid can cause skin damage, as such, it is also not used. The acids which are most commonly used are citric acid and lactic acid.

1.1.3 Alcohols

Low molecular weight alcohols also have astringent properties. Most commonly used alcohol of this class is ethyl alcohol. Sometimes, isopropyl alcohol is also used. Isopropyl alcohol has very pungent smell. Aqueous solutions of alcohols upto a concentration of 60% are used.

2. FORMULATION

2.1 Skin Toners

Skin toners are aqueous or aqueous-alcoholic lotions and these have become part of the facial skin treatment. Since these can remove oiliness, they are recommended for use after cleaning and before application of moisturizing cream. Mild toners can be formulated by dissolving metallic salts in water and fragrant waters. Formulae 1 to 3 are examples of such toners.

Formula 1

		%
Potassium alum.		2.0
Zinc Sulphate		0.5
Glycerin		5.0
Rose Water		50.0
Water	to make	100.0
Perfume and preservatives		q.s.

Formula 2

		%
Zinc Sulphate		1.0
Zinc Phenol Sulphonate		1.5
Rose Water		55.0
Water	to make	100.0
Perfume and preservatives		q.s.

Formula 3

		%
Potassium alum.		4.0
Glycerin		5.0
Rose Water		30.0
Orange flower water		30.0
Water	to make	100.0
Perfume and preservatives		q.s.

Ethyl alcohol can be used upto 60%. Usually denatured spirit is used. Toners with higher alcoholic strengths are used for oily skin while toners with lower alcoholic strengths are used for dry skin. Formulae 4 and 5 are examples of such toners.

		Formula 4	Formula 5
		per cent	per cent
Aluminium chlorohydrate (50% solution)		20.0	10.0
Glycerin		7.0	–
Propylene glycol		–	3.0
Denatured spirit		20.0	50.0
Borax		2.0	1.0
Water	to make	100.0	100.0
Perfume and preservatives		q.s.	q.s.

2.2 Skin Tonics

Skin tonics contain some auxiliary additives like menthol, camphor, allantoin etc. in addition to the ingredients of skin toners. Allantoin is considered to have regenerative, healing, softening, soothing and keratolytic properties. Allantoin combination compounds, chlorohydroxy aluminium allantoinate and dihydroxy aluminium allantoinate have mild astringent properties also. Therefore, these compounds will be useful in the formulation of skin tonics. The formulation of skin tonics may also contain thickening agents like hydroxypropyl methyl cellulose. Formula 6 is an example of body lotion of skin tonic type.

Formula 6

		%
Aluminium chlorhydroxy allantoinate		0.2
Propylene glycol		4.0
Menthol		0.05
Aluminium chlorhydrate (50%)		6.0
Hydroxy propyl methyl cellulose (3%)		45.0
Titanium dioxide		1.0
Alcohol	to make	100.0
Perfume, colour and preservatives		q.s.

Astringent creams can be prepared by incorporating astringents into aqueous phase. However, it should be ensured that emulsifying agent is compatible with astringent. Formulae 7 and 8 are examples of astringent creams.

Formula 7

		%
Sodium magnesium silicate		2.0
Isopropyl myristate		3.0
Triethanolamine		0.7
Stearic acid		5.0
Cetyl alcohol		0.5
Triclosan		0.1
Alcohol		20.0
Water	to make	100.0
Colour and perfume		q.s.

Formula 8

		%
Stearic acid		13.0
Mineral oil		1.0
Beeswax		3.0
Sorbitan stearate		4.0
Polysorbate 60		5.0
Aluminium chlorhydrate (50% solution)		30.0
Water	to make	100.0
Colour, perfume and preservatives		q.s.

An astringent-cream with witch-hazel be prepared with Formula 9.

Formula 9

		%
Cetyl alcohol		2.5
Propylene glycol stearate		12.5
Sorbitol		5.0
Isopropyl myristate		1.5
Witch-hazel extract		10.0
Water	to make	100.0
Preservatives		q.s.
Perfume		q.s.

Astringent sticks can be prepared with alcohol and sodium stearate. A basic formula for alcohol sodium stearate soap gel stick is given below (see Formula 10).

Formula 10

		%
Sodium stearate		6.0
Sorbitol		2.5
Aqueous solution of alcohol	to make	100.0
Colour and perfume		q.s.

In this formulation, water soluble astringent can be added. Antiperspirant is also added usually. In the above mentioned formulation, sodium aluminum chlorhydroxy lactate can be incorporated in concentration of about 10%.

The gel may be formed by preparing sodium stearate *in situ* with the help of stearic acid and sodium hydroxide by reflux.

Styptic sticks can be prepared from traditional alcohol soap gel. But those sticks have tendency to dry out quickly. Therefore, these are usually prepared from potassium alum crystal by melting and then incorporating a filler like talc. A humectant is also incorporated in these sticks. Finally the molten mass is poured into previously heated moulds and allowed to solidify. Sticks are taken out and are polished with moist cloth.

3. MANUFACTURE

Skin toners are solutions of soluble salts like Potassium alum., zinc sulphate, zinc phenol sulphonate and are prepared in mixing tank having an agitator. However, when alcohol (denatured spirit) is used, precautions needed for use of alcohol should be observed.

Astringent creams are manufactured in the same way as other creams. Astringent should be dissolved in aqueous phase. As mentioned earlier compatibility of astringent and emulsifier should be ascertained before taking production of commercial batch.

16

Antiperspirants and Deodorants

1. GENERAL

Perspiration is a phenomenon which the body have for regulation of body temperature and for protection of the skin from dryness. Perspiration also eliminates lactic acid which is formed during muscular exercise. Perspiration takes place because of sweat glands. Sweat glands are of two types; one, eccrine glands; two, apocrine glands. The eccrine glands occur over almost all body surface. These glands originate in deeper layers of dermis and open on skin surface through a thin duct. The other sweat glands, apocrine glands are associated with sexual development and occur after puberty. These glands are found in areas like axillar, pelvic region, around the nipples. The secretion by eccrine glands is highly dilute aqueous solution and the secretion by apocrine glands is oily sticky material. Although the axilla is an area where apocrine glands occur, but profuse flow of sweat in this area is the result of intense activity of eccrine glands. A hyperhydrotic individual can sweat more than 12 gm in each armpit per hour.

Sweats from both eccrine and apocrine glands are odourless when discharged. Later, sweat from apocrine glands which contains several fatty substances like lower fatty acids, steroids, lactones etc. is decomposed by resident bacteria producing odorous substances. Eccrine sweat helps in growth of bacteria by providing required moisture.

Obvious ways to control or reduce odour could be:

- reduction in apocrine sweating;
- removal of secretions of both types of sweat glands as quickly as possible;
- checking bacterial growth;
- absorption of body odours.

Out of the above mentioned ways, the second is not practicable way. Therefore, while developing deodorants other options are made use of.

1.1 Antiperspirant Ingredients

As mentioned in chapter 10, many metallic salts have astringent properties, but because of toxicity and other adverse reactions salts of aluminium and zirconium are used as astringent. Commonly used aluminium and zirconium salts are:

- Aluminium chlorhydrate;
- Aluminium chloride;
- Aluminium sulphate;
- Aluminium zirconium chlorhydrates.

In 1955, sodium zirconyl lactate was used in deodourant stick containing an alcoholic soap gel. But in 1956, cases of granulomatous eruptions in the axillae of users of the products containing sodium zirconyl lactate were reported. In 1977, USFDA banned zirconium based aerosol antiperspirants. However, zirconium containing non aerosol products were not banned.

Stiallian, in 1916, observed that a 25% solution of aluminium chloride hexahydrate in distilled water dabbed on the armpit every second or third day would reduce excessive sweating. This was the beginning of modern story of topical antiperspirants.

Aluminium chloride is not toxic and is not allergenic. But it is irritating to the skin of some individuals and its high acidity is damaging to clothing. Because of these disadvantages, its use was discontinued in 1940 when a less acidic salt of aluminum, aluminum chlorhydroxide was discovered. The latter reduced irritation to the skin markedly and also lessened damage to clothing. However, it had reduced antiperspirant effect.

Since the odour is produced by the bacterial action on sweat, the compounds which inhibit the growth of bacteria, are likely to exhibit deodorant properties. Antibacterials which are used in cosmetic/toiletrics include:

- Benzethonium chloride;
- Chlorhexidine acetate;
- Hexane acetate;
- Triclosan.

Ethyl alcohol which is used as vehicle in deodorant products is also antibacterial agent.

As stated earlier axillary odour is produced mainly by the action of bacteria on nutrients present in apocrine secretion. Any substance which will inhibit the growth of bacteria will exhibit deodorant properties.

Before World War II cresols were popular as bacteriostatic agents. But their objectionable odour limited their use. Use of sodium bicarbonate (baking soda) as deodourant has been known for many years. Chemically it can act either as a mild alkali or mild acid. Under arm odours are mainly due to volatile substances. It can absorb these forming stable odorless salts. In 1941, researchers at Givaudan Corporation discovered that a halogenated bisphenol, hexachlorophene exhibited bacteriostatic properties when incorporated in soap. But in 1972 US FDA banned its use in cosmetics following reports of brain lesions in test animals. In India also, use of hexachlorophene is banned except in toilet soaps. Even in toilet soaps, its concentration should not be more than 1%. Other antibacterials which are used in deodorant soaps include trichlorocarbanilide (TCC), Triclosan, cloflucarbon.

Antibacterial properties of essential oils have been known for a long time. However essential oils can vary considerably in chemical structure. Thus they lack uniformity in antibacterial activity. Therefore, these can not be used alone, but can be used in combination with other antimicrobial agents.

2. FORMULATION

2.1 Antiperspirants

Several materials which have astringent properties have been used as antiperspirants. Of them most commonly used are salts of aluminium and zinc. Earlier formulations contained aluminium chloride or sulphate in solution. Since solutions of these salts had low pH (2.0 to 3.0), these were irritating to skin and could damage fabric, these were replaced by aluminium chlorhydrate. In solutions, aluminium chlorhydrate has pH of 4.0-4.5 which is close to the pH value of skin surface. However, it can damage the fabric, if not washed away as heat during ironing the fabric can hydrolyze it. The risk of damage to fabric can be reduced by including urea or borax in the formulations. Aluminium chlorhydrate in powder form is difficult to handle unless solutions are made by adding small amounts of powder to water and mixing well after each addition. It is also available as 50% aqueous solution. It is miscible with ethyl alcohol, propylene glycol and glycerin. Antiperspirants can be formulated in the form of liquid, cream, lotion, stick and powder.

(i) Liquid Antiperspirants

A simple type of antiperspirant can be formulated as represented by Formula 1.

Formula 1

		%
Aluminium chlorhydrate (50% solution)		25.0
Glycerin		5.0
Alcohol		45.0
Borax		20
Water	to make	100.0
Perfume		q.s.

Liquid antiperspirants, generally, are applied as sprays. These are aqueous or hydro-alcoholic solutions of astringent salts with humectants. A small amount of tween 40 will disperse perfume. Alcohol present tends to prevent hydrolysis of astringent in solution and also helps in evaporation. The above mentioned formulation can be used for spray.

Quaternary ammonium salts such as cetyl pyridinium chloride, cetyl trimethyl ammonium bromide or chlorhexidine can also be used as deodorants in antiperspirants. See formulae 2 and 3.

Formula 2

		%
Aluminium chlorhydrate (50% solution)		35.0
Cetyl pyridinium chloride		0.5
Propylene glycol		5.0
Alcohol		40.0
Water	to make	100.0
Perfume		q.s.

Formula 3

		%
Aluminium chlorhydrate (50% solution)		30.0
Propylene glycol		4.0
Glycerine		3.0
Chlorhexidine acetate		0.5
Alcohol		50.0
Water	to make	100.0
Perfume		q.s.

Since antiperspirants are acidic in reaction, such perfumes should be selected which are acid stable. Preparation should be tested at room temperature and at slightly elevated temperature (40-45°C) to find out stability of perfume.

(ii) Cream Antiperspirants

Antiperspirant creams which found acceptance with the users were of vanishing cream type. Due to acidic nature of antiperspirants, usual type of vanishing cream formulated with soap emulsions do not give satisfactory results. Acid stable emulsifier, compatible with antiperspirant should be used in the formulations of cream antiperspirants. Acid stabilized glyceryl monostearate can be used as emulsifier in such creams with or without other emulsifier(s). Anionic emulsifiers which can be used in such creams are: sodium lauryl sulphate, sodium cetyl sulphate. Non-ionics such as hexitol esters of fatty acids (spans) and their polyoxyethylene derivatives (Tween) can also be used. Usually glycerol and/or glycol esters of fatty acids are used as fatty phase.

Other fatty materials like cetyl alcohol, white petroleum jelly or mineral oil can also be added in small amounts. If fabric damage inhibitor is not included in formulation, it can damage fabric. Therefore, a fabric damage inhibitor is often used in such creams. Urea can be used in concentration of 5-10% in case of aluminium salts. Humectants like glycerin, propylene glycol, sorbitol are used in concentration of 3-10%. Vanishing creams in which propylene glycol is used, generally show more crustation on long exposure to air than those in which sorbitol or glycerin is used.

Titanium dioxide can be used as whitener or opacifier. Titanium dioxide in concentration more than 1% can rub off on clothing can cause staining.

Perfume to be used in such cream should be acid stable and should also be compatible with emulsion.

Basic formulae which can be used for development of astringent creams are given below.

Formula 4

		%
Glyceryl monostearate (acid stabilized)		15.0
Spermaceti		5.0
Sodium lauryl sulphate		1.5
Propylene glycol		6.0
Aluminium sulphate		7.5
Urea		5.0
Titanium dioxide		0.5
Water	to make	100.0
Perfume and preservatives		q.s.

Formula 5

		%
Glycryl monostearate (acid stabilized)		15.0
Mineral oil		3.0
Cetyl alcohol		2.0
Glycerin		5.0
Aluminium chlorhydrate (50% solution)		35.0
Titanium dioxide		0.5
Water	to make	100.0
Perfume and preservatives		q.s

Formula VI illustrates the use of mixture of zirconium and aluminium salt. In this formula glycine has been used as a buffer for fabric protection. Glycine is more stable than urea under normal storage conditions.

Formula 6

		%
Zirconyl hydroxy chloride		5.5
Aluminium chlorhydroxide		6.5
Glycine		2.0
Glyceryl monostearate (acid stable)		12.0
Spermaceti		3.0
Mineral oil		3.0
Polyoxyethylene 50 stearate		4.0
Glycerin		5.0
Titanium dioxide		0.3
Water	to make	100.0

(iii) Lotion antiperspirants

Antiperspirants in lotion form have not been very popular. Manufacture of lotions, basically, is the same as that used for cream. Incorporation of astringent salts in lotions requires careful control. Lotions should be tested for stability. Formula 7 is basic formula for development of antiperspirant lotion.

Formula 7

		%
Glyceryl monostearate (acid stable)		15.0
Mineral oil		5.0
Petroleum jelly		2.5
Spermaceti		5.0
Glycerin		6.0
Aluminium chlorhydrate (50% solution)		40.0
Water	to make	100.0
Perfume and preservatives		q.s.

(iv) Antiperspirant Sti

Antiperspirant sticks usually consist of wax like matrix which acts as carrier for aluminium chlorhydrate and volatile silicone. Stearyl alcohol is preferred over stearic acid because of its lower melting point. Formulae 8 and 9 are typical formula of antiperspirant sticks.

Formula	**8**	**9**
	per cent	per cent
Aluminium chlorhydrate (powder)	18.0	20.0
Volatile silicone	45.0	45.0
Stearyl alcohol	25.0	25.0
Polyethylene glycol distearate (6000)	5.0	5.0
*Carbowax PEG 1540	4.0	–
*Carbowax PEG 1000	–	3.0

Sodium aluminium chlorhydroxy lactate complex and sodium aluminium lactate have been found to be useful as antiperspirants and can be used in sticks. Sodium aluminium chlorhydroxy lactate is compatible with components of alcohol gel type of stick. See Formula 10.

Formula 10

Sodium aluminium chlorhydroxy lactate complex (10% solution)	50g
Ethyl alcohol	12cc
Propylene glycol	3g
Sodium stearate	6g
Perfume	q.s.

The stick may be made by dissolving sodium stearate and other ingredients in alcohol under a reflux or by forming soap with stearic acid and sodium hydroxide. Sodium aluminium lactate which is available as 40% solution can also be used in alcohol-soap sticks.

(v) Anti-perspirant Powders

Antiperspirant powders are the least effective of the antiperspirants. These can be prepared by mixing antiperspirant salt with talcum powder. Formula 11 is an example of antiperspirant powder.

Formula 11

	%
Buffered aluminium sulphate	8.0
Sodium aluminium lactate	8.0

Talcum powder to make	100.0
Perfume	q.s.

Finely divided aluminium chlorhydroxide can also be used and will give a reasonably satisfactory result when used on body or feet. An antiseptic deodorant is usually included in powder formulations. The powders can also be pressed into powder cakes using binders.

2.2 Deodorants

As mentioned earlier, axially odour is produced, to a large extent, by bacterial action on apocrine secretion. Therefore, theoretically any compound which has antibacterial action can be used as deodorant. Antibacterial agents which have been used in cosmetics and toiletries include:

- zinc compounds e.g., zinc phenosulphonate, zinc oxide, zinc peroxide.
- organic acids e.g., benzoic acid, salicylic acid.
- quaternary ammonium compounds (e.g., cetrimide, benzethonium chloride),
- cationic compounds (e.g., chlorhexidine acetate),
- bisphenols (e.g. hexachlorophene),
- phenols (e.g. parachlorometaxylenol, dichloro-metaxylenol).

Sodium bicarbonate has also been used as deodorant. Sodium bicarbonate is an acid salt and can act either as mild acid or alkali. Axillary odours are largely caused by acid compounds. These compounds are absorbed by sodium bicarbonate and stable odourless salts are formed.

Deodorants can be incorporated in different cosmetic formulations like lotions, creams, powders, sticks and soaps. Formulations of these will be discussed briefly.

(i) Deodorant Liquids

Many of the quaternary ammonium compounds have been found nontoxic and sufficiently non-irritating. Such compounds can be used in deodorant liquids. Some such compounds are:

- hyamines [di-isobutyl phenoxy (or cresoxy) ethyl diemthyl benzyl-ammonium chloride],

– trimethyl long chain alkyl ammonium bromide (e.g. cetab),
– alkyl dimethyl benzyl ammonium chloride (e.g. Benzalkonium chloride).

Liquid deodorants may be prepared by dissolving quaternaries in water or 50% denatured spirit. Humectant and perfume may also be added if required.

The water soluble derivatives of chlorophyl and chlorophyllins (e.g., potassium, copper chlorophyllin, sodium, magnesium chlorophyllin) also have deodorant properties. Water soluble chlorophyllins can be used in concentration of 0.05%.

Formula 12 is a simple deodorant liquid. Liquid deodorants are generally available as sprays.

Formula 12

		%
Chlorhexidine diacetate		0.5
Propylene glycol		2.0
Denatured spirit (50%)	to make	100.0
Perfume		q.s.

(ii) Deodorant Creams

A potassium stearate-stearic acid vanishing cream base can be used for such creams. If chlorinated phenols are used in this type of creams, non-ionic emulsifiers should be avoided as these inhibit bacteriostatic properties of these products.

Formula 13 can be used to develop a deodorant cream.

Formula 13

		%
Glyceryl monostearate		10.0
Stearic acid		5.0
Cetyl alcohol		3.0
Isopropyl myristate		2.0
Potassium hydroxide		0.8
Propylene glycol		10.0
Triclosan		0.2
Water	to make	100.0
Perfume and preservatives		q.s.

Cream deodorants are not popular as more convenient forms of deodorants are available.

(iii) Deodorant Sticks

Popular type of deodorant sticks can be prepared with sodium stearate, humectant, alcohol and perfume. This type of formulations form gel. These may be prepared by dissolving soap in warm alcohol or by saponification of alcoholic solution of stearic acid with sodium hydroxide adding into it humectant, deodorant and perfume and then finally pouring the solution in moulds to obtain sticks of soap gels. Formula 14 is a typical formula of deodorant stick.

Formula 14

		%
Sodium stearate		8.0
Sorbitol (solution)		5.0
Isopropyl myristate		3.0
Triclosan		0.2
Alcohol	to make	100.0
Perfume		q.s.

Chlorhexidine diacetate or bithional are other effective non-irritant bactericide which can be used in stearate soaps. If a bright, clear transparent product is desired, high quality grade sodium stearate will be required. The proportion of stearate varies from 5 to 8.5. However, when lower proportion is used, cetyl alcohol is usually incorporated to give rigidity to the stick, otherwise a soft stick will be formed. Formula 15 is an example of such a formulation.

Formula 15

		%
Sodium stearate		7.0
Cetyl alcohol		1.5
Propylene glycol		6.0
Chlorhexidine diacetate		0.5
Alcohol		82.0
Water	to make	100.0
Perfume		q.s.

Method of Preparation

Put all the materials together and heat in an equipment having reflux condenser. Heat till all the soap is dissolved. Allow to cool the mixture. When temperature drops to about 60°C, add perfume and mix. Transfer the solution to moulds.

A non-alcoholic product suitable for hot climates can be prepared as per Formula 16.

Formula 16

		%
Sodium stearate		10.0
Urea		0.25
Propylene glycol		50.0
Chlorhexidine diacetate		0.5
Benzyl alcohol		5.0
Water	to make	100.0
Perfume		q.s.

Method of Preparation

Dissolve urea in water and chlorhexidine diacetate in propylene glycol and mix them together. Add sodium stearate and warm gently to affect solution. Add benzyl alcohol and mix well. Allow to cool, add perfume while cooling and mix. Transfer solution to moulds.

Since aluminium chlorhydrate is incompatible with sodium stearate and other soaps, an antiperspirant and deodorant stick can be prepared using sodium aluminium chlorhydroxy lactate. Sodium aluminium chlorhydroxy lactate is prepared by complex aluminium chlorhydrate with sodium lactate. Sodium aluminium chlorhydroxy lactate is available as 40% aqueous solution. Formula 17 is example of such a formulation.

Formula 17

	%
Sodium aluminium chlorhydroxy lactate (40% aqueous solution)	40.0
Propylene glycol	5.0
Sodium stearate	12.0
Chlorhexidine diacetate	0.5

isopropyl myristate		2.0
Alcohol	to make	100.0
Perfume		q.s.

Method of Preparation

Heat the sodium stearate with alcohol in an equipment having reflux condenser till it dissolves. Dissolve chlorhexidine diacetate in propylene glycol and add to alcoholic solution of soap. Add isopropyl myrate, mix well and allow to cool. Add isopropyl myrate, mix well and allow to cool. Add perfume while cooling. Mix well and transfer to moulds.

(iv) Deodorant Powder

Dispersion of deodorant in powder is of utmost importance in powder deodorants. This can be achieved by mixing and grinding. Dry ingredients should be mixed in suitable blender. The active ingredient should be dissolved in suitable solvent and should be distributed through powder mix. The perfume may be blended with talc first and then may be incorporated into the powder. Compatibility of perfumes may be studied before selecting a perfume for deodorant powders. Formula 18 is an illustrative formula of powder deodorant.

Formula 18

	%
Talc	67.0
Light precipitated chalk	12.0
Boric acid	5.0
Zinc oxide	5.0
Zinc phenol sulphonate	1.0
Perfume	q.s.

A much more uniform powder can be obtained by passing the powder through a micropulverizer after preliminary mixing.

In a patent, use of cation exchange resin (carboxylic type), has been suggested.

Deodorant foot powders may contain alum which acts as astringent. These powders generally contain a fungicidal agent. Propionic acid and its salts and undecylenic acid and its salts have been found useful in such powders.

(v) Deodorant soaps

Market of toilet soaps is an important market in all countries. Earlier, hexachlorophene was frequently used in deodorants including soaps. But its use was banned in USA in 1972 in all non-prescription products. In India, use of hexachlorophene is banned in all cosmetics except in toilet soaps. Even in the toilet soaps, concentration has been restricted to 1% W/W.

The most frequently used anti-microbial in soaps include trichlorocarbanilide (TCC), cloflucarban (CF3) and triclosan. In the presence of soap, all anti-microbials except triclosen are active against Gram positive organisms. Triclosan is active against both Gram positive and Gram negative organisms.

3. MANUFACTURE

Antiperspirant lotions and creams are manufactured according to general method of manufacturing of creams and lotions. However, incorporation of astringent salts in creams and lotions should be carefully controlled to avoid breaking of emulsion. Emulsion stability should also be tested on ageing.

Waxy antiperspirant sticks can be manufactured by blending antiperspirant salts and other solid materials in a lipstick type base and pouring the molten mixture into the moulds. More popular, alcohol-soap sticks are manufactured by refluxing soap and other ingredients with alcohol and then pouring the material in the moulds or by preparing soap in *situ* adding alkali solution.

Antiperspirant powders are manufactured in the same way as skin powders.

Liquid detergent deodorants are often marketed as aerosols. These can be manufactured by selecting suitable container, valve and propellent. When manufactured as aerosol, generally alcohol is used as solvent. If non-alcoholic spray is to be manufactured, small amount of non-ionic wetting agent is used to disperse perfume.

Perfume selected should be tested for compatibility both at room temperature and at slightly elevated temperature (40-50°C) for reasonable period of time. Since perfume could be irritating to skin, the finished product should be tested for skin irritation or sensitization test. If polyethylene containers are used for packaging spray, such perfumes should be used which are least permeable. Many perfumes are permeable to polyethylene. However, rate of permeation is determined by the vehicle used. Alcoholic preparations lose less perfume than water or mineral oil.

Though not popular, deodorant creams are manufactured in the same way as vanishing creams. Many non-ionics (emulsifiers) inhibit the activity of antibacterials. Therefore, emulsifier and antibacterial agent compatibility studies should be carried out. The creams are manufactured in the general way of manufacture of creams.

In manufacturing deodorant powders, it is important that active ingredient is uniformly dispersed. This may be achieved by mixing and grinding. The ingredients (except active ingredient) should be well blended in a ribbon-type mixer. The active ingredient should be dissolved in suitable solvent and should be distributed throughout the powder mix. Perfume can be first blended with a part of talcum powder and then blended into the batch. Deodorants used in the formulation can affect the perfume. Therefore, compatibility of deodorant and perfume should be studied before marketing the product. A fine textured powder can be obtained if after preliminary mixing, the powder is passed through micropulverizer.

The base of deodorant sticks is same as that of antiperspirant sticks i.e., alcohol-soap based. Deodorant sticks are manufactured in the same way as antiperspirant sticks. Solidifying temperature of stick varies with soap content. Addition of small amount of tri-isopropanolamine myristate to a sodium stearate alcohol gel stick improves application properties. Tackiness may be reduced by the addition of tri-isopropanolamine.

17

Face Powders and Other Coloured Make-up Preparations

1. FACE POWDERS

1.1 General

Functions of face powder include imparting of smooth finish to the skin, masking of minor visible imperfections, masking of shine due to moisture or grease. Desired qualities in a face powder are:

- it should look natural;
- it should have lasting properties;
- it should be reasonably resistant to mixed secretions of the skin;
- it should serve as a vehicle for perfume to be disseminated by intimate contact of perfume containing particles over a warm and relatively large area.

To achieve these objectives the powder should have covering power, slip, absorbency, adhesiveness and bloom. No. Single substance possesses all these properties. Therefore face powder is a blend of several substances. Good covering power is an important attribute to face powders. A face powder having good covering power helps in concealing various defects of the facial skin like scars, blemishes, enlarged pores etc. The other important attribute of face powder is absorbency. It should be capable of absorbing sebaceous secretions and perspiration. If adhesion is poor, powder will fall easily. This may require user to re-powder the face frequently.

1.2 Raw Materials

As mentioned earlier, no single, substance possesses all the desired properties, therefore, different substances have to be selected for formulation of face powders. Raw materials to be used in face powders will be discussed under different desired properties.

1.2.1 Covering power

Oxides of metals such as titanium dioxide, zinc oxide, magnesium oxide enhance covering power of face powders. Kaolin is another material which also enhances covering power of face powders. Titanium dioxide has greater covering power than zinc oxide. However, sometimes, difficulties may be encountered in blending titanium dioxide with other constituents. This difficulty may be overcome by using it in conjunction with zinc oxide. Zinc oxide is frequently used in face powders. It is a mild astringent and antiseptic and has soothing properties.

1.2.2 Absorbency

The substances which impart this property in face powders include colloidal kaolin, starch, precipitated chalk and magnesium carbonate.

Kaolin is a naturally occurring substance. Colloidal kaolin is prepared from the naturally occurring kaolin. It has high moisture absorbing capacity. Besides this, it also has good covering property. Another desired property that kaolin has is excellent grease resisting property. It imparts greater skin adhesion property to the finished product. It has all above mentioned good qualities but lacks slip and inclines to be somewhat harsh. Its proportion, therefore in face powders should not exceed 30%.

Rice starch has been used almost exclusively as the base of face powder because of its good qualities such as absorbency, covering power and smoothness it imparts to the skin. But its tendency to cake when exposed to humid conditions of atmosphere or to secretions to the skin made it less desirable as base for face powders. It was replaced by talc. However, when any degree of bloom is required, there is not a material which can surpass it. Special grade of treated starches have been developed which do not swell or agglutinate in the presence of moisture.

Precipitated calcium carbonate is another substance that has been used in face powders for its excellent absorption properties. It also reduces the inherent shine of talc. But because of its 'chalky' feeling it has adverse effect on slip and impart 'dry' feel. Only special grade of precipitated chalk should be used. A proportion of more than 15% is not recommended.

Magnesium carbonate is about three times more absorbent than precipitated chalk. It also imparts fluffiness to face powders. It is also one of the preferred materials for incorporating and maturing selected perfume. A proportion of 5% is good enough for this purpose.

1.2.3 Slip

Slip is that quality of powder which makes it easy to spread and imparts a characteristic smooth feeling on the skin. Slip is mainly imparted by talc. Metallic soaps like zinc stearate can also be used. Starch or modified starches can also be used to a lesser extent. Talc is hydrated magnesium silicate. Talc of very good quality is required for making face powders. Finely divided pure silica (e.g. Aerosil) exerts a marked effect in increasing slip of the powder.

1.2.4 Adhesion

Adhesion is yet another property that is required in face powders. This property in face powders can be imparted by talc, some metallic soaps of stearic acid like zinc stearate, magnesium stearate. Recommended proportions of stearates are 3-10%. This property can also be improved by inclusion of emollient substances like cetyl or stearyl alcohols and glyceryl monostearate in small proportions (0.5-1.5%).

1.2.5 Bloom

The requirement for bloom may vary according to fashion. The materials which are used to impart bloom include rice starch, prepared starch and chalk. These materials have already been discussed.

1.2.6 Colour

There are some general and some specific properties a colouring material should have before it could be used in face powders. The general properties being:

- colouring material should be light fast i.e., it should not fade easily when exposed to light;
- colouring material should be stable;
- colouring material should not be heat sensitive (modern powder milling machines sometimes develop heat).

Since face powder remains on the skin for hours, colouring material is bound to come in contact with the skin secretions. It is desirable that colour should not change either with water wetting or oil wetting. Water soluble or oil soluble dye stuffs should, therefore, be avoided otherwise 'bleeding' may occur. The colour should also not be affected by variation in pH. A dye is either soluble in water or oil or partly soluble in water and partly in oil. Therefore, dye is not suitable for use in face powders. On the other hand, majority of pigments are insoluble colouring materials. Broadly, pigments can be divided in two categories, inorganic pigments and organic pigments. Inorganic pigments are available in vast range of colours. They are light fat, stable and non-bleeding. But many of the inorganic pigments are salts of heavy metals some of which are toxic (e.g., salts of lead and arsenic).

The other class of pigments is organic pigments. Now a days, organic pigments are made synthetically. Earlier natural products like carmine and indigo were available. For face powders, organic pigments are made available as 'lakes', organic toners and reduced toners (for explanation of these terms, see section 7 of Ch. 2). These lakes are available in various brilliant colours like red, pink, orange etc. However, these pigments are not as light fast as inorganic pigments. But these are used because inorganic pigments give dull shades. Lakes are also subject to bleeding. If there is any appreciable bleeding in water by a lake that should be rejected for use in face powders. Testing for bleeding can be done by mixing given amount of lake in distilled water or alcohol for several hours at about 48°C and by examining the supernatant liquid. Colouring even to small extent indicates bleeding.

The shade of face powder depends on particle size of colour and blending. Therefore, particle size of pigments to be used in face powders is also very important. For achieving proper particle size of colours, grinding is carried out.

1.3 Formulation

As mentioned earlier face powders are made by blending different materials having one or two pronounced properties which are of importance in face powders. Powders can be classified according to these properties namely covering power, absorbing power, adhesive quality and slip. Formula 1 can be considered a basic face powder formula which has reasonable covering power, absorbency and slip.

Formula 1

	%
Kaolin	12.0
Calcium carbonate (Light)	8.0
Zinc oxide	15.0
Zinc stearate	5.0
Magnesium carbonate	5.0
Talc	55.0
Perfume	q.s.

Method of preparation of face powders will be given at the end of this part of the section.

To make a lighter and more absorbent face powder, carbonates can be increased at the expense of Kaolin (see formula 2 and 3)

	Formula 2	Formula 3
	%	%
Kaolin	10.0	8.0
Calcium carbonate (Light)	14.0	10.0
Zinc oxide	15.0	15.0
Zinc stearate	5.0	7.0
Magnesium carbonate	6.0	10.0
Talc	50.0	50.0
Perfume	q.s.	q.s.

If lighter powder with less covering power is required, proportion of zinc oxide is reduced and zinc stearate is replaced with magnesium stearate. Formula 4 is an example of such a powder.

Formula 4

	%
Kaolin	15.0
Calcium carbonate (Light)	8.0
Zinc oxide	10.0
Magnesium stearate	50
Magnesium carbonate	7.0
Talc	55.0
Perfume	q.s.

If less absorbent powder is desired Calcium Carbonate is replaced by talc (see Formula 5).

Formula 5

	%
Kaolin	14.0
Zinc oxide	15.0
Zinc stearate	6.0
Magnesium Carbonate	5.0
Talc	60.0
Perfume	q.s.

If more covering power is desired, proportion of Zinc Oxide is increased and in addition, titanium dioxide is also added. See formula 6 and 7 for such powders.

	Formula 6	Formula 7
	%	%
Kaolin	12.0	10.0
Calcium Carbonate (Light)	10.0	8.0
Zinc oxide	18.0	22.0
Titanium dioxide	10.0	10.0
Zinc stearate	5.0	5.0
Magnesium Carbonate	5.0	5.0
Talc	40.0	40.0
Perfume	q.s.	q.s.

Likewise, if powder with more adhesion is required, proportion of stearate is increased. Formula 8 is an example of such a powder.

Formula 8

	%
Kaolin	10.0
Calcium Carbonate (Light)	12.0
Zinc oxide	15.0
Zinc/Magnesium stearate	10.0
Magnesium Carbonate	5.0
Talc	48.0
Perfume	q.s.

There can be many more variations in the formulations and numerous finished products can be prepared. Usually face powders tend to have drying effect. The drying effect is due to use of porous materials like carbonates which absorb moisture and oils of the skin and also because of use of zinc oxide which is drying material itself.

Silk powder can also be used in face powders (see Formula 9).

Formula 9

	%
Talc	46.0
Silk Powder	5.0
Kaolin	14.0
Zinc oxide	24.0
Titanium dioxide	6.0
Zinc stearate	5.0
Colour (pigment)	q.s.
Perfume	q.s.

Face powders are often coloured. Most commonly organic pigments are used, sometimes, inorganic pigments are also used e.g. iron oxides. These may be used in combinations of more than one. Suggested combinations are given below. Ultramarine can also be used in combination.

	(1)	(2)	(3)
Iron oxide, brown	3.0	–	3.0
Iron oxide, russet	1.0	0.2	1.0
Iron oxide, yellow	0.9	0.6	0.7
Iron oxide, black	–	–	0.1
Ultramarine, blue	0.1	–	–
Titanium dioxide and mica	–	10.0	–

If pearling effect is required in face powders, pearl made from Bismuth oxychloride and mica may be used. Readymade pearl powders are available in the market. For example, Shinju white 100A (Mearl), Flamenco Pearl 100 (Mearl).

Climate of the areas where product is to be marketed will also influence the formulation. A product which is suitable for cold and dry areas will not be suitable for hot and humid areas. The powders having absorbents and zinc oxide will be suitable for hot and humid areas. While for cold and dry areas formulation with less drying will be more suitable. A powder can be made less drying by reducing carbonates or by increasing stearates or by adding small amounts of fatty material. Introduction of small amount of fatty materials into the powder is called superfatting. However, care should be taken to disperse facts evenly throughout the powder. Usually fats are dissolved in volatile solvent and slurry is prepared with a part of powder. Solvent is then allowed to evaporate and this powder is then blended with rest of the powder. In case, solvent is not volatile, fat solution is poured on to such quantity of talc as will not produce dough but will produce dry and friable mass. This is then mixed thoroughly and passed through 20-mesh screen and added to the rest of the powder. The proportion of fats may vary from 0-6%. Proportions beyond this may result in caking. If fats are vulnerable to rancidity, antioxidants should be used.

Appropriate perfuming of face powder is also an important aspect. While selecting perfume for face powder, it should be ensured that perfume

- is stable during shelf-life;
- does not become stale or rancid;
- does not change its characteristics;

– does not discolour the powder;

– does not irritate skin.

Materials like zinc oxide, titanium dioxide, impurities like iron in raw materials, fats (if present) and colour may affect the perfume. If there is change in perfume with time, systematic studies should be undertaken. One way of doing it is given hereunder.

Perfume in the same percentage in which it is to be incorporated in the finished product should be mixed with each ingredient except magnesium carbonate and stored for observation. In case of magnesium carbonate, proportion of perfume in the same ratio as is the ratio of perfume and magnesium carbonate in finished product should be used. If after storage, it is observed that there is interaction with any ingredient, one of the following options may be used:

– the perfume may be replaced by another perfume which does not interact with any of the ingredients;

– the ingredient with which interaction has taken place may be replaced by another ingredient without affecting the quality of the powder significantly;

– perfume may be modified and retested with all the ingredients.

Blending of perfume can be done by mixing perfume with raw materials like magnesium carbonate, calcium carbonate which have absorbent properties. There should be an excess of absorbent material so that greasy or wet spots are not formed. The mix is then sifted through 15-mesh screen and is allowed to macerate in hermetically sealed stainless steel container for a few days. This perfumed absorbent is then blended with other ingredients.

2. COMPACT POWDERS

2.1 General

Compact powders are marketed in cake form and are applied to the face with the help of a powder puff. These powders can be considered as face powders compacted in the form of a cake. Either compressed cake is placed in metallic or plastic receptacle or cake is directly compressed into the container. The following points need attention while planning to manufacture compact powders:

- when rubbed with powder puff, it should come off easily;
- after application of powder, effect must be comparable to that of face powder;
- cake must not break or get damaged during transportation or use.

To produce a cake that will not break or get damaged during transportation or use, the formulation is required to possess a quality known as "binding". Binding quality of each raw material to be used may be useful in deciding the formulation. This can be assessed by compressing the selected ingredients one by one. It will be observed that some materials compact very well, while others do not. Compactibility of the formulation will depend on the raw materials selected. A delicate balance has to be made by adding different raw materials in appropriate proportions.

2.2 Formulation

Basically, all those raw materials which are used in loose powder are used in compact powder. If loose powder is compressed directly, it will not form a cake which has all desirable attributes. Therefore, binders are used to form a cake of desirable quality. Thus, while discussing formulation of compact face powder discussion on binders becomes important. There are five basic types of binders which are used in compression of face powders:

- dry binders,
- oil binders,
- water soluble binders,
- water repellent binders,
- emulsion binders.

Materials like zinc stearate, magnesium stearate act as dry binders.

Oily materials like mineral oil, isoporopyl myristate, lanolin derivatives can be used as binders and are examples of oil binders.

Amongst the water soluble binders, solution of natural gums like gum tragacanth, gum arabic, gum karaya have been used. These binders may present bacterial growth problems. Use of suitable preservatives in adequate quantity is essential. Synthetic materials like poly-vinyl pyrollidone (PVP), methyl cellulose, carboxy methyl cellulose (CMC) have also been used.

Water repellent binders are the most commonly used binders in case of compact face powders. The materials which can be used include mineral oil, fatty esters of all types and lanolin derivatives. Addition of small quantity of water facilitates formation of smooth and solidly pressed cake. When using water, addition of small amount of wetting agent helps in distribution of moisture throughout.

Difficulties encountered during incorporation of oil repellent binders led to development of emulsion binders. This type of binders allow uniform distribution of oil and water phase, which is necessary for satisfactory compression of the cake. Therefore, this type of binders are preferred over other types. For making emulsion, emulsifying agents like soaps (e.g., triethanolamine stearate) non-ionic emulsifiers (e.g., polyoxyethylene sorbitan mono-stearate), glyceryl monostearate can be used.

Formulae of water soluble binders and emulsion binders are given below:

Formula 10

		%
Gum tragacanth		2.0
Glycerin		5.0
Water	to make	100.0
Preservatives		q.s.

Formula 11

		%
Gum tragacanth		2.0
Glucose		5.0
Water	to make	100.0

Formula 12

		%
Gum tragacanth		2.0
Glyceryl monostearate		5.0
Mineral oil		5.0
Sorbitol		5.0
Water	to make	100.0
Preservatives		q.s.

Formula 13

		%
Mineral oil		1.0
Polyoxyethylene sorbitan monostearate		2.0
Water	to make	100.0
Preservatives		q.s.

Percentage of binding solution that should be used depends on composition of binding solution and the composition of powder. Appropriate amounts of binding solutions have to be found out by trial and error method. However, experiments can be started by using 100 parts of powder and 5 parts of binding solution.

A combination of oil/fats, emulsifying agents and gum can also be used. (See Formula 14).

Formula 14

	%
Part-1	
Glyceryl stearate	6.0
Lanolin	18.0
Propyl paraben	0.05
Part-2	
Methyl paraben	0.1
Sorbitol (70% solution)	10.0
Cellulose gum (2% solution)	65.85

Some formulae which can be used as starting formula are given below:

Formula 5

		%
Kaolin		17.0
Titanium dioxide		7.0
Zinc stearate		5.0
Talc	to make	100.0
Colour pigment, binder and perfume		q.s.

Formula 16

	%
Calcium Carbonate	10.0
Zinc oxide	5.0
Zinc stearate	5.0

Talc	to make	100.0
Colour pigment, binder and perfume		q.s.

Formula 17

		%
Kaolin		10.0
Precipitated chalk		10.0
Titanium dioxide		10.0
Zinc stearate		5.0
Talc	to make	100.0
Colour pigment, binder and perfume		q.s.

Formula 18

		%
Kaolin		10.0
Zinc oxide		12.0
Zinc stearate		5.0
Magnesium Carbonate		8.0
Talc	to make	100.0
Colour pigment, binder and perfume		q.s.

Formula 19

		%
Zinc oxide		18.0
Titanium dioxide		7.0
Magnesium stearate		6.0
Magnesium carbonate		7.0
Talc	to make	100.0
Colour pigment, binder and perfume		q.s.

Soap alone can be used as compact binder. Formula 20 is an example of such a formulation.

Formula 20

	%
Kaolin	18.0
Zinc oxide	15.0
Percipitated chalk	20.0
Magnesium carbonate	5.0
Soap	8.0
Talc	34.0
Colour pigment and perfume	q.s.

Silk powder can also be used in compact face powders. An example of such formulation is given below (See Formula 21).

Formula 21

	%
Cetyl acetate (and) Acetylated lanolin alcohol[1]	3.0
Zinc stearate	6.0
Kaolin	3.0
Silk powder	5.0
Talc	82.0
Magnesium carbonate	1.0
Pigments	q.s.
Titanium dioxide	q.s.

A wet/dry face powder can be prepared using diazolidinyl urea (see Formula 22).

Formula 22

	%
Mica (and) Dimethicone (and) mineral oil	50.0
Bismuth oxychloride (Pearl)	20.0
Mica	10.0
Synthetic wax (and) Corn gluten protein	8.0
Diazolidinyl urea pigments including titanium dioxide	11.6
Preservatives (Methyl paraben/Propyl paraben)	0.4

To manufacture this formulation the following procedure may be adopted:

(i) Load all ingredients of part-1 in a blender or mixer and mix for one hour.

(ii) Add part 2 to part 1 through a spraying process.

(iii) Pass the entire batch through a micro-pulverizer with or without screen. Any shade adjustment should be done at this stage.

(iv) Pass through pulverizer again after adjustment of shade.

(v) Compress cakes at 1000 psi.

3. ROUGL

3.1 General

Rouge is a cosmetic preparation which is used to simulate the rosy freshness of young and healthy skin. Although rouges are made in liquid, cream forms also but the compact cake form is the most popular. But compact rouge is most difficult to produce. Compact rouge can be considered a pigmented powder containing a binder which helps in compacting the powder. A good compact rouge is expected to have the following characteristics:

- smooth texture;
- evenly distributed colour;
- good covering power;
- ease of application;
- perfect blending on skin;
- good adhesiveness;
- ease of removal without residual stain;
- well formed cake which will not flake, crack or crumble or be too hard.

3.2 Formulation

Although the raw materials for rouge and face powder are similar, but same type of powders in same proportions cannot be used.

Selection of binder is the most important factor in producing a good compact rouge. Binder could be a water soluble, water repellent, emulsion or dry binder. Like binders for compact face powder, water soluble binder can be made with natural gums (e.g., gum tragacanth, gum karaya) or synthetic gums (e.g., methyl cellulose, carboxy methyl cellulose, poly-vinyl pyrolidone). Concentration of gums may vary from 0.1% to 3% depending upon overall composition. These binders have disadvantage of "spotting" by water. Therefore, water repellent binders have been used. These binders could be liquids, semi-solids or solids. Semi-solids and solids are used in molten state. The materials which can be used are:

- mineral oil;
- petroleum jelly;
- fatty acid esters;
- lanolin;
- lanolin derivatives.

Concentration of these materials may vary from 0.2% to 2%. Usually, the quantity of these materials may not be sufficient for the formation of a solid cake, water may be required to be mixed with powder. Incorporation of water (usually about 10%) may require use of wetting agent. This limitation gave rise to development of emulsion binders. This type of binders also take care of problems like glazing and lumps which may be formed when oils are added to the powder. Emulsion binders have both bulk and moisture content to allow perfect distribution of aqueous phase and fatty phase. If soaps are used as emulsifying agent, adhesion of the powder is good. However, they have potential for skin irritation. Sorbitol derivatives can be used successfully in preparing emulsion binders. A good emulsion binder can be prepared by using glyceryl monostearate, mineral oil and water. Metallic stearates can be used as dry binders. When dry binders are used compression force has to be increased.

Compact rouges are made from talc, kaolin, zinc oxide, calcium carbonate and inorganic pigments like titanium dioxide and iron oxide by compressing with the help of binder. As mentioned above, binder could be water soluble, water repellent, emulsion cr dry binder. Emulsion binders are used in preference to water soluble and water repellent binders.

Formula 23 is typical formula of emulsion binder.

Formula 23

	%
Stearic acid	35.0
Mineral oil	20.0
Triethanolamine	10.0
Water	35.0

Powder and pigment blend can be prepared with kaolin, zinc oxide, talc, titanium dioxide, calcium carbonate and iron oxide colours (see Formula 24).

Formula 24

	%
Kaolin	18.0
Zinc oxide	10.0
Calcium carbonate	6.0
Talc	60.0
Titanium dioxide	6.0
Iron oxide colours	q.s.

For starting experiments, powder and emulsion binder can be used in ratio of 100 parts and 8 parts.

Metallic stearates can be used as dry binder. Formula 25is an example of dry rouge powder.

Formula 25

	%
Kaolin	15.0
Calcium carbonate (Light)	5.0
Magnesium carbonate	4.0
Zinc stearate	40
Talc	50.0
Titanium dioxide	12.0
Colour pigment	10.0
Perfume	q.s.

Rouges in other forms are not very popular. However, these will be discussed briefly in proceeding paragraphs.

(i) Liquid Rouges

Liquid rouges can be either suspension type or emulsion type. In suspension type liquid rouges, suspending agents like carboxy methyl cellulose, polyvinyl pyrolidone, polyvinyl alcohol are used. Formula 26 is an example of suspension type rouge.

Formula 26

	%
Propylene glycol	34.0
Polyvinyl alcohol (2% solution)	25.0
Sorbitol hexa-acetate (2% solution)	25.0
Titanium dioxide	6.0
Chalk	4.0

Zinc stearate	3.0
Colour pigment	3.0
Perfume	q.s.

Emulsion type of liquid rouge though has advantage of ease of application and desirable appearance in bottle, but has problem of stability. Further, emulsion type rouges being alkaline in nature, only a few organic lake colours, toners can be used. The scope of choice of colours can, however, be increased by using non-ionic emulsifiers. Formula 27 is an example of emulsion type liquid rouge.

Formula 27

	%
Mineral oil	40.0
Oleic acid	7.0
Titanium dioxide	0.7
Zinc stearate	0.5
Pigment	0.4
Aluminium hydroxide	0.4
Water	47.0
Triethanolamine	4.0
Preservative and Perfume	q.s.

(ii) Cream Rouges

Cream rouges can be made either anhydrous cream base on emulsified cream base. Earlier, anhydrous cream bases consisted of mineral oil and waxes. Now the anhydrous cream bases consist of lower alkyl fatty acid esters, hardened with carnauba wax. Carnauba wax, in the presence of talc, chalk, kaolin and pigments stiffens isopropyl palmitate and other such esters to desired consistency. This mixture is quite solid, but becomes fluid when rubbed gently with circular motion.

Both types of these formulations exude tiny oil droplets. However, this phenomenon can be minimized by adding beeswax, ozokerite or lanolin. Pigments are mixed in molten base and the mixture is poured into containers. Pouring temperature and cooling rate affect the feel and stability of anhydrous cream rouge. Formula 28 is an example of anhydrous cream rouge of former type, Formula 29 is an example of latter type.

Formula 28

	%
Petroleum jelly	77.0
Mineral oil	7.0
Lanolin	3.0
Zinc oxide	5.0
Pigments	8.0
Perfume	q.s.

Formula 29

	%
Isopropyl palmitate	25.0
Mineral oil	22.0
Carnauba wax	8.0
Ozokerite wax	10.0
Talc	10.0
Tiranium dioxide	20.0
Colour pigment	5.0
Perfume	q.s.

Pigments can be incorporated into emulsified creams also. By making rouges in emulsified cream bases, shortcoming of anhydrous cream i.e., 'greasy feeling' can be overcome. Practically all types of creams can be adopted for use as rouge bases. Formula 30 and 31 are examples of vanishing and cold cream type creams respectively which have been used as base for rouge.

Formula 30

		%
Stearic acid		18.0
Cetyl alcohol		3.0
Glycerin		10.0
Potassium hydroxide		0.9
Pigment		8.5
Water	to make	100.0
Preservatives and perfume		q.s.

Method of Preparation

Heat stearic acid and cetyl alcohol together to about 70°C. Add potassium hydroxide to water and then glycerine and heat to about 70°C. Add aqueous phase to fatty phase with stirring. Allow to cool gradually and continue stirring, and perfume when temperature drops to 45°C. Remove a small amount of cream and mix pigments. Add this pigment and cream mixture to remainder of the cream and mix thoroughly.

Formula 31

		%
White beeswax		10.0
Petroleum jelly		25.0
Spermaceti		9.0
Mineral oil		20.0
Borax		0.8
Pigment		3.0
Water	to make	100.0
Preservatives and perfume		q.s.

Method of Preparation

Heat white beeswax, petroleum jelly, spermaceti and mineral oil together to about 80°C. Add borax to water and heat to about 80°C. Add aqueous phase to fatty phase with stirring. Continue stirring and allow to cool. Add perfume when temperature drops to 45°C. Mix pigment with a small amount of cream and add to the remaining cream with continuous stirring. Mix thoroughly before filling.

(iii) Solid oil and wax rouges

Rouges in the form similar to lipsticks can be prepared in the same way as lipsticks. But these have not been very popular. Formula 32 is an example of such a formulation.

Formula 32

	%
Cator oil	77.0
Candelilla wax	10.0
Carnauba wax	3.0
Colour pigment	10.0
Perfume	q.s.

4. MANUFACTURE

4.1 General Method of Manufacture of Pigmented Powders

If a well processed pigmented powder is examined under microscope it appears as consisting of small agglomerates of pigments or single particles of pigments adhering to and covering the surface of large particles of talc. Improperly processed pigmented powder appears as consisting of large agglomerates of pigments separate from talc particles. From this, it may be made but that particle size of pigments should be reduced to appropriate size. The desired particle size is smaller than 75μ.

One of the oldest methods of manufacture of pigmented coloured powders is combination of mixing and sifting. Different types of machines are used for these operations. In some machines sifting is done before mixing, while in others, sifting is done after mixing. Finally, extension of pigment particles on the talc particles is done with the help of harmmer or pebble mills. Air grinding and fluid energy will can also be used which are modern developments. A procedure usually followed for manufacture of pigmented coloured powders is given below:

Step 1 All the powder ingredients individually are passed through a coarse screen (e.g., 40 mesh) to remove any foreign particles from packaging material or any other source. All the screened powders except colours are successively added to a stainless steel ribbon-type blender and are mixed for 1-3 hours depending on the quantity of powder and size of blender.

Step 2 Pigments to be used in powder are prepared by blending colour (pigment) and white base in a ribbon blender. These are mixed till full colour development. The colour extender is pulverized and screened. This may be compared with a standard.

Step 3 The white base prepared in step 1 and required quantity of colour extender is added to a blender and blended for several hours. When full colour development has occurred and proper shade adjustments have been made, the entire batch is pulverized, screened, mixed and is compared with the standard. Pulverization can be effected with the help of hammer mill, pebble mill or any other suitable equipment.

Step 4 Perfume is blended by absorbing it on absorbents like calcium carbonate, magnesium carbonate which usually are the ingredients of face powder. The absorbent should be pulverized before absorbing the perfume.

Step 5 If the face powder is to be manufactured in cake form binders are added and mixing is continued till the binders have been uniformly distributed throughout the batch.

Step 6 After thoroughly mixing the binder, the powder mix is passed on for compression. When ready for compression, the powder mix should be agitated to exclude as much air as is possible. If air is not excluded, cornpact tablets will break. Powder is compressed into tablets with the help of compacting machines. Compacting machines (presses) which are commonly used are hydraulic type and ram type. Hydraulic type machine is used where high speed is required. The ram press is used where high speed is not required. It is cheaper than hydraulic press. Amount of pressure required for compacting will vary depending on the basic formulation, type and quantity of binder used, moisture content of powder and other variables.

The next operation in manufacture of pigmented powder is packaging. Container for use of loose powder must be selected carefully and it should be ensured that there is no interaction between any of the ingredients of powder and material of the container. It should also be ascertained that on ageing there will not be any development of odour.

In case of compact powder, the pans being glued into the compact must be regulated against under-filling and over-filling. Underfilling will result in cakes not desirable aesthetically and overfilling will result in breakage of cakes and dusting of powders in the compact. Quality of glue used should be good or else, pan may fall out of the compact.

5. FOUNDATION MAKE-UP

Some theatrical products like 'wet white' have been used for whitening neck and arms. These are also known as liquid powders.

The basic components of liquid powders are zinc oxide, chalk, kaolin, bismuth oxychloride subnitrate. Pigments can be used for preparing different shades to match with the skin. Often glycerin is included in these preparations. Formula 33 represents a simple formulation.

Formula 33

		%
Zinc oxide		3.0
Calcium carbonate (Light)		14.0
Kaolin		1.5
Glycerin		15.0
Water	to make	100.0
Preservatives and perfume		q.s.

In such preparations, powders settle in the bottom, as such, these are required to be shaken before application. This may be reduced to some extent by incorporating suspending agents like gum tragacanth (see Formula 34).

Formula 34

		%
Zinc oxide		5.0
Titanium dioxide		12.0
Talc		12.0
Gum tragacanth (0.5% solution)		26.0
Glycerin		15.0
Water	to make	100.0
Colour, preservative and perfume		q.s.

With the availability of certain fatty acids esters new preparations were developed which were easy to apply, did not dry on skin, and gave better finish. This type of preparation is illustrated by Formula 35.

Formula 35

	%
Isopropyl myristate	55.0
Lanolin	3.0
Dry powder blend (titanium dioxide, talc, inorganic pigments)	42.0
Perfume and preservatives	q.s.

The products which find universal acceptance are suspension of pigments in emulsified lotions. While preparing such preparations, first emulsions are formed then pigments are added with stirring when emulsion cools to about 50-55°C. Formula 36 and 36 are examples of such products.

Formula 36

		%
Glycerol mono and distearate		2.0
PEG 400 monostearate		1.0
Stearic acid		12.0
Cetyl alcohol		0.5
Isopropyl myristate or palmitate		1.5
Proylene glycol		10.0
Sorbitol solution		5.0
Tatanium dioxide		2.0
Talc		10.0
Pigment		1.0
Water	to make	100.0
Preservatives and perfume		q.s.

Formula 37

		%
Stearic acid		3.0
Propylene glycol monostearate		3.0
Mineral oil		24.0
glyceryl monostearate		3.0
Triethanolamine		1.5
Sodium lauryl sulphate		1.5
Dry powder blend (Talc, titanium dioxide and pigment)		10.0
Water	to make	100.0
Perfume and Preservatives		q.s.

Method of Preparation

Heat stearic acid, propylene glycol monostearate, mineral oil and glyceryl monostearate together to about 75°C. Add triethanolamine and preservatives (para hydroxy benzoates) to water and heat to about 75°C. Add aqueous phase to fatty phase with stirring, continue stirring and allow to cool. When temperature reaches about 50-55°C, add pulverized sodium lauryl sulphate and dry powder and mix thoroughly. Pass the product through colloid mill and allow to age before filling.

Although it is very difficult to prepare cosmetic preparation for every demand of beautician, but it has been possible to manufacture preparations for concealing facial blemishes such as "port wine", birth marks, chloasma, lack of pigmentation etc. Blemish concealers are available in cream or stick form. Cream formulations have already been discussed. Desired variations can be made in those formulations.

Formula 38

	%
Butyl stearate	12.0
Petroleum jelly	6.0
Beeswax	10.5
Ozokerite	7.0
Paraffin	3.5
Titanium dioxide, Pigment and magnesium carbonate	30.0
Castor oil	31.0
Perfume and Preservatives	q.s.

Formula 38 is a representative formula of stick blemish concealer. Quantities of carnauba wax, candelilla wax, micro crystalline wax, lanolin, propylene glycol monostearate and other fatty materials can be varied according to requirement.

As in the case of face powders, silk powder can also be used in foundation make up. A formula of silky make-up base is given below (see Formula 39).

Formula 39

	%
Part 1	
Stearic acid	15.0
Part 2	
Silk Powder	5.0
Pigments	9.0
Sorbitan stearate	2.5
Isopropyl palmitate	2.5
Part 3	
Polysorbate-60	1.5
Propylene glycol	10.0

Water	54.5
Perfume	q.s.
Preservatives	q.s.

To manufacture this product, the following procedure may be adopted:

(i) Prepare silk concentrate using ingredients given in Part 2 of the formulation.

(ii) Heat Part 1 to 85°C.

(iii) Add Part 2 to Part 1 with stirring.

(iv) Heat Part 3 to 85°C.

(v) Add Part 3 to the mixture of Part 1 and Part 2 and continue mixing until the product cools down to room temperature.

A product made with Magnesium aluminium silicate (Veegum) is used for highlights either over or under make up. It is known by the name of pearly film (see Formula 40).

Formula 40

Part 1	%
Clycerin	3.0
Alcohol (Ethanol)	10.0
Pearl	10.0
Part 2	
Magnesium aluminium silicate	3.5
Water	73.5
Part 3	
Preservatives	q.s.

To manufacture this product, the following procedure may be adopted:

(i) Slowly add Veegum to water while agitating vigorously. Continue mixing until smooth.

(ii) Add Part 1 to Part 2. Mix until smooth and uniform.

High levels of opaque pigments can be used to prepare cover creams. This type of creams provide blemish cover. (See Formula 41).

Formula 41

	%
Cyclo-methicone	44.0
Lanolin, Anhydrous	6.0
Carnauba wax	10.0
Bees wax	3.0
Mineral oil	8.0
Cetyl alcohol	2.5
Pigments/extenders	26.5

Acne caused by cosmetics has become a recognized complaint in women (particularly over 25 years) and can be attributed to certain oils like isopropyl myristate used in cosmetics. Effects of these oils are pronounced when used in anhydrous products. Emollient ester derived from castor oil, cetyl acetyl ricinoleate is known to be non-acne promoting. A cover stick formula using cetyl acetyl ricinoleate is given below (See Formula 42).

Formula 42

Part 1	%
Ozokerite wax	15.0
Candelilla wax	5.0
Hydrogenated castor oil	7.0
Sorbitan sesquioleate	2.0
BHA	0.2
Mineral oil	12.0
Wheat germ oil	1.0
Part 2	
Cetyl acetyl ricinoleate	10.0
Mineral oil	22.3
Titanium dioxide	23.0
Iron oxides	2.5

To manufacture this product, the following procedure may be adopted:

(i) Combine Part 1except wheat germ oil and heat to 85-87°C. Mix until uniform.

(ii) Combine Part 2 and mix into a slurry. Roller mill can be used for this purpose.

(iii) Add Part 2 to Part 1, heat to 80-85°C and mix until uniform.

(iv) Add wheat germ oil, mix and pour into moulds at 80°C.

In Europe and the United States of America, liquidcream foundation are the main type but in Japan, compact foundations are more common. After applying a foundation cream, powder foundation is applied to the skin with the help of a sponge. It makes it so easy to touch up the make up this way.

Powder foundations consist of extender pigments, whitening pigments, colouring pigments, binding agents, perfumes, etc. Extender pigments like talc, mica, sericite are used to make them spread and feel smooth. For enhancing the skin colour, powder foundations contain more colouring pigments than compact face powder. The main colouring pigment which is used is iron oxide. High chroma organic pigments are also sometimes used. If lustre is required with finished product, titanium dioxide mica can be used. Usually oil is used as binding agent. It may be a natural animal or plant oil or synthetic oil like liquid paraffin or a synthetic ester oil. Silicone oil is used to reduce the spread of the foundation and to make it water repellant. To improve mouldability, semi-solid oils like lanolin or hydrocarbon waxes may be added. Formula 43 is a typical formula os powder foundation.

Formula 43

	%
Talc	20.0
Kaolin	5.0
Mica	33.0
Titanium dioxide	12.0
Zinc stearate	2.0
Nylon powder	10.0
Squalane	5.0
Lanolin acetate	1.0
Octyl dodecyl myristate	2.0
Neopentyl glycol octanoate	2.0
Sorbitan mono-oleate	0.5
Red iron oxide	2.0

Yellow iron oxide	2.0
Black iron oxide	0.2
Titanium dioxide coated mica	3.3
Antioxidant	q.s.
Preservatives	q.s.
Perfumes	q.s.

Dual use foundations have also have developed. When powder formulation are used with a sponge, the powder in them cake up being hydrophilic. As such powder foundation without modification cannot be used as dual purpose foundation. This caking can be prevented by subjecting powders to a process which make them hydrophobic. This may be achieved by silicon treatment. Thus the basic ingredients of dual purpose foundations are silicone treated powders. These are mainly used in summer. Therefore, these also contain ultrafine titanium dioxide and UV-screen agents. Formula 44 is a typical formula of dual purpose foundation.

Formula 44

	%
Silicone treated talc	20.0
Silicone treated titanium dioxide	14.0
Silicon treated mica	40.0
Silicone treated ultrafine TiO_2	5.0
Zinc stearate	0.5
Nylon powder	2.0
Silicone treated iron pigments	4.5
Squalane	4.0
Solid paraffin	0.5
Dimethyl polysiloxane	5.0
Glyceryl tri-iso-octanoate	3.5
Ocyl methoxy cinnamate	1.0
Antioxidants and preservatives	q.s.
Perfume	q.s.

Dual purpose foundations can be used either on a dry or wet sponge. When used with wet sponge, these give cool and refreshing feeling.

18

Body Powders (Talcum Powders)

1. GENERAL

Talcum powder is used to absorb moisture after bathing. In warmer countries, it is also used to absorb perspiration. Such powders contain a large proportion of talc. Therefore, certain points relating to talc which should be given attention to are:

- best quality of talc is white and other qualities are greyish-white to distinctly greyish;
- a good quality of talc exhibit requisite 'slip';
- a good quality of talc is lustrous and does not exhibit undue amount of glitter.

Physical properties of talc vary with its origin. Talc of Italian origin is considered to be the best. Next to Italian talc are Indian and American talc. Bacteriological examination of talc has been recommended as certain qualities are heavily contaminated with bacteria. If such a talc is used, it should be sterilised before use.

It is advisable to subject talc to chemical examination. Test for acid soluble matter is an important test. Any material containing more than 4% acid (hydrochloric acid) soluble matter should be discarded. Material containing more than 4% acid soluble matter may adversely affect perfume and may also cause irritation.

2. FORMULATION

As mentioned earlier talcum powders contain a large proportion of talc. There are certain products in market which are nothing but perfumed talc. However, good quality of talcum powder contain other ingredients like mettalic stearates, zinc oxide, light magnesium carbonate or calcium carbonate which impart additional quality in the product. Metallic stearates give additional lubricating properties. Zinc stearate, besides imparting additional lubricating property, makes the product soothing and mildly antiseptic and is used in preference to magnesium stearate. Light calcium carbonate or magnesium carbonate is used to give fluffiness to the powder. The carbonates being absorbent in nature also help in addition of perfume. Formula 1 is an example of talcum powder in which zinc stearate and light calcium carbonate have been used.

Formula 1

	%
Zinc stearate	6.0
Light calcium carbonate	24.0
Talc	70.0
Perfume	q.s.

Zinc oxide is also used in talcum powders. It is mild astringent and also has antiseptic properties. It also helps in relieving pricking caused by prickly heat during summer and rainy seasons. Formula 2 is an example to talcum powder containing Zinc oxide.

Formula 2

	%
Zinc stearate	4.5
Zinc oxide	4.5
Light Magnesium Carbonate	15.0
Talc	76.0
Perfume	q.s.

If a deodorant powder is to be prepared, it includes a suitable bactericide like chlor-hexidine or bithional (see formula 3 and 4).

Formula 3

		%
Zinc oxide		6.0
Zinc stearate		4.0
Chlorhexidine di-acetate		0.3
Magnesium Carbonate		10.0
Talc	to make	100.0
Perfume		q.s.

Formula 4

	%
Zinc oxide	9.0
Zinc stearate	5.5
Bithional	0.5
Calcium Carbonate (Light)	5.0
Talc	80.0

Good perfume in a talcum powder is a desirable quality. As mentioned earlier, a good quality of talc should be used. Impurities like iron in talc or other ingredients have deleterious influence on perfume. Perfume should be mixed with Calcium Carbonate or Magnesium Carbonate and should be allowed to stand overnight. Then it should be mixed with the rest of powder blend.

Dioctyl maleate is an emollient and a flow additive and therefore may be used in body powders. It's use has been shown in Formula 5.

Formula 5

		%
Kaolin		5.0
Zinc stearate		2.0
Imidazolidinyl urea		0.15
Dioctyl maleate		1.0
Talc	to make	100.0
Perfume		q.s.
Preservatives		q.s.

A product in the form of lotion, when applied, dries to leave a pleasant powder on the skin has been reported in the literature. Formulation of this product has been given below (see Formula 6).

Formula 6

Part 1		%
Cetearyl alcohol		0.5
PPG-2 Myristyl ether propionate		025
Emulsifying wax		2.50
Part 2		
Carbomer 940		0.15
Alcohol (ethanol)		20.0
Polysorbate 80 (and) Cetyl acetate (and)		
Acetylated lanolin alcohol		0.25
Water	to make	100.0
Part 3		
Triethanolamine		0.15
Corn starch		5.0
Silk powder		1.0
Talc		15
Preservatives		q.s.
Perfume		q.s.

Method of preparation

Hydrate carbomer 940 in ethanol-water mixture and then heat part 2 to 80°C. Heat waxes mentioned in part 1 to 60°C and add to part 2. Neutralize with triethanolamine. Add remaining ingredients with stirring until cool. Fill in the containers.

3. MANUFACTURE

Suitable mixers for mixing different powders to manufacture talcum powder are single spiral or double spiral ribbon mixers. However, vertical blenders and horizontal drum mixers are also used. In selecting mixer, attention should also be given to ease of cleaning of equipment. Mixing time can be greatly reduce by pulverizing the powders before mixing.

If extremely fine powders are to be manufactured, the powder mix should be sifted through silk bolting cloth of 300 mesh. Such sifter usually are of oscillating type containing a shallow box fitted with fine screen and rubber balls in between frames of upper screen and the lower screen which is one fourth in mesh size. The oscillating motion of frames and rolling motion of rubber balls prevent clogging of the screen. Larger particles which are not able to pass through the screen are carried to the end of the sifter and are collected. Nowadays stainless steel screens of fine mesh are available and silk cloth has been replaced by these screens. Other type of sifter like vibrator on centrifugal type can also be used.

Perfume can be mixed either by absorbing it on an ingredient, like Magnesium Carbonate, maturing it and mixing it with powder mix or by incorporating it directly into the batch. In the former method, Perfume is mixed with Magnesium Carbonate/Calcium Carbonate and is allowed to mature overnight in stainless steel container completely closed. This is then mixed with powder mix in the blender. In the latter method, Perfume oils are sprayed onto the powder mix in blender. For spraying, regular paint spray gun can be used. To prevent "balling up", perfume should be fogged in over a period of time (30 mins. of one hour) and perfume oils should be mixed with enough air to create fine mist.

In large units powder manufacturing areas are located directly over the powder filling room and powder is transferred to filling equipment by gravity or air pressure. However, it is not necessary to locate powder mixer directly over filling machine(s). Powder can be transferred to filling machines manually or by vibrators or by vacuum and air. Commonly used filling machines are augur or vacuum type. In small scale units powder is filled manually.

19

Face Packs and Masks

1. GENERAL

Face packs have been used by women from very early times. In antiquity, some earths believed to be possessing miraculous healing power were used. Face packs/masks are applied either in the form of liquid or paste and are allowed to dry. With drying, tightening effect and warmth is experienced. This produces stimulating sensation of rejuvenation. Some of the face packs contain adsorptive clays. As such, when these are removed, skin debris and blackheads may be removed alongwith them.

Such preparations are expected to possess the following properties:

* They should form a smooth paste (free from gritty particles) and should have pleasant odour.
* When applied to the face, they should dry out rapidly to form an adherent coating on face. However, the coating should be such which can be removed either by peeling off the face or by gentle washing without causing pain.
* They should produce a sensation of tightening of the skin after application.
* They should be capable of producing significant cleansing of the skin.
* They should be non-toxic to the skin.

2. FORMULATION

While formulating a face pack/mask there should be an effort to produce which will have properties mentioned above. There are five basic systems which can produce products having above-mentioned properties. These systems are based on:

- waxes,
- rubbers,
- vinyl resins,
- hydrocolloids,
- earths.

2.1 Wax Based Formulations

Usually wax based systems consist of paraffin wax, petroleum jelly and polar materials like stearyl and cetyl alcohols. Paraffin wax may be replaced with a mixture of waxes. These products are solid and are required to be melted before application. These may be applied with a brush while hot. When the waxes solidify, a sensation of tightness is felt. Since moisture-proof coating of waxes is formed on the skin, profuse perspiration occurs. This perspiration flushes out dirt and impurities from follicular openings in the skin. To facilitate application, thixotropy can be imparted to the formulation by adding a small quantity of bentonite.

Formula 1

	%
Paraffin wax	60.0
Microcrystalline wax	12.0
Mineral oil	22.0
Cetyl alcohol	4.0
Isopropyl alcohol	0.5
Bentonite	1.5

Formula I is an example of wax based mask.

2.2 Rubber Based Formulations

These formulations are based on rubber latex. To facilitate application, latex emulsions are used. These packs form a continuous and elastic film on the skin. Since so formed film is water-impermeable, it interferes with skin respiration and causes rise in temperature. Rise in temperature results in increased blood supply to the skin. Formula 2 is an example of formulation based on rubber latex.

Formula 2

		%
Latex emulsion		27.0
Methyl cellulose		8.0
Sorbitol		6.0
Kaolin		4.0
Borax		1.0
Water	to make	100.0
Preservatives		q.s.

2.3 Vinyl Resins Based Formulations

Vinyl resins like polyvinyl alcohol or polyvinyl acetate can form continuous film. This property of these resins is made use of. Adsorbents like kaolin, titanium dioxide are also added. Formula 3 is an example of face mask based on polyvinyl alcohol.

Formula 3

		%
Polyvinyl alcohol		14.0
Propylene glycol		10.0
Magnesium aluminium silicate (veegum)		0.5
Kaolin		0.7
Titanium dioxide		0.3
Ethyl alcohol		20.0
Water	to make	100.0

2.4 HYDROCOLLOIDS BASED FORMULATIONS

Hydrocolloids based face packs/masks can be prepared in the form of high viscosity solutions or in the form of solid gels. If the formulation is in the form of solid gel, it is required to be melted before application. Feeling of tightness is felt because of shrinkage of gel as drying occurs. For formulating this type of face packs/masks, a variety of gums can be used including gum acacia, gum tragacanth, guar gum, gelatin, carboxy methyl cellulose, polyvinyl pyrolidone etc. For plasticizing the film, humectants such as glycerine, propylene glycol, sorbitol solution are used. Viscosity of gels can be varied to great extent by changing gum and its concentration.

Face packs/masks based on hydrocolloids are easy to apply. But their cleansing action is inferior to face packs/masks which contain adsorbents like kaolin. If rapid drying is required, ethyl alcohol can be added to the formulation. However, when alcohol is added, only those hydrocolloids should be used which are soluble in aqueous-alcoholic solution. Certain grades of methyl cellulose and polyvinyl pyrolidone are soluble in aqueous-alcoholic solutions. Small quantities of solids in the form of fine powder can be added which act as opacifiers. Formula 4 and 5 are examples of face masks based on hydrocolloids.

Formula 4

		%
Gum tragacanth		2.0
Glycerin		3.0
Gelatin		2.5
Zinc oxide		2.0
Water	to make	100.0
Preservative and Perfume		q.s.

Formula 5

		%
Polyvinyl pyrolidone (PVP)		2.5
Methyl cellulose		10.0
Glycerin		8.0
Water	to make	100.0
Opacifiers, Perfume and Preservatives		q.s.

Winter suggested a formula containing gelatin in face pack (see Formula 6).

Formula 6

	parts
Gelatin	10.0
Camphor (dissolved is alcohol)	0.05
Zinc oxide	3.0
Kaolin	5.0
Titanium dioxide	2.0
Water	50.0

2.5 Earths Based Formulations

Earths based face packs/masks contain high percentage of solids. Earths which are used in their preparation include china clay, colloidal kaolin, fuller's earth, bentonite etc. These may be prepared either as powders or as pasters. Water is required to be mixed before application, if the mask is in powder form. These masks, on drying, harden on the skin and contract giving a sensation of mechanical astringency. Absorbent clays present in the formulation produce cleaning effect. Hydrocolloids may be added to stabilize the suspension of solids. Humaectants when added in such formulations act as plasticizers. These face packs/ masks may also contain ingredients like astringents, bleaching agents etc. if an added attribute is required. Formulae 7 to 9 are examples of face packs/masks based on earths.

Formula 7

		%
Kaolin		33.0
Bentonite		6.0
Cetyl alcohol		2.0
Sodium lauryl sulphate		0.1
Glycerin		12.0
Water	to make	100.0
Preservatives and Perfume		q.s.

Formula 8

	%
Kaolin	80.0
Magnesium Carbonate	15.0
Starch	4.0
Gum Tragacanth	1.5
Glycerin	8.0
Water sufficient to make paste	
Perfume and Preservatives	q.s.

Formula 9

	%
Kaolin	12.0
Titanium dioxide	4.5
3 Veegum	7.5

Sodium lauryl sulphate		2.0
Propylene glycol		6.0
Liquid lanolin		1.5
Isopropyl myristate		2.0
Glyceryl monostearate		3.5
Water	to make	100.0
Preservatives and Perfume		q.s.

An 'oxygenated' facemask can be prepared by incorporating peroxide like magnesium peroxide. Bergwein has suggested the following formula:

Formula 10

	Parts
Colloidal kaolin	800
Salicylic acid	20
Magnesium peroxide	200

Oxygenated masks have been recommended for use by the persons having oily skin or sallow skin. These can also be used by persons having skin blemishes.

In powder-form peel-off type alginates can also be used. Use of alginate has been illustrated in Formula 11.

Formula 11

	%
Kaolin	28.0
Talc	22.0
Sodium alginate	10.0
Calcium sulphate	35.0
Sodium carbonate	5.0
Colour	q.s.
Perfume	q.s.

When water is added to this formulation a calcium alginate gel is formed. This gel forms a film. Sodium Carbonate acts as gelling regulator.

Sodium alginate can also be used as gelling agent in powder form peel-off type packs. Calcium sulphate can be used as gelling reactant when sodium alginate is used. When sodium alginate is used, it should be coupled with gelling regulator like sodium carbonate. Use of sodium alginate has been illustrated in Formula 12.

Formula 12

	%
Kaolin	32.0
Talc	18.0
Sodium alginate	10.0
Calcium sulphate	35.0
Sodium carbonate	5.0
Preservatives, colour and perfume	q.s.

When this type of pack is mixed with water, calcium alginate gel is produced which forms the film.

Earths are heavily contaminated with micro-organisms. It is advisable to decontaminate them before use. The simple method to decontaminate earths is to heat them in oven for appropriate time. Decontamination by ethylene oxide gas can be successfully carried out without loss of any physical property of the earths. Gas sterilizers are available in the market. These are used in pharmaceutical industry.

A product which though strictly does not satisfy the attributes mentioned in the beginning of this chapter but can be placed in general classification of masks is scrubber. Its acceptance in market is not for tightening action but for its cleansing action. In such a product which can be called as cleansing masks or scrubber, a slightly abrasive material is included. It is formulated in nondrying vehicle. It is used by applying the product on skin and massaging on to the skin. Then it is allowed to remain on skin for about 10-20 minutes. Thereafter, it is removed with the help of wet towel. Formula 13 is an illustrative formula. Grain meal may be from either one or more grains like oat, rye, millet, barley, wheat, corn.

Formula 13

		%
Grain meal		23.0
Almond meal		12.0
Talc		14.0
Glycerin		20.0
Sorbitol (70% solution)		6.0
Water	to make	100.0
Colour, Perfume and Preservatives		q.s.

Zinc oxide is usually added to almond meal. These preparations should be adequately preserved as grain meal is highly susceptible to microbial growth. Opacity of formulation can be modified by use of titanium dioxide and zinc oxide. Cellulose type thickeners can also be used to modify plasticity of the finished product.

3. MANUFACTURE OF FACE PACKS/MASKS

If face packs/masks are to be manufactured in powder form, all powders are blended in a blender like ribbon blender. The powder mix is then transferred to filling machine. These may either be filled in bulk containers or in sachets.

Since paste masks form heavy compact masses, mixing equipment should have sufficient power so that thorough blending is achieved. Planetary dough mixers are suitable for this purpose. Wide bowl-tops of such mixers facilitate transfer of bulky materials to these. Most of such equipments have detachable mixing tank and tilting device which makes easy to remove semi-finished product.

Required quantities of dry materials are weighed and transferred to a blender (usually ribbon blender). The material is then transferred to planetary mixer. Blending of dry materials can also be accomplished in planetary mixer. If the liquid phase contains humectants and other water soluble ingredients, these may be mixed with water prior to addition of liquid phase. Liquid phase is added in small additions to the dry solids in planetary mixer with continuous agitation. Initially, these additions produce very viscous dough. Subsequently, with more additions viscosity decreases. Towards end of process, additions may be made at shorter time intervals.

If there are esters or waxes in the formulation, these should be molten. If the formulation contains both, fatty materials and water, these should be heated to almost same temperature. The same procedure as is used in manufacture of emulsion containing dispersed solids should be used for manufacture of such products. If pigments also form constituents of formulation, these should be dispersed in small quantity of solids and then into the powder mix.

20

Nail Lacquers and Removers

1. GENERAL

Nail lacquer or nail enamel is one of the most important group of the nail cosmetics. A lot of progress has been made in the formulation of these products. At one time, transparent uncoloured or pale pink natural colour were available. But now, a variety of shades are available.

A model nail lacquer should have the following properties:

* It should be harmless to the skin and nails.
* It should be convenient and easy to apply.
* It should be stable on storage.
* It should form a satisfactory film on nails.

To achieve a satisfactory film it should have the following characteristics:

* It should have proper viscosity (neither too thin nor too thick) and good wetting and flow properties so that the film formed is even.
* It should have uniform colour (which will require finely divided pigment intimately grounded and wetted by the solvent).
* It should have good gloss.
* It should have good adhesive properties.

* It should have sufficient flexibility so that it does not crack or become brittle.
* It should have sufficient hard surface which is resistant to impact and scratch.
* It should have reasonable drying time (1-2 minutes) without developing bloom.
* It should be able to maintain the above-mentioned properties for a reasonable time (about 1 week).

The above-mentioned characteristics may be achieved by careful selection of essential ingredients of nail enamels. These are:

- film formers;
- resins;
- plasticizers;
- solvents;
- pigments.

It will be appropriate to briefly discuss these ingredients.

Film Formers

A number of film forming substances have been suggested for nail enamels. These include cellulose acetate, cellulose acetate butylate, ethyl cellulose, vinyl polymers, and various polymers of methacrylate. But none of these is as acceptable as nitrocellulose. Nitrocellulose is available as solution in different viscosity (solution is effected by industrial spirit or solvent like butyl acetate). Special grades of nitrocellulose are available for nail lacquers. Films produced by nitrocellulose are hard and water-proof and these also resist abrasion. But when used alone, nitrocellulose has drawbacks like poor gloss, tendency to shrink, moderate adhesion. Therefore, other substances are used along with it which have been mentioned in proceeding paragraphs.

There are two standard types of nitrocellulose for lacquer work. These are designated as "RS" and "SS". The RS type contains 11.2 to 12.8% of nitrogen and is soluble in esters, ketones and glycol ethers. The SS type contains 10.7 to 11.2% nitrogen and is soluble in mixture of alcohol and toluene.

RS nitrocellulose is generally used in nail lacquer compositions. It is available in a range of viscosities. The viscosities are expressed in terms of time (usually seconds) required for a metal ball to fall through standard solution. Viscosity grades vary from 10 cps to 5000 sec.

The stability of nitrocellulose is indicative of the relative rate at which the material breaks down chemically. Stability of nitrocellulose is important to a cosmetic chemist as, instability of nitrocellulose may cause severe discolouration of nails of user. The chemist should also be careful in selecting other ingredients. Other ingredients should not adversely affect stability of nitrocellulose.

Resins

Resins impart adhesion and improve gloss. Resins used in industrial enamels were found unsuitable in nail enamels. Around Nineteen Hundred thirties, aryl sulphonamide for maldehyde type resins were introduced. These resins were good luster to nail varnish films and also improved resistance in detergent solutions. Since then, these resins have been used in nail enamels. Examples of two commercially available such resins are santolite MHP and santolite MS 80 percent. These resins are claimed to increase the hardness of the nitrocellulose film and impart gloss to it. They are also claimed to increase moisture resistance.

These resins are soluble in majority of solvents used for manufacture of nail enamels. However, their solvent release for higher alcohols is slow. Therefore, amount of high alcohols should be kept minimum.

The other resins that have been used are maleic alkyd resins. These resins are compatible with nitro-cellulose. Other resins that could be experimented include styrene alkyds, melamine-formaldehyde, urea formaldehyde and the acrylics.

Plasticizers

As mentioned above, nitro-cellulose alone gives a brittle film and therefore, other substances are added to the formulation of nail enamels. Plasticizers are one of them. Even resins which have been discussed in foregoing paragraphs will not impart necessary flexibility to lacquer films. As such, plasticizers are required to be used. Platicizers impart flexibility and adhesive properties to the film.

There are two types of plasticizers, namely, solvent plasticizers and non-solvent plasticizers. As the name suggests, the former are solvents for nitro-cellulose and main of them are high molecular weight esters having fairly high boiling point and low volatility (e.g., butyl acetyl ricenoleate). The latter are not solvents for nitro-cellulose and are not compatible with nitro-cellulose. These cannot be used alone, because, if used alone, after evaporation of solvent they often form droplets on the film. Therefore, these should be used in conjunction with solvent plasticizers. The most commonly used non-solvent plasticizer is castor oil. If used in proportion of 1:1, it produces a very flexible film.

The amount of plasticizers which can be used in nail lacquers varies widely and may vary from about 25% to 50% of dry nitro-cellulose. The amount depends on flexibility of the film required. Formulation may contain one, two or sometimes more than two plasticizers. Dibutyl phthálate is the most widely used plasticizer. The main group of plasticizers are constituted by phthalates, phosphates, phthalyl glycollates, sulphonamides and citrates. Some commonly used plasticizers are listed below:

Table 20.1: Plasticizers for nail lacquers

Tricresyl phosphate
Benzyl benzoate
Tributyl phosphate
Butyl acetyl ricenoleate
Dibutyl phthalate
Butyl glycollate
Dioctyl phthalate
Butyl stearate
Triphenyl phosphate
Triethyl citrate
Camphor
Castor oil
Dibutoxy ethyl phthalate
Dibutyl tartrate
Diamyl phthalate.

Glycollate plasticizers give better hardness to film, better feel and good adhesion on the nail.

Solvents

Although evaporation characteristics of solvents are of prime importance in nail lacquers, but too rapid rate of evaporation causes a poor flow of enamel resulting in uneven and streaky application. Very quickly evaporating solvents may cause intense cooling, this may cause precipiration of moisture from surrounding atmosphere making the film dull with unattractive finish. This is called 'blushing' of the lacquer. On the other hand, if solvent evaporates too slow, it will result in poor pick-up of nail enamel on the brush, thin application and extension of time of setting and hardening of the enamel. Solvents are generally classified according to their boiling points and are listed in the table.

Table 20.2: Solvents for nail lacquers

Solvent	Boiling range °C
Low boiling point Solvents	
Ethyl ether	34-35
Petroleum ether	40-60 and 60-80
Methyl acetate	56-59
Acetone	55-56
Cyclohexane	81
Ethyl acetate	74-79
Methyl ethyl ketone	79
Carbon tetrachloride	77
Ethyl alcohol	78
Isopropyl alcohol	80
Medium boiling point Solvents	
n-Butyl acetate	124-128
Amyl acetate	137-142
Xylol	138
n-Butyl alcohol	115-118
Diethylene glycol monoethyl ether	135
High boiling point Solvents	
Ethyl lactate	150-160
Cellosolve acetate	145-165
Butyl cellosolve	166-173
Carbitol	185-205

Rate of evaporation depends on many factors such as specific heat, latent heat of evaporation, molecular weight, degree of association etc. Other factors, besides the rate of evaporation, which will influence the selection of solvent include solvent capacity for non-volatile components, odour, (initial and residual), effect on viscosity of finished product.

Usually a mixture of solvents is used to achieve desired characteristics. There can be very many combinations and a correct solvent balance is a matter os experimentation. The solvents can be placed into three inter-related categories:

- active solvents,
- couplers, and
- diluents.

Solvents like esters, ketones and glycol ethers are true solvents for nitro-cellulose. These are active solvents. These may be fast, medium and slow evaporating. Couplers are not solvents for nitro-cellulose in themselves but when used in conjunction, they increase the strength of active solvents. Diluents are non-solvents for nitrocellulose. These are used to stabilize viscosity, to carry resins in solution and to reduce the effect of subsequent applications on the coat of enamel already applied. Aromatic and aliphatic hydrocarbons and alcohols are commonly used diluents (e.g., toluene, light petroleum ether). Only such amount of diluent should be used which will not precipitate ellulose solution. The amount of diluent which can be tolerated by cellulose solution is known tolerance. The actual tolerance ratio for solvent and diluent can be found out by titrating a given volume of the nitro-cellulose solution with diluent until the solution becomes turbid. Nail lacquers in which solvent-diluent ratio approximates to the tolerance ratio, have higher viscosity than the nail lacquers in which smaller amount of diluent has been used.

Alcohols, particularly ethyl, isopropyl and butyl are very efficient diluents. Ethyl alcohol is a controlled item and also produces chill, it is not used. Butyl alcohol evaporates neither too rapidly nor too slowly, but tends to lower the viscosity of nitro-cellulose solutions. Isopropyl alcohol, because of its lower cost and easy availability, is used widely. In nail varnishes, aromatic hydrocarbons like toluene and xylene are used, but they tend to increase the viscosity of nitro-cellulose solutions and also tend to impart poor flow property.

This may be overcome by using a mixture of toluene and isopropyl alcohol.

Pigments

Pigments used in nail enamels should have the same properties as required in other cosmetics, namely:

- these should be non-toxic and non-irritating;
- these should be non-staining;
- these should be substantially insoluble in lacquers;
- these should not exhibit bleeding tendency;
- these should be compatible with other ingredients of the lacquer;
- these should be moderately stable when exposed to light.

Once soluble dyes like erythrosine, carmosine and rhodamines were used but were found to stain surrounding skin. As such, the use of these dyes was abandoned. Insoluble lakes are incorporated in the nail lacquers to produce suitable shades. Colour lakes mentioned in the Schedule Q to the Drugs and Cosmetics Rules should be used.

The main inorganic pigments which can be used in nail enamels are:

- Titanium dioxide
- Yellow iron oxide
- Red iron oxide
- Iron blue
- Iron black
- Ultramarine blue
- Chrome oxide greens.

However, iron oxides and chrome greens have tendency to settle. In addition to coloured pigments, iridescent materials like 'pearl essence' can be incorporated into nail enamels. Pearl essence is a suspension of crystalline guanine (2-amino-6-hydroxy purine) in nitro-cellulose and solvents. Thus its is ready for use on dilution with finished lacquer. Owing to the high cost of pearl essence, synthetic pearl pigments are available, the most popular being bismuth oxychloride. Bismuth oxychloride is generally available as suspension (12.5-25.0%) in nitro-cellulose butyl acetate-toluene mixture to which a small amount of colloidal pre-treated clay is added. Another material which is gaining popularity is mica coated with titanium dioxide. Being less dense than bismuth oxychloride is easy to suspend. However, it is less brilliant than bismuth oxychloride and has less covering power.

Suspending Agents

Insoluble pigments and iridescent materials have tendency to settle. This is not considered good by the consumers. Therefore, developments have been made to avoid sedimentation. Suspending properties have been achieved by developing thixotropic system using pre-treated colloidal clays [e.g., benzyl dimethyl hydrogenated tallow, ammonium montmorillonite (bentone 27), dimethyl dioctadecyl ammonium bentonite (Bentone 34)]. These clays increase the viscosity to a great extent and heavy oxides remain suspended. Begin thixotropic, viscosity drops when either the bottle is shaken or when the product is applied with a brush on the nail. The concentration of bentone ranges from 0.5 to 2.0%. Viscosity can be further enhanced by adding small quantities of polyvalent acid e.g., orthophosphoric acid.

2. FORMULATION

Gloss, fullness of film and resistance to wear mainly depend on thickness of the nail lacquer. From the point of view of convenience and solvent economy it will be preferred that a thick film is achieved in single application. But practically, it may not be possible and more than one application may be required to achieve the desired thickness of the film.

The film thickness for single application depends upon non-volatile matter and the viscosity of the enamel applied. In this context it will be relevant to mention here that Indian Standards IS: 9245-1979 [Specifications for Nail Polish (Nail Enamel)] require that the nail enamel should contain at least 25% non-volatile matter. The viscosity range for easy application falls between 300 and 400 centipoises (cp). Products having viscosity less than 300 cp are likely to be so thin as not to remain on brush and products having viscosity substantially over 400 cp are likely to be thick and will give streaky and lumpy application.

As mentioned earlier, nitro-cellulose of RS type is used in the formulation of nail lacquers. Of the nitro-cellulose of several viscosities, RS 1/2 Sec., Rs 1/4 Sec. and RS 5-6 Sec. serve the purpose of a cosmetic chemist. RS 1/4 Sec. gives high solid content, RS 1/2 Sec. has better wear resistance and Rs 5-6 Sec. has high viscosity.

As mentioned in general discussion that innumerable combinations of different ingredients of nail enamels can be made, experimentation should be made to achieve the products of desired characteristics. Therefore, various tests should be devised to ascertain the following:

- flow characteristics of formulation;
- rate of drying of the lacquer film;
- compatibility of the constituents during drying;
- appearance and hardness;
- adhesion,
- resistance to soap and detergents

Selection of solvents for nail lacquers is an important task. Solvents for nail lacquers consist of a mixture of solvents suitably balanced so that rate of evaporation is neither too fast nor too slow. A blend of solvents given in Formula 1 and 2 can be used as solvent for lacquers.

Formula 1

	%
Methylated spirit	10.0
Ethyl acetate	20.0
Butyl acetate	15.0
Toluene	55.0

Formula 2

	%
Butyl alcohol	10.0
Butyl acetate	40.0
Toluene	50.0

A solution of nitro-cellulose (10-20%) in solvent blend like the one mentioned above provides the basis of a nail lacquer. But the film produced by such a lacquer will shrink on drying, will be brittle and dull. Therefore, suitable plasticizer(s) should be added to give the film flexibility. To impart gloss and hardness, some resin should be added. The resins which are most commonly used are condensation products of *para*-toluene sulphonamide and formaldehyde (santolites). Two commonly used resins of this type are santolite MS 80 and santolite MHP. Formula 3 is a typical nail lacquer base.

Formula 3

	%
Nitro-cellulose	18.5
Dibutyl phthalate	3.0
Santolite MS 80	6.5
Ethyl acetate	10.0
Butyl acetate	25.0
Isopropyl alcohol	10.0
Toluene	27.0

After a suitable solvent-plasticizer mix has been achieved, it can be further improved by addition of small amount of castor oil or a liquid acetylated monoglyceride. These materials impart additional plasticizing effect and make the film longer lasting with less tendency to chip.

In order to prepare the nail for better acceptance of the enamel, base coats have been developed. These contain higher quantities of resin to increase adhesion and quick drying solvents. A lower non-volatile content and lower viscosity are considered desirable characteristics for base coats. Formula 4 is an example of base coat lacquer. Small amount of pigment can be added to the base coat.

Formula 4

	%
Nitro-cellulose	10.0
Santolite	10.0
Dibutyl phthalate	3.0
Ethyl alcohol	6.0
Ethyl acetate	20.0
Butyl acetate	15.0
Toluene	36.0

For increased thickness of film, greater lustre and resistance to abrasion and wear, topcoats are applied. Formulations of topcoats contain higher percentage of nitro-cellulose and plasticizer and lower percentage resin. They also contain relatively higher percentage of diluent. Formula 5 is an example of topcoat.

Formula 5

	%
Nitro-cellulose	18.0
Santolite	4.0
Dibutyl phthalate	5.0
Isopropyl alcohol	11.0
Ethyl acetate	10.0
Butyl acetate	10.0
Toluene	42.0

Pigments are added to the lacquer base to prepare final product. The concentration of pigments varies from about 3-5% in the final product. Usually the pigments are first dispersed by milling in suitable vehicle and are converted into coloured chips. These coloured chips are dissolved in lacquer base when required. Alternatively, concentrated tint bases, known as concentrated tinters can be prepared by dissolving coloured chips in lacquer base and these can then be blended with lacquer to achieve the final product.

Thick or cream type enamels can be prepared by including titanium dioxide in the formulation. It also helps in varying shades. For pearly or iridescent type of products special additives like pearl essence, bismuth, oxychloride, mica coated with titanium dioxide are added. These materials are available as concentrated dispersions in enamel base and can be blended with the lacquer for desired effect.

Keither proposes in interesting formula which does not contain nitro-cellulose and contains chlorinated biphenol as plasticizer (see formula 6).

Formula 6

	%
Polyvinyl chloride-acetate co-polymer	10.7
Polymethyl methacrylate	7.0
Methyl ethyl ketone	21.5
Sorbitol	20.0

Arochlor 5460	15.0
Tricresyl phosphate	8.0
Ethyl acetate	22.3
Colours	0.5

Frosted nail enamels can be prepared by incorporating frosted nail enamel concentrates. These are viscous nitrocellulose pastes containing quaternary ammonium modified clay as thixotropic agent. On dilution with correct amount of clear lacquer, a non-setting pearlescent nail enamel is obtained. The recommended dilution ratio must be followed in order to produce nail enamel of desired quality. The formulator should reach the manufacturers bulletin. Pearl concentrates are based on (i) synthetic pearl (Bismuth oxychloride) and (ii) natural pearl essence (Guanine). Paste concentrates containing 25% of pigment are also available. These are diluted with suspending lacquer to form stable enamel.

Since Bismuth oxychloride may darken in UV radiation, it must be stabilized. The supplier of pearl concentrates can advise on the type of UV absorber and its concentration. Formula 7 is an example of frosted nail enamel.

Formula 7

		%
Pearl concentrate		16.0
UV absorber		q.s.
Diluting lacquer	to make	100.0

Diluting lacquer may be prepared with the following formula:

	%
Nitrocellulose (RS type)	15.0
Toluene sulphonamide/Formaldehyde Resin	10.0
Camphor	2.0
Dibutyl phthalate	5.0
Isopropyl alcohol, anhydrous	7.0
Butyl acetate	33.0
Ethyl acetate	5.0
n-Butyl alcohol	2.0
Methoxy propanol acetate	2.0
Toluene	19.0

3. MANUFACTURE ON NAIL LACQUERS OR ENAMELS

Manufacturing of nail enamels involves following distinct processes.

3.1 Grinding of Pigments

Finely divided pigments particles have tendency to form aggregates. These aggregates can be broken down by shearing force. Dispersion of aggregates can be carried out either in ball mill or roller mill (double or triple roller). The roller mill of the type which is used in rubber compounding is suitable for dispersion of pigments for nail enamels. The grinding charge consists of pigment, nitro-cellulose, plasticizer and sufficient solvent to make a plastic mass. This plastic mass is then charged on to the rollers and passed through them to formulation sheet. The sheet is passed and repassed through rollers till dispersion of desired degree has been achieved. Generally, all the solvent and a part of plasticizer evaporates during milling because of the heat generated during milling.

The sheet, while hot is soft and plastic and can be dissolved easily in the lacquer. However, if it is not to be used immediately, the sheet, on cooling, hardens and can be broken into chips and can be stored for use in future. To ascertain dispersion of pigments, a small piece out of the sheet can be dissolved on a glass slide and examined under microscope for aggregates.

3.2 Manufacture of Nail Lacquer

Manufacture of nail lacquer involves simple mixing process. Mixing tanks for manufacture of nail lacquers should be made of either aluminium or stainless steel. Other metals can cause discolouration of lacquer. The mixing tanks may have potable or stationary stirrer (propeller type or turbine type). For manufacturing clear lacquers, diluent(s) are first charged into the mixing tank. Nitro-cellulose is then added with stirrer on and is wetted thoroughly with diluent(s). Subsequently, solvent is added, then plasticizer is added and next resin is added. Mixing is continued for several hours until solution of all ingredients is complete. Thus formed clear lacquer is passed through filter press or alternatively is centrifuged. The clear lacquer is stored in suitable containers until required for use. Filtration on centrifugation is an important step as it removes foreign particles and insoluble particles imparting clarity and brilliance to the lacquer.

3.3 Mixing of Pigments with Lacquer

For manufacturing nail enamels, required amount of clear lacquer is charged into the mixing tank and stirrer is switched on. To this are added pigments chips or concentrated tinters and mixing is continued. The product is filled into containers and containers are closed and screw sealed immediately.

3.4 Safety Aspects

Solvents used in the manufacture of lacquers are highly inflammable. Therefore, proper precautions must be taken to avoid perils of fire and explosion. All equipments used in the manufacture of nail lacquers should be explosion-proof. Some important precautions are as under:

* Storage of raw materials should be reasonably far from manufacturing area.
* Similarly storage of finished products should be reasonably far from raw material storage area and manufacturing area.
* Nitro-cellulose should not be stored in open sun. It should preferably be stored in a separate building about 100 ft. away from any other building. Such a building should also be protected by a sprinkler system.
* Unloading station for solvents should be located away from storage and handling area.
* If solvents are to be transferred from tank car, solvent should be unloaded through top connection and never by bottom connections.
* Engines of truck car should be shut off before unloading operation is commenced to avoid accident because of spark from engine or exhaust.
* Buildings in which solvents are handled should be very well-ventilated by means of fans and ducts so that vapour concentrations of solvents do not build up to dangerous levels.
* Floors of buildings in which solvents are handled should be made of non-sparking and non-conductive materials.
* Tools and auxiliary equipments should be constructed of metals other than iron to minimise the danger of struck sparks.

* Mixing tanks, storage tanks and other fixed equipments should be installed by adequately grounding them so as to pervent discharge of sparks by static electricity.
* In addition to sprinkler system, there should be carbon dioxide systems to flood the individual equipment with carbon dioxide.

Personnel working in lacquer manufacturing should be educated about the hazards and should be trained in fire fighting including means of escape from burning building.

4. ENAMEL REMOVERS

4.1 General

Usually nail enamel removers are mixtures of solvents containing small amount of fats. As the name suggests, these products are used to remove nail enamel. Enamel removers are generally available as liquids. However, cream nail enamels removers are also marketed.

4.2 Formulation

As mentioned above, nail enamel removers may be formulated with suitable solvents like acetone, ethyl acetate, toluene etc. More volatile solvents like acetone, ethyl acetate cause dehydration and remove natural fat from nails. Dehydration of nails can be reduced to some extent by either using solvent blends or by adding a small percentage of oily material. Castor oil has been used in earlier formulations. Formula 8 is an example of such formulation.

Formula 8

	%
Castor oil	2.5
Diethylene glycol monoethyl ether	14.5
Acetone	83.0

Other oils which have been mentioned in literature include almond oil, olive oil, cottonseed oil and even mineral oil. Some other fatty additives which are used in nail enamel removers are dibutyl phthalate, butyl stearate, glycol monolaurate, glyceryl monoricinoleate and lanolin derivatives. Still other substances, the use of which has been mentioned in the literature are cetyl alcohol, glycol stearate, triethanolamine stearate and magnesium oleate. Formula 9 is based on butyl stearate and solvent blend.

Formula 9

	%
Butyl stearate	3.0
Ethyl acetate	15.0
Butyl acetate	25.0
Acetone	27.0
Toluene	30.0

The products can be made more attractive, if these could be perfumed. Because of objectionable odour of solvents a higher percentage of perfume will be required. A heavy floral type perfume can be used in concentration upto 3.0%.

A different type of nail enamel remover, so called non-smearing remover can be formulated with a mixture of water and water-miscible solvent. This type of removers do not dissolve enamel but loosen and dis-integrate it. A simple remover of this type can be prepared with water and ethyl acetate as shown in Formula 10.

Formula 10

	%
Water	10.0
Ethyl acetate	90.0

Nail enamel removers can be prepared in cream form by dissolving waxes in lacquer solvents. For these formulations fairly high boiling point lacquer solvents are used, e.g., Methyl ethyl ketone. In the formulations based on solvent and waxes alone, solvent tends to break away from the wax during use. This can be reduced by addition of acetylated monoglycerides. Addition of small amount of bentonite helps to keep the product in cream form. Formula 11 is an example of such a product.

Formula 11

	%
Beeswax	8.0
Carnauba wax	12.0
Acetylated monoglycerides (solid and liquid type in equal parts)	10.0
Bentonite	1.0

Methyl ethyl ketone	69.0

A cream type nail enamel remover can be prepared with solvent, waxes and soap (like triethanolamine stearate). Formula 12 is an example of such a product.

Formula 12

	%
Beeswax	3.0
Micro-crystalline wax	1.0
Acetylated monoglycerides (solid type)	10.0
Diethylene glycol monoethyl ether	52.0
Ethyl acetate	15.0
Stearic acid	15.0
Triethanolamine	4.0

Method of Preparation

Put all the ingredients together except triethanolamine and melt them. Add triethanolamine to the mixture with stirring and allow to cool.

A gel type nail varnish remover may be formulated using hydroxy propyl cellulose. Formula 13 is an illustrative example.

Formula 13

		%
Hydroxy propyl cellulose		1.0
Butyrol acetone		75.0
PPG-12-PEG-50 lanolin		1.0
Pigment (in Butyrol acetone)		0.1
Sodium hydroxide (5% aqueous) (to adjust pH to 7.0)		q.s.
Water	to make	100.0

Method of Preparation

Mix all ingredients except hydroxy propyl cellulose. Add hydroxy propyl cellulose to vortex of well agitated liquid at room temperature. Addition of the cellulose should be slow enough to permit particles to separate in the liquid. However, all the powder should be added before appreciable viscosity build up is obtained. Disperse for 10 minutes and then allow wet for 30 minutes.

Thereafter, stir for 5 minutes.

A conditioning nail polish remover can be prepared with Malleated Soybean oil and acetone (see Formula 14).

Formula 14

	%
Malleated Soybean oil	10.0
Acetone	90.0

4.3 Manufacture of Enamel Remover

As may be seen from the formulae of liquid nail enamel remover, these contain solvents and substances soluble in solvents. These can be manufactured in mixing tanks having an agitator.

Cream formulations are dispersions of waxes in solvents which may be achieved by melting waxes with gentle heat and stirring in a mixing tank.

All safety precautions mentioned in earlier section of this chapter should be observed in the manufacture of enamel removers.

21

Toothpastes

1. GENERAL

Food debris and plaque seem to be the causes for tooth problems. These and tooth surface stains can be removed in a part if not altogether by the use of a cleansing dentifrice in conjunction with tooth brush. Dentifrices can be prepared in the form of paste, powder, liquid and block. Although primary function of a dentifrice is to clean accessible surfaces of the teeth but secondary results of this cleansing affect the incidence of tooth decay, gingival health and mouth odours. Thus dentifrices are not only cosmetics but are also preventive measures for teeth problems.

Minimum requirements for a dentifrice are listed below:

* When used with a tooth brush in should adequately clean teeth of food debris, plaque and stains.
* It should leave a sensation of cleanliness and freshness in mouth.
* It should be non-toxic, pleasant and convenient to use.
* It should be stable during its commercial shelf life.
* It should be economic in cost so as to encourage its use by all sections of the society.
* It should conform to national standards for its abrasivity to enamel and dentine.
* Any claims made should be substantiated by appropriate data.

To achieve these minimum and additional requirements dentifrices have been formulated in different forms. Out of these toothpaste is the most popular form of dentifrice.

2. FORMULATION

To achieve the characteristics mentioned above and other desired characteristics various materials have been used in the formulation of toothpastes. These materials can be divided into the following groups:

- Abrasives,
- Detergents and foaming materials,
- Humectants,
- Binding agents,
- Sweetening and flavouring agents,
- Miscellaneous agents-preservatives, therapeutic agents, etc.

(i) Abrasives

Abrasives in dentifrices are used to remove food debris and residual stains of the teeth and to polish the teeth surface. The abrasives used in dentifrices should possess the following properties:

- they should be compatible with other ingredients of dentifrice;
- they should not produce dust, if used as powder, all the same they should be small enough not to be gritty in the mouth;
- they should be free from earthy taste;
- they should be non-toxic.

The most widely used abrasives include precipitated calcium carbonate, dibasic calcium phosphate dihydrate, anhydrous dibasic calcium phosphate, tricalcium phosphate, calcium pyrophosphate, insoluble sodium metaphosphate and hydrated alumina.

Precipitated Chalk

Precipitated chalk or precipitated calcium carbonate is available in a number of grades. These grades differ in crystalline form, particle size and surface area. Detailed information can be obtained from the manufacturers. Two common crystal types are:

– aragonite (orthorhombic crystals);
– calcite (rhombohedral crystals).

Particle sizes vary from 2-20 μm. Grades containing particle size more than 20 μm may produce scratching on enamel surface and therefore, should not be used. It is common to use small proportion of chalk with large proportion of less abrasive phosphates.

Calcium Phosphates

Various phosphates of calcium which have been used in dentifrices are:

– dicalcium phosphate dihydrate,
– anhydrous dicalcium phosphate,
– tricalcium phosphate,
– calcium pyrophosphate.

Out of these dicalcium phosphate dihydrate (DCP) is most commonly used in dentifrices. Taste of toothpastes made with DCP is better than made with chalk. DCP being in the metastable state reverts to the anhydrous form resulting in hardening of the paste. This change is accelerated, if fluoride ions are present. Usually stabilized DCP is supplied. Stabilization is achieved by addition of stabilizers like trimagnesium phosphate, calcium sodium pyrophosphate, tetrasodium pyrophosphate.

Anhydrous DCP is more abrasive than DCP and therefore, it should be used in small proportions. It is less soluble than DCP dihydrate and is of advantage in toothpastes containing fluorides.

Tricalcium phosphate is not used that commonly. It is also less soluble than DCP.

Calcium pyrophosphate was developed for use in tooth pastes containing fluorides (sodium fluoride, stannous fluoride). It is insoluble in water. In fact, it is claimed that low availability of calcium ions is a contributory factor to the stability of fluorides.

Other Phosphates

The other phosphates which have been used in dentifrices are insoluble sodium metaphosphate and ammonium phosphate dibasic. Since insoluble sodium metaphosphate does not contain calcium ion, it is used in fluoride containing tooth pastes. Its main disadvantage as abrasive is that it contains small proportion of soluble phosphates. Ammonium phosphate dibasic occurs as white crystals or powder. This being soluble in water is not frequently used but sometimes it is used as an ingredient of ammoniated dentifrices.

Hydrated alumina ($Al_2O_3.3H_2O$)

Hydrated alumina is available in two forms, as a white micro-crystalline powder and as a gel (suspension). Powder is used for its abrasive and cleansing properties. Gel is used in medicines as antacid.

(ii) Detergents and other foaming materials

Detergents and foaming materials in tooth pastes are used for their cleansing action. These materials lower surface tension, thereby promote penetration of paste and help in removal of deposits and debris. These also remove mucus by emulsification.

Soap is the earliest used foaming material. But it had disadvantage of alkaline pH, bad taste and incompatibility with many materials. The disadvantages of soaps were overcome by synthetic detergents. A large number of synthetic detergents are available. But only those detergents can be used in dentifrices which are tasteless, non-toxic and non-irritant to oral mucosa. The commonly used synthetic detergents in dentifrices include sodium lauryl sulphate (SLS), magnesium lauryl sulphate, sodium lauryl sarcosinate, sodium lauryl sulphoacetate, dioctyl-sodium sulphosuccinate, monoglycerides, sulphates and sulphonates. Properties of the most commonly used detergents are mentioned below in brief.

Sodium Lauryl Sulphate

Sodium lauryl sulphate is available in various grades. While selecting sodium lauryl sulphate for tooth paste, particular attention should be given to its taste. Taste is influenced by free alcohol content. A low content of inorganic salts are desirable. Recrystallized grades are very good but these are expensive.

Sodium Lauryl Sarcosinate

Sodium lauryl sarcosinate is another detergent which has been widely used. A Colgate patent claims prophylectic effects due to its anti-enzymatic activity. It is highly soluble and therefore, is preferred in oral products.

Sodium Lauryl Sulphoacetate

Sodium lauryl sulphoacetate occurs as white powder having coconut like odour. Its aqueous solution has acrid taste and is neutral or slightly alkaline in pH.

(iii) Humectants

Humectants in tooth pastes are used to prevent their drying out. They also impart some plasticity to toothpastes. Earlier, glycerin was the only humectant that was used in toothpastes. Later on, other humectants were also used and these include propylene glycol and sorbital solution. Glycerin is still most commonly used because it produces glossy product, its behaviour is well-known with other ingredients and also acts as sweetening agent. Propylene glycol tends to produce pastes of softer consistency. It also has slightly bitter taste. Sorbitol solution (70%) can replace glycerin as it has high viscosity and produces firmer toothpastes with good plasticity.

(iv) Binding Agents

Solid and liquid phases of toothpastes tend to separate in absence of binding agents particularly during storage. All binding agents essentially are hydrophilic colloids. Biding agents disperse, swell or absorb water to form viscous liquid phases. Binding agents which have been used in toothpastes include natural gums (e.g., gum tragacanth, gum arabic), cellulose derivatives (e.g., carboxymethyl cellulose, sodium carboxymethyl cellulose, hyroxyethyl cellulose), starch ethers and synthetic resins.

At one time, glycerin of starch, liquid glucose and simple syrup were used in toothpastes. Subsequently, mucilages prepared from natural gums like gum tragacanth, gum arabic, gum karaya were used. Another natural material, Irish Moss also known as carrageen has been used. A 3% solution in boiling water forms a thick jelly on cooling. Pastes made with Irish Moss have soft and attractive texture. These materials have been largely replaced by cellulose derivatives.

Cellulose derivatives are the most commonly used binding agents for toothpastes. Important ones are mentioned below in brief.

Carboxymethyl Cellulose (CMC) and Sodium Carboxymethyl Cellulose (SCMC)

SMC is the most widely used cellulose derivative. It is anionic in nature. It is sensitive to pH values outside 5.5-9.5. Gel produced by SCMC is reasonably stable in the presence of electrolytes and calcium ions. Because of its anionic nature, SCMC is not suitable for toothpastes containing cationic anti-bacterials.

Cellulose ethers

The most widely used cellulose ethers are methy and hydroxyethyl. By varying the degree of substitution their properties can be changed and can be tailormade for desired purpose. These are non-ionic in nature. These are stable over a wide range of pH and are not affected by metallic ions. These can be used in toothpastes containing cationic anti-bacterials.

Methyl cellulose is more soluble in cold water than not water. Glycerin should not be used when methyl cellulose is a binding agent as it is somewhat incompatible with it.

Hydroxyethyl cellulose has general properties of cellulose ethers. Toothpastes made with hydroxyethyl cellulose disperse slower than those made with SCMC. It is usually used in toothpastes which contain cations.

Synthetic Resins

Use of two resins namely Polyox (an ethylenoxide polymer) and carbopol (a carboxy vinyl polymer) has been suggested. These resins have thickening and suspending properties.

(v) Sweetening and Flavouring Agents

Sweetening and flavouring agents are, by far, the most important ingredients in toothpaste as they have great influence on the acceptance of the product.

Amongst the sweetening agents which have been commonly used in toothpaste include saccharin sodium (0.05 to 0.3%) and chloroform. The concentration of sodium saccharin will also depend on the humectant used. For example, if glycerin is used as humectant a low concentration of saccharin sodium will be required. Chlorofom is also a good sweetening and flavouring agents as it covers chalky taste and dry feeling in the mouth. It gives a sharp, fresh sweetness Apart from its sweetening property, it also has anti-bacterial property.

Although flavouring of toothpastes is done by blending suitable oils but it needs can expertise to prepare the desired flavour. The flavour should leave a pleasant, clean and refreshing feeling in the mouth after use. The flavours which have attained popularity are spearmint, peppermint, wintergreen, cinnamon-mint. Principal flavouring agent is not used alone. It is blended with other essential oils to modify the flavour and to give a distinctive note. The essential oils which are used to modify flavours are oils of clove, anise, caraway, coriander, pimento, eucalyptus, nutmeg, thyme. Some other oils which have also been used are citrus oils, eugenol, eucalyptol, ionone, orris and menthol.

The proportion in which the flavour should be used will depend on the other ingredients like sweetening agent, detergent etc. and may vary from 0.5 to 3.0%. Since the abrasives are generally absorptive materials, it is necessary to evaluate product after storing for a period (several weeks). Trial batches should be evaluated when freshly prepared as well as after ageing as suggested above.

(vi) Miscellaneous Agents

Amongst miscellaneous dentifrice agents are included preservatives and substances included for specific action like astringent, anti-bacterial etc. Though some preserving action is imparted by essential oils and chloroform (if added) but it is always advisable to add preservatives. Commonly used preservatives are methyl *parahydroxy* benzoate (0.15%) and propyl *para*hydroxy benzoate (0.02%). Use of sodium benzoate is not recommended in toothpastes. Other anti-microbials like formaldehyde, dichlorophene can also be used.

Additives like astingents (e.g., zinc chloride), oxidizing agents (e.g., potassium chlorate, sodium perborate) have been used. Chlorophyll is sometimes included for its deodorizing effect. It is understood that stannous fluoride combines with tooth enamel to form insoluble film of tin oxide, tin phosphates and calcium fluoride which is resistant to acid attack.

Fosdick and co-workers suggested that one of the most effective ways of preventing dental caries would be use of enzyme inhibitors (or anti-enzyme). A large number of compounds were screened for this property. Only a few compounds were found having this property. Of those three substances have been tested in vivo. These are penicillin, sodium N-lauroyl sarcosinate and sodium dehydroacetate. Mouthwashes containing these substances decreased rate of fermentation significantly. Sodium N-lauroyl sarcosinate has been used as foaming agent in dentifrices. Such formulations are referred to as anti-enzyme dentifrice.

After discussing briefly the various ingredients it will be appropriate to give a basic formula showing the proportions of various ingredients that have been discussed in preceding paragraphs. Formula 1 represents such a basic formula.

Formula 1

		%
Abrasives		40.0-60.0
Detergents/foaming agents		1.50-3.00
Humectants		5.00-30.0
Binding agents		0.50-2.50
Sweetening and flavouring agents		0.50-3.00
Miscellaneous ingredients		0.15-0.50
Water	to make	100.0

A formula in which calcium carbonate has been used as abrasive is shown in Formula 2.

Formula 2

		%
Precipitated calcium carbonate		42.0
Glycerin		30.0
Propylene glycol		3.0
Gum tragacanth		1.2
Saccharin sodium		0.05
Sodium lauryl sulphate		1.3
Water	to make	100.0
Flavour, chloroform, preservatives		q.s.

In formula 3, a part of calcium carbonate has been replaced with di-calcium phosphate and gum tragacanth has been replaced by sodium carboxymethyl cellulose.

Formula 3

	%
Di-calcium phosphate	30.0
Precipitated calcium carbonate	15.0

Glycerin		25.0
Saccharin sodium		0.05
Sodium lauryl sulphate		1.2
Sodium carboxymethyl cellulose		1.0
Water	to make	100.0
Flavour, chloroform, preservatives		q.s.

In formula 4, calcium carbonate has been completely replaced with di-calcium phosphate, gum tragacanth has been replaced by Irish Moss extract and sodium lauryl sulphate has been replaced with sodium coconut monoglyceride sulphonate.

Formula 4

		%
Di-calcium phosphate		42.0
Glycerin		25.0
Saccharin sodium		0.05
Irish Moss		1.5
Water	to make	100.0
Flavour and Preservatives		q.s.

Sodium lauryl sarcosinate is claimed to have anti-enzymatic activity. Formula 5 represents the use of this substance.

Formula 5

		%
Precipitated calcium carbonate		12.0
Di-calcium phosphate dihydrate		38.0
Sodium lauryl sacrosinate		2.0
Glycerin		30.0
Irish Moss		1.0
Water	to make	100.0
Flavours, sweetening agent, preservatives		q.s.

In a British patent flouride toothpaste has been suggested with micro-crystalline aluminium hydroxide (325 mesh) as abrasive and is shown in formula 6.

Formula 6

	%
Microcrystalline aluminium hydroxide	38.2
Aluminium hydroxide (325 mesh)	5.0

Sodium fluoride	0.1
Sodium alginate	1.0
Glycerol	15.3
Sorbo (70% aqueous sorbitol)	15.3
Water	20.8
Colour	0.004
Saccharin soluble	0.25
Flavour	1.2
Sodium lauryl sulphate	2.2
Orthophosphoric acid to adjust pH 7.3	q.s.

Fluoride in toothpastes in India has been restricted to 1000 ppm. This requirement is laid down under the Drugs and Cosmetics Rules. Fluoride toothpastes are also required to have date of expiry on the label.

Formula 7 is an example where sodium monofluoro phosphate has been used as source of fluoride.

Formula 7

		%
Insoluble sodium metaphosphate		40.0
Di-calcium phosphate, anhydrous		7.0
Hydrated alumina		1.0
Glycerin		15.0
Sorbitol Solution (70%)		12.0
Irish Moss		1.0
Titanium dioxide		0.5
Saccharin		0.1
Sodium monofluoro-phosphate		0.76
Sodium N-lauroyl sarcosinate		2.0
Water	to make	100.0
Flavour		q.s.
	pH adjusted to	6-6.5

When fluoride tooth pastes are to be formulated, abrasive material should be chosen with care. Use of calcium carbonate with sodium monofluoro-phosphate will result in formation of calcium fluoride and the formulation will lose its cariostatic activity. Insoluble sodium metaphosphate and special grade of calcium pyrophosphate are usually used in the formulation of fluoride tooth paste. The following concentrations of commonly used fluorides corresponds to 1000 ppm.

Fluoride	Concentration
Sodium fluoride	0.2%
Stannous fluoride	0.4%
Sodium monofluoro-phosphate	0.76%

Formula 8 is an example of tooth paste illustrating use of calcium pyrophosphate and stannous fluoride.

Formula 8

		%
Calcium pyrophosphate		38.0
Stannous pyrophosphate		2.0
Stannous fluoride		0.4
Glycerin		25.0
Sorbitol solution		12.5
Irish Moss		1.5
Sodium saccharin		0.05
Sodium lauryl sulphate		2.0
Water	to make	100.0
Flavour		q.s.
Orthophosphoric acid		q.s
	to adjust pH to	7.3

Other additives like soluble chlorophyll derivatives (e.g., sodium copper chlorophyllin) anti-enzyme substance and oxidizing agents (e.g., potassium chlorate) have also been used. Formula 9 is an example of toothpaste containing chlorophyll derivative.

Formula 9

	%
Isoluble sodium polymetaphosphate	30.0
Di-calcium phosphate	25.0
Gum tragacanth	1.5
Sodium lauryl sulphate	1.0
Saccharin sodium	0.2
Glycerin	20.0
Sodium copper chlorophyllin	0.1

Water	to make	100.0
Flavour		q.s.

Ammoniated toothpastes can be prepared by adding ammonium compounds like urea, di-ammonium phosphates, aminoacetic acid etc. Formula 10 is an example of ammoniated tooth paste.

Formula 10

		%
Tri-calcium phosphate		28.0
Sodium lauryl sulphoacetate		2.5
Glycerin		40.0
Gum tragacanth		1.0
Sodium saccharin		0.1
Di-ammonium phosphate		5.0
Urea		3.0
Water	to make	100.0

Anti-enzyme toothpaste can be formulated using sodium N-lauroyl sarcosinate (see Formula 11).

Formula 11

		%
Di-calcium phosphate dihydrate		38.0
Calcium carbonate		12.0
Glycerin		30.0
Irish Moss		1.0
Sodium N-lauryol sarcosinate		2.0
Water	to make	100.0
Flavouring and sweetening agents and preservatives		q.s.

Now a days, toothpastes in gel form are available. Formula 12 is a typical example of toothpaste in gel form.

Formula 12

	%
Silica	20.0
Sorbitol solution (70%)	50.0
Glycerin	12.0
Sodium lauryl sulphate	1.5
Sodium carboxymethyl cellulose	1.5

Sodium saccharin		0.05
Water	to make	100.0
Flavour, colour and preservatives		q.s.

Though not popular, liquid form dentifrice can be prepared in water and alcohol mixture. See Formula 13.

Formula 13

		%
Sodium lauryl sulphate		1.0
Glycerin		6.0
Polyoxyethylene polypropylene glycol		0.5
Sodium saccharin		0.1
Ethanol		10.0
Water	to make	100.0
Flavour, colour and preservatives		q.s.

Method of Preparation

Dissolve glycerin, sodium lauryl sulphate and Polyoxyethylene polypropylene glycol in purified water. Dissolve flavour in ethanol and add to the aqueous solution. Add to this mixture colour, preservatives and sweetening agents.

3. MANUFACTURE OF TOOTH PASTES

Manufacture of tooth pastes should be carried out either in stainless steel vessel or tin lined vessel. For mixing either a kneading machine or a dough mixer with slowly rotating blades can be used. Common practice in the manufacture of tooth pates is to prepare an aqueous gel or mucilage. If gum tragacanth is being used for preparing mucilage, it is advisable to first disperse it in appropriate quantity of humectant and then add water. Sodium carboxy methyl cellulose should be wetted with hot water to get better results. On the contrary, methyl cellulose should be wetted with cold water. After wetting remaining water should be added and mixed. The mix is usually allowed to stand overnight. If the mix is to be left overnight, preservatives are dissolved in water before it is added to the wetted cellulose derivatives. Part of humectant can also be added while preparing the mix.

Next, powder ingredients except detergent are sifted together and are added gradually to the aqueous mucilaginous mixture with slow but continuous stirring. Addition of powders and humectant(s) may be alternated which will maintain the mix in a creamy form. While adding powder or humectant it should be ensured that the consistency of paste does not become too soft or too hard. After addition of all powders, flavouring agent(s) is/ are added. Surface active agent is added in the last. Flavours and surface active agent influence thixotrophic properties. Therefore, if the final texture of the paste becomes too soft, the formula should be revised. Aeration or foaming should be avoided during mixing. If the formula is well-balanced, gentle agitation does not cause aeration or foaming. Vacuum mixing is also employed to prevent aeration or foaming. Mixing should be continued till all the constituents are evenly distributed. The finished product thus obtained is allowed to stand for 24 hours. During the period, though the paste becomes firmer but more elastic. The paste is finally filled into collapsible tubes.

In an alternate method the binder is pre-mixed with solid abrasives and introduced simultaneously with an aqueous solution of humectant, preservatives and saccharin into a suitable mixer. The mass is mixed into a homogeneous paste. Thereafter flavouring agent and detergent are mixed and mixing is completed. The rest of the method is the same as described above. Before employing this method of manufacture it should be ascertained that binder would swell adequately during mixing process to form an uniform paste.

Earlier, tin tubes were used for packaging tooth paste. Tin coated lead tubes were also used. Aluminium tubes being light and strong are now being used. However, aluminium is subject to corrosion. Corrosion of tubes can be minimised by internally waxing or lacquering the tubes. Addition of inhibitors of corrosion such as sodium silicate also reduce corrosion. Stannous fluoride attacks aluminium. Therefore, pastes containing stannous fluoride should not be packed in aluminium tubes. Collapsible tubes made of polyolefins are also used. Currently many toothpastes are available in polyolifins collapsible tubes.

22

Tooth Powders

1. GENERAL

Tooth powders are original form of dentifrice. Though less popular than tooth paste, tooth powders are also used in India. Tooth powders are more popular in suburban and rural areas. The constituents of tooth powder and tooth paste are same except that tooth powders do not contain humectants, water and binding agents. Camphorated chalk (calcium carbonate containing camphor) was an early dentifrice but was discontinued as it had the potential of cracking of the tooth enamel on continued use. Carbolic tooth powders (tooth powders containing phenol) were popular at one time. Most of the modern tooth powders contain abrasives, detergent, flavouring and sweetening agents. They may also contain additional additives.

In India black tooth powders are also available. Black tooth powders usually contain burnt seed kernel, bark or other plant materials. Plant materials are burnt to the extent that these are converted into coal. The coal is powdered to produce fine charcoal particles. They usually contain other additives like, salt, flavours etc.

2. FORMULATION

Tooth powders contain abrasives, detergents or other foaming agents, sweetening and flavouring agents. Most commonly used abrasives include calcium carbonate, tri-calcium phosphate, insoluble sodium metaphosphate. Soaps and detergents, both have been used in tooth powders. Dental soap powder is prepared from selected fatty acids. These powders are white or creamy white and are tasteless. When soap is to be used as foaming agent, it should be ensured that it has not been made from unsuitable fats because soap from such fats have strong odour and soapy taste. One of the soaps that has been used is sodium palmitate. Amongst the detergents, sodium lauryl sulphate has been used extensively.

Tooth powders are usually flavoured with essential oils. Flavouring oils include peppermint oil, spearmint oil, clove oil, cinnamon oil, anise oil.

Tooth powders also contain sweetening agent. Sodium saccharin is the most commonly used sweetening agent in tooth powders.

Use of these constituents has been illustrated in the formulae 1 to 3.

Formula 1

	%
Calcium carbonate (precipitated)	94.0
Sodium palmitate (soap)	5.0
Flavouring oils	1.0
Sweetening agent (sodium saccharin)	q.s.

Formula 2

	%
Di-calcium phosphate (di-hydrate)	80.0
Calcium carbonate (precipitated	19.0
Sodium lauryl sulphate	1.0
Flavouring agent(s)	q.s.
Sweetening agent	q.s.

Formula 3

	%
Insoluble sodium metaphosphate	78.8
Tri-calcium phosphate	20.0
Sodium lauryl sulphate	1.2
Flavouring agent(s)	q.s.
Sweetening agent	q.s.

Like toothpastes, other additives are also used in tooth powders e.g., peroxides, ammonia compounds, fluorides, chlorophyll derivatives. Examples of tooth powders containing additives mentioned above are shown in formulae 4 to 6.

Formula 4

	%
Calcium carbonate (precipitated)	96.2
Sodium lauryl sulphate	1.8
Magnesium peroxide	2.0
Flavouring agent(s)	q.s.
Sweetening agent	q.s.

Formula 5

	%
Di-basic ammonium phosphate	5.0
Carbamide	3.0
Bentonite	4.0
Calcium carbonate (precipitated)	87.0
Sodium lauryl sulphate	1.0
Flavouring agent(s)	q.s.
Sweetening agent	q.s.

Formula 6

	%
Di-calcium phosphate (dihydrate)	77.2
Calcium carbonate (precipitated)	21.0
Sodium lauryl sulphate	1.0
Sodium monofluorophosphate	08
Flavouring agent(s)	q.s.
Sweetening agent	q.s.

Formula 7

	%
Di-calcium phosphate (dihydrate)	93.8
Sodium copper chlorophyllin	0.2
Sodium tripoly phosphate	4.0
Sodium lauryl sulphate	2.0
Flavouring agent(s)	q.s.

Anti-enzyme tooth powder can be formulated using sodium N-lauroyl sarcosinate. Formula 8 is an example of such a product.

Formula 8

	%
Sodium N-lauroyl sarcosinate	3.0
Di-calcium phosphate dihydrate	94.5
Saccharin	0.25
Flavour	2.25

Smokers' teeth are stained with tobacco stains. A powder containing sodium benzoate is considered to be effective for removing tobacco stains and tartar. Use of sodium benzoate has been illustrated in Formula 9.

Formula 9

	%
Calcium carbonate (precipitated)	52.0
Kieselguhr	38.0
Sodium palmitate	5.0
Sodium benzoate	5.0
Flavouring agent(s)	q.s.
Sweetening agent	q.s.

Tooth powders containing ammonium compounds and peroxides can also be used for removing stains and tartar.

Flavours can be prepared by mixing different essential oils or other flavouring substances. Illustrative formulae of flavours are shown in Formula 10 and 11.

Formula 10

	%
Peppermint oil	68.0
Thymol	1.0
Anethol	20.0
Eugenol	8.5
Cinnamon oil	2.5

Formula 11

	%
Peppermint oil	38.0
Anise oil	38.0
Cinnamon oil	9.0
Clove oil	15.0

Since abrasives are generally absorptive materials it is necessary to evaluate preparation after a few weeks. Usually all flavours are blended with sweetening agent. The most commonly used sweetening agent is saccharin and is generally present in concentrations 0.05 to 0.25 of the finished product.

3. MANUFACTURE OF TOOTH POWDERS

Manufacture of tooth powders is comparatively simple operation. Primary object of the operation is to achieve uniform distribution of all ingredients. Ingredients which are in small amounts are mixed first and are mixed with remaining ingredients. Mixing of tooth powder can be conveniently done in ribbon mixer. Flavour can either be sprayed during mixing of the powder or it can be adsorbed on to polishing agents like calcium carbonate. This mix is finally screened before filling into hopper of filling machine.

Some tooth powders are not free flowing or ten to agglomerate. This problem can be overcome by granulating and then comminuting after drying. The powder so obtained is flavoured.

Tooth powders are generally packed into metal cans with a dispensing top closed with either metallic or plastic cap. Cans are generally made of tin-plated or chemically treated steel. These can be coated with a suitable lacquer. Now-a-days tooth powders are also packed in plastic containers.

It has been recommended under the Drugs & Cosmetics Rules that facilities for manufacture of black tooth powder should be separate from white tooth powder.

23

Mouthwashes

1. GENERAL

Mouthwashes are generally liquid dentifrices and can be formulated either in ready to use form or in concentrated form. Mouthwashes in concentrated form are required to be diluted as per directions on label. In general three types of mouthwashes are prepared:

- mouthwashes containing anti-bacterials;
- mouthwashes containing fluoride;
- mouthwashes containing minerals (astringents).

Mouthwashes containing anti-bacterials reduce bacterial population of the mouth. Mouthwashes containing fluoride help to reinforce the fluoride layer of the enamel of the teeth. Mineralizing mouthwashes help to repair early carious lessions. Of these three types, mouthwashes containing anti-bacterials are more popular than other two and are generally manufactured as drugs rather than cosmetics.

Though anti-bacterial mouthwashes have been marketed for clean breath but some mouthwashes like those containing chlorhexidine may have anti-plaque and even anti-caries properties also.

Mouthwashes perform three functions:

- rinsing of food debris from the mouth;
- reduction in total bacterial count in mouth;

– imparting flavour to mouth cavity and thereby imparting flavour to breath.

2. FORMULATION

Mouthwashes can be formulated with aqueous-alcoholic solutions of flavouring oils. Such mouthwashes are used for removing bad odours and to give a refreshing feeling in the mouth. They may or may not contain soap or detergent. Formula 1 is an example of aqueous-alcoholic solution of flavouring oils containing sodium lauryl sulphate.

Formula 1

		%
Sodium lauryl sulphate		1.0
Alcohol		5.0
Flavouring oils		2.0
Water	to make	100.0

But such mouthwashes are not very popular. Generally therapeutic agents like anti-bacterials, astringents etc. are added to mouthwashes and these are manufactured as drugs. Anti-bacterial agents that have been used include chlorinated phenol (e.g., *para*-chloro *meta*-cresol, *para*-chloro *meta*-xylenol), thymol, quaternary ammonium compounds (e.g., benzalkonium chloride), chlorhexidine, peroxides (e.g., hydrogen peroxide).

Essential oils, apart from having flavour also have anti-bacterial action and when used in anti-bacterial mouthwashes have synergistic anti-bacterial effect. These include cinnamon oil, clove oil, eucalyptus oil, peppermint oil, anise oil, winter-green oil etc. Some constituents of these oils are also used. For example, menthol, thymol, eucalyptol, anethole, methyl salicylate etc.

Thymol (isopropyl *meta*-cresol) has anti-bacterial action, but it is not very soluble in water. It is solubilized in water by using borax or suitable alcohols. Formula 2 is an example of thymol containing mouthwash.

Formula 2

	%
Thymol	0.03
Alcohol	3.5
Borax	2.0

Sodium bicarbonate		1.0
Glycerin		8.0
Water	to make	100.0
Flavour		q.s.

Astringent mouthwash can be prepared by using metallic compounds. Most commonly used compounds are zinc and aluminium compounds (e.g., zinc chloride, zinc acetate, aluminium potassium sulphate). These compounds can be used in concentrations of 0.05 to 0.2%. However, zinc phenol sulphonate can be used in concentration of 0.1 to 0.3%. Copper salts are not employed because of their emetic effect. Salts of iron and manganese are also not used as these may stain the teeth. Other substances that can be used as astringent include tannic acid (and its derivatives), citric acid, lactic acid and acetic acid. Formula 3 is an example of astringent mouthwash.

Formula 3

		%
Zinc chloride		0.12
Saccharin sodium		0.1
Menthol		0.05
Alcohol		20.0
Water	to make	100.0
Flavour		q.s.

Alkaline mouthwashes can be formulated using sodium bi-carbonate. Formula 4 is an example of alkaline mouthwash.

Formula 4

		%
Sodium bi-carbonate		2.0
Sodium chloride		0.5
Alcohol		20.0
Water	to make	100.0
Flavour		q.s.

An anti-enzyme mouthwash can be prepared with sodium N-lauroyl sarcosinate (0.1%).

Mouthfresheners can also be prepared in aerosol form. Usually, these are solutions of antiseptic material in alcohol containing some percentage of water. Formula 5 is an illustrative of mouthfreshner base for aerosol.

Formula 5

	%
Flavour	1.0
Alcohol	94.0
Water	5.0

A container charge may contain 30-35 of mouthfreshner base and the best propellent.

3. Manufacture of Mouthwashes

Glass-lined mixing vessels are the most suitable vessels for all types of mouthwashes. However, stainless steel (SS 316) vessels can be used in majority of mouthwashes. Mixing vessel preferably should have refrigerant chilling coils so that formulations in which solubility of components is at a borderline level, can be chilled before filteration. Alternatively, clean ice can be substituted for water in the formulation. All mouthwashes should be filtered before filling. Filter aids like fuller's earth, pure talc etc. are used for filtering mouthwashes. Pressure filters are suitable filtering machines. Filtered preparation is then filled into suitable containers. Glass containers are the most suitable containers.

Usually mouthwashes are manufactured in concentrated form. Directions for use indicating the dilution etc. should be given conspicuously. Warning and cautions, if any, should also appear on the label of mouthwashes.

24

Hair Oils and Hair Lotions

Hair oils are combination of oils and suitable perfumes. The base oils like Castor oil, coconut oil and seasamum oil are mostly used vegetable based oils. Besides vegetable based oils another class of base oils which are used in Hair Oils are florol oils such as Bela oil, chameli oil, Henna oil etc. which posses most delicate fragrances. Vegetable oils are refined before using it in the Hair Oil formulations. The natural scents added to hair oil such as balsom peru, cantharidin and fly cantharides help to invigorate the growth of hairs and prevent baldness.

HERBAL HAIR OILS

Some of the important herbal hair oils are based upon following:

1. Amla
2. Brahmi
3. Bhringraj
4. Bhangra
5. Kaddu Seeds
6. Soya Lecithin
7. Henna

HERBAL HAIR OIL EXTRACT

Herbal well known for use in hair oils are processed into thick pulp which is soluble in both vegetable and mineral oils. These are:

Common Name	Sanskrit Name	Botanical Name	Part Used
Amla	Amarphalam	*Emblica officienalis*	Dried Fruit
	Amalakam	*Phyllanthus emblica*	
Brahmi	Mandukaparni	*Centella asiatica*	Herb
Bhringraj	Bringraja	*Ecliptica alba/eracta*	Herb
Bhangra	Kesaraja	*Wadellie calandulacea*	Herb
Kaddu seeds	Alabu	*Legenarie sinceraria*	seeds

EFFICACY OF HERBAL HAIR OILS

Hair oil containing any one or combination of herbs mentioned above have been used in India since time immemorial and are highly spoken of in folklore and books on indigenous drugs.

Amla: Fruits are rich in tannins; Fixed oil in berries strengthen and promotes growth of hair.

Brahmi: Local stimulant useful for skin erruption, Eczema. The extract is a remedy in ulcers, eczema and Psoriasis.

Bhringraj: Antispetic; excellent for head; renders hair black and promotes luxurious growth; paste of herb in oil is useful for skin diseases, itch, headache and also for dying hair black.

Bhangra: Contains oil soluble dye useful in alopecia and skin diseases.

Kaddu seeds: Have Fatty oil which is applied in headache, oil of seed is cooling and emolient.

Henna leaves: Have colouring matter, for external appl... tion in headache; astringent; detergent and deodorant, applied to hair to promote growth.

TYPICAL FORMULATION & PROCEDURES FOR HAIR OIL

A few typical recipes for making scented hair oils follow:

Formulation 1

Ingredients	Quantity
Refined Coconut or Seasamum Oil	5 seers
Balsam Peru	2.50 oz.
Fly Cantharides	5 dr.

Sandal Oil	15 dr.
Alkanet Root	15 dr.
Otto of Henna	5 dr.
Oil Rosemary	10 dr.

Procedure

First of all the oil is treated with alkanet root and allowed to remain undisturbed for 2 days for colouring. Then strain the oil through cloth. The fly cantharides are next fried in about one chhatak of fresh coconut or sesamum oil and when these are well fried and discoloured, these are allowed to cool. Afterwards add the previously coloured oil, and the Balsam Peru (after melting it over a slow fire). Finally add the other ingredients one by one with constant shaking.

Formulation 2

Ingredients	Quantity
Refined Seasamum Oil	24 oz.
Alkanet Root	2 dr.
Oil Bergamot	6 dr.
Oil Lemon	3 dr.
Oil Rosemary	2 dr.
Oil Neroli	1 dr.
Oil Lavender (English)	2 dr.
Oil Orange	1 dr.
Oil Rose Geranium	2 dr.
Cantharidin	3 grains
Balsam Peru	2 dr.

Procedure

The best quality of refined sesamum oil is taken and into it is added 2 dr. of alkanet root previously cut into small pieces. The whole is then allowed to stand undisturbed for 2 days and then filtered through a piece of fine cloth. Next add the other ingredients one after another in the order they appear in the recipe and shake the whole for 15 minutes after each such addition. Balsam Peru, the last ingredient, is to be melted over a slow fire before incorporation. When the ingredients are all incorporated, the whole is kept aside air-tight in a vessel for a fortnight and then packed.

Formulation 3

Ingredients	Quantity
Chemeli Oil	2 litre
Almond Oil	1 litre
Alkanet Root	1 oz.
Cantharidin	12 grains
Balsam Peru	5 oz.
Sandal Oil	3 oz.
Flora Jasmine	12 dr.
English Lavender	2 oz.

Procedure

Mix the *Chameli* and almond oil together and drop into this the alkanet root in small pieces and let the oil remain undisturbed for 2 days. Then strain through a piece of cloth and add the ingredients one after another with constant shaking. While adding the balsam peru take care that it is melted over a slow fire before addition. When all the ingredients are well incorporated, pack in a vessel with the mouth well-covered and put in the strong sunlight for 20 days together. Finally strain and pack into phials.

Formulation 4

Ingredients	Quantity
Sesamum Oil	6 litre
Alkanet Root	2 oz.
Otto Keora	1 oz.
Oil Lavender	2 oz.
Oil Rosemary	1 oz.

Procedure

The sesamum oil is first of all treated with animal charcoal and put in the sun for a fortnight. This is then filtered through a filter paper or through flannel. To the oil thus refined add the alkanet root in small bits and strain after two days. Then incorporate the other ingredients one after another with constant stirring and let the wholestand for 7 days in vessel tightly corked. Finally strain again and pack into phials.

This oil keeps the brain cool and stimulates the growth of hair.

Formulation 5

Ingredients	Quantity
Coconut Oil	12 ch.
White Oil	4 ch.
Oil Lavender	3 dr.
Oil Sandal	3 dr.
Oil Bergamot	3 dr.
Alkanet Root	1.5 dr.

Procedure

First refine the coconut oil and add the alkanet roots. The whole is left for colouring for 2 days. Now filter and add the essential oils one by one and shake well before the addition of the next one. The whole is left well corked for 7 days for ripening, then phial.

Formulation 6

Ingredients	Quantity
Til, Coconut or Castor oil	500 parts
Balsam Peru	15 parts
Oil of Jasmine	60 parts
Oil of Roses	30 parts
Oil of Bitter Almonds	30 parts
Oil of Vanilla	60 parts
Oil of Ambergris	30 parts
Oil of Musk	30 parts

Procedure

The balsam Peru is first of all digested for 14 days in the oil, shaking the vessel frequently. When the mixture is clear, add the essential oils one by one. The oil keeps for a long time and resembles very much the heliotrope oil in odour.

Formulation 7

Ingredients	Quantity
Benzoated Oil	20 oz.
Otto of Rose	25 minims
Heliotropin	20 dr.

Procedure

The benzoated oil is made by digesting an ounce of bruised benzoin, preferably of Siam, in a pint of almond or olive oil for three hours, and filtering through filter paper. Finally add the scent, shake and phial. The oil does not become rancid.

In the preparation of these scented hair oils, precautions are to be taken that procedures are to be followed strictly so that desired quality is achieved. The addition of scents and colouring of hair oils are two important steps.

ADDITION OF SCENTS

The addition of the perfumes also must be methodical. They should be added one after another in the order they are put in the recipes. The order should not be changed by any means. Moreover a few minutes' time should be allowed to the fixation of one scent before the next one is incorporated and if possible the whole mass should be agitated carefully so that the scent may be intimately incorporated, absorbed by the oil itself and sweetly tempered. After the whole preparation is finished, the mass is recommended to be set aside for a certain period of time before final bottling. This is a most important matter that should not be overlooked by the manufacturers. It is found that on keeping the preparation substantially improves in quality, and hence whenever excellent quality is desired to be attained, the preparation should be allowed to stand for a number of days before final packing.

COLOURING HAIR OILS

The colouration of the hair oils is not a difficult affair. For red, the alkanet root is mostly in vogue. This is cheap and being of vegetable origin is perfectly non-neurosis. For yellow shade saffron may be added but this is rarely done as this is rather costly. Now-a-days all tints in hair oils except red are produced by the incorporation of aniline dyes. But from hygienic point of view these are not non-injurious to health and their use should be as much restricted as permissible.

PACKAGING

Finally for packaging the hair oils, decent phials should be used. These should be nicely corked and capsuled and balelled and put in decent paper cartons.

HERBAL HAIR DYES

Henna dyes give dark hair a reddish colour. But the exact colour result in very difficult to predict so a test dye is very essential. Henna dye can be made following the undermentioned method:

Henna powder	2 cups
Hot water	1 cup
Vinegar	1 tsp

Stir them all to a thick paste and let this stand for 1 hour. Pour it into a bowl and put this bowl in a saucepan filled with water. Keep the paste stirring till the water in the bottom of the saucepan bubbles freely. Let the mixture stand for another hour, then apply the mixture into each strand of the hair by parting hair with a comb. Start applying henna from one side of the head and working to the other end. Leave the henna on your head for 3-6 hours.

Some of the formulations for Henna and other herbal hair dyes are described as under:

HENNA HAIR DYE

Henna	200 gm
Coffee powder	1 tsp
Egg yolk	1 eg
Rum/Brandy	1 tbsp

Procedure

Mix coffee powder in the water and make a paste of henna with this water. Beat the egg yok and mix this into henna. Also add brandy to it. Apply the paste and leave it on for 3-4 hours before washing it with lukewarm water.

SAFFRON HAIR DYE

Saffron	1 pinch
Boiling water	500 ml

Soak saffron in water for 10 minutes. Strain and use it on the hair. Grey hair will acquire a rich golden tint.

WALNUT HAIR DYE

Walnut husk	500 gm
Water	500 ml

Boil husk in the water for 15 minutes. Then strain and use this liquid to dye your hair. It will colour brown hair to a darker shade.

25

Preservation of Cosmetics

The cosmetics in general contain oils, fats, moisture which are subject to deterioration due to number of factors such as oxidation of fats, microbial growth. Cosmetic preparations which contain oils and fats are required to be protected against the growth of molds and from becoming rancid. By the effect of rancidity the cosmetics get discoloured and aquire undesirable odours. For preventing the cosmetics to get deteriorated, preservatives are required to be added in the cosmetic preparations.

A preservative is a substance which prevents the decomposition of the cosmetic preparation by discouraging the growth of bacterial and fungus, thereby preserving its original colour, odour and qualities.

For the growth of molds, access of the air to the cosmetics is required as these are aerobic. To prevent this is a piece of waxes paper of foil is placed on the surface and the lid of the jar is screwed as well.

The materials used for preserving the cosmetics from spoilage by microorganisms are having function to prevent the multiplication of bacteria and fungi throughout the period of its use.

ANTIOXIDANTS

Antioxidants are used to prevent the oxidation of certain materials in cosmetic preparation. These materials which are subject to oxidation are castor oil, corn oil, almond oil, olive oil sesame oil etc.

The antioxidants should have following properties:

1. It should have no odour of its own.
2. The cosmetic preparation should not deteriorate if kept for some time.
3. It should not be toxic.
4. It should be colourless.

For dissolving the antioxidant in the oil phase, it should be warmed up to 60°-70° centigrade.

FACTORS FOR DETERIORATION OF COSMETICS

1. Presence of Molds

The molds are fungi with a filamentous type of growth; they usually reproduce by means of spores. These spores falling on a moist surface germinate and produce branching filaments or hyphae. Later fruiting bodies are formed with masses of colourless or pigmented spores.

The following are probably the most frequent molds encounteded in cosmetics.

Penicillium

Penicillium is an extremely widespread genus of fungi, most often seen as a green, velvety growth on decaying vegetables and fruits. Its vegetative growth of mycelium is a network of fine, branching tubular threads with cross walls marking off cell limits. Some of the branches are characterized by a tuft of fingerlike branches at the tip, at the end of which long chains of microscopic single celled spores occur. This fungus is able to decompose proteins, fats and carbohydrates.

Aspergilus

Aspergilus is similar to the preceding in many ways and is also seen frequently on decaying fruits and vegetables. Its colors are varied: green, yellow, brown and black. The spores are also borne in chains but in this case the tip of the mycelial branch bearing them is club shaped. The species of Aspergilus trend to grow under rather warmer conditions than Pencillium and on media containing a higher concentration of nutrients.

Rhizopus and Mucor

Rhizopus and Mucor belong to a group of fungi differing from the preceding general their mycelia show no cross walss and spores are produced inside a globe or sporagium. These fungi also produce thick walled resting cells (Zygospores) by a rudimentary sexual process.

Rhizopus nigricons

Rhizopus nigricons occurs commonly as the black bread mold. Its large black sporangla can be distinguished with the naked eye on the surface of a fluffy white network of mycelium. It is highly proflific species causing black rot of weet potatoes and storage rots of many other vegetables.

Mucor Mucdo

Mucor Mucdo grows as a silvery gray turf of mycelium. Its sporangia are grayish, and are borne on single long cheards branching off the main mycelium. It too, is widespread and may be found on a great variety of decaying organic matter. Both of these genera require more moist conditions than the Pencillia or Aspergilli.

Botrytis cincrea

Botrytis cincrea is commonly found on decaying organic material and is commonly associated with plant disease, one of its relatives is the cause of a destructive rot of onion. Vegetative growth is fluffy gray-white to dark, with small single celled spores borne on crowded fine swellings along the rounded tips of upright branches, somewhat in the manner of bunches of grapes. It has been found in creams where it subsists on the fatty acid residues of soap substances.

Species of Alternaria are found both as saprophytes and as parasites.

Alternaria

Alternaria is usually dark in colour, greenish-black with creeping vegetative mycellium which sends up short unbranched threads at the ends of which chains of large many celled dark spores are formed. Alternaria has been found by Holt and Carroll to contaminate creams and lotions the sealers of the caps providing the inoculum.

Stemphylium

Stemphylium resembles Alternaria in occurring as a dark spreading mycelium with club-shaped muriform spores. However these spores are borne singly at the tips of short upright branches rather than in chains.

Cladosporium

Cladosporium is a soil fungus withdark greenish-black mycelium. Its spores are usually olive green and they appear in chains which branch in a treelike fashion on upright mycelial threads. This fungus is found frequently among soil isolates.

Yeasts

Yeasts also occur as common contaminants; they are classified along with molds as fungi. The yeast are generally nonfilamentous spherical or ellipsoidal cells which reproduce by budding. They are found in soil and air and are common contaminants of culture media. Their greatest commercial uses are in the manufacture of bread and in the production of alcohol and alcoholic beverages.

Bacteria

The bacteria are smaller than yeasts and reproduce by fission or in some cases by formation or spores. Saprophytic forms occur widely in nature. Little informations present on the bacteria contaminating cosmetics; however, Bacillus subtilis, B mycoides, Aerobacter aerogenes, and Pseudomonas sp commonly present in air and soil and capable of vigorous growth may be taken as representatives.

2. Factors Influencing the Growth of Microorganisms

As a group, the microorganisms are the most omnivorous of living things since they are capable of supporting their metabolic processes by utilisation of the most diverse food sources. According to Lamanna and Mallette, it may be speculated that there is probably not a single naturally occurring compound for which a persistent search would not reveal one or more kinds of bacteria capable of utilizing it as a nutrient. It is remarkable that there are bacteria which can utilize organic compounds having no known existence outside the laboratory of the organic chemist.

On the other hand, many microorganisms show a remarkable specificity as to sources of food. This is true of a number of parasitic microorganisms as well as those organisms which cause decay.

The following may serve as substrates for microrganisms found in cosmetics:

1. Carbohydrats and glycosides: Natural gums and mucilages, pectinase, starches, dextrins and sugars.
2. Alcohol: glycerol, mannitol and fatty alcohols.
3. Fatty acids and their esters; animal and vegetable fats, oils and waxes.
4. Steroids; Cholesterol, ergosterol and lanolin.
5. Proteins, peptones and main acids.
6. Vitamins.

In addition to a carbon source an adequate, suitable nitrogen source is necessary. This may be organic and serve also as a source of carbon such as protein, or it may be inorganic such as ammonia. The latter is readily utilized by most molds.

3. GROWTH FACTORS

Growth factors have been defined as those organic compounds required for growth which need to be present in only minute amounts. As a rule these compounds are assumed to be functioning metabolites necessary for the chemical reactions occurring in the cell. Growth factors are considered essential if growth cannot take place without them.

4. MOISTURE CONTENT

Microorganisms can grow only when they have a sufficient water supply, since normally growing metabolizing cells of all kinds must be bathed in an aqueous phase. In addition to acting as an inert medium for vital systems, water also is a reactant in numerous essential reactions of the cell. It is of further interest that the amount of moisture present has a strong influence on the type of organisms which will grow in a particular product.

The bacteria is general require a higher water content in their immediate environment than do fungi; there is an intermediate range in which yeasts may become the dominant organisms.

5. pH

The pH has a marked effect upon the number and types of microorganisms which can grow in a given substrate. Fungi are capable of growing over a fairly wide range of pH, although the rate of growth is usually best at a pH of 4 to 6. Some acid-producing fungi can grow best in more neutral media (pH 6 to 8). In slightly acid conditions the yeast and lectic bacteria are favoured. No organism seems to be able to grow appreciably above a pH of about 9.

6. TEMPERATURE

There is a true optimum temperature for the growth of each organisms and the range of temperature ever which any particular organisms can grow is usually fairly narrow. The optima for the great majority of common saprophytic bacteria, yeasts and fungi (including most types naturally occurring in air, water and soil) appear to lie in the range of 20 to 30°C. Since this is the temperature range at which most cosmetics are stored and used, this favourable temperature obviously plays an important part in providing optimum conditions for growth of contaminants.

7. OXYGEN

The presence of oxygen or more fundamentally the oxidation reduction potential, has an includence on the type of organism which will grow in a given substrate. Those organisms which cannot develop without oxygen are called obligate aerobes. Those organisms which cannot grow in the 5 presence of oxygen are called obligate anaerobes. Those which prefer a limited access of oxygen the called microaerophiles such as the lactic acid bacteria. Finally there is a large group called facultative anaerobes which grow best in the presence of air but can grow in its absence if the medium is able to supply the missing oxygen.

Most molds are strongly aerobic and apparently none are obligate anaerobes; yeasts too, grow best in the presence of air, although they ferment material without it. The bacteria is indicated above, very greatly in their oxygen requirements. However most of the organisms of concern in the preservative of cosmetics appear to be aerobic.

8. OTHER INGREDIENTS

Other ingredients of the composition even though they do not serve as sources of food for microorgansms may influence their growth. In this category are preservative themselves. Also in this group are substances such as alcohols and glycols which in lower concentrations serve as sources of carbon and energy for microorganism but in higher concentration may inhibit their growth. Salts of various types may become inhibitory in higher concentrations.

Cosmetics preservatives may be regarded as agents which extend the storage and shelf life of cosmetics by retarding or preventing deterioration. This generally implies retardation or prevention of microbial growth, or of oxidation of fats and oils or both. To eliminate any ambiguity that might arise from this definition, the word preservative is used to refer to any compound capable of preventing growth of microorganism, antioxidant to any agent which retards oxidative deterioration in facts and oils. The term preservative is by no means synonymous with either antiseptic or germicide, although they are sometimes confused and a preservative does not necessarily fit into the category of antiseptics or germicides.

The problem of the preservation of cosmetic preparation is a complex one. The complexity is increased by the vast number of different problems and formulations with each product and formulations presenting its own particular problems, depending on a number of factors. Some of the more important of these facts are:

1. The physical form of the preparation-liquid, emulsion, ointment, powder etc.
2. Factors influencing growth of microorganism-nutritional factors, moisture, pH, temperature etc.
3. Factors affecting the action of the preservative-concentration, nature of and amount of inoculum incompatible substances etc.
4. Presence of compounds which are inherently bacteriostatic or fungistatic.

5. Purity and cleanliness of raw materials and maintenance of sanitary operations in formulating and packing and finished product.

From the foregoing, it is quite evident that deterioration may arise from several causes-physical, chemical, microbial and enymatic. Evidence of deterioration which can be detected visually or organoleptically (changes in odor, colour and texture) is of particular importance, as these changes are easily noticed by the consumer. Odor changes are due to the production of volatile substances, such as aldehydes, ketones, acids, amines, sulfides, mercaptans to colour changes may be due to growth of pigmented or pigment-producing organisms to oxidative reactions, and to other chemical reactions. Changes in texture may be due to hydrolysis of starches, solubilization of protinaceous material and microbial overgrowth. In addition destruction of active ingredients such as vitamins, hormones and the like may occur.

Most cosmetic preparations are subject to deterioration. Almost all cosmetics containing water are susceptible to microbial action. Even substantially anhydrous preparations such as lipsticks may require preservatives. Mucilages, fatty acids, lipids, albumins, hormones and vitamin in mention just a few are materials that are susceptible to microbial deterioration.

All preparations containing fats and oils are subject to oxidative as well as to microbial deterioration. Microorganisms are extremely adaptable to unfavourable conditions. To be on the safe side, a preservative should be added to each cosmetic preparation, unless it can be shown that the cosmetic is inherently resistant to the growth of microorganisms.

The selection of a preservative poses, itself a problem. An 'ideal' antimicrobial agent or antioxidant must have the following attributes:–

1. It must be effective under the conditions of use; this means that it must have few incompatibilities (physical or chemical), must retain its effectiveness over a wide pH range, and must not alter the pH of the preparation.
2. It must be soluble to an extent commensurate with its effective concentration.
3. It must be stable and capable to sustained action.

4. It must be colourless and odorless or nearly so.
5. It must be easily and economically formulated into the product.
6. It must be nontoxic and must not produce irritation or sensitization in the concentrations employed.

This last attribute is of great consequence, because every effort is made to eliminate from cosmetic preparations any possibility of irritation or sensitization even with long continued use; also any possibility of toxicity caused by inadvertent ingestion. Fortunately compounds now exist on which as considerable amount of data has been amassed to show their safety under a wide range of conditions.

Although there is no antimicrobial agent which meets all the requirements of the ideal, some progress has been made in the field.

Preservatives such as formaldehyde, alcohol, boric acid and salicylic acid and its derivatives which were once widely used, are now known to be useful only under limited circumstances and at concentration which make them less desirable than other compounds presently available. Numerous investigators share the opinion that of the preservatives in general use today, the esters of p-hydroxybenzoic acid are the preservatives of choice since they approach the requirements of the "ideal preservatives" most closely.

Since much of the information on the use of preservatives is empirical it is necessary to consider available information on factors affecting the growth of microorganisms in cosmetics and to inquire into the effectiveness of the preservatives from the microbiological and biochemical point of view, in order to place the choice of a preservative on a rotational basis, and to decrease the chances of unexplained and costly failures.

26

Plant and Equipment for Herbal Cosmetics Manufacture

For the preparation of herbal cosmetics of different kinds, as detailed earlier, different processes or combination of processes are adopted. Some of the basic process and equipment required for it are as under:

S.No.	Processes	Equipment
1.	Heating	Immersion heater, jacketed & non jacketed kettles
2.	Grinding or size reduction	Micropulverisers, grinders
3.	Sieving & grading	Sifter
4.	Mixing (dry)	Paddle mixer, drum mixer
5.	Mixing (wet)	Universal mixer
6.	Homogerization	Homogenizer
7.	Emulsification	Emulsification equipment
8.	Straining/filtering	Strainer/filter
9.	Filling/sealing form, fill & seal machines for pouches	Automatic liquid filling machines
10.	Labelling	Labelling Equipment

These processes and equipment are described as under:

1. HEATING EQUIPMENT

a. Immersion Heaters

An accurately controlled, electric immersion heater is fast becoming recognized in the preparation of cosmetic products of different kinds as heating applications.

Each application usually presents a separate problem in the selection of the correct immersion heater. For most cosmetic mixtures containing oils, fats, and waxes, standard heaters with steel sheaths are satisfactory; for use in materials where steel would be corroded, heaters can be supplied with the enclosing sheath of a special corrosion resisting alloy such as stainless steel.

The required heater capacity will depend upon the amount and physical constant of the material being heated, the temperature to which the material is to be heated, and the time allowed for heating, as well as upon the size and construction of the container. As a rough approximation, 30 watts of heater capacity will raise the temperature of 1 lb of a substance, similar to wax, approximately 100°F. in a period of one hour.

b. Jacketed/non-jacketed kettles

In good cosmetic practice heat (gas burner or stove) is rarely applied directly to a container. The only time direct gas heat may be used is in dissolving substances in water or similar inert solvent.

Many small manufacturers do not use water baths claiming that heating is too slow and that scorching is averted by constant attention. True heating is somewhat slower in one respect but a more even heat over the sides of the kettle is obtained in this way. Also the savings and assurance resulting from slower heating on a water bath more than repay the effort expended.

Small batch heating may be accomplished by using inexpensive aluminium jacketed kettles of the double boiler type. The removable pan is easy to handle and is suitable for small scale production.

2. GRINDERS/MICRO PULVERISERS

The process of reducing a material to finer particles is called comminution or disintegration, sometimes loosely referred to as grinding. It is one of the most important chemical engineering process in industry. The fineness of finished product determines if the process shall be called grinding, pulverizing or micropulverizing.

Fine pigments as well as pigment mixtures are prepared by grinding. Commonest form of grinding is accomplished with a mortar and pestle.

Pulverizers and micropulverizers are being used more in the manufacture of face powder, eliminating a sifting operation.

Only a rough premixing is required, the material which passes through the machine is finely ground and quite uniformly mixed. If not sufficiently uniform, it may be passed through the machine again.

Grinding can also be accomplished by the use of ball or pebble mills specially in preparing uniform blends.

3. SIEVING & GRADING EQUIPMENT

Next to grinding operation is the sifting process–the separation of large particles from small ones. Sifting is accomplished by means of suitable screens and the products to be sifted must be mixed to assure uniformity. The lighter particles pass through the screen first, the heavier particles last.

Face powder and certain make-up cosmetics are sifted atleast once before being packed. Cosmetics as a group require that a product pass through a 200 mesh sieve if they are to be considered satisfactory for consumer use. The term 200 mesh means that there are 200 holes per lineal inch. Simple sifting devices are like silk cloth of 120-160 mesh, conveniently held in position by two wooden rings, one of which fits over the other. Similarly a sieve of 25 cm diameter is suitable for small batches. With mesh sieves can also be used but as metal affects the colour of the product, silk sifter is more suitable.

4. DRY-MIXING EQUIPMENT

The dry powers commonly mixed are face powders horizontal, round bottom mixers are the most frequently used for mixing powdered ingredients in cosmetic practice. It has two twisted paddles for agitating the central mass effecting thorough mixing of the ingredients.

5. WET MIXING EQUIPMENT

Mixing-Paste, Creams and Emulsions is readily accomplished with a push-pull type of portable agitators.

Simplicity of construction, ruggedness and adaptability of this kind of agitation makes it a common sight in cosmetic plants. It can be used successfully in making liquid emulsions, emulsified cold creams and other medium-heavy mixes.

Not as commonly seed as the "push-pull" or propeller type of mixing machine but very popular indeed is a blade type mixing machine. In these machines agitation and mixing are very thorough. The adaptability of the machinery will make it useful for any mixing operation.

6. HOMOGENIZING EQUIPMENT

The principle upon which all homogenizers are based is the forcing of substance under pressure, through a minute opening regulated by a spring needle valve. The substance passes the needle valve into discharge chamber where the pressure is released. The material in effect "explodes," producing a very fine dispersion.

A complete unit of universal vacutherm mixer comprising of mixer kettle, mixing baffle, dosing funnel & valves, jacket heating vacuum condensor is used for efficient mixing of different ingredient in liquid state.

7. EMULSIFICATION EQUIPMENT

An emulsion consists of two immiscible liquids, one being dispersed in the other. These are known as the internal, and external phases respectively. Cosmetic emulsions are generally creams.

Most cosmetic emulsions are oil and water systems, of which there are two types. The type of emulsion obtained depends on the proportion of oil and water used. When the oil or fatty phase is dispersed in the aqueous or water phase, it is known as an oil in water (O/W) system. When the aqueous phase is dispersed in the oil phase it is referred to as a water in oil (W/O) system.

The two types of emulsions may be distinguished by several means. An oil in water emulsion is less greasy than a water in oil emulsion because water is the external phase. An oil in water emulsion is dispersible in water. It is also more easily washed than a water in oil emulsion, which is not so readily water dispersible. Again because water is the external phase, an oil in water emulsion will conduct electricity, whereas a water in oil emulsion will not conduct electricity unless an electrolyte has been added.

An emulsion of oil in water should consist of oil dispersed in the water. If a very small amount of oil is added to water it is comparatively easy to reduce it to very small droplets. Once in this state the droplets do not readily coalesce. This is due to electrical charges which form on the surfaces of the droplets. If a larger quantity of oil is required, it is less easy to mix with the water, and once mixed there is a tendency for the phases to separate. To prevent this an emulsifying agent is used. The emulsifying agent stabilizes the emulsion by forming a thin film over the droplets and preventing them from coalescing.

Thus there are two main conditions which must be satisfied in the preparation of emulsions. The first is that the droplets of the internal phase must be small. This is ensured during the process of mixing, which should be designed to make the emulsion, homogenous throughout. Homoegenizing the emulsion can be done by shaking the phases in a bottle, by stirring them in a beaker or by using a mortar and pestle, depending usually on the nature of the oil phase. The second condition is that the droplets should have a thin film of emulsifying agent around them.

PREPARATION OF COSMETIC EMULSIONS

1. All cosmetic emulsions should be prepared in glass containers. In the laboratory, glass beakers are the most suitable.
2. Care should be taken to follow the correct formula. This will ensure that the preparation is of the high consistency.

Ingredients

The Water Phase should contain all the water soluble materials such as glycerine and borax. All preparations must contain a preservative and an antioxidant. The proportion of water in a stable emulsion should not fall below 50% in any formula.

Some oil phase ingredients

1. **Liquid paraffin:** This is one of the major oils used either as an ingredient in cleansing creams, or as a diluent for other fatty materials.
2. **Almond oil:** This is the best oil for cosmetic emulsions.
3. **Sesame oil:** This can be substituted for olive oil.
4. **Petroleum jelly:** This is sometimes used as an oil-thickening agent and emollient.
5. **Fatty acids-oleic acid:** This is the chief oil phase ingredient in vanishing and shaving creams.
6. **Esters:** Isopropyl myristate, iropropyl palmitate, isopropyl stearate-these are in liquid form and promote skin penetration.
7. **Spermaceti:** This is an excellent emollient.
8. **Carnauba wax:** This is the thickening agent for the oil phase.
9. **Beeswax:** This acts as an emollient and emulsifier.

Perfumes and insoluble powders are not added until after the phases have been mixed.

The choice of an emulsifying agent. The first emulsifier to be used was soap, but nowadays oil soluble materials such as fatty alcohols (e.g. cetyl alcohol) and esters (e.g. glyceryl monostearate) are used. The choice of the emulsifying agent depends on two important factors:

1. The nature of the emulsion–that is, whether it is to be an oil in water or water in oil emulsion.
2. The computability of the emulsifying agent with the rest of the substances in the emulsion.

Most emulsifying agents produce oil in water systems. Some examples are wool-fats, beeswax-borax mixture, wool alcohols and triethanolamine.

If a surfactant (i.e. a surface active agent) is used to make oily or waxy substances mix with water, the resulting emulsion may be either opaque or clear. Many detergents are classed as surfactant and are often used to stabilize oil and water emulsions.

A detergent molecule has a long hydrocarbon part which is insoluble in water but soluble in oil (hydrophobic and lipophilic). The ionic end group is insoluble in oil but soluble in water (hydrophilic and lipophobic). If a small amount of detergent is added to water, a colloidal suspension is formed. The hydrocarbon ends of the detergent molecules cluster together and leave their ionic and groups in contact with the water. If oil is then introduced and the whole stirred together, the hydrocarbon parts of the detergent molecules enter the oil droplets, leaving the ionic end groups in the water. Thus round the oil droplets is formed a film which is partly in the water and partly in the oil.

Method of preparation

The phases. As most cosmetic emulsions are prepared from waxes and other substances that are numerally solid at room temperature, the two phases must first be heated separately. The waxes and oils should be heated to about 10°C above the melting point of the highest melting wax, taking care not to overheat. This usually means heating the waxes to about 70°C. The water phase should be heated to a temperature 20°C above that of the oil phase, to allow for cooling when the phases are mixed.

Mixing and cooling. Generally the water phase should be added to the oil phase. An exception to this is made in the case of high oil content (80-90%). There must be continuous stirring with a glass rod as there is a tendency for the phases to separate if stirring is stopped. The rate of cooling should be slow, to avoid coarsening of the emulsion. Stirring should continue until the temperature reaches about 40°C. Perfumes should be added whilst stirring, when the emulsion is partially cool (35°C). If there are many insoluble powders to be used in the preparation they should be heated to 75°C and added soon after the phases have been mixed.

The finished preparation should be smooth and creamy. If this has not been achieved during the mixing process, it may be necessary to completely homogenize the emulsion at this stage. This may be done by using an ordinary whisk or, if the emulsion is semi-solid, by using a mortar and pestle. Homogenization helps to prepare a most stable emulsion by breaking up the drops of oil into smaller droplets.

O/W emulsions. In preparing these emulsions it is best to make a preliminary mixture containing a portion of the water and emulsifier with an equal amount of oil. This should be stirred with a glass rod and homogenized slowly while the remaining oil is added. When the remaining water is added slowly to the oil phase, a very heavy W/O emulsion is formed. This will thin out suddenly to the O/W type of emulsion. When this happens the water can then be added more rapidly.

Control of the thickness of emulsions

Liquid emulsions tend to thicken. They then no longer pour. This increase in viscosity may be due to one or more of the following:

1. Too high a concentration of waxes in the oil phase.
2. Too much emulsifying agent.
3. Too much homogenizing.

To lower the viscosity of the emulsion any of the following methods may be used:

1. Increase the proportion of the external phase.
2. Decrease the proportion of the internal phase.
3. Use a lower melting point ingredient in the internal phase.
4. Add a water soluble emulsifier.

To raise the viscosity use one of the following methods:

1. Increase the proportion of the internal phase.
2. Add thickeners such as emulsifiers or gums.
3. Include a higher melting point ingredient in the internal phase.

Cause of failure of emulsion preparations

1. Insufficient emulsifying agent. This is rarely the cause of trouble as the tendency is to add too much emulsifier.
2. Decomposition of the emulsifying agent. This could be due to chemical reaction or the activities of micro-organisms. The emulsifying agent may be destroyed by chemical reaction with one of the ingredients.
3. Temperature changes. An increase in temperature can cause the two phases to separate, if the emulsifier is susceptible to temperature variations. Freezing can also destroy an emulsion by the formation of ice crystals on the surface.

4. Presence of electrolytes. Occasionally, small quantities of electrolytes (e.g. calcium salts) are added to emulsions containing triethanolamine soaps. This causes the phases to separate.
5. The concentration of the phases. The concentration of the phases should be in the region of 60% water and 40% oil. A higher phase volume ratio than 60:40, i.e. too much water, tends to cause separation of the phases.
6. Rancidity of the oil. Some animal and vegetable oils may become rancid on prolonged storage and cause the phases to separate. Rancidity may be prevented by the addition of an antioxidant.

Emulsification process for preparation of herbal creams

Creams are an emulsion of oil and a water soluble liquid, allowing the final product to be readily absorbed by the skin. The easiest way to make a herbal cream is to buy an emulsifying cream from the drugstore, and heat the desired herb plant material in it.

1. To begin, melt approximately 2 tablespoons of emulsifying cream in a bowl placed over a pot of boiling water.
2. Add one large tablespoon of dried herbs to the mixture, and stir slowly until the cream takes on the colour of the herbs.
3. Remove from heat, strain, and squeeze the remaining liquid from the clamp.
4. Let cream cool in a glass bowl, and spoon into small, dark bottles.
5. Store jars in a cool, dark place for up to one year.

8. STRAINING, FILTERING & CLARIFYING

In straining only the bigger undesirable particles are removed, as through the ordinary kitchen or tea strainer. In making mucilages, with quinee seed for example, the seeds must be strained off in due time. Mucilages of most gums are too thick to filter, but can be partially cleaned by straining. Further polishing requires centrifuging.

Filtration is "more perfect straining." The more closely woven the strainer, the more nearly it approaches a filtering device.

For greater production filtering machines are now used. The material to be filtered is pumped through the discs by means of an attached pump. Such machines give good production for small as well as moderate scale manufacture.

9. FILLING LIQUIDS

After manufacture, filling of the cosmetic into containers becomes an important problem, Liquids may be filled by gravity, siphon or vacuum. Small manufacturers prefer the gravity filler as it is most useful for all round liquid filling.

Gravity fillers are best for shampoo and foaming bath preparations because vacuum filling tends to produce foam in the bottle.

Siphon fillers are based on a well known principle going back before the time of the ancient Egyptians.

Economical and simple fillers for limited production are used for "touching up" purposes. Hundreds of these little fillers are in use throughout the country in large and small manufacturing plants alike. These are available at a price within the reach of the smallest manufacture. It may also be used for filling creams in the liquid state.

Filling Pastes—Creams

Heavy creams, ointments or pastes present an entirely different problem in filling.

Ordinary pastes, such as tooth paste, can be filled with a hand operated machine. In the case of tubes, they can be folded over and crimped with inexpensive hand operated machinery.

10. LABELLING EQUIPMENT

Attaching the labels is the next step in completing a package, most manufacturers prefer to buy labels printed on plain paper stock and apply glue at the time of labelling.

This requires a lot of labour or the purchase of gluing equipment. Simple machines are available for the purpose of applying a thin, even film of glue. The label is then placed on the package and smoothed on by hand. Machines of this sort are very inexpensive. The speed of labelling is dependent on the operator.

27

Packaging of Herbal Cosmetics

Cosmetic products are in use for hundreds of years. Well before the commencement of manufacture of these products by the organised sector, many naturally occurring of homemade articles were being used. Examples of these are Shikakai and Soap-nuts for hair care, milk, cream with turmeric and gram flour for the face, and Oil (massage) for softening of skin. Most of these items were found in the kitchen or purchased in bulk and hence needed no special packaging. Thus, although these products were being used in the country for hundreds of years, systematic development and importance of packaging in true sense started only after the establishment of organised industry for cosmetic products.

With the start of cosmetics/toiletries industry in the country, home-made products slowly got replaced by products manufactured in factories e.g. creams and lotions replaced milk-cream-flour mix etc.

With the use of factory-made cosmetic products, need for the development of their effective packaging was felt. Initially most primary packages consisted of glass bottles, usually of simple round shape and metal constainers. Packaging at this stage was mostly from utility angle.

Most of the manufactures of cosmetic products in the initial stages were multinational companies or their licensing. They wanted their products of Indian origin to appear the same as those manufactured by the originating companies. This gave boost to the modernisation in packaging of cosmetics products.

Another very important reason for the need for modernisation in packaging is rapid industrialisation of our society. With more and more people in our country getting educated and working women sharing equal responsibilities with men, demand for cosmetic products has steadily increased over the last few decades. Manufacturers have now fully realised the includence of attractive and efficient packaging system in conveying quality and brand image to the consumer.

The main factors that one must consider before deciding on the package design and packaging component(s) for packaging of cosmetics are as under:-

Determining Factors for Packaging

Determining factors may be classified under three broad considerations, viz. technical, aesthetic and cost.

Technical Factors

Under technical consideration, the factors to be examined are chemicals and physical compatibility (of the product with the packaging material).

Aesthetic Factors

Presentability/appearance, technicalities and practicabilities for packaging design.

Cost Factors

Cost-effectiveness of a package is an important consideration.

Each of these important factors are analysed in greater detail in following lines.

TECHNICAL FACTORS

Chemical Compatibility

The primary container (package) and the auxiliaries coming in contact with the product (e.g., plug, wad, liner, etc.) should not react with the product or any of its ingredients. The material from which the container is made should be impermeable to the product. If the product is liable to deterioration in sunlight, then the container must have the U.V. absorbers. To meet this requirement, one has to be very familiar with the chemical properties of the products as well as the chemical properties of packaging material components.

Chemical compatibility may be ascertained by checking product stability. Stability of the product over the period for which it is expected to lie on the shelf is done by conducting accelerated ageing studies (at 38°C temperature and 90% R.H.). Stability study will also confirm whether the colour of the container (in case of coloured packaging materials) leaches out and affects the colour of the product or vice-a-versa.

Some plastic materials impart their own smell or modify the perfume. The perfume notes have to be checked after ageing the product in the container in the case of perfumed products.

PHYSICAL COMPATIBILITY

(i) Retention of volatiles

Many health care products have a high percentage of volatiles such as water or alcohol, loss of volatiles would affect the quality of the product, perfume is usually more volatile and hence its retention is very important. The volatiles should neither escape in vapour from the closure system nor permeate through container walls.

(ii) Leak Proof Caps

No container, however perfect, is of any value unless it has an efficient closure system. Ideally the closure should be easy to remove and replace, but should give a sea that prevents the diffusion of gases and vapours and the seepage of liquids. Most bottle and tube closures consist of a screw cap containing compressible wad, although wadless caps are coming into wider use of late. Leak-proof property of the cap along with the container must be checked with the intended product and not with water. As water may not leak out through many closure systems but products like shampoo, oil can find a way to come out as each of them has got peculiar characteristics.

There is increasing trend for making the closure not only leak-proof, but also tamper-indicating. This is a very desirable development.

(iii) Tamper-proof Seal

Most of the consumer products in the category of cosmetics/ toiletries attract very high duties which make them expensive.

A customer who is willing to pay a high price for such a product will naturally expect an intact product. A product having tamper proof seal will automatically assure its intactness to the customer. Most manufacturers are in the process of developing pilfer-proof seal for their products wherever it is not there. A few examples are: Many plastic containers now are seen with PVC heat-shrinkable pilfer proof sleeves; Glass and plastic bottles with ROPP caps; Cartons are either closed with cellotapes or glued, if not, the product inside is packed in a sealed poly bag. Aluminium collapsible tubes have metallic membrane seas on the nozzles.

(iv) Transport Hazards

Teritary packaging materials (shippers) are designed to take care of product damage during transit. If the shipper is made up of corrugated box, then grammage, type of paper, flute, number of primary packs to be packed are considered. Even the type of glue to be used while manufacturing corrugated box has to be specified. Cushioning material also plays important role in taking care of this factor.

AESTHETIC FACTORS

(i) Presentability/Appearance

The aesthetic side of package design is basically a marketing responsibility, but a very close liaison between marketing and packaging experts is essential to ensure that a design is aesthetically functional and technically feasible. This applies not only to the container itself but also to the labelling and printing, and to the design of the display holders too.

In packaging of cosmetic products probably the package is ten times more important than the product. Esoteric shapes of crystal clear glass bottles, fancy spray systems, oversize decorative caps, glossy sophisticated labels and eye-catching cartons made from laminated boards combine to make a pack of cosmetic product a piece of art. Its designing requires the imagination of a creative artist rather than scientific knowledge of a package engineer.

An attractive pack appeals to the consumer and contributes substantially to the initial sales of the product. An average product with appealing package can succeed. On the other hand even an excellent product with defective packaging is bound to fail. Good packaging is therefore very important for the success of a product.

(ii) Packaging Design-Technicalities

As far as technicalities of the package design are concerned, in general, the final pack must be sufficiently strong to survive the normal treatment it is liable to receive during manufacturing process, distribution, sale and actual use at customer's end. There is bound to be a certain failure of packs, largely due to accidents, but it is essential that this failure rate is very low, if the product has to be a commercial success. Typical possible problems we look for in package design are:

(a) Thin areas in containers-glass or plastic;

(b) Highly stressed areas-when polyolefins are used;

(c) Very small radius convex areas on the outside of clear packs that can act as effective lenses for focussing U.V. radiation, and so concentrate its harmful effects on to small areas of a product;

(d) Stability of the container-especially plastic containers with unstable bases can give rise to troubles on a mechanical filling line.

Apart from all the technical and aesthetic parameters of a pack, it must also dispense the product easily and be convenient for the consumer to handle. There is nothing mor infuriating to a customer than a lotion that will not come of a container because the orifice of the nozzle is too small, or a deodorant squeeze pack that squirts a direct jet of liquid rather than the expected fine spray problem of a badly judged orifice size in the first example and incorrect orifice dimensions and design in the second examples can stop the growth of the respective products. These two problems can easily be overlooked if proper attention is not paid while designing the pack. One of the solutions to avoid these problems is to do technical survey of similar packs used for similar products. Any shortcomings in the competitor's a pack can be a lesson to overcome similar problems while designing the pack.

(iii) Packaging Design–Practicability

The practicability includes easy availability of the material, presence of alternative suppliers, supplier's capacity, limitations as far as their machines are concerned and cost considerations.

Whenever any new packaging material has to be introduced its available must be checked. We must check the expertise, technical know how and capabilities of the existing supplier. It is always advisable to go for indigenously available packaging material where availability is not a problem. Packaging expert must visit the supplier's premises and check under what conditions the supplier is going to manufacture the material. It is also better to check whether more than one supplier are available. Manufacturing capacity must also be critically evaluated.

(iv) Packaging Design–Standard Weights and Measures for Packaged Rules Commodities Act and (SWAMPA Rules)

It is necessary to be aware of SWAMPAC Rule. Among other things, these rules specify product quantity that can be packed and sold, e.g., all creams except dental and shaving must be packed in 25, 30, 35, 40, 45, 50, 60, 70, 80, 90, 100, 120, 140, 160, 180, 200 and thereafter in multiples of hundreds grammes. Hence, while designing a pack, we have to inform Marketing that the product could be packed in certain specified quantities only.

Second important SWAMPAC requirement is the relation between letter height on the label and area of principal display panel of the pack.

COST FACTORS

The last but not the last factor to be considered is cost. Selection of design, material shape, weight, etc. must be appropriate. Every paise saved in packaging is the real profit.

Secondly, cost economy can be achieved by minimising the handling of the packaging material, e.g., corrugated boxes can be delivered to the plastic container manufacture who in turn will pack them in the desired manner and despatch them to the factory. In this process we can avoid loading unloading, opening-closing of the shippers. Moreover containers packed uniformly will help on-line operations (i.e. stamping., conveying) easier.

Another example we can take is that of printing. One can go for four colour off-set printing or settle with two colours. As three colour off-set printing machines are to available in our country. Either we can print on four colour machine or print twice on two colour machine.

It is true that cost holds the balance between aesthetic and functional considerations. When this equilibrium is attained, the we can say the pack is cost-effective.

PACKAGING MATERIALS COMMONLY USE FOR COSMETICS

(a) Cartons: Coated boards, varnished, laminated embossed, E-fluted boards

(b) Flexibles: Paper, cellophene, LDPE, HDPE, BOPP, PP, PET, aluminium foil, nylon, HIP, shrink and stretch films and laminates of various combinations.

(c) Rigid Plastic containers (Jars, bottles etc.) Blow moulded, injection blow moulded, stretch blow moulded, injection moulded and rotatinal blow moulded.

(d) Form fill and seal pouches from multilayer films.

(e) Corrugated boxes; Virgin, semi-virgin, B-grade kraft papers, A,B,C, E-fluted.

(f) Collapsible Tubes: Aluminium and multilayer (lami tubes)-coextruded plastic tubes or soft squeeze tubes.

(g) Aerosol systems: Aluminium tin.

(h) Glass Bottles; Plain transparent, amber coloured.

(i) Cushioning Material: Corrugated material, expanded LDPE and PS.

(j) Labels, Stickers, shrink sleeves; Papers, PVC material, etc.

Out of all the above mentioned packaging materials, plastic materials have the major share and it is growing at a very fast rate. There has been many new developments in plastic packaging like development of multilayer pouches, multilayer co-extruded tubes (Lami tubes), Stretch blow moulded pet containers of various sizes and shapes besides the development of sophisticated and fast packaging machinery and equipment. A suitable packaging system and packaging machinery is adopted depending upon the cosmetic product to be packed and various factors detailed earlier.

28

Miscellaneous Formulae

PEROXIDE GEL DENTIFRICE

Component	Composition (W/W)%
Carbopol 940	1.50
Polyethylene glycol 400	30.00
glycerine 99.6%	25.00
Butylated hydroxy anisole	0.50
Hydrogen peroxide (35% solution)	10.00
Sodium saccharin	0.50
Mixed flavour oils	1.00
Calcium pyrophosphate	29.00
Sodium lauroyl sacrosinate	1.50
Tetrasodium pyrophosphate	1.00

HIGH LATHER CREAM

Rinse Shampoo

Component	Composition (W/W)%
Sodium lauroyl sacrosinate, 30%	20.0
Coco betaine, 35%	10.0
Lauramide DEA	5.0

Component	Composition (W/W)%
Cetrimonium chloride, 30%	0.8
Steralkonium chloride, 25%	0.1
Disodium EDTA	0.2
Water, perfume, preservative	q.s.
Adjust pH to 6.7	

Antidandruff Shampoo

Component	Composition (W/W)%
Sodium lauroyl sacrosinate, 30%	4.0
Colloidal sulfur	4.0
Sodium chloride	6.0
Sodium coconut alkyl glyceryl sulfonate	30.0
N-cocoyl sarcosine	0.7
FD&C blue dye no. 1	0.4
Perfume	0.5
Succuinic Acid	1.0
Disodium cupric ethylenediaminet-etraacetate	0.5
Distilled water	q.s

Antidandruff Shampoo for Only Hair

Component	Composition (W/W)%
Sodium lauroyl sarcosinate, 30%	10.0
Tea dedecyl sulfate, 40%	25.0
Zinc pyrithione, 48%	4.2
Magnesium aluminium silicate	1.0
Hydroxypropylmethyl cellulose, E4,000	1.25
Water, perfume, colour	q.s.

Disperse magnesium aluminium silicate and HPMC, E4,000 in water and allow to stand overnight. Add the rest of the ingredients.

Crystal Clear, Acid Balanced Shampoo

Component	Composition (W/W)%
Part 1	
Sodium lauroyl sarcosinate, 30%	30.0
Lauryl dimethyl amine oxide, 30%	5.0
Polyquaternium 7 (Merquat 550)	1.0
Part 2	
Polyol alkoxy ester (Crothix)	0.7
Disodium EDTA	0.3
Water	64.0

Disperse Crothix in hot water add with strong agitation to Part 1. A clear solution forms. While still hot, adjust pH to 5.7 by adding citric acid solution with strong agitation.

Sarcosinate Shampoo

Component	Composition (W/W)%
Triethanolamine lauryl ether sulfate (3 moles ethylene oxide)	4.0
Triethanolamine cocoyl sarcosinate	10.0
Monoethanolamide of coconut fatty acids	3.0
Diethanolamide of coconut fatty acids	3.0
EDTA, partialthiethanolamine salt	0.65
Ethanol	7.0
Methyl cellulose (4000 cps)	0.75
Perfume	0.75
Water	q.s.
pH adjusted to 6.7	

Clear Facial cleansing Gel

Component	Composition (W/W)%
Sodium cocoyl glutamate	40.0
Sodium lauroyl sarcosinate	10.0

Component	Composition (W/W)%
Coacamide DEA	10.0
Glycerol	5.0
Water, perfume, preservative	q.s.

Mix ingredients, heat to 50°C until clear, cool.

Mild Shower Gel

Component	Composition (W/W)%
Cocoamphoglycinate	23.0
Sodium lauryl sarcosinate, 30%	20.0
Sodium dodecyl sulfate, 30%	20.0
Hydroxyprpyl methylcellulose (E4M)	0.3
Water, perfume, preservative,	q.s.

Mix ingredients, Heat to 50°C and adjust pH to 7.0 with lactic acid, cool.

Liquid Both Foam

Component	Composition (W/W)%
Na.alpha-olefin sulfonate, 40%	10.0
Ammonium lauryl sulfate, 30%	30.0
Cocoyl sarcosine	3.0
Ammonium chloride	3.0
Water, preservative, etc.	q.s.

Mix surfactants, dissolve ammonium chloride in warm water, and add. Adjust pH to 4.8.

Liquid Toilet Soap

Component	Composition (W/W)%
Sodium (C14-16) olefin sulfonate, 40%	20.0
Sodium lauroyl sarcosinate, 30%	10.0
Cocamide MEA	3.0

Ammonium chloride	2.0
Disodium EDTA	0.2
Water, perfume, colour, opacifier, preservative	q.s.

Add first two ingredients to water, heating to 80ºC. add cocamide MEA and heat with stirring until clear. Add remaining ingredients and adjust pH to 5.5 with citric acid.

Cationic Skin Cleanser

Component	Composition (W/W)%
Sodium lauroyl sarcosinate, 30%	50.0
Oleoyl sarcosine	1.0
Lauramide DEA	5.0
Tetrasodium EDTA	0.4
Cetrimonium chloride, 29%	3.4
Water	q.s.

Surgical Scrub Liquid

Component	Composition (W/W)%
Sodium C14-16 olefinsulfonate, 40%	20.0
Sodium lauroylsarcosinate, 30%	10.0
Cocamide MEA	3.0
Choroxylenol	1.0
Ammonium chloride	2.0
Disodium EDTA	0.2
Water	q.s.
Adjust to pH 5.5	

Facial Cleanser for Oily Skin

Component	Composition (W/W)%
TEA lauroyl sarcosinate, 40%	20.0
Hydroxypropylmethyl cellulose, E4000	2.0

Component	**Composition (W/W)%**
Salicylic acid	1.0
Methyl paraben	0.2
EDTA	0.2
Water	q.s.

Disperse thickener in hot water before adding other ingredients.

Acne Lather Scrub Gel with 10% Benzoyl Peroxide

Component	Composition (W/W)%
Sodium lauroyl sarcosinate, 30%	30.0
Oleth-10	15.0
Benzoyl peroxide, 70%	14.3
Magnesium aluminum silicate (Veegum-R.T. Vanderbilt Co.)	1.0
Disodium EDTA	0.2
Water	q.s.

Disperse Veegum in hot water with high shear mixing and allow to stand overnight. Mill benzoyl peroxide with Veegum suspension. Mix remaining ingredients, heat to 50°C and mill to uniform texture. Fill warm into containers. A stiffer gel may be obtained by increasing the oleth-10 to 20.0%.

Emollient Gel

Component	Composition (W/W)%
Coal tar extract	50 mg
N-lauroyl sarcosine	30 mg
Glyceryl capric/caprylic ester	800 mg
Propylene glycol	20 mg
Glyceryl tris 12-hydroxy stearate	100 mg

Sunscreen Lotion

Component	Composition (W/W)%
A:	
Veegum	1.5
Water	78.5
Triethanolamine	4.0
B:	
Myvacet 9-40	4.0
Cetyl alcohol	0.5
Stearic acid	1.5
Cocoyl sarcosine	5.0
C:	
P-aminobenzoic acid	5.0

I. Rehydrate Veegum in water. Add Tea and heat to 65°C.

II. Heat B to 70°C, then add to 1 with agitation.

III. Add paba with agitation until 35°C is reached.

Note: Because of the possible formation of suspected cancer causing compounds. p-Aminobenzoic Acid (PABA) should be replaced with some other UV blocker, such as Benzophenone-4 or Octyl Methoxycinnamate.

Aerosol Shave Cream

Component	Composition (W/W)%
A:	
Veegum	1.5
Water	76.0
Sorbitol (70% solution)	3.0
Triethanolamine	6.0
B:	
Stearic acid	6.5
Cocoyl sarcosine	7.0
Preservative	q.s.
Perfume	q.s.

I. Add the VEEGUM to water slowly, agi-tating continually until smooth. Add sorbitol and triethanolamine. Heat to 70°C.

II. Heat B to 75°C.

III. Add 11 to 1 and mix until cool.

Aerosol Depilatory Spray

Component	Composition (W/W)%
Sodium N-lauroyl sarcosinate	1.5
Sodium metasilicate penthydrate	1.0
Thioglycolic acid (80% solution)	7.5
Sodium hydroxide	5.36
Urea	10.0
Perfume	0.45
Water	q.s.

Deodorant Stick

Component	Composition (W/W)%
A:	
Veegum	2.0
Water	q.s.
B:	
Zinic stearate	5.0
C:	
Cocoyl sarcosine	2.0
D:	
Pyrax B	90.5
Vancide 89RE	0.5

Add the Veegum to about 30 parts water, agitating continually until smooth. Add the zinc stearate with agitation. Add the cocoyl sarcosinate to the paste. Premix D, add to A, B and C and work into a smooth paste (add more water if necessary to get a paste). Pack into stick mold and allow to dry. (Final pH should be about 5.0)

Analgesic Cream

Component	Composition (W/W)%
A:	
Hectabrite DP	1.75
Klucel J	1.75
Water	40.75
Ethanol	36.75
B:	
Eucalyptus oil	0.20
Menthol	0.40
Peppermint oil	0.40
Triethanolamine	3.00
Methyl salicylate	5.00
Cocoyl sarcosine	10.00
Preservative	q.s.

Phase A: Dry blend Hectabrite DP and Klucel J and add to the water and ethanol slowly, agitating continually until smooth.

Phase B: Combine, stiring to dissolve crystals, and add to Phase A: with slow mixing. Mix until unifrom.

Surfactant Base Shower Gel Formulation

Ingredient	Chemical Name	A-1785	B-1352
Phase A			
Empicol ESB3/A&W	SLES (30%)	30.0	30.0
Oramix NS10/Seppic	Decyl Glucoside (50%)	5.0	5.0
Amonyl 380 BA/Seppic	Cocamidoporpylbetaine (30%)	10.0	10.0
Brij 30/ICI	Laureth-4	2.0	2.0
Sepigel 305/Seppic	—	2.0	2.0
Water		Up to 100	
Phase B			
DC 1785/Dow Corning	Silicone Emulsion	8.3	0.0
DC 1352 DowCorning	Silicone Emulsion	0.0	3.0
Phase C			
NaCl		0.5	0.5

Soap Base Shower Gel Formulation

Ingredient	Chemical Name	Ratio (%)
Natrosol 250HR/Aqualon	Hydroxyethylcellulose	0.65
Edenor C 18 98/100/Henkel	Stearic Acid	2.00
Edenor C 14 98/100/Henkel	Myristic Acid	9.00
Edenor C 12 98/100/Henkel	Lauric Acid	14.00
K0H 85% flake	—	7.06
Propylene Glycol	—	2.00
Glycerin	—	2.00
Ethylene Glycol Monostearate	—	2.00
EDTA-4Na	—	0.10
Citric Acid	—	0.20
Germall II	—	0.20
Perfume	—	1.50
DC 1497 Emulsion	Silicone Emulsion	2.50
Water	—	Up to 100

Procedure

* Dissolve HEC into 40% weight of water.
* Add 0.1% KOH, mix until uniform.
* Heat to 70°C, add PG and Glycerin-A.
* Heat all acid to 70°C and agitation until uniform-B.
* Add B into A, mixed and maintain 70°C.
* Add residue KOH (50% solution) slowly, mixed and maintain 80c, mixed 10 min more after finished neutralization.
* Add EGMS when 60c, get well dissolution and start cooling system Add DC 1497 emulsion when 50c
* Add residue ingredient like citric acid, EDTA-4NA, Germall 11 and perfume when 40c or below.

Mixed Base Shower gel Formulation

Ingredient	Chemical Name	Ratio (%)
Phase A		
Aculyn 33/ISP	Acrylates Copolymer	1.4
Aculyn 22/ISP	Acrylates/Steareth-20 Methacrylate Copolymer	1.4
Water	—	10.0
TEA	—	0.8
Phase B		
Liquid Soap SFP/Goodway	Potassium Soap (30%)	38.9
Mirataine BET C-30/Rhodia	Cocamidoporpylbetaine (35%)	3.4
Texapon N70/Henkel	Sodium Laureth Sulfate (18%)	32.2
Plantacare 1200/Henkel	Lauryl Polyglucosides (50%)	1.0

Mixed Base Shower Gel Formulation

Ingredient	Chemical Name	Ratio (%)
Phase C		
Cetyl Alcohol/Merk	—	1.0
EGMS	—	1.4
EGDS	—	0.5
Phase D		
Liquid Germall Plus/ISP	—	0.5
DC 1352/DC 1497 Emulsion/Dow Corning		3.3
Perfume	—	0.6
Water	—	Up to 100

<u>Procedure</u>

1. Mixed part A and B separately and agitate together until uniform.
2. Heat to 70°C, add ingredient of group C, cool the whole system.
3. Add part D by mild mixing.
4. Adjust pH value to 8.3-8.7 with citric acid or TEA, add salt to adjust viscosity.

Soap Base Shower Gel Formulation

Formulation	A	B	D	E
D.I. Water	41 14	43.64	46.14	46.44
Natrosol 250HR	0.65	0.65	0.65	0.65
C18 Fatty Acid (99%)	2	2	2	2
C14 Fatty Acid (99%)	14	14	14	14
C12 Fatty Acid (99%)	9	9	9	9
K0H (85-%)	7.49	7.49	7.49	7.49
Propylene Glycol	2	2	2	0
Glycerine	2	2	2	6
EGMS	2	2	2	2
FDTA-4Na	0.1	0.1	0.1	0.1
Citric acid	0.2	0.2	0.2	0.2
Germall II	0.2	0.2	0.2	0.2
PCA-Na	0	0	0	0.3
Perfume	1.5	1.5	1.5	1.5
DC 2-1497	0	2.5	5	3

Suractant Base Shower Gel Formulation

Ingredient	Chemical Name	Ratio (%)
Phase A		
Empicol LS 30P/A&W	SLS(30%)	25.0
Empilan Fd/A&W	Coconut diethanolamide	3.0
Empigen BS-AU/A&W	Cocamidoporpylbetaine (30%)	5.0
Extrapone Seaweed/Dragoco	Plant Extract	3.0
Carbopol 2020 (4%)/BF	Acrylic copolymer (4%)	15.0
Water		44.0
Phase B		
Suttocide A/ISP	Sodium Hydroxy Methyl Glycinate	0.8
Phase C		
DC 1227 emulsion/Dow Corning	Silicone Emulsion	4.0
Perfume		0.2
Colour		q.s.

Daily Protection Facial Lotion (SPF 25)

K 18/1-22026/E

Ingredients	INCI Name	% (w/w)
Part A		
Crodafos MCA	Cetyl Phosphate	1,50
Cutina MD	Gyceryl Stearate	2,00
Lanette 16	Cetyl Alcohol	1,00
Catiol SN	Cetearyl Isonanoate	4,00
Myritol 318	caprylic/Capric Triglyceride	5,00
Witconol TN	C12/15 Alkylbenzoate	5,00
Prisorine 3505	Isostearic Acid	1,00
Copherol 1250	Tocopheryl Acetate	0,50
Solbrol P	Propyl Paraben	0,10
Neo Heliopan BB	Benzophenone 3	1,50
Neo Heliopan 303	Octocrylene	5,00
Part B		
Dermineralized Water	Water	QS
Neo Helopan Hydro	Phenylbenzimidazole Sulfonic Acid	2.00
NaOH Solution	Sodium Hydroxide Solution	QS
Glycerin 99%	Glycerin	3.00
Solbrol M	Methyl Paraben	0.20
Carbopol ETD 2050	Carbomer	0.20
Phenoxyethanol	Phenoxyethanol	0.70
Part C		
Alpha Bisabol Nat H&R	Bisabolol	0.10
Perfume Oil	Fragrance (Parfum)	0.30

Dental Cream

Component	Composition (W/W)%
Calcium Carbonate	12.1
Dicalcium phosphate dihydrate	36.2
Sodium N-lauryl sarcosinate	2.0
Glycerine	30.6
Water	15.3
Irish moss	1.0

Mouthwash

Component	Composition (W/W)%
Sodium N-lauroyl sarcosinate	0.2
Ethyl alcohol	10.0
Flavor	0.15
Saccharin (Soluble)	0.012
Distilled water	q.s.

Dental Cream

Component	Composition (W/W)%
Sodium lauroyl sarcosinate	41.
Stannous fluoride	0.2
Sec. calcium phosphate dihydrats	86.0
Magnesium silicate	7.0
Flavoring materials	2.5
Saccharin (Soluble)	0.2

Mouth Rinse

Component	Composition (W/W)%
Disobutyl cresoxyethoxlethyl-dimenthylbenzyl ammonium chloride	0.03
Sodium N-lauroyl sarcosinate	0.20
Polyoxyethylene tridrcyl alcohol (EO12)	0.25
Ethanol	15.0
Adjuvants (colours, flavour, fragance)	0.20
Water (distilled)	84.32

Commercial Baby Shampoo

PEG-80 Sorbitan Laurate

Cocamidopropyl Betaine

Sodium Trideceth Sulfate

lauroamphoglycinate
PEG-150 Distearate
Sodium Laureth-13 Carboxylate

Performance:

Lather Drainage Time	
(2% Solids)	15 Seconds
ET-50 (10% Solids)	8 Hours

Formula 1

Component	Composition (W/W)%
Hampshire Sodium LED3A	32.
Sodium Myristoyl Sarcosinate (Hamposyl@M-30)	3.2
Sodium Lauryl Ether Sulfate	3.2
Polyquaternium 7	0.4
Water	100
Performance:	
Lather Drainage Time	
(2% Solids)	101 Seconds
ET-50 (10% Solids):	15 Hours

Formula 2

Component	Composition (W/W)%
Hampshire Tris LED3A	5.0
Cocamphodiacetate	5.0
Water	90.0
	100.0
Performance:	
Lather Drainage Time	
(2% Solids)	103 Seconds
ET-50 (10% Solids):	5.3 Hours

Formula 3

Component	Composition (W/W)%
Hampshire Sodium LED3A	5.0
Alkylppolyglycoside 1200	5.0
Water	90.0
Performance:	
Lather Drainage Time (2% Solid)	50 Seconds
ET-50 (10% Solids):	19 Hours

Formula 4

Component	Composition (W/W)%
Hampshire Sodium LED3A	3.3
Sodium Lauryl Ether Sulfate	3.3
Sodium Cocamidopropyl Betaine	3.4
Water	90
	100.0
Performance:	
Lather Drainage Time	
(2% Solids)	57 Seconds
ET-50 (10% Solids):	24 Hours

Formula 5

Component	Composition (W/W)%
Hampshire Sodium LED3A	3.3
Sodium Lauryl Ether Sulfate	3.3
Sodium Cocamidopropyl Betaine	3.4
Water	90
Ca/Mg Hardness to 3,000 ppm	—
	100
Performance:	
Lather Drainge Time	
(2% Solids)	49 Seconds
ET-50 (10% Solids):	24 Hours

Instant Polish

Ingradients	(W/W)%
Phase A	
Lxxsol D40 (ExxonMobil)	25.0
DC 200 Fluid, 350 cSt (Dow Corning)	1.4
DC 200 Fluid, 1,000 cSt (Dow Corning)	1.0
DC 5200 Formulation Aid (Dow Corning)	2.0
Phase B	
Water	57.6
Sillikolloid P.87 (Hoffmann Minerals)	8.5
Wax emulsion (35% activeblend of soft/hard waxes)	2.5
50% sodium citrate in water	2.0

Procedure: Blend phase A ingredients in the main vessel under low shear. In an auxiliary vessel, load phase B ingredients in the order listed. Mix with low shear. Add phase B to phase A very slowly under high shear until the emulsion begins to form. The remainder of phase B can then be added at a faster rate. When addition is complete, mix with high shear.

Comments: The blend of fluids in this formulation yields high gloss in an easy-to-use product form.

Amide-free Liquid Dishwash

Ingradients	(W/W)%
Dodecylbenzene sulfonic acid	21.5
Caustic soda	5.4
Sodium laureth sulfate (60%)	4.0
Mackam 35UL (McIntyre Group) (cocamidopropyl betaine)	5.5
Sodium xylene sulfonate (40%)	8.0
Water, dye, fragrance	q.s. to 100

Procedure: Add caustic soda to water and adjust pH to 7.0-8.0 with dodecylbenzene sulfonic acid. Add remaining components and adjust pH to 6.5-7.0 with citric acid. If necessary, lower viscosity with sodium xylene sulfonate, or raise viscosity with sodium chloride.

Comments: Solids, %: 30+/- 1.0 pH: 6.5-7.0 viscosity (cps, 25°C): 260-350.

Aloe Vera SPF 10 Sun Protection Gel

Ingradients	(W/W)%
CoVera (RTD Hall Star) (aloe barbadensis leaf juice)	14.77
Triethanolamine	2.18
Phenylbenzimidazole sulfonic acid	4.00
Allantoin	0.10
RTD Glycerin 99.5% (RDT Hall Star) (glycerin)	5.00
CoSept M (RTD HallStar) (methylparaben)	0.20
Imidazolidinyl urea	0.15
Water (deionized)	1.00
Carbopol 940 (carbomer)	1.50
Water (deionized)	(to 100) 58.10
Triethanolamine	3.00
Water (deionized)	10.00

Procedure: Add CoVera to Vessel one and with good mixing, add triethanolamine (2.18% of formula) and then phenylbenzimidazole sulfonic acid. When homogeneous, add allantoin, RTD Glycerin 99.5% and CoSept M in order and heat batch to 70°C. Maintain until homogeneous (but at least 15 minutes) and then start cooling. Dissolve imidazolidinyl urea in water (1% of formula) and when batch is at 45°C, add it to the batch. In vessel two, disperse Carbopol 940 in deionized water (58.10% of formula) and mix until uniform. In vessel three, dissolve triethanolamine (3% of formula) in deionized water (10% of formula). Add vessel three to vessel two with strong mixing but without aeration. When homogeneous, add the batch in vessel one to vessel two and mix to homogeneity. Continue cooling and mixing until the completed batch is at desired filling temperature. Perform quality assurance checks.

Comments: pH: 6.0. Viscosity: 24 cps.

Gentle Baby Shampoo

Ingradients	(W/W)%
Deionized water	q.s. to 100
Tego Betaine L-7 (cocamidopropyl betaine)	18.5
Neosorb 70/20 (sorbitol)	16.9
Plantaren 1200 UP (lauryl glucoside)	15.9

Plantaren 818 UP (coco glucoside)	12.5
Amisoft LS-11 (sodium lauroyl glutamate)	5.0
Antil 141 (propylene glycol (and) PEG-55 propyleneglycol oleate)	2.2
D-panthenol SP (D-panthenol)	1.0
Sensomer CI-50 (Ondeo Nalco) (hydroxypropyltrimonium chloride)	0.5
Crotein HKP Powder (keratin amino acid)	0.4
Fragrance	0.1
Preservative	q.s.

Procedure: Add water first and heat to approximately 40°C. Add the remaining ingredients to the water in the order listed. Mix until uniform at a low speed (under 100 rpm). Cool to room temperature.

Comments: Makes a clear, colourless shampoo formulation.

Vitamin Skin Lotion

Ingradients	(W/W)%
Deionized water	79.1
Carbomer 941	0.2
Glycerine	5.0
Paragon G-2	0.5
Fancorsil Lim-1	0.5
Mackstat DM	0.5
Triethanolamine	0.2
Hydrobrite 1000 (Crompton)	10.0
crodafos CES	2.0
Shea butter	1.0
Uvinul MC-80	0.2
Vitamin E acetate	0.3
Fragrance No. 225404	0.5

Procedure: Premix deionized water and Carbomer 941 cold with high agitation. Heat to 70°C and add glycerine, Paragon G-2, Fancorsil Lim-1 and Mackstat DM in order. Add triethanolamine and maintain heat at 70°C. Premix Hydrobrite 1000, Crodafos CES, shea butter and Uvinul MC-80 in oil kettle; heat to 70°C. Add oil phase to water phase at 70°C. Mix for 30 minutes; cool to 50°C. Add vitamin E acetate and fragrance. Mix and package at room temperature.

Kids Foaming Conditioning Shampoo

Ingradients	(W/W)%
Deionized water	72.27
Celquat L-200 (National Starch((polyquatemium-4)	1.00
Amaze (National Starch) (corn starch modified)	1.00
Tego Betaine L-7 30% (Goldschmidt) (cocamidopropyl betaine)	13.33
Mackanate El 40% (Mclntyre Group) (disodium laureth sulfosuccinate)	5.00
Tween 20 (Uniquma) (polysorbate 20)	1.00
Glydant (Lonza) (DMDM hydntoin)	0.40
Isobutane	6.00

Procedure: In a mixing vessel, add deionized water and Celquat L-200. Mix until dispersed, and add Amaze. Once dispersed, add remaining inuredients are at time until homogeneous. Filter and fill aerosol containers. Charge with propellants.

Comments: Valve type: Seaquist VX-81 Stem: 018 Length: 0.343" Gasket: Buna-P 0.045" THK Code: 150 Spring: SS Cup: High profile OS OD, epoxy top, laminate bottom, dimpled, Taperseal; Code: 1625 Actuator: Mousse spout short neck, short spt (S4LS OFF)

Gel Sanitizing Vertical Surface Cleaner

Ingradients	(W/W)%
Deionized water	40.0
50% NaOH	5.0
DeMox CSG-30 (DeForest)	15.0
Sodium hypochlorite 10%	40.0

Procedure: Add first three ingredients and mix well until thick and fully dissolved. Add the chlorine bleach last, mixing well as it is added. A visco-elastic gel is formed.

29

Indigenious Materials and Technologies for Herbal Cosmetics

Cosmetics or personal care products is a broad spectrum of products and it is increasing in an exponential way. In the present topic a few will be discussed, leaving guidelines for other category of products. Skin being the largest part of the body, skin care products are proportionately large in their percentage or ratio to the other personal care products like hair, nails, and teeth. As such there is no proper definition for herbal cosmetics, neither defined specifications nor stipulated quality controlled proformas developed in a global way.

Creams have a major share in commercially personal care products. The details of this category of products is undertaken. At the outset of the raw materials of creams for both types i.e., o/w type or w/o type.

NATURAL WAXES

Spermacetic and oils

Vegetables fats and oils	Exotic fat sources
Shea butter (*butyrosperum parkil*)	Suitable melting range
Cocoa butter or Shorea butter	Pleasant fragrance

Mangoferan idica	Inherent properties of emolliency
Palm kernel fats	
Rice bran oil sediment	
Coconut oil	
Almond oil	
Apricot kernel oil	
Natural waxes	**Spermacetic**
Vegetable fats and oils	Exotic fat sources
Shea butter (*butyrosperum parkil*)	Suitable melting range
Cocoa butter or Shorea butter	Pleasant fragrance
Mangoferan idica	Inherent properties of emolliency
Coconut oil hydrogenated	
Palm kernel fats	
Rice bran oil sediment	
Coconut oil	
Almond oil	
Apricot kernel oil	
Palm oil	

The adsorption/penetration/spreadability for creams made out of pure vegetable oils is also much lighter than synthetic, wax based creams. No doubt polymers give additional elegance to a cream, but the skin benefits by vegetable oil absorption only.

Vegetable oils are reserve skin foods and tonics. E.g. Indian vegetable oils like sesame and saffola. There is not much difference in physical properties except for the odour in sesame oil and olive oil. However deodorised sesame oil can be used as a substitute to olive oil.

CREAMS

A wide range of creams are available in commerce. Generally bases for all creams are of four types:

A. Oil/Water

B. Water/Oil

C. Mineral base creams

D. Gels

Based on the site of application and action they are classified as:

Face cream

Body creams

Hand creams

Moisturiser

Cleansing creams

Protective creams

Anti acne creams

Sun screen creams

Anti wrinkle creams

Facial treatment creams

Blemishes and spot removal creams

Pore cleansing creams

Table No. 1

The raw material for the manufacture of herbal cosmetics can be broadly divided into three categories.

1. Vehicles/carriers of therapeutic agents.
2. Therapeutic agents from herbs and other natural sources.
3. Additives for formulation stability.
4. Miscellaneous (any auxiliary materials).

VEHICLES/BASES

Face creams	**Herbs**
Choice of base/vehicles	for improving complexion
Vegetable oils	Chamomile
Natural waxes	Calendula (Marigold)
Water	Rose petal extract
Preservatives	*Ficus bengalenses* bark extract

Stabilisers	Comfrey/orange flower extract
Colours	
Perfumes	
Vegetables oils	**Antiwrinkles Herbs**
Sweet almond oil	Cucumber
Til oil (deoodrised)	Carrot juice
Olive oil	Coconut water
Cotton seed oil	Papaya milk oil makes skin more supple
Sunflower oil	
Butter	
Apricot	
Kernel oil	
Base	Anti acne
Mineral paste or cream	Scented turmeric
	Beriberis
	Red sanders
	Urtica dioica

Table 2: Herbal Sources for Cosmetics

	Name of plant	
1.	Neem	Hair, Lice Dandruff
2.	Orris Root	Face Powder
3.	Papaya Milk	Facial Mask
4.	Priangu Phool	Face Brightener
5.	Pudina	Under Eye
6.	Rakta Chandan	Anti Septic for facial preparations
7.	Shatavari	Pimples
8.	Sallaki	Facial Anti-Wrinkler
9.	Tulsi	Antiseptic, for spots and pimples
10.	Vettiver	Skin antiseptic preparations
11.	Liquorice	Skin and Hair preparations
12.	Ganja	Hair preparations
13.	Indigo	Hair preparations

Table 3: Plant Extracts for Natural Colouring Materials

Pterocarpus Santalinas :(Southern region of the Indian subcontinent)—ground heartwood of the tree is used as a traditional colouring (orange) in acidic media.

Oil soluble colours rendered water dispersible through emulsion technology.

Porphyrine (Chlorophyll)	
Cocchineal	
Grape Skin	
Elderberry	Commercially Exploited
Hibiscus	Sources
Red Cabbage	
Beetroot–Betavulgaris	
Vulgaxanthin–Yellow Colour	
Betanin–Red	
Annatto Seeds–(Orange powder)	
yellow powder	
Crocus Sativus	
Gardenia Substitute	
Marigold Extract–Yellow	
oil soluble colour	
Calendula Officinails–pot,	
Marigold	
Carrot	
Algae	
Curcumin	

RECENT HERBAL APPLICATIONS

Spirulina: For face creams and lotions β carotene Vitamin A, B group and E – All essential for maintaining a healthy skin

Applications: Anti wrinkling creams, pimple creams Rejuvenating marks and face packs Phycocyanin pigment of spirulina–Biolipsticks in Japan, Eye–liners, Eye Shadows

Unpasteurized Aloe Vera Living Juice

Preparation by crushing whole leaves between rollers and then filtering.

Biogenic Applications Rejuvenator

Sun burn cream

Scars, stretch marks, acne, age, spots

Dandruff and scpal problems.

Quality Control: Physical (Creams)

1. A stable emulsion.
2. Uniform distribution of herbal extract.
3. Spreading and penetration in case of massage creams with minimum quality and maximum spreading.
4. Becoming non greasy on the skin within a short time i.e. 3 min. (indicates absorption into skin).

In the case of cleansing creams.

1. No pore blocking indicated by best dissipation and cleansing.
2. Non greasy/no tackiness.
3. Cleansing by removing collected dirt on the face/body.
4. Pore cleansing (by immediate perspiration pore opening etc.)
5. Rheological Standards.
6. No discoloration of extract on shelf life.

Challenges to Indian Scientists in Post Gatt Era

1. The product patent will be in force in the country from 2005 and before and end of a 10 year period the government will have to introduce the necessary legislation to amend the Indian Patent Act. Once the product patent system comes into force, one can definitely expect inflow of other countries into Cosmetic Industries line also. With the stupendous technical and monetary advantage at their disposal they might attempt to do research on Indian herbal heritage and go for Patents. Thus Indian plant potential is open to universal/global research and vulnerable to foreign take over.

   Before this our scientists should gear themselves and get the credit first from our rich heritage and wealth of herbal knowledge in literature.

2. The research should be planned by recognised bodies like CSIR, ICMR, UGC, ICAR, etc.
3. Herbs are Natures gifts out not the monopoly of any individual/organisation. At the same time the processing of plants into extracts or incorporates into cosmetics can be permitted for patents.

The absorption/penetration/spreadability for creams made out of pure vegetable oils is also much lighter than synthetic, wax based creams. No doubt polymers give additional elegance to a cream, but the skin benefits by vegetable oil absorption only.

Vegetable oils are reserve skin foods and tonics e.g. Indian vegetable oils like sesame and saffola. There is not much difference in physical properties except for the odour in sesame oil and olive oil. However deodorised sesame oil can be used as a substitute to olive oil.

SUGGESTIONS

Scientific approach based on the performance of the herbs selected in formulation is to be encouraged for a standard cosmetic manufacturing.

Official standards to these herbal cosmetics should come out. Consisting of monographs for all the raw materials and also specific standards for different cosmetics (qualitative, objective, quantitative).

Objectionable advertisement acts should be made applicable to herbal cosmetics also. Process patenting for more herbs used in the cosmetics should be launched on a massive scale, before product patenting start from 2005.

As all cosmetic preparation mentioned in Schedule S should conform to the Bureau of Indian Standards (BIS) laid down from time to time by ISI, herbal cosmetics should also fall in line for such type of standards.

Statistical Information About Indian Patents

No. of patents published during period 1972-1995	–	104
Inventions relating to materials from plant source	–	101

Patents relating to processes of isolation of Extracts of medicines	–	101
Patents filed by Indians	–	72%
Patents filed by Foreigners	–	28%
Patents only "Neem"	–	14
Indian patents on "Neem"	–	12
Foreign patents on "Neem"	–	2

30

Present Manufacturers of Cosmetic Products

Allied Sales
19-2, Abdul Kadar Chamber,
St. Xavier's St. Parel,
Mumbai-400012

Anil Ayurpharma (I) Ltd.
Lagdiwala Estate,
Hingwala Lane, Ghatkopar (East),
Mumbai-400077

Anubhav Industries (L)
106, Shivam Industrial Estate,
Near Govandi Station Road,
Govandi, Mumbai-400088

Apex Cosmetics (L)
M-2718(1) Camawadi,
Din Quarry Road, Chembur,
Mumbai-400088

Asian Aerosol Pvt. Ltd.
228, Pragati Industrial Estate,
N.M. Joshi Marg, Lower Patel,
Mumbai-400011

Attari Brothers (Al-Hayat Group of Cos)
Hasham Building, P.O. Box No. 3008,
107-D, Mohammad Ali Road,
Mumbai-400003

Any & Getty Inns Pvt. Ltd.
Kusum Villa, 14 K.N. Marg,
Gamdevi, Mumbai-400007

Ayushakti Ayurved (P) Ltd.
A/5, Rishikesh, Haridas Nagar,
Opp. Avanti, Shimpoli Road,
Borivali (West),
Mumbai-400092

Arno Cosmetics (L)
C-Block, Amar Nivas,
Punjabi Wadi, Deonar,
Chembur, Mumbai-400088

Argus Cosmetics Ltd. (L)
"Sujatha Centre" 2nd Floor,
No. 4 Sheshadri Road,
Alwarpet, Chennai-600018

Arjun Pharmachem (L)
12, Kanya Kumari Apt.
Agashi Road,
Behind Desai Hospital,
Virar (West), Thane-401303

Baccarose Perfumes & Beauty Products Ltd.
66, Maker Chamber VI,
Nariman Point, Mumbai-400021

Barkur Surfactants Pvt. Ltd. (L)
Sony Apt.
Opp. St. Jode's High School,
Off Andheri Kurla Road,
Jarimari,
Mumbai-400072

Beauty Basic
286, Sher-E-Punjab Society,
Mahakali Caves Road,
Andheri (East),
Mumbai-400093

Beauty Cosmetics Ltd. (L)
37, Whites Road,
Chennai-600014

Beeta Chemicals
B-31, Nandjyot Industrial Estate,
Safed Pool, Andheri Kurla Road,
Near I.B.M.,
Mumbai-400072

Bendale Chemicals
2, Jalgaon Hsg. Soc.
Jilha Road,
Jalgaon-425001 (Mah.)

Body Care
14/15, Vishal Indl. Estate,
Near Gas Godown,
Goddev Road,
Bhayander (E), Thane-401105

Chemhouse Marketing
12, Gokul, Krishna Dham Society,
Sant Dnyaneshwar Path,
Panch Pakhadi, Thane (w)-400602

Chaganlal & Co.
Daya Vira House, Shop No. 3,
Near Laxmi Nivas,
Below Elphinstone Bridge,
Mumbai-400013

Cosmiks Mfg. Co. (L)
37, Agarwal Indl. Estate,
2nd Floor, S.V. Road, Dahisar (East),
Mumbai-400068

Cosmolene Laboratories (India) (L)
301, Owners Indl. Estate,
Gabrial Road,
7, Agarwal Pitamber lane,
Mahim (W),
Mumbai-400016

Choice Laboratories
999, State Highway,
Unjha -384170N. Gujarat

Choloayil Pharmaceuticals (L)
M Block No. 4,
Anna Nagar East, -Chennai-600102

Desai Agencies
B-38 Bagree Market,
71, Canning Street,
Kolkata-700001

Danyal Engineering Co.
3022, Gali Nal Badan
Shahganj, Agmeri Gate,
Delhi-110006

Dr. P.R. Dingaonkar
7, Shefali Phirozshah Road,
Santacruz (West),
Mumbai-400054

Dura Chemical Corpn. Ltd. (L)
11, Sprott Road,
Weikfield House, 2nd Floor,
Ballard Estate,
P. Box No. 395,
Mumbai-400038

Debon Herbal Products (L)
Jamma Cottage,
Geondevi Road, Poisar, Kandivali (West),
Mumbai-400067

Deepa Ceramics
K-49/51, Sonal Heavy Indl. Estate,
Ramchandra Lane,
Malad (East),
Mumbai-400064

Dimple International
Plot No. 619-4B, Asha Bhavan,
14th Road, Khar (West),
Mumbai-400052

Emami Limited
207, Chartered House,
297/299, Dr. Cawasji Hormasji Street,
Near New Marin Lines, Churchgate,
Mumbai-400002

Espee Herbals
101, Liberty Apt. Sarojini Road,
Vile Parle (West),
Mumbai-400056

Eveslynk Industries
H/Block Unit No. 225,
Ansa Ind. Estate, Sakivihar Road,
Mumbai-400072

Evershine International
Gala NO. 5, 1st Floor,
Vora Ind. Estate,
Navghar, Vasai (East),
Thane-401202

Eva Green Creation/Oyatab Fibre Pvt. Ltd.
15/5, Harinivas,
Dattatraya Road,
Santacruz (West),
Mumbai-400054

Emami Limited (L)
8, Bentnck Street,
10th Floor,
Kolkata-700001

E-Merck (India) Ltd.
Shiv Sagar Estate,
Dr. Annie Besant Road, Worli,
Mumbai-400018

Fine Organic Industries
Fine House, Anandji Street,
Off. M.G. Road,
Ghatkopar (East),
Mumbai-400077

FFC Aromas Pvt. Ltd. (L)
C-11, Udyog Sadan No. 1
Moral Ind. Area, Andheri (East),
Mumbai-400093

Flora Super Prints
131/132, Dewan & Sons Ind. Estate No. 6,
Vasai (East),
Thane

Flower Valley Perfumes P. Ltd.
4/13, Kamal Mension,
Arthur Bunder Road,
Colaba, Mumbai-400005

Fortune Laboratories Pvt. Ltd.
B/572, Sarita Vihar,
Mathura Road,
New Delhi-110044

Fem Care Pharma Ltd. (L)
Fem House, Plot No. 3/A,
Ram Mandir Road,
Kherwadi, Bandra (East),
Mumbai-400051

Grip Engineers
Gala No. 12,
Shree Mahalaxmi Kripa Sadan,
Near IT Colony, Meghwadi,
Jogeshwari (East),
Mumbai-400060

Gujarat Petrochem P. Ltd.
508, Faiz-E-Qutbi,
375, Narsi Natha Street,
Mumbai-400009

Gazelle Beauty Parlour
16, D.D.A. Market,
Defence Enclave,
Vivek Marg,
Delhi-110092

H.A.G. Soaps & Chemical Works Pvt. Ltd.
145, Keshab Chandra Sen Street,
Kolkata-700009

Health Products
363, Kalindas Udyog Bhavan,
Near Century Bazar, Worli,
Mumbai-400025

Hind Bottles Stores (L)
127, Sheriff Devji (Chakla) Street,
Mumbai-400003

Hemani Aromatics
Minerva Estate, 2nd Floor,
Bunder Road, Sewree (East),
Mumbai-400015

Hesh Pharma (L)
B-3/4/5/, Singh Ind. Esate,
Ram Mandir Road,
Goregaon (West),
Mumbai-400104

Hindustan Perfumery
M.C. Compound,
S.V. Road, Dahisar (East),
Mumbai-400068

Hygienic Research Institute (L)
Crystal plaza,
Unit No. 406-409,
4th Floor, New Link Road,
Andheri (W),
Mumbai-400053

Indo Plast P. Ltd. (L)
Acme House, 2nd Floor, K.D. Road,
Behind Rasraj restaurant,
Vile Parle (West),
Mumbai-400056

J.B.J. International P. Ltd. (L)
F/18, Swastik Ind. Estate,
Ghoddev Road,
Bhayander (East), Thane

J.B. Shah & Co. (L)
28, Pankaj Society,
Near Bhattha Anand Nagar,
Ahmedabad-380007

J.P. Pharma
301, Triumph Industrial Estate,
Motilal Nehru Marg,
Panch Bawdi, W.E. Highway,
Goregaon (E),
Mumbai-400063

Kemco Chemicals (L)
18, R.N. Mukherjee Road,
Kolkata-700001

Kesavardhini Products (L)
Chaudhary Nagar,
Arcot Road,
Chennai-600087

Kamal Home Products P. Ltd. (L)
112/1, Shivam Apts.,
A-40, Ashok Chakravarti Road,
Kandivali (East),
Mumbai-400101

Khushboo Chemical
101, Pooja Apt. Asha Nagar,
Western Express Highway,
Kandivali (East),
Mumbai-400101

Komal Manufacturing Chemists Ltd.
Wacco House, Masrani Lane,
Kurla (West), Mumbai-400070

Kushmi Cosmetics (L)
F-3A, Shri Laxmi Woolen Mills Comp.
1st Floor, Shakti Mill Lane,
Mahalaxmi,
Mumbai-400011

Kinnari Padflex
14, Aroto House, P.K. Road,
Nr. Saidham, Mulund (West),
Mumbai-400080

L.D.G. International
Plot No. 1-2-3-Khasra No. 43/2/5,
Village Badli,
Delhi-110042

Laxicon Laboratories
56, Shakespear Sarani,
Kolkata-700017

Lason Engg. Co. Pvt. Ltd.
8, New Jagruti, 227, S.V. Road,
Bandra (West),
Mumbai-400050

Malbros Aromatic Co. Pvt. Ltd. (L)
Anugraha, Palayoor,
Chavakkad,
Kerala-680506

Mod Cosmetics
1975, MIDC-2, Dalatpara,
Junagadh-362037

Modern Cosmetics Pvt. Ltd. (L)
Mehta Apt. Agashi Road,
Virar (West),
Thane-401303

Marico Industries Limited
"P" Plot, Fosberry Road,
Sewri, Mumbai-400033

Mansee Product
6-A, 3rd Floor, Vimal Udyog Bhavan,
Opp. Badal Bijli Cinema,
Mahim, Mumbai-400016

Menaxi Pharmaceuticals (L)
P.O. Box 16778,
200-A, Samir,
Sion (East), Mumbai-400022

Mehsons (India) Ltd.
Kamla Bhavan,
Madari Gate, Bareilly-243003

Mr. Madhukar
Mahant Kumar Co. Opp. Hsg. Soc.
Bldg. No. 4, Block No. 3,
Near Utkarsh Mandal,
Vile Parle (East),
Mumbai-400057

Mohini Organics Pvt. Ltd.
208, Mukund Bldg., 1st Floor,
137, Dadiseth Agyari Lane,
Mumbai-400002

Mr. Parchure S.W.
2, Asawaso, 887-B, Raichand Wadi,
Opp. Datta Rawoot Maidan,
Near Gokhale Road,
Dadar, Mumbai-400028

Mysore Sales International Ltd.
Arun Chambers,
Tardeo,
Mumbai-400034

Merphy Corporation (L)
Shrol Villa, Paili Pada,
Trombay,
Mumbai-400081

Nanoomal Issardas Motiwalla (L)
257, Janjikar Street,
Mumbai-400002

Neha Herbal
F-2328, Rajajipurarm,
Lucknow-226017

Nogi & Co. Pvt. Ltd.
Suren Road,
Andheri (East),
Mumbai-400093

National Trading Company
P.B. No. 2622,
57, Velachery Road,
Chennai-600032

New Look Cosmetics Pvt. Ltd.
4-C, Govind Chandra, Dhar Lane,
Khoja Mansion, 4th Floor,
Kolkata-700001

Neel Trading Company
3, Motisagar, Kaluskar Road,
South Shivaji Park, Dadar,
Mumbai-400028

Neha Soap Industries (L)
2/3, Raffique Ind. Estate,
Krishna Nagar, Opp. Wireless,
Dahisar (East),
Mumbai-400068

O.S.R. International (L)
E/6, Sukhdayak, J.B. Nagar,
Andheri (East),
Mumbai-400059

Pragna Organics
Mr. Anil Gondalia/Mr. Lalit Vedi
Plot No. 2907, Phase IV, GIDC,
Vapi-396195

Parijat Products
201, Adarsh Ind. Estate,
Sahar Road, Andheri (East),
Mumbai-400099

Preeti Plastics (L)
3121, Tata Nagar,
Near Qureshi Masjid,
Govandi (W),
Mumbai-400043

Patel Enterprises
150, Venubhuvan Bldg.,
2nd Floor, Room No. 15,
Lamington Road Cross Lane,
Mumbai-400007

Pretty ma'am Herbal Cosmetics
32/637, MKV Road,
Palarivattom,
Cochin-682025 (Kerala)

Reliance Silicons (I) Ltd.
Off. 95, Mittal Tower "B"
210, Nariman Point,
Mumbai-400021

Rockside Research Laboratory

Association
198/27-C, Ramesh Market,
East of Kailash,
New Delhi-110065

Rajendra Enterprises (L)
63, Yusuf Building,
Delema Street, Dockyard Road,
Mumbai-400010

Roopash Cosmetics
7/6 & 7/8, Panchali,
Amman Koil St.,
Arumbakkam,
Chennai-600106

Remedies Pharmaceuticals
127 Wadala Udyog Bhavan, 1st Floor,
Naigaon Cross Road, Wadala,
Mumbai-400031

S.T.C. Agencies (L)
9-D, Devrajeurs Road,
Mysore-570001

Salone-Di-Bellezza
607-A, Dolat Manzil,
Dr. Ambedkar Road, Dadar,
Mumbai-400014

Sara Chemical Corporation
12, Beezzade Commercial Complex,
Sion Trombay Road, Chembur,
Mumbai-400072

Savla Enterprises (L)
80/88, D.L. Nagar
Kalachowki,
Mumbai-400033

Shah & Salim Products (L)
1, Pavwala Chawl,
44-E, Down Elphinstone Bridge,
Mumbai-400013

Shalom Personal Care Products
Opp. Govt. Colony,
Saru Saction Road,
Jamnagar-361008

Shrimad Corporation
23, Navyug Society,
Surendra Mangaldas Road,
Ambawadi,
Ahmedabad-380015

Shahnaz Herbals
C-89, Okhla Industrial Area, Phase-I,
New Delhi-110020

Spac Aromas
Room No. 236, 2nd Floor,
38, Mangaldas Bldg.,
29 Mangaldas Road,
Mumbai-400002

Style Cosmetics (L)
3/17, Gajanan Colony,'
Jawahar Nagar,
Goregaon (West),
Mumbai-400062

Subhash Chemicals Company
"S" Block, Shed W-2, MIDC,
Bhosari,
Pune-411026

Sansheel Herbals
C/o. Morarji Bros.
(Imports & Exports Pvt. Ltd.)
Prospect Chambers,
317-21, Dr. D.N. Road, Fort,
Mumbai-400001

Standard Surfactants Ltd.
240B, New Sector Industrial Area,
Mandi Deep,
Madhya Pradesh-462046

Star Glass Works (L)
299, Kurla Andheri Road,
Zari Mari,
Mumbai-400072

Star Industrial Corporation
13/14, G.B. Shops, O.T. Section,
Ulhasnagar-4 Thane
(Maharashtra)

Super Cosmetics
Goma Bhavan,
Datta Patil Estate,
Veer Savarkar Road,
Near Surekha Hotel,
Virar (East) Thane.

Sonarome Chemicals P. Ltd.
C-133/136, Peenya 2nd Stage,
Bangalore-560058

Supreme Perfumery (L)
C/o. Jaybharat Cutlery Stores
117, Walchand Hirachand Marg,
Fort, Mumbai-400001

Suzuki Products (L)
A/5, Samarth Ind. Estate,
Godev Raod,
Bhaynder (East),
Thane

Seth Brothers (Perfumers) Pvt. Ltd. (L)
C-197, Naraina Industrial Area,
Phase-1,
New Delhi-110028

S.J. Enterprises
14/3, Mahavir Cottages
125, Garodia Nagar,
Ghatkopar (East),
Mumbai-400077

Sanjog Herbs & Foods (I) Pvt. Ltd. (L)
112/1, Shivam Apt. Ashok Nagar,
Ashok Chakravorty Road,
Kandivali (East),
Mumbai-400101

Sunny Engineerings & Consultants
A-201, Sharda Gram,
Opp. Shiv Mahal, Mathuradas Road,
Kandivali (West),
Mumbai-400067

Tershco Incorporation (L)
2&3 Saraf Kaskar Ind. Estate,
S.V. Road, Jogeshwari (West),
Mumbai-400102

Sumangalam Industries (L)
4-A, Council House Street,
Kolkata-700001

Ultra International Ltd.
304, Avg Bhavan,
M-3, Cannaught Circus,
New Delhi-110001

Velvette International Pharma Products Ltd.
8-A, Dr. Ambedkar Road,
Kodambakkam,
Chennai-600024

Venus Herbo Aromatics P. Ltd.
Muhavoor Road, Virudhu Nagar,
Tal. Rajapalayam,
Seithur-626121

Yukti Cosmetics India Pvt. Ltd.
2-A, Sun & Sea Apartment
Near Royal Lane,
Juhu Tara Road,
Santacruz (West),
Mumbai-400049

Argus Cosmetics Ltd. (L)
"Sujatha Centre" 2nd Floor,
No. 4 Sheshadri Road,
Alwarpet, Chennai-600018

Arjun Pharmachem (L)
12, Kanya Kumari Apt.
Agashi Road,
Behind Desai Hospital,
Virar (West), Thane-401303

Baccarose Perfumes & Beauty Products Ltd.
66, Maker Chamber VI,
Nariman Point,
Mumbai-400021

Barkur Surfactants Pvt. Ltd. (L)
Sony Apt.
Opp. St. Jode's High School,
Off Andheri Kurla Road, Jarimari,
Mumbai-400072

Beauty Basic
286, Sher-E-Punjab Society,
Mahakali Caves Road, Andheri (East),
Mumbai-400093

Beauty Cosmetics Ltd. (L)
37, Whites Road,
Chennai-600014

Beeta Chemicals
B-31, Nandjyot Industrial Estate,
Safed Pool, Andheri Kurla Road,
Near I.B.M.,
Mumbai-400072

Bendale Chemicals
2, Jalgaon Hsg. Soc.
Jilha Road,
Jalgaon-425001 (Mah.)

Body Care
14/15, Vishal Indl. Estate,
Near Gas Godown,
Goddev Road,
Bhayander (E),
Thane-401105

Chemhouse Marketing
12, Gokul, Krishna Dham Society,
Sant Dnyaneshwar Path,
Panch Pakhadi,
Thane (w)-400602

Chaganlal & Co.
Daya Vira House, Shop No. 3,
Near Laxmi Nivas,
Below Elphinstone Bridge,
Mumbai-400013

Cosmiks Mfg. Co. (L)
37, Agarwal Indl. Estate,
2nd Floor,
S.V. Road, Dahisar (East),
Mumbai-400068

Cosmolene Laboratories (India) (L)
301, Owners Indl. Estate,
Gabrial Road,
7, Agarwal Pitamber lane,
Mahim (W), Mumbai-400016

Choice Laboratories
999, State Highway,
Unjha -384170N. Gujarat

Choloayil Pharmaceuticals (L)
M Block No. 4,
Anna Nagar east,
Chennai-600102

Desai Agencies
B-38 Bagree Market,
71, Canning Street,
Kolkata-700001

Danyal Engineering Co.
3022, Gali Nal Badan
Shahganj, Agmeri Gate,
Delhi-110006

Dr. P.R. Dingaonkar
7, Shefali Phirozshah Road,
Santacruz (West),
Mumbai-400054

Dura Chemical Corpn. Ltd. (L)
11, Sprott Road,
Weikfield House, 2nd Floor,
Ballard Estate,
P. Box No. 395,
Mumbai-400038

Debon Herbal Products (L)
Jamma Cottage,
Geondevi Road, Poisar, Kandivali (West),
Mumbai-400067

Deepa Ceramics
K-49/51, Sonal Heavy Indl. Estate,
Ramchandra Lane, Malad (East),
Mumbai-400064

Dimple International
Plot No. 619-4B, Asha Bhavan,
14th Road, Khar (West),
Mumbai-400052

Emami Limited
207, Chartered House,
297/299, Dr. Cawasji Hormasji Street,
Near New Marin Lines, Churchgate,
Mumbai-400002

Espee Herbals
101, Liberty Apt. Sarojini Road,
Vile Parle (West),
Navghar, Vasai (East),
Thane-401202

Eveslynk Industries
H/Block Unit No. 225,
Ansa Ind. Estate, Sakivihar Road,
Mumbai-400072

Eva Green Creation/Oyatab Fibre Pvt. Ltd.
15/5, Harinivas,
Dattatraya Road,
Santacruz (West),
Mumbai-400054

Emami Limited (L)
8, Bentnck Street,
10th Floor,
Kolkata-700001

E-Merck (India) Ltd.
Shiv Sagar Estate,
Dr. Annie Besant Road, Worli,
Mumbai-400018

Fine Organic Industries
Fine House, Anandji Street,
Off. M.G. Road,
Ghatkopar (East),
Mumbai-400077

FFC Aromas Pvt. Ltd. (L)
C-11, Udyog Sadan No. 1
Moral Ind. Area, Andheri (East),
Mumbai-400093

Flora Super Prints
131/132, Dewan & Sons Ind. Estate No. 6,
Vasai (East),
Thane

Flower Valley Perfumes P. Ltd.
4/13, Kamal Mension,
Arthur Bunder Road,
Colaba, Mumbai-400005

Fortune Laboratories Pvt. Ltd.
B/572, Sarita Vihar,
Mathura Road,
New Delhi-110044

Fem Care Pharma Ltd. (L)
Fem House, Plot No. 3/A,
Ram Mandir Road,
Khirwadi, Bandra (East),
Mumbai-400051

Grip Engineers
Gala No. 12,
Shree Mahalaxmi Kripa Sadan,
Near IT Colony, Meghwadi,
Jogeshwari (East),
Mumbai-400060

Gujarat Petrochem P. Ltd.
508, Faiz-E-Qutbi,
375, Narsi Natha Street,
Mumbai-400009

Gazelle Beauty Parlour
16, D.D.A. Market,
Defence Enclave,
Vivek Marg,
Delhi-110092

S.A.G. Soaps & Chemical Works Pvt. Ltd.
145, Keshab Chandra Sen Street,
Kolkata-700009

Health Products
363, Kalindas Udyog Bhavan,
Near Century Bazar, Worli,
Mumbai-400025

Hind Bottles Stores (L)
127, Sheriff Devji (Chakla) Street,
Mumbai-400003

Hemani Aromatics
Minerva Estate,
2nd Floor,
Bunder Road, Sewree (East),
Mumbai-400015

Hesh Pharma (L)
B-3/4/5/, Singh Ind. Esate,
Ram Mandir Road,
Goregaon (West),
Mumbai-400014

Hindustan Perfumery
M.C. Compound,
S.V. Road, Dahisar (East),
Mumbai-400068

Hygienic Research Institute (L)
Crystal plaza,
Unit No. 406-409,
4th Floor, New Link Road,
Andheri (W),
Mumbai-400053

Indo Plast P. Ltd. (L)
Acme House, 2nd Floor, K.D. Road,
Behind Rasraj restaurant,
Vile Parle (West),
Mumbai-400056

J.B.J. International P. Ltd. (L)
F/18, Swastik Ind. Estate,
Ghoddev Road,
Bhayander (East),
Thane

J.B. Shah & Co. (L)
28, Pankaj Society,
Near Bhattha Anand Nagar,
Ahmedabad-380007

J.P. Pharma
301, Triumph Industrial Estate,
Motilal Nehru Marg,
Panch Bawdi, W.E. Highway,
Goregaon (E),
Mumbai-400063

Kemco Chemicals (L)
18, R.N. Mukherjee Road,
Kolkata-700001

Kesavardhini Products (L)
Chaudhary Nagar,
Arcot Road, Chennai-600087

Kamal Home Products P. Ltd. (L)
112/1, Shivam Apts.,
A-40, Ashok Chakravarti Road,
Kandivali (East), Mumbai-400101

Khushboo Chemical
101, Pooja Apt. Asha Nagar,
Western Express Highway,
Kandivali (East),
Mumbai-400101

Komal Manufacturing Chemists Ltd.
Wacco House, Masrani Lane,
Kurla (West),
Mumbai-400070

Kushmi Cosmetics (L)
F-3A, Shri Laxmi Woolen Mills Comp.
1st Floor, Shakti Mill Lane,
Mahalaxmi,
Mumbai-400011

Kinnari Padflex
14, Aroto House, P.K. Road,
Nr. Saidham, Mulund (West),
Mumbai-400080

L.D.G. International
Plot No. 1-2-3-Khasra No. 43/2/5,
Village Badli,
Delhi-110042

Laxicon Laboratories
56, Shakespear Sarani,
Kolkata-700017

Lason Engg. Co. Pvt. Ltd.
8, New Jagruti, 227, S.V. Road,
Bandra (West),
Mumbai-400050

Malbros Aromatic Co. Pvt. Ltd. (L)
Anugraha, Palayoor,
Chavakkad,
Kerala-680506

Mod Cosmetics
1975, MIDC-2, Dalatpara,
Junagadh-362037

Modern Cosmetics Pvt. Ltd. (L)
Mehta Apt. Agashi Road,
Virar (West),
Thane-401303

Marico Industries Limited
"P" Plot, Fosberry Road,
Sewri,
Mumbai-400033

Mansee Product
6-A, 3rd Floor, Vimal Udyog Bhavan,
Opp. Badal Bijli Cinema,
Mahim, Mumbai-400016

Menaxi Pharmaceuticals (L)
P.O. Box 16778,
200-A, Samir,
Sin (East),
Mumbai-400022

Mehsons (India) Ltd.
Kamla Bhavan,
Madari Gate,
Bareilly-243003

Mr. Madhukar
Mahant Kumar Co. Opp. Hsg. Soc.
Bldg. No. 4, Block No. 3,
Near Utkarsh Mandal,
Vile Parle (East),
Mumbai-400057

Mohini Organics Pvt. Ltd.
208, Mukund Bldg., 1st Floor,
137, Dadiseth Agyari Lane,
Mumbai-400002

Mr. Parchure S.W.
2, Asawaso, 887-B, Raichand Wadi,
Opp. Datta Rawoot Maidan,
Near Gokhale Road,
Dadar,
Mumbai-400028

Mysore Sales International Ltd.
Arun Chambers,
Tardeo,
Mumbai-400034

Merphy Corporation (L)
Shrol Villa, Paili Pada,
Trombay,

Mumbai-400081

Nanoomal Issardas Motiwalla (L)
257, Janjikar Street,
Mumbai-400002

Neha Herbal
F-2328, Rajajipurarm,
Lucknow-226017

Nogi & Co. Pvt. Ltd.
Suren Road,
Andheri (East),
Mumbai-400093

National Trading Company
P.B. No. 2622,
57, Velachery Road,
Chennai-600032

New Look Cosmetics Pvt. Ltd.
4-C, Govind Chandra, Dhar Lane,
Khoja Mansion, 4th Floor,
Kolkata-700001

Neel Trading Company
3, Motisagar, Kaluskar Road,
South Shivaji Park, Dadar,
Mumbai-400028

Neha Soap Industries (L)
2/3, Raffique Ind. Estate,
Krishna Nagar, Opp. Wireless,
Dahisar (East),
Mumbai-400068

O.S.R. International (L)
E/6, Sukhdayak, J.B. Nagar,
Andheri (East),
Mumbai-400059

Pragna Organics
Mr. Anil Gondalia/Mr. Lalit Vedi
Plot No. 2907, Phase IV, GIDC,
Vapi-396195

Parijat Products
201, Adarsh Ind. Estate,
Sahar Road, Andheri (East),
Mumbai-400099

Preeti Plastics (L)
3121, Tata Nagar,
Near Qureshi Masjid,
Govandi (W),
Mumbai-400043

Patel Enterprises
150, Venubhuvan Bldg.,
2nd Floor, Room No. 15,
Lamington Road Cross Lane,
Mumbai-400007

Pretty ma'am Herbal Cosmetics
32/637, MKV Road,
Palarivattom, Cochin-682025 (Kerala)

Reliance Silicons (I) Ltd.
Off. 95, Mittal Tower "B"
210, Nariman Point,
Mumbai-400021

Rockside Research Laboratory Association
198/27-C, Ramesh Market,
East of Kailash,
New Delhi-110065

Rajendra Enterprises (L)
63, Yusuf Building,
Delema Street, Dockyard Road,
Mumbai-400010

Roopash Cosmetics
7/6 & 7/8, Panchali,
Amman Koil St., Arumbakkam,
Chennai-600106

Remedies Pharmaceuticals
127 Wadala Udyog Bhavan, 1st Floor,
Naigaon Cross Road, Wadala,
Mumbai-400031

S.T.C. Agencies (L)
9-D, Devrajeurs Road,
Mysore-570001

Salone-Di-Bellezza
607-A, Dolat Manzil,
Dr. Ambedkar Road, Dadar,

Mumbai-400014

Sara Chemical Corporation
12, Beezzade Commercial Complex,
Sion Trombay Road, Chembur,
Mumbai-400072

Savla Enterprises (L)
80/88, D.L. Nagar
Kalachowki,
Mumbai-400033

Shah & Salim Products (L)
1, Pavwala Chawl,
44-E, Down Elphinstone Bridge,
Mumbai-400013

Shalom Personal Care Products
Opp. Govt. Colony,
Saru Saction Road,
Jamnagar-361008

Shrimad Corporation
23, Navyug Society,
Surendra Mangaldas Road,
Ambawadi,
Ahmedabad-380015

Shahnaz Herbals
C-89, Okhla Industrial Area, Phase-I,
New Delhi-110020

Spac Aromas
Room No. 236, 2nd Floor,
38, Mangaldas Bldg.,
29 Mangaldas Road,
Mumbai-400002

Style Cosmetics (L)
3/17, Gajanan Colony,'
Jawahar Nagar,
Goregaon (West),
Mumbai-400062

Subhash Chemicals Company
"S" Block, Shed W-2, MIDC,
Bhosari,
Pune-411026

Sansheel Herbals
C/o. Morarji Bros.
(Imports & Exports Pvt. Ltd.)
Prospect Chambers,
317-21, Dr. D.N. Road,
Fort,
Mumbai-400001

Standard Surfactants Ltd.
240B, New Sector Industrial Area,
Mandi Deep,
Madhya Pradesh-462046

Star Glass Works (L)
299, Kurla Andheri Road,
Zari Mari,
Mumbai-400072

Star Industrial Corporation
13/14, G.B. Shops, O.T. Section,
Ulhasnagar-4 Thane
(Maharashtra)

Super Cosmetics
Goma Bhavan, Datta Patil Estate,
Veer Savarkar Road,
Near Surekha Hotel,
Virar (East) Thane.

Sonarome Chemicals P. Ltd.
C-133/136; Peenya 2nd Stage,
Bangalore-560058

Supreme Perfumery (L)
C/o. Jaybharat Cutlery Stores
117, Walchand Hirachand Marg,
Fort, Mumbai-400001

Suzuki Products (L)
A/5, Samarth Ind. Estate,
Godev Raod,
Bhaynder (East),
Thane

Seth Brothers (Perfumers) Pvt. Ltd. (L)
C-197,
Naraina Industrial Area,
Phase-1,
New Delhi-110028

S.J. Enterprises
14/3, Mahavir Cottages
125, Garodia Nagar,
Ghatkopar (East),
Mumbai-400077

Sanjog Herbs & Foods (I) Pvt. Ltd. (L)
112/1, Shivam Apt. Ashok Nagar,
Ashok Chakravorty Road,
Kandivali (East),
Mumbai-400101

Sunny Engineerings & Consultants
A-201, Sharda Gram,
Opp. Shiv Mahal, Mathuradas Road,
Kandivali (West),
Mumbai-400067

Tershco Incorporation (L)
2&3 Saraf Kaskar Ind. Estate,
S.V. Road, Jogeshwari (West),
Mumbai-400102

Sumangalam Industries (L)
4-A, Council House Street,
Kolkata-700001

Ultra International Ltd.
304, Avg Bhavan,
M-3, Cannaught Circus,
New Delhi-110001

Velvette International Pharma Products Ltd.
8-A, Dr. Ambedkar Road,
Kodambakkam,
Chennai-600024

Venus Herbo Aromatics P. Ltd.
Muhavoor Road, Virudhu Nagar,
Tal. Rajapalayam,
Seithur-626121

Yukti Cosmetics India Pvt. Ltd.
2-A, Sun & Sea Apartment
Near Royal Lane,
Juhu Tara Road,
Santacruz (West),
Mumbai-400049

31

Suppliers of Plant and Equipments

A.R.V. Engineering
8/7, Rao Wadi, Gopi Tank Road,
Mahim, Mumbai 400 016.
Tel: 2446 4776
Products / Services: Paste Filling Equipment, S.S. Tanks

AAHAN Engineers Pvt. Ltd.
5C/204, Mittal Indl. Estate,
Andheri-Kurla Road,
Andheri (E),
Mumbai 400 059
Tel: 2850 2400 / 2850 0008
Fax: (022) 2850 6785
Email: sbecton@bom3.vsnl.net.in
Products / Services: Dryers & Drying Ovens, Mill Colloid/Ball Multi/Cone, Sieving & Sifting Machine, Stirrers, Bottle Drying & Washing Machines.

Ace Industries
14 Apline Industries Estate,
Marol Military Road,
Andheri (E),
Mumbai-400 059
Tel:2 580 5763
Fax: 2580 4939
Email: ace_centrifuges@yahoo.co.in
Products / Services: Ace Four-point Suspended Bottom Discharge Centrifuge

Acmefil Engineering Industries
65/1/B, Phase-II, G.I.D.C.
Vatva
Ahmedabad.
Tel: 2583 4111 / 2589 0365
Fax: (079) 2583 4111 (R) 2589 6950
Products / Services: Spray Driers, Fluidized Spray Driers, Fluid Bed Driers, Flash Driers, Wook Free Driers, Evaporators, Spin Flash Driers, Pilot Plant Facilities.

Aditya Agencies
151, Lekhraj Market-III,
Indiranagar, Faizabad Road,
Lucknow 226 016,
Tel: 2386 876 / 2386 704
Fax: (0522) 2388 656
Products / Services: Bottles, Caps & Closers.

Adsum Pharma Engineers
Hanuman Bhagda,
Valsad 396 030.
Tel: 02638-253653, 243959
Fax: 02638 243959
Products / Services: Fluid Bed Dryers, Stirrers, Bottle Filling & Sealing Machines, Bottle drying & Washing Machines, Lable Gumming & Pasting Machines.

Advance International
G-1, Ruchi Tower, 60 ft. Road,
Bhayander (W), Thane 401 101.
Tel: 2818 9132 / 33
Fax: 2818 9134 / 2814 2477
Email: nffi@bom5.vsnl.net.in
Website: http./www.al-can.com
Products / Services: Spray Pumps and Dispensers for the cosmetics industry.

Aero Therm Systems Pvt. Ltd.
Plot: 1517, Phase III, GIDC-Vatva,
Ahmedabad 382 445.
Tel: 2583 4987/2589 0158
Fax: (079) 2583 4987
Products / Services: Fluid Bed Dryers

AIMIL Ltd.
Naimex House, Mathura Road,
A-8, Mohan co-op. Indl. Estate,
New Delhi 110 044
Tel: (011) 2695 0001-9
Fax: (011)2 695 0011
Email: sanjaymiglani@aimil.com
Products / Services: Testing Equipment

Akshay Engineering
20-21, Nathalal Estate
Jashodanagar Cross Rds.
Besides Canal. N.H. 8,
Ahmedabad 380 002.
Tel: (079) 2583 5756
Fax: (079) 2287 0875
Products / Services: Batch Numbering & Printing Machines, Lable Gumming & Pasting Machines.

Alexandra Scale P. Ltd.
12/2, Amee Bazar,
B/h Jyolisangh Patthar Kuva,
Ahmedabad 380 001.
Tel: (079) 2535 5777/3482
Fax: (022) 2532 1859
Email: alexandra@ad1.vsnl.net.in
Products / Services: Weighing Machines/Balances

Alfa Laval (India) Ltd.
Mumbai-Pune Road, Dapodi,
Pune 411 012.
Tel: (020) 2797 721
Fax: (020) 2797 711
Website: http.//www.alfalaval.com.in
Products / Services: Evaporators, Separators

Allied Equipment Corporation
215/216A, Suyog,
D.K. Sanshu Marg,
Station Avenue, Chembur,
Mumbai 400 071.
Tel: (022) 2652 6495/2652 8921/ 2652 8399
Fax: (022) 652 8385
Email: kunal.aecorp@axcess.net.in
Products / Services: Condensers

Allied Sales Corporation
37, Gr. Floor, Swastik Indl. Estate
178, Vidya Nagari Marg, Kalina,
Santacruz (E), Mumbai 400 098
Tel: 2610 5906 / 2616 2745
Products / Services: Filter Press, Bottle Filling & Sealing Machines, Caps & Closers

Amar Engineers Works
B-6, Gupta Palace, A-2/42,
Rajouri Garden,
New Delhi 110 027.
Tel: 2543 1105 / 2546 4291
Fax: (011) 2546 9291
Email: sbecton@bom3.vsnl.net.in
Products / Services: Dryers & Drying Ovens, Fluid Bed Dryers, Mill Colloid/ Ball Multi/ Cone, Paste /Filling Equipment,

Rotary Filling Machines, Sieving & Sifting Machine, Stirrers, Bottle Filling & Sealing Machines, Bottle Drying & Washing Machines.

Amar Equipments Pvt. Ltd.
6, Parmar Ind. Estate, Bel-Bazar,
Kurla (W), Mumbai
Tel: 2514 0169 / 2510 9565 / 2595 3029
Fax: 595 3028
Email: amarengg@vsnl.com
Website: www.amarequip.com
Products / Services: Laboratory Autoclave for high pressure & temperature, Horizontal Filter Press (Zero hold up Sparkler type).

Ambalika Engineers
62, Ghanshyam Estate,
B/H Margha Farm, Rakhail,
Ahmedabad 380 2089
Tel: (079) 2274 2098
Fax: (079) 2274 3668
Products / Services: Bottle Filling & Sealing Machines, Bottle Packing Machines

Amba Machines
Plot No. A-12, Phase II
G.I.D.C. Estate,
Vatva, Ahmedabad 382 445.
Tel: (079) 2583 1346 / 2589 3253
Fax: (079) 2583 5885
Email: labelling@vsnl.com
Website: www.ambicalabelling.com
Products / Services: Marking and Labelling Systems

Ambica Labelling P. Ltd.
Plot No. A12, Phase II,
G.I.D.C. Estate
Vatva, Ahmedabad 382 445.
Tel: (079) 2589 1182 / 25831346
Fax: (079) 2583 5885
Email: ambica@ad1.vsnl.net.in
Website: www.ambicalabelling.com
Products / Services: Bottle Filling/ Sealing Machines

Ambica Machine Tools Co.
Plot No. 1, Phase II, G.I.D.C. Estate,
Vatva, Ahmedabad 382 445,
Tel: (079) 2583 0153 / 2583 2988
Fax: (079) 2583 2396
Email: amtic@icenet.net
Products / Services: Bottle Filling Sealing Machines

Ambica Engineering Works
Bhgyodaya Estate,
Chakudia Mahadev Road,
Rakhail,
Ahmedabad 380 023.
Tel: 2274 5643
Fax: (079) 2274 4262
Products / Services: Bottle Drying & Washing Machines

Anju Pharmaceuticals
111, Alankar Chambers,
2-A, Ratlam Kothi,
A.B. Road
Indore 452 001.
Tel: 2527 415 / 2523 968
Fax: (0371) 2856 142
Products / Services: Paste Filling Equipment, Rotary Filling Machines, Sieving & Sifting Machine, Stirrers, batch Numbering & Printing Machines, Bottle Filling & Sealing Machines, Bottle Packing Machines, Bottle Drying & Washing Machines

Anil Tubes
(A Div. Of Anil Chemicals & Industries Ltd.)
524, Sandhurst Bldg.,
2nd Floor,
S.V. Road,
Opera House,
Mumbai 400 004.
Tel: (91-22) 2389 6559 / 2389 6560
Fax: (91-22) 2380 2286
Email: anilchem.mktg@vsnl.net
Products / Services: Coextruded Seamless Plastic Tubes for Cosmetics

Anish Pharma Equip Pvt. Ltd.
C-6, Shardashram Bhavani Shankar Road,
Dadar (W), Mumbai 400 028.
Telefax: (022) 2436 2920 / 2422 9843
Products / Services: Dryers & Drying Ovens

Anup Engg. Ltd.
Behind 66 KV Electrical Sub-Station,
Odhav Road,
Ahmedabad 382 415.
Tel: (079) 2287 0622 / 2287 2823 / 2287 2587
Fax: (079) 287 0642
Telex: 021-26327
Products / Services: Evaporators, Separators

Apex Electromec Pharma P. Ltd.
Unit No. 8, Hare Ram Hari Krishna Indl. Estate,
1-B. Patel Road,
Goregaon (E),
Mumbai 400 063.
Tel: (022) 2876 8034 / 2873 4932
Fax: (022) 2811 6196 / 2816 0263
Email: apexin@bom2.vsnl.net.in
Website: www.apexectromec.com
Products / Services: Mixers, Packaging/Wrapping Machines

Aristo Engineers
J-3, Vikas Udyog Nagar,
Behind Kasturi Tower,
Phatak Goddeo Road,
Bhayander (E),
Dist. Thane 401 105.
Tel: (Off) 2819 2568 / 5268
Fax: 2819 1242
Cell: 98212-36157
Email: aristoeg@vsnl.com
Products / Services: Agitated Nutch Filter with hand operated or Hydraullically Up & Down of Agitator, S.S./M.S. Reaction Vessels, Condensors/Heat Exchangers, Flakers/Drum Driers, High Vacuum Distillation Plant, Ribbon Blenders with Choppers, Crystallisers, Evaporators, Lead Bonded & Rubber Lined Equipments, Heating Units, Columns & Scrubbers.

Arora Metal Industry
1st Floor, 66, Ezra Street,
Kolkata 700 001.
Tel: 2225 4357 / 2225 4170
Products / Services: Paste Filling Equipment, Batch Numbering & Printing Machines, Caps & Closers

Autopack Machines
101-C, Poonam Chambers,
Dr. A.B. Road,
Worli, Mumbai 400 018.
Tel: 2497 48 / 2492 4806 / 2493 4406
Fax: (022) 2496 4926
Products / Services: Paste Filling Equipment, Rotary Filling Machines

Automatic Devices
105/A, Hind Saurastra Indl. Estate,
Andheri Kurla Road,
Marol, Mumbai 400 059.
Tel: (022) 2850 1376
Fax: (022) 2859 3042
Products / Services: Packaging/ Wrapping Machines

Avon Engineering Works
2, Qureshi Industrial Estate,
Patel Wadi, Behrambagh,
jogeshwari (W),
Mumbai 400 102.
Tel: 2631 4456 / 26326414
Fax: (022) 2631 9117
Products / Services: Paste Filling Equipment

Baroda Lable Manufacturing Co.
FF-3, Mini Plaza,
Opp. Mental Hospital, Karelibagh
Baroda 390 018.
Tel: 2540 248

Fax: (0265) 2424 799
Products / Services: Lables

Beekay Pharmamech Industries
B-10, Shipl Sangeet,
L.T. Road,
B/H Punjab & Sindh Bank
Babhai, Borivali (W),
Mumbai 400 091.
Tel: 2801 97943
Fax: (022) 2801 0894
Products / Services: Sieving & Sifting Machine

Best Pack Industries
4, Moulavi Lane,
2nd Floor, Flat-25,
Kolkata 700 016.
Tel: 2245 2743 / 2246 6412
Fax: (033) 2245 7289
Products / Services: Bottle Packing Machines, Lable Gumming & Pasting Machines.

Bhartiya bright & Seamless Steels Ltd.
B-1/2, Gillander House,
8, Netaji Subhash Road,
Kolkata 700 001.
Tel: (033) 2220 5741 / 2220 5742
Fax: (033) 2220 7604
Telex: 021 27098 Bars In
Products / Services: Boilers, Filter

Bhuvaneshwari & Co.
Old Trunk road,
Pallavarm,
Chennai 600 043.
Tel: 2240 1716 / 2240 1767
Fax: 2236 6964
Email: bhucorp@md2.vsnl.net.in
Products / Services: Sigma Mixers for Mixing Detergent Cake.

Bifriends Engg. Works
Kim Cottage,
Sant Narsi Mehta Marg,
Parsiwadi, Ghatkopar (W),
Mumbai 400 084
Tel: (022) 2516 5675
Fax: (022) 2516 2744
Website: http://www.logonindia.combifriend
Products / Services: Separators, Vacuum Filtration Units

Birla Technical Services
B-2, B-3, Sector 16,
Noida 201 301.U.P.
Tel: (91) 2451 0833 / 2750 / 2451 2201
Fax: (91) 2451 2361
Email: htsnoida@mantraonline.com
Products / Services: Filters

Blastcarbocks P. Ltd.
224, Vardhman Chambers,
Sector-17, Vashi,
Navi Mumbai 400 705.
Tel: (022) 2789 2971 / 3854 / 3809
Fax: (022) 2789 3854 / 2979
Email: blastcarbo@hotmail.com
Products / Services: Reactor and Process Vessels

Blow-Tech Engineers
Gali No. 9, Road No. 4,
Singh Estate,
B/h. M&M Samata Nagar,
Kandivali (E), Mumbai 400 101.
Tel: (022) 2873 5122 / 2880 1813
Fax: (022) 2873 5122
Products / Services: Separators

The Bombay Engineering Works
2&7, Navyug Industries Estate,
Torkersey Jivraj Road,
Sewree, Mumbai 400 015.
Tel: 2413 7094 / 2413 5959
Fax: (022) 2413 5828
Products / Services: Filter Press, Sterilizers & Equipment

Bright Pharma Machinery
37-A, New Empire Industrial Estate,
J.B. Nagar, Andheri (E),
Mumbai 400 059.
Tel: 2837 7150 / 2821 4341
Fax: (022) 2821 0190

Products / Services: Bottle Packing Machines, Lable Gumming & Pasting Machines

Cadmach Machinery Co. Pvt. Ltd.
Plot: 3604 & 3605, Phase IV,
GIDC-Vatva, Ahmedabad 283 445.
Tel: (079) 2583 1491 / 2589 1853
Fax: (079) 2583 2602
Products / Services: Mill Colloid/ Ball Multi/Cone, Rotary Milling Machines, S.S. Tanks, Sieving & Sifting Machine, Stirrers, Caps & Closers, Granulators.

Caelsons Industries
4610, Phase IV, G.I.D.C., Vatva,
Ahmedabad 382 445.
Tel: 079-2583 5372 / 2583 4260
Fax: 079- 22743089
Email: nimachec@yahoo.com
Products / Services: Caelsons Brand Tube Filling Sealing & Coding Machine Model SAU-1 Caelsons Brand Twin head Tube Filling Sealing and Coding Machine Model SAU-2

Caps Sales India
184, Subhash Colony,
Shastri Nagar,
Jaipur 302 016.
Tel: 2301 440 / 2301 394
Fax: (0141) 2302 658
Products / Services: Bottles, Caps & Closers.

Century Environmental Services
1525 Sector 34 D,
Chandigarh 160 034
Tel: (0172) 22601 628
Fax: (0172) 22697 680
Products / Services: Decanters

Chandra Helicon Pumps Ltd.
Unit No. 8, Hare Ram Hari Krishna Indl. Estate,
I.B. Patel Road,
Goregaon (E), Mumbai 400 063.
Tel: (022) 2642 3052 / 80 43
Fax: (022) 2643 2174
Telex: 011-71077 FERT In.
Email: autoind@hotmail.com
Products / Services: Centrifugal Pumps

Chandra Helicon Pumps Ltd.
H-68, Panki Indl. Area, Site 1,
Kanpur 20 022. U.P.
Tel: (0512) 2691 554 / 692 142
Fax: (0512) 2691 235
Products / Services: Centrifugal Pumps

Chemi Duti Pumps
AB-5, II Avenue, Anna Nagar,
Chennai 600 040.
Tel: 2621 4677 / 2626 1647
Fax: 044-2621 2866
Products / Services: Chemical Pumps Centrifugal Pumps, M.O.C. –Glass filled PP, Glass Filled Noryl. Pumps with Mechanical Seal. Dosing and Metering Pumps. Sealless-Magnetic Pumps. All the Pumps are imported and of the highest quality (World leaders).

Chemiprocess Engineers
14, Laxmi Co-op. Indl. Estate Ltd.,
Near Nagarvei Hanuman Mandir,
Amraiwadi Road,
Ahmedabad 380 026.
Tel: (079) 2274 8001 / 2274 8168
Fax: (079) 2274 8001 / 2274 8168
Products / Services: Reactor and Process Vessels

Chemitherm Plants & Systems Pvt. Ltd.
No. 30, Anandha Street, Alwarpet,
Chennai 600 018.
Tel: (044) 2499 6248
Fax: (044) 2499 1778
Email: chemthrm@md2.vsnl.net.in
Website: www.Chemither.com
Products / Services: Reactor and Process Vessels

Chemac Equipment P. Ltd.
M.J. D' Souza Compound,
Saphed Pool,
Saki Naka, Andheri (E),
Mumbai 400 072.
Tel: (022) 2851 0777 / 2859 2352 / 2595 2191
Fax: (022) 2851 6986
Email: chemac@bom4.vsnl.net.in
Website: www.chemacequipments.com

Chemithon Engineers Ltd.
Shiv Anand-A, 1st Floor,
372/374, S.V. Road,
Goregaon (West),
Mumbai 400 104.
Tel: (022) 2873 2955 / 2872 0331
Fax: (022) 2874 1366
Email: trivedi@bom3.vsnl.net.in
Products / Services: Chemical Process and Environmental Equipments

Chemtex Engg. Enterprises
Plot No. 277-278,
Opp. Shed No. L-1,
G.I.D.C. Indl. Estate Odhav,
Ahmedabad 382 415.
Tel: (079) 2287 1180 / 2287 1280
Email: chemtec@ad1.vsn.net.in
Products / Services: Boilers, Mixers

Chitra Engineers
23, Narmada Estate,
N.H. No. 8 Odhav
Ahmedabad 283 415.
Tel: (079) 2289 1666 / 2289 0136
Fax: (079) 2289 1666
Products / Services: Mill Colloid/ Ball Multi/Cone

Cimmco Birla Ltd.
D-150, Okhla Indl. Area, Phase I,
New Delhi 110 020.
Tel: (011) 2681 1985 / 6 / 7 / 8 / 2681 0582
Fax: (011) 681 9418
Telex: 031-75465 CIMC In.
Products / Services: Crushers, Heat Exchangers

Clean air Engineers Pvt. Ltd.
210/B, Hind Saurashtra Indl. Estate,
Marolnaka, Andheri-Kurla Road,
Andheri (E), Mumbai 400 059.
Tel: 2850 1630 / 2850 5538
Fax: (022) 2850 5538
Products / Services: Dryers & Drying Ovens

Collapsible Tube Corporation
162, Senapathi Bapat Marg,
Opp. Phoenix Mills,
Janata Indl. Estate,
Gala No. 5, Lower Parel,
Mumbai 400 013.
Tel: 2492 1962 / 2492 3132
Fax: 2495 2334
Products / Services: Printed Aluminium Collapsible Tubes with Lacquered or Without Lacquered, Clossed nozzle as well as long nozzle.

Corres Flow Engineers
1/20, Kailash Indl. Estate,
Jay Chemicals St,
B/L. Hindustan Marbles, Odhav,
Ahmedabad 382 415.
Tel: (079) 2874 2189 / 2874 1459
Products / Services: Centrifugal Pumps

Cosywo Engineering Company
15, Laxmi Co-Op. Indl. Estate,
Nr. Nagarvel Hanuman Mandir,
Amraiwadi,
Ahmedabad 380 026
Tel: 274 8168 / 274 80001
Fax: 274 8168 / 274 80001
Email: cosywo@yahoo.com
Website: www.cosywo.com
Products / Services: High Speed Stirrer, Slow Speed Stirrer, S.S. Tank, Acid Slurry Vessel, Sand Filter.

Aybernetik Technologies Pvt. Ltd.
7, Lunkad Villa,
Law College Road,
Pune 411 004.

Tel: (020) 2528 2799 / 2800
Fax: (020) 2528 0182
Email: cybernetik@vsnl.com
Website: www.cybercyber.net.
Products / Services: Mixers

D-Parikh Engg. Works
115, Morol Co-op. Indl. Estate,
M.V. Road,
Near Sakinaka,
Mumbai 400 059.
Tel: (022) 2850 4787 (R) 2610 5766
Fax: (022) 2850 5979
Email: dparikh@bom2/vsnl.net.in
Websit: htt:///www.dporikh.com
Products / Services: Vacuum Distillation Plants

Dalco Engg. Pvt. Ltd.
H.A. Ltd. Compound, Pimpri,
Pune 411 018.
Tel: (022) 2772 187 / 2772 818
Fax: (020) 2770 832
Telex: 0146-22943
Products / Services: Dryers & Drying Ovens, Vacuum Distillation Plants, Heat Exchangers

Deepak Aerosols Ltd.
7, Community Centre,
East of Kailash,
New Delhi 110 065.
Tel: (91-11) 2621 5015 / 2629 5015
Fax: (91-11) 2648 5015
Email: DAgrawal@satyam.net.in
Products / Services: Spray Pumps, Aerosol Valves, Dispensers, Trigger Spray, Machines.

Delhi Bottle Stores
142, Tilak Bazar,
Delhi 110 006.
Tel: (011) 2251 3433 / 2398 4008
Products / Services: Bottles

Deshera Tech Pharmaceutical
204, Keytuo Ind. Estate, 2nd Floor,
Kandivita Road, Andheri (E),
Mumbai 400 059.
Tel: (022) 2383 0583 / 2832 5104
Fax: (022) 2837 7089
Products / Services: Bottle Filing / Sealing Machines

DEV Engineers
402, Nandan Complex,
Near Railway Crossing,
Mithakhali,
Ahmedabad 380 006.
Tel: (O) 2640 3839 (R) 2760 0730
Fax: (079) 2640 3839 / 273 6627
Email: devpumps@enfinet.net
Products / Services: Chemical Process Pumps, Self-Priming Mud/Sewage Pumps, Polypropylene Process Pumps, Rotary Gear Pumps

Dwarkesh Machinery
32/A, Shivshakti Estate,
Opp. Surat - Ahmedabad Transport,
Naorl,
Ahmedabad 380 405 (Gujarat)
Tel: 2532 0286 / 2216 3285 / 2211 0529
Products / Services: Blenders, Mill Colloid/Ball Multi/Cone, S.S. Tanks

Dyke Engg. Services
604, G.I.D.C. Estate, P.B. NO. 37,
Distt. Bharuch,
Ankleshwar 393022.
Tel: (02646) 222134 / 222033 (R) 240372
Fax: (02646) 250114
Products / Services: Heat Exchangers

E-Merck (India) Ltd.
Shiv Sagar Estate "A",
Dr. A.B. Road,
Worli,
Mumbai 400 018.
Tel: (022) 2496 4855
Fax: (022) 2495 4590
Email: lr.mktg@merck.co.in
Products / Services: Filters

Eimco KCP Ltd.
Ramakrishna Bldg.,
P.B. No. 5446, 183, Anna Salai,
Chennai 600 006.
Tel: (044) 2855 5171
Fax: (044) 2855 5863
Telex: 041-7310 EIMC In
Email: wmras@giasmd0.1.vsnl.net.in
Products / Services: Vacuum Filtration Unions

Emkay Engineering Works
B-33 DDA Sheds,
Okhla Industrial Area, Phase-II,
New Delhi 110 020.
Tel: 2684 4088 / 2682 1045
Fax: 2691 9913
Website: www.emkayenggworks.com
Products / Services: Manufactures & Suppliers of Machinery for Cosmetics and Toiletries

Erection & Instrumentation Engineers
2, Meena Nagar,
Rabari Colony Amraiwadi Road,
Ahmedabad 380 026.
Tel: (079) 2274 3864 / 2274 3782
Fax: (079) 2274 3782
Products / Services: Blenders

Eriez MBI India Ltd.
Whitefield P.O. Box 41,
Bangalore 560 066.
Tel: (080) 2845 5307 / 381
Fax: (080) 2845 5380
Email: emil@emil.co.in
Products / Services: Separators

Essae Teraoka Ltd.
61-A, Raj Indl. Complex,
Military Road,
Marol Moroshi Road,
Andheri (E), Mumbai 400 059.
Tel: (022) 2850 8187
Fax: (022) 2850 1409
Email: etlmum@bom5.vsnl.net.in
Website: www.essae.com
Products / Services: Weighing Machines/Balances

Europack Machine (I) P. Ltd.
Akash Business Centre, CST Road,
Kurla (W),
Mumbai 400 070.
Tel: (022) 2650 4919 / 1859 / 5928 2799 / 2800
Fax: (022) 2650 5368
Email: europack@vsnl.com
Products / Services: Packaging / Wrapping Machines

Eurrestra Industries Ltd.
Plot No. 56,
Thane Belapur Road,
Kalwe, Thane 400 605.
Tel: 2760 2711 / 12 / 13
Fax: 2790 2709 / 769 1177
Products / Services: Plant & Machinery for oils, fats, soaps, Detergents and chemical industry.

Excellent Engineers
110, Bhola Bhagawan Industries Estate,
1-B, Patel Road, Goregaon (E),
Mumbai 400 063.
Tel: (022) 2873 3759 / 2873 0299
Fax: (022) 2873 0986
Products / Services: Sterilizers & Equipment

Excellent Equipment Engineers
Plot: 4, Swamy Ayappa Colony,
108, Bazar Lane,
AOC Gate,
Secunderabad 500 015.
Tel: 2774 4290
Fax; (040) 2774 4290
Products / Services: Dryers & Drying Ovens

Famach Machinery Company
6, Gurjar Industrial Estate,
Ajod Diary Road, Rakhial,
Ahmedabad 380 023.
Tel: (079) 2274 1118
Products / Services: Blenders, Mill Colloid/Ball Multi/Cone

Febchem Engg. Works
Plot No. A/2, Sector-A,
Sanwar Road, Indl.Area,
Indore 452 003.
Tel: (0731) 2420 467 / 421 951
Fax: (0731) 2423 087
Products / Services: Vacuum Distillation Plants

Fertiplant Engg. Co. Pvt. Ltd.
Moray House, 2nd Floor
226, S.V. Road,
Bandra (W),
Mumbai 400 050.
Tel: (022) 2642 3052 / 8043
Fax: (022) 2543 2174
Telex: 011-71077 FERT In
Products / Services: Crushers

Flamingo Blow-Pack
57, Laxmanbhai Estate,
Nr. Revabhai Estate,
Nr. Shreeji Hotei,
Amraiwadi,
Ahmedabad 380 026.
Products / Services: Bottles

Fluidtech Boiler Pvt. Ltd.
2703, Phase-IV,
G.I.D.C., Vatva,
Ahmedabad 382 445.
Tel: 079-2584 0105 / 2584 0106
Fax: 079-2584 0041
Email: fluidtd@yahoo.com
Website: www.fuidtd.com
Products / Services: FBC Boiler IBR Water wall Boilers IBR Package Steam Boilers Non-IBR Steam Boilers Thermic Fluid Heaters Hot Air Generators Hot Water Generators
Note: All the models are available with multi fuel options.

Fouraar Enterprises
715, Veena Killeahr Indl. Estate,
10/14, Pais treet,
Byculla (W), Mumbai 400 001.
Tel: (022) 2309 4777 / 2309 7546
Fax: (022) 2307 1479
Email: fouraar@bam3.vsnl.net.in
Products / Services: Compressors

Frigmaires Engineers
P.O. Box 16353,
Janta Industries Estate,
Opp. Phoenix Mil,
Tulsi Pipe Road,
Lower Parel (W),
Mumbai 400 013.
Tel: 2494 4108 / 2494 5624
Fax: (022) 2469 8371
Email: tinu@bom3vsn.net.in
Products / Services: Aerosol Plants, Mill Colloid/Ball Multi/ Cone, Mixers

Gee Tee (India)
Plot-3316, Phase-IV, GIDC-Vatva,
Ahmedabad 382 445.
Tel: 2583 2232 / 2377 400
Products / Services: Rotary Filling Machines

General Pharma Machinery Co.
Mahal International, L.B.S. Marg,
Opp. Ciple Mahal House,
Vikhroli (W), Mumbai 400 083.
Tel: (022) 2578 1161 / 2578 2132 / 2579 3832
Fax: (022) 2579 3833
Email: mahal@bom3.vsnl.net.in
Products / Services: Granulators

Godrej & Boyce Mfg, Co. Ltd.
Pirojshanagar,
Vikhroli, Mumbai 400 079.
Tel: (022) 2517 2230 / 0442 / 1166 / 2576 3535
Fax: (022) 2517 1969 / 517 1457
Telex: 011-271926
Products / Services: Condensers, Reactor & Process Vessels, Storage Tanks

Gopal Engineering Works
2/4 & 5, Kailash Indl. Estate,
B/H CMC Odhav Road,
Ahmedabad 382 415.

Tel: (079) 2287 4969
Fax: (079) 2287 4969
Products / Services: Lables

Greaves Ltd.
1, Dr. V.B. Gandhi Marg,
Mumbai 400 001.
Tel: (022) 2267 1524 / 4913
Fax: (022) 2265 2853
Email:
bg5@mum.greaveslimited.com
Website: http://
www.greaveslimited.com
Products / Services: Centrifugal Pumps

Greg-Vin Engineers
301,Gold Coin, Marve Road, Orlem,
Malad (W), Mumbai 400 064.
Tel: 2807 3720 / 2347 6916
Fax: 2372 9153
Products / Services: Small Automatic Duplex Stamping for Hotel Soap, Pneumatic Controlled Duplex Stamping Machine for Bandless Soap, and Standard Duplex Stamping Machine with Parallel or right angle feed and Delivery Conveyors, EP 6 Soap Feed Pumps and Soap cutting Machines.

Gujarat Dishing P. Ltd.
7506 G.I.D.C. Indl. Estate.
Karmatur Chokdi,
Ankleshwar 393 002.
Tel: (02646) 252466 / 52564
Fax: (02646) 250610
Products / Services: Heat Exchangers

Gujarat Glass (P) Ltd.
100, Centre Point,
Dr. Ambedkar Road,
Parel, Mumbai 400 012.
Tel: (91-22) 2413 4651 / 2413 4653 / 2417 2855
Fax: (91-22) 2414 6006
Website: www.gujaratglass.com
Products / Services: Manufactures of: Sodalime Amber & Flint Glass Containers for Cosmetics/ Perfume Industry.

Haldyn Glass Limited
Off. Western Express Highway,
Goregaon (E).
Mumbai 400 063.
Tel: (91-22) 2873 0311-4 / 2874 2480-3
Fax: (91-22) 2873 5231
Email: haldyn@vsnl.com
Products / Services: Nail Polish Bottles Perfume & Cosmetics Bottles

Hari Environments Systems
12C, Stephen House 4,
B.B.D. Bag,
Kolkata 700 001.
Tel: (033) 2221 4859 / 2248 7612 / 4451
Fax: (033) 2248 7155
Email: hmlcal@cal2.vsnl.net.in
Products / Services: Settler

Harikrushna Technnocrates Engg. Co.
Plot No. C-1, 4310, Phase-IV,
Nr. Neeka Tube Chokdi,
G.I.D.C.,Vatva,
Ahmedabad 382 445
Tele/*Fax*: 079-2584 0010
Email: maulik_htec@satyam.net.in
Website: www.harikrushna.com
Products / Services: 1. Automatic Sticker Labeling Machine, Semi Automatic Sticker Labeling Machine, Single Sided, Double Sided, Top & Side, Top Bottom, Three Sided, Body Wrapping Labelling on Products is Possible with (On Line Batch Coding). 2. Automatic Visual Vial Inspection Machine. 3. On Line Coding Devices (a) Ink Coder, (b) Cassette Type Coder, (c) Hot Foil Coder. 4. Leak Check Machine. 5. Automatic Packing Line for I.V.

Fluid. 6. Semi-Automatic Stretch Wrapping Machine/ 7. Shoe Cleaner. 8. On-line Pouch Sealing (Top Sealing) Machine.

H.C. Engineers
A-6, Maroli, Udyog Nagar,
Village Nadod,
Via Marolibazar,
Navasari 296436 Gujarat
Tel: (02637) 272060 / 62 / 94
Fax: (02637) 272240
Email: newpar@vsnl.com
Products / Services: Reactor and Process Vessels

Himachal Pharmaceuticals
Dist. Kangra,
Kandori 176 402.
Tel: (0186) 268 333 / 268 377
Fax: (0886) 220 027
Products / Services: Bottles

Hi-Tech Industries
T-5, 'Shukun Plaza',
Near L.G. Hospital,
Opp. Pruthvi Hotel, Maninagar,
Ahmedabad 382 008.
Tele: (079) 2546 1828
Fax: (079) 2546 7117
Email: info@hitechmachines.com
Website: www.hitechmachines.com
Products / Services: 1. Automatic FFS Pouch Packing Machine. 2. Semi/Fully Automatic Liquid Filling Machine. 3. Semi/Fully Automatic Plastic Allu. Cap Sealing machine. 4. Semi Automatic Labeling Machine. 5. Automatic High speed Lable Code Printing Machine. 6. Stirrer 7. Mass Mixer

Hychem Laboratories
S.R.T. 31, Jawaharnagar,
Chikkadpally,
Hyderbad 500 020.
Tel: (040) 2760 1017 / 2761 8702
Fax: (040) 2766 3598
Products / Services: Weighing Machines/Balances

Industrial Filter Corporation
J/405 1&2, Road No. 4, G.I.D.C.,
Panoli 394 116, Gujarat.
Tel: (02646) 272635
Fax: (02646) 229762
Email: rkm@ic.xeebech.xeemail.com
Products / Services: Filters

Industrial Machinery Mfrs. Pvt. Ltd.
Plot: 3607-3609, Phase-IV,
GIDC, Vatva,
Ahmedabad 382 445.
Tel: 2583 1152 / 2583 1449
Fax: (079) 2583 2216
Email: sysadmin@impl.xeeahm.xeemail.ems.vsnl.net.in
Products / Services: Blender, Dryers & Drying Ovens

Is Instruments UIC
111, Parvati Indl.Estate,
Opp. PNB, Shahibaug,
Ahmedabad 380 004.
Tel: (079) 2562 004
Fax: (079) 2562 1052
Email: dharam_int@hotmail.com
Products / Services: Vacuum Distillation Plants

ITW Signode India Ltd.
5, S.P. Road,
Begampet,
Hyderabad 500 016.
Tel: 281 4892
Fax: (040) 284 9153
Products / Services: Bottle Packing Machines

Jacsons Engineers
Plot No. 4701, Phase IV,
G.I.D.C. Estate, Vatva
Ahmedabad 382 445.
Tel: 2584 0156
Fax: (079) 2583 3408
Email: jacsonsngrs@indalonline.com
Register online at:
www.jacsonsengrs.com
Products / Services: High Speed Automatic Label Carton Over Printing Machines and Systems.

Jaico Metals
Mathuradas Mill Compound,
Lower Parel,
Mumbai 400 013.
Tel: (022) 2492 3259
Fax: (022) 2494 3409
Email: vshah@bom4.vsnl.net.in
Website: www.jaicogroup.com
Products / Services: Mixers

Jay Chamunda Industries
Near Kamla Laxmi Petrol Pump,
Gandhi Ashram,
Ahmedabad 380 027.
Tel: 2755 6884 / 2755 7425
Email: jay_chamunda@yahoo.com
Products / Services: All type of Filterpress, Manual & Hydraulic, Wooden & PP Plates.

Jay Instruments & Systems Pvt. Ltd.
Lab Equipments Division,
C-043, Ground Floor,
Antop Hill Warehousing Complex Ltd.,
Near Barkatali Naka,
Wadala (E),
Mumbai 400 037.
H.O.: Plot C-64,
TTC Industries Area,
MIDC, Turbhe,
Thane-Belapur Road,
Navi Mumbai 400 705.
Products / Services: 1. Laboratory Spray Drier 2. Electric Weigh Scale & System 3. Computer Colour Matching System 4. Computer Aided Design System for Textile printing

Jay Instruments & Systems P. Ltd.
C64, TTC Indl. Area,
Turbhe,
Navi Mumbai 400 613.
Tel: (022) 2767 0092 / 2767 2955
Fax: (022) 2767 0161
Products / Services: Weighing Machines/Balances

Jet Fibre Pumps & Equipments P. Ltd.
17-B, Swagat Complex,
Selat Bhuwan,
Maninagar,
Ahmedabad 380 008.
Tel: (079) 2532 5385
Fax: (079) 2532 2513
Products / Services: Blowers

Jicon Machines
37-D, Sarita Estate Jarimari,
Kurla Andheri Road,
Mumbai 400 072.
Tel: (022) 2851 0398
Fax: (022) 2851 6488
Email: jicon@bom7.vsnl.net.in
Products / Services: Bottle Filling / Sealing Machines

JVC Separation Engineering [P] Limited
Unit No. 14, Krishna,
Lakshmi Industrial Complex,
Vartak Nagar,
Thane 400 606.
Tel: 2539 8569
Tel/fax: (022) 2542 8320
Email: japejh@vsnl.com.
5-2-1-27/1, J.N. Road,
Hyderabad 500 095.
Tel: (040) 2460 0235 / 2465 7078
Fax: (040) 2465 7078
Products / Services: (a) Vibrating Screens used for screening detergent power, (b) Water Conditioners used for treatment of 'Hard Water'

Jyotech Engg. & Marketing Consultants
H-49 A, Kalkaji,
New Delhi 110 019.
Tel: (011) 2644 7666 / 2647 3973
Fax: (011) 2648 2189 / 2646 4000
Email: jyotech@del3.vsnl.net.in
Products / Services: Filters

K.C.P. Ltd.
Ramakrishna Building,
2, Dr. P.V. Cherian Cresent,
Chennai 600 105.
Tel: (044) 2827 0678 / 2827 9533
Fax: (044) 2825 5762
Email: admin-kep@speint.rpg.ems.vsnl.net.in
Products / Services: Condensers, Evaporators

Kamal (E) Industries
Datta Bhavan,
Kashinath Duru Road,
Dadar, Mumbai 400 028.
Tel: (022) 2422 1555 / 2437 3474
Fax: (022) 2473 474
Products / Services: Paste Filling Equipment, Batch Numbering & Printing Machines

Kapoor International
22, Vishnu Indl. Estate
Halao Pool Masrani Lane,
Kurla (W),
Mumbai 400 070.
Tel: (022) 2514 2594 / 2516 8891
Fax: (022) 2650 1878
Products / Services: Packaging / Wrapping Machines

Kaps Engineering
831, G.I.D.C. Estate,
Makarpura,
Vadodara 390 010.
Tel: (0265) 2644 692 / 2642 889 / 2644 407 / 2640 785
Fax: (0265) 2643 178 / 2642 185
Telex: 011-71077 FERT In.
Products / Services: Crushers

K.D. Kumar & Co.
K-58, Kirti Nagar,
New Delhi 110 015.
Tel: (011) 2510 4762 / 2545 0061
Fax: (022) 2510 4762
Products / Services: Weighing Machines/ Balances

Kevin Engg. Pvt. Ltd.
A/1/3706 G.I.D.C. Estate,
Phase IV, Vatva,
Ahmedabad 382 445.
Tel: (079) 2589 1503
Fax: (079) 2589 4243
Email: kevin@ad.vsnl.net.in
Products / Services: Testing Equipment

Kilburn Engineering Ltd.
Subhash Nagar, Bhandup,
Mumbai 400 078.
Tel: (022) 2611 6314 / 26137 / 2613 0413 / 2618 4881
Fax: (022) 2617 5119
Telex: 011-278117 PT PL In
Email: pramod@giasbm0.1vsnl.net.in
Products / Services: Blowers

Kothari Pharma
C/11, M.K. Bros. Indl. Estate
Jarimari, Andheri-Kurla Road,
Andheri (E),
Mumbai 400 072.
Tel: (022) 2589 2888 / 2851 0837
Fax: (022) 2851 3584 / 2838 9961
Products / Services: Paste Filling Equipment, Bottle Filling/ Sealing Machines

Kothari Pharma Machines Eqpts Pvt. Ltd.
23/C, Vaibhav Indl. Estate,
Saki Vihar Road,
Andheri (E),
Mumbai 400072.
Tel: (022) 2857 1874 / 2857 0597
Fax: (022) 2857 0597 / 2838 9961
Products / Services: Fluid Bed Dryers, Paste Filling Equipment

Krebs Cie (India) Ltd.
60B, Pretoria Street,
Kolkata 600 105.
Tel: (033) 2242 3175 / 2242 3175
Fax: (033) 2242 8472
Telex: 021-7586 KRBS In.
Products / Services: Condensers, Mixers

Krimson Petrochem Pvt. Ltd.
A2/10, Rana Pratap Bagh,
Delhi 110 007.
Tel: (011) 2293 3772 / 2718 0807
Fax: (011) 2718 0805 / 2293 3773
Products / Services: Lables

Labtronik
10, 11 Harikrupa Shopping Centre,
Near Dipali Cinema, Ashram Road,
Ahmedabad 380 009.
Tel: (079) 2658 3613 / 2856 8565
Fax: (079) 2658 0729
Products / Services:
Weighing Machines/Balances

Larsen & Toubro Ltd.
GR II, Project,
Chem P & S,
Saki Vihar Road, Powai,
Mumbai 400 072.
Tel: (022) 2858 1401 / 1411
Fax: (022) 2858 1890
Products / Services: Packaging / Wrapping Machines

Magumps
Trisandhya 'A',
97, D. Phalke Road,
Dadar (E),
Mumbai 400 014.
Tel: 2411 3572 / 2415 4474
Fax: 2413 7648 / 2413 8307
Email: magumps@vsnl.com
Products / Services: Filtration United, Bottle Washing Machines, S.S. Transfer Pumps, S.S. Tanks, Bottle Filling Machines, Homoginisers, Label Gumming Machines, Mini Print Master Hand Operated and Mini Print Master Electrically Operated.

Maharshi Udyoc
4, Ruchi, 36, Swastik Society
Navrangpura
Ahmedabad 380 009.
Tel: 2656 3612 / 2644 1079 / 2640 2816 / 2642 4883
Fax: (079) 642 5456
Email: info@maharshi.com
Products / Services: 1. Labelling & Lables. Manufacturer of Sticker Labelling Machines in Various models and Sticker labels in Roll form. 2. Liquid Filling and Sealing Equipments.

Manmech Industries
Unit-219, II-B, Mittal Indl. Estate,
2nd Floor, Andheri-Kurla Road,
Andheri (E), Mumbai 400 059.
Tel: 2850 0527
Fax: (022) 2850 0527
Products / Services: Fluid Bed Dryers, Mill Colloid/Ball Multi/Cone

Max Numbering Company
326, Sri Tikaram Mandir,
Marg, Aligarh 202, 002.
Tel: (0571) 2509 056 / 2502 156
Fax: (0571) 2502 156
Products / Services: Batch Numbering & Printing Machines

Mect Metal Corporation
181/1, Phase III,
GIDC Vatva,
Ahmedabad 283 445.
Tel: 2583 3078 / 2532 0654
Products / Services: Mill Colloid/ Ball Multi/Cone

Mettler-Taledo India Pvt. Ltd.
Amar Hill,
Saki Vihar Road, Powai,
Mumbai 400 072.
Tel: (022) 2857 0808 / 2857 1238
Fax: (022) 2857 5071
Email: sales.mtn@mt.com
Website: www.mt.com
Products / Services: Weighing Machines/Balances

Micro Machines
Plot No.2,
Dharmajivan Industries Estate,
Gokuldham Main Road,

Rajkot 360 004.
Tel: (281) 2368 564
Fax: (281) 2366 010
Email: micro_machines@yahoo.com
Products / Services: Manufacturers and Exporters of Soap Plant and Machinery

Mixo Fill (India)
28669-Bulbuli Khana.
Turkman Gate,
Delhi 110 006.
Tel: 2327 0735 / 2327 4460
Fax: (011) 2327 5278
Fac: 2226 3362 / 2226 3446
Products / Services: All Types of Machines for Pharmaceutical, Paint, Food, Cosmetics Oil and Allied Industries. Dryers & Drying Ovens.

Mixsep
1 Matrochhaya,
Off Gulmohar Cross Road No. 6,
JVPD Scheme,
Mumbai 400 049.
Tel: 2625 0262
Fax: 2620 7911
Email: wish@vsnl.com
Visit our Webstie at: www.mixsep.net
Products / Services: Versatile Mixer Batch or continuous designed and manufactured for applications ranging from solid, solid mixing, solid, liquid mixing granulation drying and reaction.

Mix-Wel Engineering Pvt. Ltd.
2, Yamuna Bhuvan,
14-A, Road, Khar (W),
Mumbai 400 052.
Tel: 26498477 / 2605 1372
Fax: 2648 7620
Email: mixwel@vsnl.net
Products / Services: Solutions to mixing problems with latest proven technology. Expert in Bio-Technology agitation system.

Modern Printer's House
5040-A, Roshanara Road,
Delhi 100 007.
Tel: (011) 2369 3652
Products / Services:Lable Gumming & Pasting Machines

Mojj Engg. Systems Ltd.
81-B/15, M.I.D.C. Bhosari,
Pune 411 026.
Tel: (020) 2712 0835 / 360
Fax: (020) 2712 2836 / 7198
Email: majjpune@p.et.net
Products / Services: Evaporators

M.M. Aqua Technologies Ltd.
Behrampur Road, Khandsa,
Gurgaon 122 001, Haryana.
Tel: (0124) 2371 774 / 51
Fax: (0124) 2517 626
Email: heavysal@md4.vsnl.net.in
Products / Services: Settler

MVS Engineering Limited
MVS House, E-24,
East of Kailash,
New Delhi 110 065.
Tel: 2643 1908 / 6869 / 2398
Fax: (011) 2646 4994 / 642 2654
Email: mvs@axces.net.in
Products / Services:Dryers & Drying Ovens

Mysore Pune Chemicals
1218, Vaishakhi,
Kantharaje URS Raod,
Ashoka Circle,
Mysore 570 004.
Tel: (0821) 2483 832 / 2481 757
Fax: (0821) 2481 757
Products / Services: Laboratory Equipments

Neelam Industries
Plot: 3735, Phase-IV,
GIDC-Vatva,
Ahmedabad 382 445.
Tel: (022) 2583 2894 / 2392 147
Products / Services: Sterilizers & Equipment

Neomachines Mfg. Co. Pvt. Ltd.
39/2A, Purna Das Road,
Kolkata 700 029.
Tel: 2464 4568 / 7253 / 7254
Fax: 033-2464 3473
Products / Services: Fluid Bed Dryers

Netzsch India Pvt. Ltd.
P.O. Box No. 7314,
Plot No. 1961-B, Asiad Colony,
Anna Nagar, Western Extn.,
Chennai 600 101.
Tel: (044) 2626 3750 / 2626 3751
Fax: (044) 2262 3741
Email: nim@md3.vsnl.in
Products / Services:
Centrifugal Pumps

Newtronic Equipment Co.
C-18, Bonanza Indl. Estate,
Ashok Chakravarti Road,
Kandivli (E),
Mumbai 400 101.
Tel: (022) 2887 1628 / 1850
Fax: (022) 2887 1850
Email: nutronic@bom2.vsnl.net.in
Products / Services: Laboratory Equipments

Niulab / Ashco
Lab House,
Plot No. F-13, M.I.D.C.
Opp. Seepz Andheri (E),
Mumbai 400 093.
Tel: (022) 2837 6701 / 6693 / 6697 / 6698
Fax: (022) 2836 8275
Email: nulab@bom3.vsnl.net.in
Products / Services: Laboratory Equipments

Nimach Engineering Company
6, Rajani Ind. Estate
Opp. Gujarat Bottling Co; Rakhial,
Ahmedabad 380 023.
Tel: 2276 0596
Tele/*Fax*: (079) 2274 3083
Website: http://nimach.8m.com
Products / Services: Nimach Brand High Speed Lable Code Printing Machine Type AU-1 Nimach Brand High Speed Carton Printing Machine Type AU-2

N.S. International
4, Anurag Apartments,
RNP Park, Plot No. 28,
B/h Jassl Park,
Bhayander (E),
Mumbai 401 105.
Tel: (022) 2816 1127 / 3005
Fax: (022) 2816 5894
Products / Services: Packaging/ Wrapping Machines

NSI Equipments Private Limited
734, Mount Road,
Chennai 600 006.
Tel: (044) 2852 4539
Fax: (044) 2852 0217
Email ID: nsie@vsnl.net
Products / Services: Mixers, Reactors, Centrifuges, Rotary Vacuum Drier, Rotary Vacuum Filter, Rotary Driers, Rotary Kiln, Vibro Sieve, Spin Flash Driers, Tray Driers, Fluid Bed Driers, Ultrafine Air Classifiers (ACM), Heat Exchangers, Evaporators, Pollution Control Equipments etc.

Otoklin Plants & Equipments Ltd.
Plot No. 1, Shah Indl. Area,
Veera Desai Road,
Azad Nagar Post,
Andheri (W), Mumbai 400 053.
Tel: (022) 2636 7476 / 7281
Fax: (022) 2636 7172
Email: otoklin@bom3.vsnl.net.in
Products / Services: Filters

Parksan Filters Pvt. Ltd.
3, Saraswati Industries Estate,
Navghar, Vasai Road (E),
Dist. Thane 410 210.
Tel: (0250) 2391 413
Fax: (022) 2899 5838
Telefax: (0250) 390 818

Email: parksan@bom5.vsnl.net.in
Website: http://
www.parksanfilters.com
Products: Process & Filtration equipment, Plate & Frame Type Filter Press, Cartridge Filter, Bag Filter, Pipe Fittings, Centrifugal Pump.

Parth Enterprise
12/3, Shanti Sadan Estate,
Opp. Dinbai Towers,
Mirzapur Road, Lal Darwaja,
Ahmedabad 380 001.
Tel: 2550 6193 / 2583 1128
Fax: (079) 2583 5885
Products / Services: Sterilizers & Equipment

Pennwalt India Ltd.
507, Kakad Chambers,
132, Dr. Annie Besant Road,
Worli, Mumbai 400 018.
Tel: (022) 2493 2702 / 2493 0494 / 2267
Fax: (022) 2493 6255
Telex: 011-75091 PENN In
Email: pennwalt@bari3./vsnl.net.in
Products / Services: Chlorination Plants, Decanters

Pharma Fab Industires
B-11, Hariyali Industries Centre
B/H Shivkrupa Estate,
L.B.S. Marg, Vikhroli(W),
Mumbai 400 083.
Tel: 2579 1504 / 2579 2116
Fax: (022) 2579 1504
Products / Services: Fluid Bed Dryers

Pharma Tech
Gala No. 1, Bhide Compound,
Dutta Mandir Road,
Bhandup (W), Mumbai 400 078.
Tel: 2591 3466 / 2591 1704
Fax: (022) 2591 3466
Products / Services: Blenders

Pharmatech Engineering Pvt. Ltd.
T-1699, Malka Ganj Road,
Sabzi Mandi, Delhi 110 007.
Tel: 2252 0381
Fax: (011) 2252 0381
Products / Services: Dryers & Drying Ovens, Fluid Bed Dryers

Pragati Engineering Works
Plot No. N-8, Street No. W88 (A),
Chikhaloli, MIDC, Ambernath 421 505.
Tel: (0251) 2682 961
Fax: (0251) 2685 054
Email: shantaflaker@vsnl.com
Products / Services: Flaker/Dryer, Fluid Bed Dyer, Centrifuges, Aerosol Plants

Precise Packaging Machines
Ashirwad Industries Estate,
Building No.4, Gala No. 5,
Ram Mandir Road, Goregaon (W),
Mumbai 400 104
Tel/Fax: 2868 7919 (R) 2839 2843
Products / Services: Machines for Soap Cakes & Detergent Bars, Liquid Filling & Pouch Packing with latest technology

Premier Rolls (Regd.)
Factory: Raikot Road,
Malerkotla 148 023.
Tel: (0) 2365 3645 (R) 2365 6785 (F) 2365 3785
Fax: (0167) 2365 9785
Mobile: 09814153645
Products / Services:Chilled Rolls Solid (One Piece) & Barrels. Special Quality Rolls for Soap Factories and Chemical Industries.

Process Instruments & Controls
305, Galaxy Complex Wadi Wadi,
Opp. Sarabhai Main Gate,
Vadodara 390 007.
Tel: (0265) 2357 228
Fax: (0265) 2335 429

Products / Services: Marking and Labelling Systems

Proton Engineering Works
Plot No. W-28, Phase-II,
M.I.D.C. Dombivli (E) 421 204.
Tel: (251) 2879 459
Tele/*Fax*: (251) 2871 060
Email: protonengg@yahoo.com
Products / Services: Flaker/Drum Dryers.

R. Squar & Co.
Brij Complex, 101, 1st Floor,
Old Bendipada,
Ambernath 421 501.
Tel: (0251) 2683 037 / 2682 785
Fax: (0251) 2682 785 / 2683 272
Products / Services: Granulators

Rank & Company
A/953, Wazirpur Industries Area,
Delhi 110 052.
Tel: 2754 6101 / 2745 6102
Fax: (011) 2723 4126
Email: rank@poboxes.com
Products / Services: Fluid Bed Dryers

Reva Pharma Machinery
Plot: 429/4, GIDC-Makarpura,
Baroda 390 010.
Tel: 2640 982 / 2380 750
Products / Services: Paste Filling Equipment

Rupen Engineers P. Ltd.
5, Pushpa,
Oswal Apartment,
Opp. Johnson Tiles,
Thane 400 604.
Tel: (022) 2582 1432 / 2580 1958
Fax: (022) 2582 0323
Email: patelpro@hotmail.com
Products / Services: Separators

S.C. Brothers
Western Express Highway,
Goregaon (E),
Mumbai 400 063.
Tel: (022) 2873 3738 / 23229 / 1768
Fax: (022) 2873 2478
Telex: 011-270043 SCB In.
Products / Services: Granulators, Vacuum Fitration Units

Sabnil Packaging Machines Pvt. Ltd.
B-2, Bijli Society Bombay Forging,
C.S.T. Road, Kalina,
Mumabi 400 091.
Tel: 2617 8312 / 2618 3739
Fax: (022) 2617 8314
Products / Services: Paste Filling Equipment

Sadana Brothers
B-210, Ashok Vihar Phase-I,
Delhi 110 052.
Tel: (011) 2721 0771 / 2722 8108
Fax: (011) 2723 1161
Email: sadana@del2.vsnl.net.in
Products / Services: Laboratory Equipments

Saideep
A-11, Laghu Udyog Kendra,
I.B. Patel Road, Goregaon (E),
Mumbai 400 063.
Tel: 2873 0429
Fax: 2635 3080/89
Telefax: 2873 2233
Email: saideep1@bom5.vsnl.net.in
Website: www.saideeponline.com
Products / Services: Vibro Sifter to Sieve upto 50 Microns

Sakun Engineers
33/A, New Arbuda Estate,
Near G.S.T. Crossing Road,
Post-Digvijaynagar,
Ranip, Ahmebadad 382 580
Tel: (F) (079) 2752 2886 (R) (079) 2741 7487
Products / Services: Equipments for detergents cake and power, Cake Ploder Machine, Cake Mixer Machines 'U' Type, Powder Mixer Machine, Powder Screening Machine and Cake Cutting and Stamping Machine.

Sanira Associates
Precitch Compound,
C-1877/3, GIDC, Makarpura,
Baroda 390 010.
Tel: 2643 280
Fax: (0265) 2642 416
Products/ Services:

Sanjay Scientific Corporation
B-11/12, Bhiwandiwala
Terrace,Ground Floor,
618, Jagannath Shanker Seth Road,
Mumbai 400 002.
Tel: (022) 2201 6490 / 25859 /
2200 4908
Fax: (022) 2206 5334
Email: sscorp@bom3.vsnl.net.in
Products / Services:Weighing
Machines/Balances

Sanum Plastics
W-59 (C), MIDC-Hingna,
Nagpur 400 016
Tel: 232 159 / 232 158
Fax: (07104) 232 159
Products / Services:Lables

Sapphire Machines Pvt. Ltd.
Kalpataru, Plot: 1263-B,
Prabhadevi, Mumbai 400 025.
Tel: 2422 1478 / 2442 5674
Fax: (022) 2578 5329
Products / Services:Sterilizers &
Equipment

Sarbi Engg. & Whg. P. Ltd.
9, Moonstone, 65/E, Linking Road,
Santacruz (E), Mumbai 400 054.
Tel: (022) 2604 3722 / 9548
Email: sarbi1@vsnl.com
Products / Services:Testing
Equipment

SBP International Private Ptd.
19-A, Ansari Road, Darya Ganj,
New Delhi 110 002.
Tel: (91-11) 2328 4212 / 2324 3075 /
2324 3078
Fax: (91-11) 2324 3078
Email: sbpcon.@ndf.vsnl.net.in
Sales@sbpprojectfinder.com
Portal www.sbpprojectfinder.com
Products / Services: Complete
finishing line for toilet soap,
detergent cake and powder,
sulphonation, plants, wrapping
machines, plodders & mixers of
all types and sizers, reaction
vessels, formulations of various
products on turnkey basis.

Scientific Equipment Work (India)
1/777, Nicholson Road,
Kashmere Gate,
Delhi 110 006.
Tel: 2292 8572 / 2396 7039 /
2397 7309
Fax: (011) 2396 7039
Products / Services:Mill Colloid/Ball
Multi/Cone

Shakti Laboratory Equipment &
Chemicals
Plot No. 5215, G.I.D.C. Estate,
Near Water Tank,
Ankleshwar 393 002.
Tel: (02646) 224337
Fax: (02646) 224337
Products / Services: Laboratory
Equipments

Shanta Flaker & Dryer Co. Pvt. Ltd.
Plot No. 114,
New Chikholi, MIDC,
Ambernath (W),421 505.
Tel: (0251) 2682 961 / 7407 /
2892 564
Fax: 2685 054
Email: shantaflaker@vsnl.com
Website: http./www.shantaflaker.com
Products / Services:

**Sharplex Agro Process (India)
Pvt.Ltd.**
302, Hill View industries Estate,
L.B.S. Marg,
Ghatkopar (W),
Mumbai 400 086.
Tel: 2500 8808 / 2500 7606 /
2500 7008

Fax: 2500 8239
Email: sharplex@bom3.vsnl.net.in
Website: www.sharplex.com
Products / Services:Fitration Equipment Self-Cleaning Filter, Vertical/Horizontal Pressure Leaf Filter, Tubular Centrifuge, Candle Filter, Horizontal Plate Filters.

Sheerang Technologies Pvt. Ltd.
No. 61. KSRTC Layout, 4th Cross,
1st Main, J.P. Nagar, 2nd Phase
Bangalore 560 078.
Tel: 2658 8472 / 2658 8560
Fax: (91-80) 758 3951
Products / Services: Electro Pneumatic Inkcoder SR-100 Coding Device Sold Dual Print Mechanical SoloUnit

Shree Krishna Industries
18, Shree Kanta Estate,
Khodiyar Nagar, Bapunagar,
N.H. No. 8 Road,
Ahmedabad 380 024
(Gujarat)
Tel: (O) 2270 0471, (R) 2289 3447
Products / Services: Soaps, Detergents Machine.

SMD Pump & Engineering India (P) Ltd.
96-A, T.T.K. Road, Alwarpet,
Chennai 600 018.
Tel: (044) 2499 7392, 2467 9060
Fax: (044) 2499 0966
Email: jsdesai@eth.net.
Products / Services: Air Operated Double Diaphragm Pumps Magnetic Coupled Sealless Pumps Barrel/Drum Pumps

Solace Engineers (MKTG) Pvt. Ltd.
S/25, Suraj Moti Complex,
Nr. Hariom Nagar
High Tension Road,
Subhanpura Baroda.
Tel: 33 5969
Fax: (0265) 233 2448
Products / Services: Blenders

S.P. Automatics
Sita Estate, Unit No. 5,
1st Floor, 'B' Wing,
Ghatkopar Mahul Road,
Chembur, Mumbai 400 074.
Tel: 2554 3921
Tele/*Fax*: 2554 6648
Email: spauto@vsnl.com
Products / Services: Chemicals, Cosmetics and Food-Processing
Machines.

Spanpack Systems
B-136, Ghatkopar Indl. Estate,
Opp. L.B.S. Marg, Ghatkopar (W),
Mumbai 400086.
Tel: (022) 2517 0184 / 0144
Fax: (022) 2517 3352
Email:
spanpack.filling@axcess.net.in
Website: www.cybercyber.net.
Products / Services: Packaging / Wrapping Machines

Swan Packaging
Plot No. A-15,
Sinnar Co-op. Indl.Estate,
Sinnar, Dist. Nashik 422 103.
Tel: (02551) 2293 3772 / 2718 0807
Fax: (02551) 2718 0805 / 1293 3773
Mumbai Contact:
53/54, Unique Estate,
Dr. R.P. Road, Mulund (E),
Mumbai 400 080.
Products / Services: Manufacturers of Multicolour Printed, Laminated & Hotmelt Coated Toiled Soap Wrappers Printed Multiayer Laminated Waxed, Polycoated Papers, Flexible Packaging Materials in Rolls, Sheets & Pouches.

Techno Engineering Works
V-77, Street No. 24,Vijay Park,
Mauzpur, Sahadra Delhi.
Tel: (011) 2219 2115
Products / Services: Testing Equipment

Toshniwal Process Instruments Pvt. Ltd.
Kutchery Road,
Ajmer 305 001.
Tel: (0145) 2420 506 / 7 / 8
Fax: (0145) 2420 505
Email: toshcon@jpl.dot.net.in
Products / Services: Laboratory Equipments

Trema Raj Process P. Ltd.
Jukaso House,
Andheri Kurla Road,
Saki Naka, Andheri (E),
Mumbai 400 072.
Tel: (022) 2851 0171 / 2851 1171 / 2851 1514
Fax: (022) 2851 1515 / 2851 5814
Email: rjasso@glasbm01.vsnl.net.in
Products / Services: Separators

Unitop Engineers P. Ltd.
78/1, G.I.D.C. Indl. Estate,
P.O. Box 761,
Makarpura,
Vadodara 390 010.
Tel: (0265) 2642 161 / 162
Fax: (0265) 2644 697
Telex: 0175-26443 UNTPIN
Products / Services: Evaporators

V.P. Engineering
Plot No. D-25/8, TTC Industrial Area,
Opp. Hindustan Petroleum Turbhe,
Navi Mumbai 400 705.
Tel: 2763 4907 / 08 / 2768 3626 / 2790 3633 / 3743 / 44
Fax: 2790 3634
Email: vpengg@satyam.net.in
Products / Services: Project Engineers & Erection Contractors, Fabrication & Installation of Chemical Plant& Equipments

Zanjrukiya Engineering Cons.
C-1/37, Aji Industrial Estate,
Rajkot 360 003. (Gujarat)
Tel: 2388 181
Fax: (0281) 2387 785
Email: zanjrukiya@yahoo.com
Website: www.zanjrukiya.com
Products / Services: 1. Turnkey Project-From Noodle to Finis h Soap OR Small Scale Boiling System in Toilet Soap Plant. 2. Minimum Machinery/ Power/ Manpower in Detergent Cake Plant

32

Cosmetics Consultants

Ala Cosmetology
B 44, Girdhar Nagar, Jivdaya Lane,
Ghatkopar (West),
Mumbai-400086
Maharashtra
Tel: 25131955
Deals in: Cosmetologist

Anacons
Padmakung, 882 B Bhandarkar Road,
Pune-411004
Maharashtra
Tel: 020-25654192
Fax: 020-25654192
Email: gemgraph@axcess.com
Deals in: Product Development,
Aroma Therapy, Lab Facility

Ankur Publishing Co.
C/1, Anandvan, Anandpark,
Thana (w), 400601
Maharashtra
Tel: 25369907
Fax: 25432817
Email: ankur.kul@axcess.net.in
Deals in: Packaging Technology

Aviance Beauty Solutions
Q2, Cuffe Castle, Cuffe Parade,
Mumbai-400 005 Maharashtra
Tel: 22187683

Axicom International Projects Ltd.
1C, Neelamber, 28B,
Shakespeare Sarani,
Kolkata-700017 (West Bengal)
Fax: 22476166

B K Products
39, Radha Madhab Saha Lane
P.o. box 6850,
Kolkata-700097
West Bengal
Tel: 22413361 / 31001942
Deals in: Cosmetic Perfume

Balson Laboratories
A-9, Naraina Industrial Area, Ph. 1,
New Delhi-110028
Tel:-91-11-25791299, 25798134,
55494506
Fax: 91-11-25891299
Email: balsonlab@yahoo.co.in

Cleopetras Aroma
66/A, SA Sadan, Sumangal Society,
Panic Colony,
Jamnagar-361008,
Gujarat
Tel: 0288-2675515
Email: bhatrajma@rediffmail.com

Cosmic Healers Pvt. Ltd.
7393, B-10, Vasant Kung,
New Delhi-110070,
Tel: 26890747, (M)9891198133
Fax: 26122509
Email: simer78@rediff.com
Website: www.ki2health.com
Deals in: Homeopathic Medicines, Ayurvedic Medicines, Biotique Cosmetics, Forest Essential Products, Natural Way Products, Livfit Products, Aroma Therapy Products, Cds and Audio Cassettes On Mediation & Yoga, Herbal and Health Related Books

Dr. Kipti Patel
154 Hindu Colony,
7 Laxmi Nivas, Dadar,
Mumbai-4141234
Maharashtra
Fax: 241260674
Email: dpate@bol.net.in
Deals in: Herbal Products

Dr. Vijay Sharma's Cosmetics
Surgery Centre Of India
Plot No. 350, Vishal Mandir 6th Road,
Opp. Pizza Hut, Kharwest,
Mumbai-400052
Maharashtra
Tel: 002-26491022 / 26044543
Fax: 022-26041353
Email: drvijaysharma@vsnl.com
Website: www.changinglooks.com

Global Marketing
First Floor, Prithivi Singh Market,
Roorkee 247667
Uttaranchal
Tel: 91-01332-261442
Email:
globalmarketing@indiatmes.com

Jayshree Consultancy
B304 Shivdarshan Chst
Kastur Park, Shimpoli Road
Borivali (west),
Mumbai-400 092
Maharashtra
Tel: 28996544
Deals in: Project Consultant

JMD (Indian) Trading Company
WZ-70-A, (G-16), School Road,
Opp, M.C.D.
Dispensary Uttam Nagar,
New Delhi-110059
Tel: 011-25638350
Mob.: 9811451699
Email: veenavneet@yahoo.com

Khattri Fragances & Flavours Ltd.
Lucknow Kanpur Road,
P.O. Sohramau Distt.
Unnao,
Lucknow-209859
Uttar Pradesh
Tel: mb:-98390-75353 / 75555 / 75454
Email: khattri@khattri.com
Website: www.khattri.com

Krishna & Saurashtri
74F, Venus, Worli Seaface,
Mumbai-400018
Maharashtra
Tel: 2672158
Fax: 2641774
Email: injo@krishnaandsaurastri.com
Deals in: Trademark & Ipr Regn.

Kumar Process Const. & Chem P Ltd.
230/4 Ashoka House,
Behind Sheetal Arch,
Linking Road, Bandra)w),
Mumbai-400 050
Maharashtra
Tel:2 6451964 / 26432512
Fax: 26420637
Email: kumarfil@bom3.vsnl.net.in
Deals in: Filter Media

Link Pharmaceutical Consultancy
C 6, Om Kailash, Devi Dayal Road,
Mulund (w),
Mumbai-400 080
Maharashtra
Tel: 25672974

Deals in: Formulation Development, Film Coatings

Manisha Analytics Labs P Ltd.
219221, Ashirwad Indestate No.3,
Ram Mandir
Road, Goregaon (w),
Mumbai-400104
Maharashtra
Tel: 28720919
Fax: 28759539
Deals in: Technical Anylists

Manisha Risbud
Vama Clinic, Suvarna Complex,
Oppambar Hall and Cosmos Band,
Karve Road, Ko,
Pune-411 029
Maharashtra
Tel: 25453198

Miss. Vineeta Joshi
66/A, Sai Sadan,
Sumangal Society,
Park C Colony,
Jamnagar-361008
Gujarat
Tel: 0288-2675515
Email: bhatrajma@redffmall.com
Deals in: Books On Aromatherepy, Fengshui Etc.

Mr. Kirit Doshi
G4, Patel Society,
M Gxroad No.4,
Kandivli (w),
Mumbai-400 067
Maharashtra
Tel: 28050909
Email: abkind@yahoo.com
Deals in: Marketing Consultant for Dubai

Mr. Madhukar Y B
C4/3, Kumar, Mahant Road,
Mumbai-400 057
Maharashtra
Tel: 26960009
Deals in: Cosmetic Technologist

Ms. Neera Agarwal
511 Devika Tower
6 Nehru Place,
New Delhi-11019
Tel: 26216145 / 2621646
Fax: 26211003
Email: incosmesi@vsnl.com
Deals in: Physiocosmetician, Nail Technician

Mr. Sonu Bakshi
Hempee House, B 3 Union Part,
Near RK Studio, Chembur,
Mumbari-400 071
Maharashtra
Tel: 25551857
Deals in: Cosmetologist, Aroma Therapy

MSD Labs
9339 Calumet Ave,
Munster-46321,
United States of America
Tel: 219-836-8331
Fax: 219-836-8331
Email: msdlabs@yahoo.com

Oscar Consultants
122, Ganesh Tower, Oppostation,
Thane 400602
Maharashtra
Tel: 25433417
Email: trademark@rediffmail.com
Deals in: Trademark Regn.

Pacheria Trading Co.
Y 450 Janta Market, Camp No. 1
Nangloi,
New Delhi-110041
Tel: 25472997
Deals in: C and F Agents

Packaging Solutions Group
E-94, Ekta Apartments,
Saket,
New Delhi-110017
Tel: 91-11-265110870, 26560767
Fax: 91-11-26531405
Email: pkgsolutions@indiatimes.com
Website: www.pkgsolutions.com

Deals in: Design & Development of All Types of Packaging Machines & Materials

Rajkamal Herbs And Aromatics P. Ltd.
307, Chitr Rath,
Behind Hotel President, C.G. Road,
Ahmedabad-380009
Gujarat
Tel: 079-26566911
Fax: 097-26566811
Email: rajkamal@aloeveraindia.com
Website: www.aloeveraindia.com

Ramu & Assoiates
253 Shantivan, New Link Road,
Andheri (w),
Mumbai-400 053
Maharashtra
Tel: 26827650/246405901
Fax: 6302201
Email: vedaraman@vsnl.com
Deals in: Patent & Design Regn.

S.S. Trading Company
M.G. Road. Opp. Union Club,
P.B. No. 21.
Bijapur-586101
Kamataka
Tel: 08352-2251443/2222939

Sheyna Cosmetics. Intl
205 Birch Road,
Peachtree City-30269,
United States of America
Tel: 770-632-7567
Email: mannings@ycos.com

Subhash Chemical Industries
'S' Block, Shed W2, MIDC, Bhosari,
Pune-411 026
Maharashtra
Tel: 20-27120632
Fax: 20-27122554
Email: pkothari@giaspn0.1vsnl.net.in
Deals in: Consulting Chemical Engineer

Sugand Aromatics
No. 12, First Floor,
89 Mohamadai, Road,
Mumbai-400 003,
Maharashtra
Tel: 23400310
Fax: 23412942
Email: webmaster@Indiaolichem.com
Deals in: Aromatic Chemical & Ayurvedic Herbs, Medicines Etc

Sunrise International
Green Field,
Ludhiana 141 001
Punjab
Tel: 2404425/2403024
Fax: 404425
Email: specvin@usa.net
Deals in: Export Agents for Ayurveic Herbs, Medicines etc.

Tech Know Consultants
3, Anant Chhayar Bmehta Maarg
Ghatkopar (E),
Mumbai-400 077,
Maharashtra
Tel: 25161215/25119236
Fax: 022-5173018/5153774
Deals in: Technical Advice

The Me Cosmetics
55, Canning Street, Block-B,
No. 26, IInd Floor,
Kolkata-700001
West Bengal
Tel: 228630491 / 232020737
Email: the_me_cosmetics@yahoo.com

Tradax Worldwide
103/43, Silvern Oaks, DLF Phase-1
Gurgaon-122002
Harayana
Tel: 0214-5051569
Fax: 0124-5051569
Email: acbansal@mantraonline.com

Trade India Exports
PB No. 15,
Ootacamund 643-4143
Deals in: Essential Oils

Trans Techno Consultants
'siddharth Arcade",
Oppholiday Camp, Station Road,
Aurangabad 431 005
Maharashtra
Tel: 240-354912
Fax: 240-332111

Vimkuda Consultants Private Limited
80/64 Gr. Floor, Malviya Nagar
New Delhi-110017
Fax: +(91)-(11)-26680386

Wintage Engineers And Consultants
1591, DDA Flats, G.t.b. Enclave,
New Delhi

33

Raw Materials and Chemicals Manufacturers/Suppliers

Ace International
13/21, Laura Bldg, 1st Floor,
Dhobi Talao,
Mumbai-400002
Maharashtra
Tel: 22008169
Fax: 22093240
Email: acearomatic@yahoo.com
Deals in: Guar Gum-accacia Gum-arabic

Acme Synthetic Chemicals
308, Veer Savarkar Marg,
Dadra (west),
Mumbai-400028
Maharashtra
Tel: 022-24465127, 022-24452706
Fax: 022-24440282, 28729918
Email: acmecham@vsnl.com
Website: www.acmecham.com
Deals in: Silica Gel and Aluminium Oxide For Thin-layer & Column Chromatography

Acroma Chemical Corpn.
308, Veer Savarkar Road
Dadra (west),
Mumbai-400028
Maharashtra
Tel: 24465127
Deals in; Aromatic Chemicals

Adithya Natural Products
Plot No 44, Flat No 506,
Om Towers, Om Nagar,
Langar House,
Hyderabad-500028
Andhra Pradesh
Tel: 23518220
Deals in: Crude Herbs

Advance Chemical Sales Corporation
138, 1st Floor, Pul Mithai, Teliwara,
New Delhi-110006
Tel: 011-23629151, 23529151
Fax: 011-23625660
Email: advchem@vsnl.com

Adya Oil & Chemicals Ltd.
55, Manjirekar Compound, Worli
Mumbai-400018
Maharashtra
Tel: 24918401 / 5
Fax: 24919831
Deals in: Cosmetic Chemicals

Agro Bi-Chem (India) Pvt. Ltd.
No.2281/b, 14th 'a' Main Hal,
IInd Stage, Indira Nagar,
Bangalore- 560008
Karnataka

Tel: (080)5296190 / 5297664
Fax: 25297664
Email: agrobio.bir@rmd

Alchemy Import & Export P. Ltd.
J93, Sector 25,
Gautam Budha Nagar,
Noida
Uttar Pradesh
Tel: 24535258
Fax: 24444092
Deals in: Cosmetic Raw Materials Importers & Exporters

Alkon International
11, Bombay Treekies Compound,
Malad (W),
Mumbai-400064,
Maharashtra
Tel: 022-28820626
Fax: 022-228820626
Email: alkoninternational@hotmail.com
Deals in: Spl:- Aloe Vera Juice, Gel, power

Ambika Enterprises
B/51, Om Pushpanjali Chs.
Borsapada Road,
Poisar,
Kandivali (W),
Mumbai-400 067,
Maharashtra
Tel: 28059592
Fax: 28059592
Email: ambikaent.hotmail.com
Deals in: Aloe Vera, Jojoba Oil & Other Herbal Products

Amit Fine Chem
A-32, Siddhi Apartment
Off A.c. Road, Ashok
Nagar, Kandivali (E),
Mumbai-400101,
Maharashtra
Tel: 022-28870920
Fax: 022-28871551
Email: amit170@rediffmail.com
Deals in: Dirs, Raw Materials for Cosmetics & Ayurveda

Amrut Bio-Tech Pvt. Ltd.
Plot No 21, Kotwalnagar
Nagpur 440 022
Maharashtra
Tel: 227 446
Fax: (0712) 2541 900
Deals in: Neem Extracts, Neem Formulations

Ansar Industries
4/3367, Hkstreet Zampa Bazar,
Surat 395 003
Gujarat
Tel: 2432645 / 2433522
Fax: (0261) 2432645
Deals in: Herbal Extracts

Anthurium Agrowealth P Ltd.
B/2, Rudrakash Apartment,
Oppramvan Nehur
Park, Vastrapur,
Ahmedabad-380051
Gujarat
Tel: 26762501
Fax: 26565243
Email: nbildhalya@hotmail.com

Anupam Colours & Chemical Ind.
145 Span Landmark,
Andheri Kurla Road,
Andheri (e),
Mumbai-400 093
Maharashtra
Tel: 23864389
Deals in: Pigments & Colours

Apurva Herbs
B/104 Labh Ashish, Old Police Lane,
Andheri (east),
Mumbai-400 069
Maharashtra
Tel: 28392557
Deals in: Ayurvedic Raw Materials

Arihant Trading Company
268/70 Shahid Bharat Singh Road,
6& 9 Chandresh Bhavan,
Mumbai-400 001
Maharashtra
Tel: 22690707 / 22618443

Fax: 2614778
Email: arihantt@vsnl.com
Deals in: Cosmetic Raw Materials & intermediates

Arjuna Natural Extracts Limited
Bypss Road,
Awaye 683 101
Kerala
Tel: 2622 612 / 2622 204
Fax: (0484) 2532 404 / 2622 612
Email: mail@arjunatural.com

Arochem Silvassa Ltd.
Scent House, Station Road,
Goregaon (w),
Mumbai-400 062
Maharashtra
Tel: 28722280
Fax: 28720818
Deals in: Aromatic Chemicals

Aromatic Agencies (I)P Ltd.
41 Manoj Indlestate,
G Dambedkar Road,
Wadala,
Mumbai-400 031
Maharashtra
Tel: 2413541 / 24135889
Fax: 24135786
Deals in: Aromatic Chemicals

Barkur Surfactants Pvt. Ltd
Sony Apartments,
1st Floor Opp.ak Road,
Jarimari,
Mumbai-400072
Maharashtra
Tel: 022-28510275 / 28511541
Fax: 91-022-2851324 / 25810275
Deals in: Mfrs of Shampoo Bases & Cosmetic Additives

Bharat Chemicals Enterprises
D 171, West Patel Nagar,
New Delhi-110008
Tel: 257321169/25751747
Fax: 25767255
Deals in: Cosmetic Raw Material

Blulux Laboratories
79/66-B, I.H.I. Complex,
Indl. Area, N.I.T,
Faridabad-121001
Haryana
Tel: 91-129-25021360, 2444433
Fax: 91-129-2237762
Email: blulxu@rediffmail.com
Website: www.blulux.com
Deals in: Manufacturers & Exporters of Laboratory Chemicals

Chawla Trading Company
C2B-113/A, Janak Puri
New Delhi-110058
Tel: 91-11-25522680
Fax: 91-11-25522680
Deals in: Raw Materials For Cosmetics (Cream, Shampoo, Oil etc.)

Chemical Traders
188/1, Gali Sarawali
Tilak Bazar,
New Delhi-110006
Tel: 011-23913177, 23926470, 35913177
Deals in: Dealers of All Cosmetics Chemicals

Chemical & Polymers
212, Allied House,
Old Rohtak Road,
New Delhi-110035
Tel: 23658508
Deals in: Cosmetic Raw Materials

Chemico
10/18, Old Hanuman Lane,
Princess Street,
Mumbai-400002
Maharashtra
Tel: 022-56312452
Fax: 022-22407623
Email: virang@vsnl.com
Website: www.chemico.net
Deals in: Cosmetic Chemicals

Chowdhry Rubber & Company
1403, Pan Mandi,
Sadra Bazar,
New Delhi-110006
Tel: 91-011-23656680/8709/9055/
23646364
Fax: 011-23646014
Email: crcc@vsnl.com

Classic Medi Herbs
3/2270, 4th main Begur Road,
Bangalore-560 068
Karnataka
Tel: 5721558
Deals in: Herbel Extract

Continental Chemicals
M67, Street-4,
Shastri Nagar,
New Delhi-110052
Tel: 91-11-23642111, 23655346
Fax: 91-11-23649176
Email: coschem@ndf.vsnl.net.in
Deals in: Cosmetics Chemicals, essential Oils, Preservatives and Others

Deepak & Co.
333 Narsi Natha Street,
Katha Bazar, Masjid,
Mumbai-400 009
Maharashtra
Tel: 340719
Fax: 3421581
Email: vnd@bom7.vsnl.net.in
Deals in: Bees Wax, Carnawba Wax, Petrolleum Jelly

Dishman Pharmaceuticals & Chemicals Limited
401, Sangeet Plaza,
Marol Maroshi Road,
Andheri (E),
Mumbai-400059,
Maharashtra
Tel: 022-28592120, 56964055
Fax: 022-28528758, 56964054
Email: mumbai@dishmangroup.com

Encee Aromatics (P) Ltd.
14-1-68 & 69 Main Road,
Mettupalayam 641
301 Tamil Nadu
Tel: 24254-23863
Fax: 24254-22569
Deals in: Aromatic Chemicals

Flavex Aromats (India) Ltd.
B2/17 Satvatra Society,
Paud Road,
Pune-411 029
Maharashtra
Tel: 20-5439974
Fax: 20-5380580
Email: consafe@satyam.net.in

Globe Chemical Company
A-12, 13 Sardar Nagar,
New Delhi-110009
Tel: 91-11-23941380, 23945839
Fax: 91-11-23956222
Email: kkt@satyam.net.in.
Deals in: Cosmetic Chemicals Imports

Gogia Chemical Industries Pvt. Ltd.
A-127, Okhla Industries Area,
Phase-II,
New Delhi-110020
Tel: 91-11-26385194, 26383329,
26385664
Fax: 91-11-26386485
Email: gcipl@vsnl.com
Website: www.gogia.com
Deals in: Natural Essential Oils, Aromatic Chemicals, Fragrances, Essential Oils

Gotewala Brothers
148 Mint Street,
Chennai-600 079
Tamil Nadu
Tel: 25387399
Fax: 25355000
Deals in: Cosmetic Raw Materials

Green Valley Herbal Forms Limited
D No3 4531/1a Narayanaguda,
Hyderabad-500027
Andhra Pradesh
Tel: 2756 1188
Fax: 040-27567648
Email: greenherbs@coolmail.com
Deals in: Herbal Raw Material

H.K. Chemicals & Pharmaceticals
Post Box No. 27698, Shop No. 4,
Indraprastha 1-A,
Opp Ashoka Hospital
Jitendra Road, Malad (East),
Mumbai-400097
Maharashtra
Tel: 91-22-28775829, 28774445
Fax: 91-22-28773079, 28728835
Email: nkc@vsnl.com
Website: www.hkoverseas.com
Deals in: Cosmetic Chemical-Triclosan

Hertz Chemicals Limited
2/3 Sant Kaskar Indlestate,
SV Road,
Oshiwara, Jogeshwari (w),
Mumbai-400 102
Maharashtra
Tel: 26786931/26780057
Fax: 26783852
Email: hertz@vsnl.com
Deals in: Perfumes & Cosmetics

Hindustan Pharmaceuticals
Kot Mit Singh, Tarn Taran Road
Amritsar 143 022
Punjab
Tel: 2482 240
Fax: 0183-2482671
Email: hindphrm@del2vsnl.net.in
Deals in: Herbal Extracts

ICI India Limited
20, 2nd Block, Koramangala,
Bangalore-560034
Karnataka
Tel: 225522709
Deals in: Cosmetics Raw Materials

Indfrag Limited
1320, 12th Cross Indirangar li Sta,
Bangalore-560-038
Karnataka
Tel: 2528-5365/2528 5366
Fax: 080-2528 4636
Email: indfrag@vsnl.com
Deals in: Herbal Extracts

India Glycols Limited
C-124, Okhla Industrial Area
Phase 1,
New Delhi-110020
Tel: 26815772, 26810768, 26810834, 26810838
Fax: 91-01126810390, 26819410
Deals in: Cosmetics Chemicals

Indian Ayurherbs Pvt. Ltd.
2/4A, Kengsington Road
Banglore 560 042
Karnataka
Tel: 25547110
Fax: 080-2536 3487
Email: ayurtherb@blr.vsnl.net.in
Deals in: Herb Extracts, Natural Food Colours

Indian Drug & Botanical Co.
103, Ram Nagar,
Krishna Nagar,
New Delhi-110051
Tel: 2242 3579/2243 2443
Fax: 011-23953182
Email: groinfotele@bol.net.in
Deals in: Herbal Extracts, Natural Essential Oils

Indo World Trading Corporation
303, Prakash Chambers,
6, Netaji Subhash Marg,
Daryaganj,
New Delhi-110002
Tel: 23278050
Fax: 23274521
Email: indoworld@vsnl.com
Deals in: Herbal Extract, **Deals in** Herbs/ botanicals, Herbal Extracts

Jaggi Cosmetic Store
1423, Gali Telian,
Tilak Bazar,
New Delhi-110006
Tel: 23937610
Deals in: Chemicals for Cosmetic Toiletries

Jay Kay Dyes & Chemicals
2136, Tilak Bazar
Khari Baoli,
New Delhi-110006
Tel: 23929230
Fax: 23929231
Deals in: Cosmetics

Jaykay Resources
A 13 Shivam Park,
B/h Akashwani, Makarpura Road
Vadodara 390 005
Gujarat
Tel: 265-646370
Fax: 265-654483
Email: jaykayresour@satyam.net.in
Deals in: Herbs & Herbal Extracts

K P Corporation
B 305, Sita Park,
Mandeeshwar Road,
Borivali (w),
Mumbai-400103
Maharashtra
Tel: 28951828
Deals in: Petroleum Jelly

Kajal Chemicals
4 Ballkrishan Chambers
¼ Issaji, Street, 1st Floor,
Vadgadi,
Mumbai-400 003
Maharashtra
Tel: 23421570/23442434
Fax: 234215670
Deals in: Chemicals & Solvents

Kancor Flavours & Extracts Ltd.
Xvii/138, Kanakkankadvu Road
Angamally
South, Angamally-682 573
Kerala
Tel: 0484-2452236/2452237
Fax: 2452 662/2453376
Email: mail@kancoflavours.com
Deals in: Oleoresins, Extracts, Essential Oils

Kavens India
30/4, Third Trust Cross Street,
Mandavelipakkam,
Chennai-600 028
Tamil Nadu
Tel: 246115558
Email: kavens@eth.net

Khedut Utkrash Mandal
Valaki Farm, Zanzmer Road,
Pithalpur 364135
Gujarat
Tel: 2842-87820
Email: srosto;ab@indiainfo.com
Deals in: Aloevera and Aloein

Koel Colours P Ltd.
824 Mangal Prabhat
Gujarat Mandal Road
vile Parle (e),
Mumbai-400 057
Maharashtra
Tel: 26151334
Deals in: Colourants

Krishan Baldev & Company
Majith Mandi,
Amritsar 143001
Punjab
Tel: 183-2530351/2558795
Fax: 183-2545673
Email: sudhird@del3.vsnl.net.in
Deals in: Indian Herbs

Krishna Traders
20, Hara Chandra Mullick Street
Kolkata-700005,
West Bengal
Tel: 91-33-25434494
Mb:9831008941
Fax: 91-33-25543793/22153095
Email: tmohan@gias.cl0.1.vns.net.in

Kunj Enterprises
P O Box 1282, General Post Office
Mumbai-400 001,
Maharashtra
Tel: 22664116
Fax: 22664116
Deals in: Perfumery Raw Materials

Laila Impex
40-15-14, Brindavan City labbipet
Vijayawada 520 010
Andhra Pradesh
Tel: 2473468/476561
Fax: 0866-475278
Email: Herbal Extracts

Mas Enterprises
93/1, 7th Cross Road, 3rd Main,
Chamrajpet, Bangalore-560 018
Karnataka
Tel: 26618933
Fax: 26612749
Deals in: Perfumery Raw Material

Maulik Dye Chem Industries
A/501, Jagannath Appt.
Rokadia Lane, Borivli (W),
Mumbai-400092
Maharashtra
Tel: 022-28933422, 28952947
Fax: 022-28941419
Email: maulikdyecham@hotmail.com
Website: www.maulikdyechem.7.com
Deals in: Cosmetics Raw Materials Like Sles. Coco-diethanolamide, Coco-Monoethanolamide, IPM, IPP Etc.

Mewani Exports
111/52 Mulund Clny Malabar Hill Rd,
Mumbai-4000 028
Maharashtra
Tel: 25670734
Deals in: Perfumery Compounds

Millennium Resource
B29, S G Barve Marg,
Nehru Nagar, Kurla (east),
Mumbai 400 024
Maharashtra
Tel: 25225678
Fax: 25225678
Email: milleniumresource@us.net

Minex Agencies
71, Ganesh Chandra avenue,
Kolkata-700013
West Bengal
Tel: 22216791/22361178
Fax: 033-22250162
Email: mins@cal.vsnl.net.in
Deals in: Dried Plants Medicinal Herbs

Mokashi Aromas Pvt. Ltd.
W81, Addl Ambermath Midc,
Ambemath (east) 421506,
Dist Thane
Maharashtra
Tel: 2680403
Fax: 2680062
Email: mokashi@livewire.net.in
Deals in: Aroma Chemicals, Perfumery Compounds

Monisha Sales Corporation
112 Apollo Chambes, Mogra Lane,
Andheri (E),
Mumbai-400 093,
Maharashtra
Tel: 28228034
Deals: Pigments and Colours

Monochem Industries
Mohatta Bhavan, Dre Moses Road,
Worli,
Mumbai-400 018
Maharashtra
Tel: 24928926
Fax: 24929151
Deals in: Cosmetic Chemicals

Mr. R S Bhandari
19B, 48 Bihari Bagh,
3rd Bhoiwada,
Mumbai-400 002
Maharashtra
Tel: 23759098
Deals in: Bindi Raw Material

Nat. Con Fruit & Food Proc. P. Ltd.
No490(1), Iv Phase Peenya Industries Ar.
Bangalore-560 058
Karnataka
Tel: 28362986
Fax: 080-333 4804/836 2986
Deals in: Plant Extracts Natural Colours

Natural Collectors
267 Rabindra Sarani,
Kolkata-700007,
West bengal
Tel: 22336496
Fax: 25436852
Email: nautralcolls@hotmail.com
Deals in: Indian Herbs

Natural Products Company
Akashganga, 23 Chitra, Raboali
Thane 400601
Maharashtra
Tel: 25330654
Deals in: Herbal Extracts

Natures Bounty
3040 Sector 21 D,
Chandigarh 160022,
Haryana
Tel: 172-2710195
Email: natures_bounty@yahoo.com
Deals in: Geranium Oil and Other Herbal Oils

Naulakaha Exim P. Ltd.
14 Parkar Bldg.
12 Cawasji Patel Street, Fort,
Mumbai-400 023
Maharashtra
Tel: 2852320
Deals in: Aromatic Compounds

Neelikon Food Dyes & Chemicals Ltd.
D8, D17, Everest,
Pt. M Maiviya Marg,
Tardeo Circle,
Mumbai-400 034 Maharashtra
Tel: 24980572/24986159
Fax: 4964945
Email: neelikon@bom3.vsnl.net.in
Deals in: Colours For Cosmetics

New Bharat Chemical Works
4901, Phoota Road,
Sadar Bazar,
New Delhi-110006
Tel: 91-11-23613307, 23538310,
Mob: 9810410703
Fax: 91-11-23523602
Email: nbcworks@hotmail.com
Deals in: Deals In: chemicals, Waxes, oils, Perfumes, Fatty Acids, Petroleum Products, SLS, SLES and Others

Om Sri Sathya Sai Exports
Post Box NO 8217
Jayanag,
Bangalore-560 082
Karnataka
Tel: 2634 1008
Fax: 080-2634 1008
Email: saiaeropace@yaho.com
Deals in: Essential Oils Perfumery Compounds

Orchid Chemicals
4/28A, 1st & IInd Floor,
Kiriti Nagar Industrial Area,
New Delhi-10015
Tel: 011-25420785, 25460705
Fax: 011-25440280
Email: orchemin_rk95@rediffmail.com
Deals in: Dealers of All Cosmetics

Paxchem Ltd.
4 Yugprabhat,
N S Pathare Marg,
Off Sitliadevi
Temple Road, Mahim,
Mumbai-400 016
Maharashtra
Tel: 24449295/24449359
Fax: 24464888
Email: marketing@paxgroup.com
Deals in: Cosmetics Raw Materials

PCS Petrochem
B 11 Sidhpura Indlestate,
LBS Marg, Ghatkopar
(w), Mumbai-400 086,
Maharashtra
Tel: 25171622
Deals in: Waxes

Phyto Concentrates
24 25 D Sector C industries Area,
Sanwer Road Indore
Tel: 2701318/2282 886
Fax: 0731-2701 318
Email: phytoind@bom4.vsnl.net.com
Deals in: Herbs

Premier Chem Corporation
203, Himalaya House, 79,
Palton Road,
Mumbai-400001,
Maharashtra
Tel: 91-22-22615578,22615589
Fax: 91-22-22615538
Email: premierchem@vsnl.net
Website: www.premierchemcorp.com
Deals in: Dealers, Exporters & Importers of Cosmetics Chemicals

Quanta Chemicals P Ltd.
177 Samuel Street,
Somaya Bldg, Next
Tovadgadi P O,
Mumbai-400 009
Maharashtra
Tel: 23752145
Fax: 23739346
Deals in: Cosmetic Chemicals

R.R. Enterprises
2202, Gali Hinga Beg,
Tilak Bazar, Khari Baoli
New Delhi-110006
Tel: 91-11-239207390, 23977337
Fax: 91-11-23929312
Email: rregroup@vsnl.com
Website: www.business.vsnl.com/irregroup
Deals in: Dealer & Trader of Cosmetics Chemicals

R.S. Agencies
A-38, Gujrat Appts,
Pitam Pura,
New Delhi-1100034
Tel: 91-11-2258113, 22591578,
Mob: 9810033774
Email: rsagencs@yahoo.com

Rama Chemical Co.
1362/5, 1st Floor, Pan Mandi,
Sadar Bazar,
New Delhi-110006
Tel: 23610754,30933507
Mob: 9810135563
Deals in: Dealer & Trader of: Cosmetics Chemicals and Raw Materials

Rolex Lanolin Products Limited
52/58, Babu Gani Road,
1st Floor, 15,24-26
jivraj Shahji Bldg.,
Mumbai-400002
Maharashtra
Tel: 91-22-22012345
Fax: 91-22-22015950
Email: info@rolexlanolin.com
Website: www.rolexlanolin.com
Deals in: Raw Materials For Cosmetics/ personal Care:- lanolin(pharma/cosmetics Grade)

SV Marketing
2210/19 Aggarwal Market,
Katra Tabacco,
Khari Baoli,
New Delhi-110006
Tel: 23933003/23915500
Fax: 23915383
Email: vsm20@bol.net.in
Deals in: Raw Herbs & Herbal Extracts

S.S. Herbals
485/2, Katra Ishwar Bhawan,
Khari Baoli
New Delhi-110006
Tel: 23950471/23910274
Fax: 23964221

Email: ssherbal@bol.net.in
Deals in: Medicinal & Botanical Herbs, Herbal Extracts

Saatal Katha & Chemicals Ltd.
42, Jarora Compound
Myhospital Road,
Indore 452 001
Tel: 2701 449/702
Fax: 0731-2702018
Deals in: Herbal Extracts

Shankar Dyes & Chemicals
1209, Shankar Building,
Gali No.-11 Sadar Bazar
New Delhi-110006
Tel: 91-11-23673462, 23558239
Mob: 9810355592
Fax: 91-11-23970589
Email: shankardyes@rediffmail.com
Website:
www.shankardyesanchemicals.com
Deals in: Mfrs., Dealers & Traders of All Types of Pigments & Dyes For Colour Cosmetics

Shree Ganesh Dye Chem
Plot no.71/13, Phase-1,
GIDC Estate, Vatva,
Ahmedabad-382445
Gujarat
Tel: 91-79-25896563, 25890334, 230918109
Fax: 91-79-2589083, 25890334
Email: kayen@wiletonline.net; kayend1@sancharnet.in
Website: www.India-chemicals.com
Deals in: Dealers & Trader of:-Hair Dyes & Cosmetic Intermediate Chemicals

Shri Ram Sons Wax (P) Ltd
181, Tilak Bazar,
New Delhi-110006
Tel: 91-11-23942451
Mob: 9811076830
Fax: 91-11-23927312
Email: srs@del3.vsnl.net.in
Deals in: Dealer/trader of Cosmetic Waxes & and Other Chemicals

Subash Chemical Industries
S Block, Shed W2, Midc, Bhosari,
Pune-411 026
Maharashtra
Tel: 27120632
Fax: 27122554
Email: subhashchem@vsnl.com
Deals in: Raw Materials For Cosmetics/ Pharmaceuticals

Subash Chemical Works
4, Joymitra Ghat Lane, (1st Floor),
Kolkata-700005,
West Bengal

Sud Pines Pvt. Ltd.
B 28, D/c, Gandhi Nagar,
Jammu, Jammu & Kashmir
Tel: 191-2431606/2450258
Fax: 2431606
Email: sudpines@usa.net
Deals in: Essential Oils

Sunshine Chemicals
13, Tikona Park Market, N.I.T,
Faridabad-121001,
Haryana
Tel: 0129-2417330, 2417350,
Mob: 9818163513
Fax: 0129-2417350
Deals in: Consignment Agent, Dealer & Trade of: Cosmetics Chemicals and Raw Materials

Super Fine Aromatic Co P Ltd.
157 KK Road,
Bangalore-560 042,
Karnataka
Tel: 28360595
Deals in: Aromatic Compound

Swati Traders
XXII/232, Gali No. 7,
Near Roshanara Paints,
Opp. 4/56, Roop Nagar,
New Delhi: 110007
Tel: 91-11-23842465, 23842832
Mob: 9818806093
Deals in: Dealers & Traders of Cosmetic Chemicals, Dyes & Intermediates

Taxtron Technica S.L., Europe
Vegetable Oil, S.L.
(Plimon Group Spain)
DDA MIG 123, Pocket-B,
East of Loni Road,
New Delhi-110093
Tel: 91-11-22813657
Mob: 9810017563
Fax: 91-11-22813657
Email: sadhnasood@satyam.net.in
Deals in: Importer Of Natural Oils, Essential Oils And Otherchemicals For Cosmetics Applications

Torrel Cosmetics Pvt. Ltd.
Samudra Annexe, offc G Road,
Ahmedabad,
Gujarat
Tel: 26441189/26562718
Fax: 26425173
Email: torresl@ad1.vsnl.net.in
Deals in: Cosmetic Raw Material

Unicorn Natural Products (P) Ltd.
13/1 Rasoolpura,
Secunderabad-500 003
Andhra Pradesh
Tel: 27844162
Fax: 040-27845136
Email: unicom@hdl.vsnl.net.in
Deals in: Natural Herb, Herbal Extracts

Unique (India)
C-41A, Shivaji Park,
Punjabi Bagh
br.off: no. 123, Transport Centre,
Punjabi Bagh,
New Delhi-110026
Tel: 91-11-25917611, 255458082,
Mob: 9811052474
Fax: 91-11-25109312
Email: uniqueindia1@rediffmail.com
Deal in: Dealer & Distributers of:- HLP, LLP, Liquid Paraffin Oils, (IP), White Oil, Petroleum Jelly For Hair Oil, Massage Oil, Body Oil And Other Cosmetics

Veekay Enterprises
240 Samuel Street,
Mumbai-400 003,
Maharashtra
Tel: 23422354/2342882
Fax: 23427543
Deals in: Cosmetics Chemicals

Vinamra Oil & Herbs
41 Anupam Nagar Extn.
Gwalior 474003
Madhya Pradesh
Tel: 2751-341336
Fax: 2571-347055
Email: vivek@bitsmart.com
Deals in: Menthol Oil, White Moosli, Aawla, Tulsi, Neem Oil

Way-Link International
71, B.R.B. Basu Road, B-411,
Kalkota-700001
West Bengal
Tel: 91-33-22358933/9092
Fax: 91-33-25212082
Email: waylink@vsnl.net

34

Manufacturers/Raw Materials Suppliers of Herbs/Plants and their Extracts

A Green Earth Products
W 105, Khuranas, Greater Kailash-1,
New Delhi-110048, Delhi
Tel: 26219095
Fax: 26446921
Deals in: Herbal Products

A M N Ayurveda Centre
1st Shree Ind. Centre,
2nd Hasanabad Lane,
Santa Cruz,
Mumbai-400054 Maharashtra
Tel: 26490357
Deals in: Ayurvedic, Herbal Drugs & Medicinal Plants

A-One Agarbatti Agencies
2842, Kotni Range, Raipur Gate,
Ahmedabad-380001, Gujarat
Tel: 079-21145345, 26753018, 26753228
Email: abc@abc40.com
Deals in: Fragrances & Flavours

Aar Kay Agro Enterprise
B-11/138, Kalyani, Nadia,
Kolktat-741235,
West Bengal
Tel: 25825084
Fax: +(91)-(33)-25828039
Email: aarkay@yahoo.com
Deals in: Herbal Cosmetics, Medicinal Herbals, Crude Drugs, Etc.

Abid & Company Pvt. Ltd.
Dardar Market, Ganj Bakhsh Road,
Lahore-54000, Lahore,
Pakistan
Tel: 92-42-7115733
Fax: 92-42-7249956
Email: osmanali@jamila.com.pk
Website: www.jamila.com.pk

Achal Impex Inc.
93, Rajiv Nagar, Canal Road,
Faribadad-121002,
Haryana
Tel: 91-129-2296256, 91-11-23520838
Fax: 91-129-2296257, 91-11-23610838
Email: aii@vsn.com
Website: www.achalimpex.com
Deals in: Mfr. & Exporter or Natural

Henna, Herbal, Henna, Hair Dyes Henna Paste, Henna Shampoo, Henna Oil, Hair Regrowth Oil and Others

Active Herbal Export Pvt. Ltd.
9, Damoder Park,
Nr. Arya Kanya Vidhyalay,
Karelibaug,
Baroda-390018,
Gujarat
Tel: 91-265-234413115, 22413115

Advance High Tech Agro Product Pvt. Ltd.
49/32, Site IV, Indl. Area,
Sahibabad,
Ghaziabad-201020,
Uttar Pradesh
Tel: 2776388/77429
Fax: (0575)2776399
Email: advnace@ndf.vnsl.net.in
Deals in: Essential Oils

Ajit Traders
6629, Main Bazar,
Khari Baoli,
New Delhi-110006
Tel: 2235146/23849242
Fax: 23946756
Deals in: Aromatic Chemicals, Natural Essential Oil, Resinoids

Akash Export
913, 8th Floor, Brigade Tower,
Brigade Road,
Bangalore-560025,
Karnataka
Tel: 2292710/2292710
Fax: +(91)-(80)_23430087/22244506
Deals in: Natural Essential Oils:- Sandal Wood Oil, Davana Oil Etc.

Al-Kowzer Exports
65/B/1, Periyar Nagar
Bindigul-424001,
Tamil Nadu
Tel: 0451-2402413
Fax: 0451-2438070
Email: alkowzer@yahoo.com
Deals in: Herbs

Alarsin Mktg. Pvt. Ltd.
A/32, MIDC, 3, Andheri (e),
Mumbai-400093,
Maharashtra
Tel: 28367084/282216836
Deals in: Ayurvedic, Herbal Drugs & Medicinal Plants

Albatross Herbals
A-1/58, Mahipalpur, Extn.,
New Delhi-110037
Tel: 91-11-267833326
Fax: 91-11-26783326
Email: herbalba@hotmail.com
Deals in: Herbal Havan Samagri/ poojan Samagri/Agarbatti

Alchem International Limited
201, Empire Plaza Mehrauli,
Gurgaon Road
Sultanpur,
New Delhi
Fax: (011) 2780 2423/2102
Email: reman.mehta@elnet.ems.vsnl.net.in
Deals in: Herbal Extract

Alicon Pharmaceutical Pvt. Ltd.
14, Ranchod Dham,
Y.r. Tawre Road, Dahisar (w),
Mumbai-400068,
Maharashtra
Tel: 28930030
Deals in: Ayurvedic, Herbal Drugs & Medicinal Plants

Alka Chemi-Cosmetic
1578, Lallu Raiji's Vanda,
Opp. Jansatta
Building, Mirzapur,
Ahmedabad-380001,
Gujarat
Tel: 079-255051/25500346
Fax: 079-25351022, 25351150
Email: asit@alkachemi.com
Deals in Mfrs. & Exporters of:-

fragrances, incense Sticks, Cosmetics, Herbal Cosmetics

Alkon International
11, Bombay Talkies Compound, Malad (W),
Mumbai-400064,
Maharashtra
Tel: 022-232948713, 28820626
Fax: 022-28820626
Email:
alkoninternational@hotmail.com
Deals in: Spl:- Aloe Vera Juice, Gel, Powder

All India Drugs Suly. Co.
22, Darayasthan St. Masjid Bunder Road,
Mumbai-400003,
Maharashtra
Tel: 23422313

Alps Containers Pvt. Ltd.
Plot. No. 16, Govt. Industrial Estate Kandivli (w),
Mumbai-400067, Maharashtra
Tel: 022-28670891
Fax: 022-286770891
Email: alpscontainers@yahoo.com
Website: www.alpscontainers.com
Deals in: All Types of Tooth Paste, All Aloe Vera, Herbal & Ayurvedic Products

Alps Industries Ltd.
57/2, Site-IV, Industrial Area, Sahibabad,
Ghaziabad-201010, Uttar Pradesh
Tel: 91-120-2896022/22/24
Fax: 91-120-2895299, 2896041
Email: alpsind@del2.vsnl.net.in ;kkagarwal@alpsindustries.com
Website: www.alpsind.com
Deals in: Herbal Gulal For Holi, food Colours, Natural Dyes For Textiles

LIST OF THE READY AVAILABLE DETAILED PROJECT REPORTS

AUTOMOBILES, MECHANICAL & METALLURGICAL

1. AGRICULTRAL EQUIPMENTS
2. AGRICULTRAL EQUIPMENTS INCLUDING THRESHERS
3. AIR BRAKE HELICAL COIL
4. AIR COOLER
5. AIR FILTERS(FOR SCOOTER CAR & EXCAVATORS ETC.)
6. ALUMINIUM & ALUMINIUM ALLOYS FROM ALUMINIUM SCRAP TO MAKE UTENSILS (INDUCTION FURNACE MELTED)
7. ALUMINIUM ALLOY WHEELS
8. ALUMINIUM ALLOYS FROM ALUMINIUM SCRAP TO MAKE UTENSILS (INDUCTION FURNACE)
9. ALUMINIUM HOT & COLD ROLLING MILL
10. ALUMINIUM BOTTLE MANUFACTURING (COLD EXTRUSION OF ALUMINIUM)
11. ALUMINIUM/COPPER CABLE LUGS
12. ALUMINIUM CANS FOR BEER PACKAGING
13. ALUMINIUM CANS FOR CAPACITORS
14. ALUMINIUM CAPS FOR INJECTION VIALS
15. ALUMINIUM EXTRUSION
16. ALUMINIUM FURNITURE & HARDWARE
17. ALUMINIUM SHEET ROLLING MILL
18. ALUMINIUM UTENSILS
19. ALUMINIUM UTENSILS & SCHOOL BOXES
20. ALUMINIUM WIRE DRAWING AND SUPER ENAMELLING FOR WINDING
21. ANODISED ALUMINIUM UTENSILS
22. ANODIZING OF ALUMINIUM
23. ANTIMONY OXIDE FROM LEAD SCRAP
24. ARC WELDING FILTER GLASS
25. ALUMINIUM FOIL CUTTING & ROLL MAKING
26. AUTO FLAPS FOR TRUCKS & BUSES
27. AUTOMOBILE WORKSHOP (GARAGE & SERVICE CENTRE)
28. AUTO GEARS
29. AUTO HORNS
30. AUTO LEAF SPRING
31. AUTO TUBES
32. AUTO PISTON RING
33. AUTO PISTON
34. BAKERY AND BISCUITS EQUIPMENTS FABRICATION
35. BALL POINT PEN REFILLS
36. BALL ROLLER & TAPER BEARING
37. BAND SAW BLADES
38. BARBED WIRE
39. BICYCLE SPOKES
40. BRAKE LINING ASBESTOES/ RESIN BASED & ASBESTOES FREE
41. BRASS ARTWARE/HOLLOW WARE CASTING (WITH THE HELP OF PHENOLIC RESIN)
42. BRASS CASTING
43. BRASS PIPES FROM BRASS SHEET WITH LONGITUDINALLY WELDING
44. BRASS WARE BY CASTING METHOD (BRASS ARTICLES VIZ. BRASS POOJA LAMPS AND OTHER CASTED)
45. BRIGHT BARS
46. BUFFING AND POLISHING INDUSTRY (JOB WORK)
47. BUTT HINGE (BRASS SHEET)
48. CARBON BRUSH HOLDER & SLIP RING
49. CO_2 WELDING WIRE ELECTRODES (COPPER/ COPPER ALLOY COATED M.S.WIRE)
50. CARBON FILM RESISTORS
51. CARBURETTORS
52. CAST STEEL PANES FOR MELTING FURNACE
53. CHEMICAL ETCHING OF STAINLESS STEEL
54. CHEMICAL RESISTANT IRON & STEEL
55. COLD FORM SECTION MILL
56. COLD ROLLED FORMING OF SECTION AND OTHER SECTIONS
57. COLD ROLLING OF MS STRIP
58. COLD TWISTED DE-FORMED RIBBED STEEL
59. COMPRESSOR (HERMETIC) FOR AIR CONDITIONERS
60. COMPRESSED NATURAL GAS (CNG KIT) FOR AUTOVEHICLE
61. CONTINUOUSLY CAST STEEL WIRE RODS (5 mm)
62. CONTINUOUS CASTING COPPER WIRE RODS
63. CONVEYOR BELTINGS
64. CONVEYOR BELT, TRANSM -ISSION BELT & V BELTS
65. COOKING RANGES
66. COPPER/BRASS SHEETS, CIRCLE & UTENSILS
67. COPPER FOIL
68. COPPER INGOTS, RODS MAKING & WIRE DRAWING
69. COPPER PRODUCTS FROM COPPER SCRAP
70. COPPER SMELTING PLANT
71. COPPER WIRE RODS FROM COPPER SCRAP
72. CORRUGATED BOX MAKING MACHINERY AND OTHER THEIR PARTS
73. CYLINDER LINER FOR AUTOMOBILES
74. DOOR LOCKS/PAD LOCKS
75. DRILL BITS & TOOL BITS
76. DRUM CLOSURES
77. ERW STEEL CONDUIT PIPE
78. EARTH MOVING EQPT.
79. ENGINE VALVES FOR AUTOMOBILES
80. FABRICATION OF HEAT EXCHANGER
81. FABRICATION OF STORAGE TANKS AND M.S. DRUM
82. FERROUS ALLOY NI-HARDY I.V CASTING
83. FERROUS Mn ALLOY CASTING BY ALUMINA THERMIC PROCESS
84. FERRO ALLOYS
85. FERRO SILICON & FERRO MANGANESE FROM DOLOMITE (SMS GRADE)
86. FIRE EXTINGUISHERS
87. FLIP-TONE CANS
88. FORGED CONECTING ROD
89. FORGING UNIT
90. FOUNTAIN PEN NIBS
91. FOUNDRY SAND
92. FUEL INJECTION SYSTEM
93. GALVANIZED M.S.STRIPS
94. GALVANIZING PLANT
95. GALVANIZED IRON WIRE
96. GAS WELDING TORCHES AND NOZZLES
97. GASKET SHEET
98. GATE GRILLS & WINDOW FRAMES
99. GENERATING SET (DIESEL)
100. HARD ANODISED ALUMINIUM
101. HOSPITAL WARES
102. HOSPITAL FURNITURES
103. HOT DIP GALVANIZING
104. HOT FORGED FASTENERS
105. HOT MIX PLANT
106. INJECTION MOULDED PLASTIC COMPOUNDS WITH TOOL ROOM
107. INJECTION MOULDED PLASTIC COMPONENTS AND METAL PIPE SPINNING UNIT
108. INVESTMENT CASTING
109. IRON/STEEL WIRE GAUGE
110. IRON TAWA
111. KNIVES (S.S.KNIVES)
112. KITCHEN SINK (S.S.)
113. L.P.G REGULATORS
114. MACHINE SCREWS & SELF TAPPING SCREWS
115. MARUTI WORKSHOP CUM SERVICE STATION
116. MAGNESIUM INGOTS & BULLETS CASTING

Above all the "Detailed Project Reports" are available at *"ENGINEERS INDIA RESEARCH INSTITUTE"*. 4449, Nai Sarak (D), Main Road Delhi - 110 006 (India) ● Ph : 91-11-23918117, 2391 6431, 2384 0361 ● Fax : 91-11- 2391 6431 ●E-Mail : eirisidi@bol.net.in ● WebSite : www.eiriindia.org

117. MANUFACTURE OF TIN CONTAINERS
118. MANUFACTURE OF STORAGE TANKS, PRESSURE VESSELS, HEAT EXCHANGERS
119. MARK II HAND PUMPS
120. MARUTI WORKSHOP CUM - SERVICE STATION
121. MECHANICAL JACKS
122. METAL CUTTING DIE DESIGN
123. METAL CUTTING OF AND GRINDING WHEELS (ABBRASIVE CUTTING WHEELS)
124. METAL HOOKS & CLIPS
125. METAL SEPARATION (COPPER, TIN, LEAD) FROM SPENT WASH ACID
126. METALLIC RING JOINTS
127. METALLIC GASKET (SPIRAL WOUND)
128. MICROVEE & ABSOLUTE FILTER
129. MICROWAVE OVEN
130. MILD STEEL INGOTS
131. MINI STEEL PLANT
132. MODERN VEHICLE WORKSHOP
133. MOPED
134. M.S.HINGES
135. M.S.INGOT AND HR. STEEL STRUCTURALS
136. M.S.INGOT BY INDUCTION FURNACES
137. M.S.PIPES
138. M.S. WELDING ELECTRODE
139. MUFFLERS & SILENCERS FOR THREE WHEELERS
140. NAIL CUTTER WITH FILER & MANICURE
141. NICHROME WIRE
142. NICKEL LINED SCREENS
143. NON-FERROUS ALLOY ROLLING
144. NON-FERROUS FORGING
145. NON-FERROUS FOUNDRY
146. NON PRESSURE
147. INCANDESCENT LAMP
148. NUMBER COMBINATION LOCKS FOR LUGGAGES
149. NUTS & BOLTS
150. PAPER COATED ALUMINIUM AND COPPER WIRE
151. PETROMAX CONTAINER
152. PHOTO ETCHING OF STAINLESS STEEL PLATES
153. PIPE GALVANIZING PLANT
154. PISTON RING-AUTOMOBILE
155. PLANT PROTECTION EQUIPMENTS
156. PLATINUM LABORATORY APPARATUS
157. PRESSURE COOKER & ALUMINIUM UTENSILS
158. PRESSURE COOKER (ALUMINIUM)
159. PRESSURE DIE CASTING
160. PRINTED ALUMINIUM COLLAPSIBLE TUBES
161. PRINTED TIN CONTAINERS
162. PRINTING PRESS (CYLINDER MACHINE)
163. PUMPS FOR CHEMICAL INDUSTRY (SPECIAL)
164. RAILWAY SLEEPERS (M.S.)
165. RAZOR TWIN BLADE
166. R.C.C SPUN PIPES
167. RECONDITIONING OF M.S. DRUMS/BARRELS
168. RE-ROLLING COPPER AND BRASS SHEET AND RODS
169. RE-ROLLING MILLS
170. RESIN COATED SAND
171. RESIN CORED SOFT SOLDER WIRES
172. ROLLING MILL (BY INDUCTION FURNACE) & MANUFACTURE OF BARS, ANGLES, SQUARES, TUBES AND OTHERS
173. ROLLER BEARING & FORGING
174. ROLLING OF STAINLESS STEEL PATTA
175. RUBBER INSULATED PLIERS (HAND TOOLS)
176. RUBBING COMPOUND FOR AUTOMOBILES
177. SCIENTIFIC LABORATORY EQUIPMENTS
178. SCOOTER ASSEMBLING
179. SECONDARY LEAD EXTRACTION BY SCRAP BATTERY PLATES, PIPES & SHEET
180. SEAMLESS M.S. TUBES & PIPES
181. SELF TAPPING STEEL SCREW
182. SEWING NEEDLES
183. S.G. IRON & ALLOY STEEL
184. SHEET METAL PRODUCTS, (FERROUS/NON-FERROUS)
185. SHIP/MARINE CONTAINER
186. SHOCK ABSORBERS
187. SHOE EYELETS
188. SHOT AND GRITS BY AUTOMIZATION PROCESS
189. SHOVELS
190. SILICO MANGANESE ALLOYS
191. SILENCERS (MUFFLERS) EXHAUST & TAIL PIPE FOR ALL TYPES OF VEHICLES
192. SINTERED BEARING
193. SINTERED BUSHES
194. SINTERED METAL PRODUCTS
195. SOFT AND HARD FERRITES
196. SPANNERS
197. SPARK PLUGS
198. STEEL PLANT (ELECTRIC ARC FURNACE BASED- EAF)
199. SPHERIODAL GRAPHITE CAST IRON
200. SPRAY DRYER
201. STAINLESS STEEL HINGES
202. STAINLESS STEEL SHEET ROLLING TO PRODUCE STAINLESS STEEL UTENSILS
203. STAINLESS STEEL UTENSILS
204. STAPLE PINS, PAPER PIN, GEM CLIPS ETC.
205. STEEL CASTINGS
206. STEEL CHAIN
207. STEEL FOUNDRY
208. STEEL FURNITURES AND ELECTRICAL APPLIANCES
209. STEEL PLANT (MINI)
210. STEEL RODS AND COILS FROM SCRAPS
211. STEEL ROLLING MILL
212. STEEL STRIPS (COLD ROLLED) SILICON WITH GRAIN RIENTED FOR ELECTRIC USE
213. STEEL TRANSMISSION LINE TOWERS & ROLLING MILL TO PRODUCE STEEL SECTION
214. STEEL FURNITURES AND ELECTRICAL APPLIANCES
215. STEEL WIRE DRAWING AND GALVANIZING
216. STEEL WOOL
217. SUBMERGED ARC WELDED PIPES
218. SUBMERSIBLE PUMP MANUFACTURING
219. SUPER ENAMELLED COPPER WIRE
220. THREE WHEELERS
221. TIE-ROD ENDS
222. TIN CONTAINERS
223. TOOLROOM AND SHEET METAL PRODUCTS
224. TRACTOR TRAILERS
225. TRANSMISSION POWER FITTING
226. TUBULAR POLES
227. SUPER ENAMELLED COPPER WIRES
228. TUBULAR POLES FOR ELECTRICAL TRANSMISSION (BY FABRICATION PROCESS)
229. TUBULAR POLES OF M.S. & HIGH TENSILE STEEL
230. VACUUM CLEANERS
231. VACUUM FLASK (STAINLESS STEEL)
232. VALVES FOR REFRIGERATION AND AIR-CONDITION
233. VEHICLE WELDING & PAINTING
234. VENETION BLIND
235. WASHING MACHINES (AUTOMATIC & COMPUTERISED)
236. WATER CONTROLLER (AUTOMATIC)
237. WATCH STRAPS/CHAINS/ BRACELETS/BELT BRASS & STAINLESS STEEL
238. WATER COOLERS
239. WELDED WIRE MESH
240. WELDING ELECTRODES
241. WICK STOVES
242. WIND MILL WINDOW FRAME (FERROUS & NON-FERROUS)
243. WRIST WATCH

359. DI ETHYL OXALATE
360. DI METHYL ORTHOPHTHALATE
361. DI-METHYL PHTHALATE
362. DICLOFENAC GEL
363. DIOCTYL PHTHALATE (DOP)
364. DI PHENYL GLYCERINE
365. DI PHENYL OXIDE
366. DINITRO-CHLORO BENZENE
367. DISTILLED WATER
368. DODECYL BENZENE SULPHONATE
369. DUSTLESS CHALK
370. EDTA & ITS SALTS
371. ELECTROLESS NICKEL PLATING ON PLASTICS
372. ENDOSULFAN
373. EPOXY RESIN BASED COMPOUND
374. ETHYL ACETATE
375. EHTYL ETHER
376. ETHYL ALCOHOL (POTABLE LIQUOR)
377. ETHYL HEXANOL
378. EXTRACTION OF ESSENTIAL OILS BY SUGAR CRITICAL FLUID (CARBON DIOXIDE) METHOD FROM FLOWERS, HERBAL & SPICES
379. FERRIC ALUM
380. FERRO CHROME LIGNO SULPHONATE
381. FERRO MANGANESE
382. FERRO SILICONE
383. FERRO VANADIUM FROM VANADIUM SLUDGE
384. FERROUS SILICATE
385. FERROUS SULPHATE
386. FERTILIZER FROM ANIMAL BLOOD & LEATHER WASTE
387. FLUORESCENT TUBE LIGHT POWDER
388. FOAMED PVC COMPOUNDING & ITS PRODUCTS
389. FORMALDEHYDE
390. FRACTIONAL DISTILLATION OF D.M.O (DEMENTHOLIZED OIL)
391. FRACTIONAL DISTILLATION OF ESSENTIAL OIL & MEDICINAL PLANT EXTRACT
392. FRICTION DUST (LIQUID & POWDER) FROM CNSL
393. FRUIT FLAVOURS
394. FURFURAL FROM RICE HUSK
395. GARLIC ACID
396. GASKET SHELLAC COMPOUND
397. GEAR OIL
398. GIBBERELLIC ACID
399. GLASS PUTTY
400. GLYCERINE
401. GOSSYPOL (POLY PHENOL) FROM COTTON SEED OIL
402. GUAR GUM POWDER
403. HAIR FIXER (HAIR GEL TYPE)
404. H - ACID
405. HENNA PASTE MAKING
406. HEPTAL DEHYDE
407. HIGH CARBON FERRO CHROME
408. HYDRATED CALCIUM SILICATE BRICK
409. HYDRATED LIME FROM SEA SHELL
410. HYDROCHLORIC ACID
411. HYDRO FLUORIC ACID
412. HYDROGEN PEROXIDE (BY AUTO-OXIDATION PROCESS)
413. ICE PACKS (SOLUTIONS TYPE, WHITE GEL TYPE, VIOLET SEMI SOLID POLYMER TYPE)
414. IMPROVING DROP POINT PARAFFIN WAX FROM 45-50^{0}C TO 75-80^{0}C
415. INDUSTRIAL ALCOHOL
416. INTEGERATED COMPLEX OF EASTER & ALLIED PRODUCTS (D.O.P, D.B.P, ETHYL ACETATE WIRE ENAMEL & CABLE JELLY)
417. IMFL (WHISKY) & COUNTRY LIQUOR
418. IRON OXIDE FOR MAKING FERITTE
419. IRON SULPHIDE
420. JUTE BATCHING OIL
421. KESH KALA TEL (HAIR DYE LOTION) (VASMOL 33, BLACK NITE TYPE)
422. L-LYSINE MONOHYDROCHLORIDE
423. LACTIC ACID FROM WHITE SUGAR BY FERMENTATION PROCESS
424. LDPE GRANULES FROM VIRGIN (LDPE RESIN)
425. LEAD EXTRACTION FROM BATTERY SCRAP
426. LEAD OXIDE (A) LEAD MONOXIDE
(B) LEAD TETRA OXIDE
(C) GREYLEAD OXIDE
427. LIQUID GLUCOSE & ITS BY PRODUCTS
428. LIQUID OXYGEN BOTTLING PLANT
429. LIQUID SHOE POLISH
430. LIQUID FLOOR POLISH
431. LUBE OIL VISCOSITY IMPROVED FOR P.P.G/P.E.G.
432. LUBRICANTS ASHLESS 100% COMBUSTION
433. MAGNESIUM CARBONATE AND MAGNESIUM BICARMONATE
434. MAGNESIUM HYDROXIDE POWDER
435. MAGNESIUM SILICATE
436. MAGNESIUM SULPHATE
437. MALACHITE GREEN
438. MALEIC ANHYDRIDE
439. MANGANESE SULPHATE
440. MANUFACTURING OF CARBON MONO-OXIDE WATER GAS
441. MENTHOL BOLD CRYSTALS FROM FLAKES
442. MENTHOL CRYSTAL & MENTHA OIL
443. MERCURIC OXIDE
444. METAL PRE-TREATMENT CHEMICALS
445. METHANE GAS BY SODIUM ACETATE & SODA LIME
446. METHYL ACETYL RICINOLATE
447. METOL
448. METOL FROM HYDROQUI-NONE & METHYLAMINE
449. MICANITE
450. MICRO NUTRIENT MIXTURE
451. MINERAL WATER
452. MINERAL WATER AND PET BOTTILNG PLANT
453. MINERAL WATER IN BOTTLES, GLASS AND POUCHES
454. MINI CEMENT PLANT (BY ROTARY KILN PROCESS)
455. MIXED FERTILIZER
456. MOSQUITO & FLIES REPELLENT AGARBATTI (INCENSE STICKS)
457. MONO CHLORO ACETIC ACID
458. MONOCROTOPHOS (TECHNICAL)
459. MOSQUITO COIL
460. MOSQUITO COIL & MAT
461. MOSQUITO MAT
462. MOTHER TINCTURE & BIO CHEMIC MEDICINES
463. NAPHTHALENE & PHENYL (INTEGRATED UNIT)
464. NATURAL MINERAL WATER BY REVERSE OSMOSIS PROCESS
465. NICKEL PLATING BRIGHTNER (PRIMARY OR CARRIER BRIGHTNER & SECONDARY BRIGHTNER)
466. NICKEL SULPHATE
467. NICOTINE FROM TOBACCO WASTE
468. NICOTINE SULPHATE FROM TOBACCO WASTE
469. NITRO BENZENE
470. NITRO CELLULOSE SANDING SEALER/LACQUER
471. NITRO MUSK
472. NITROGEN & OXYGEN GAS PLANT
473. NON-IONIC SURFACTANT (WETTING AGENT)
474. NO-CARB PASTE
475. OCTANOL
476. ORTHO NITRO PHENOL
477. OXALIC ACID FROM MOLASSES
478. OXALIC ACID FROMRICE HUSK
479. OXALIC ACID FROM TREE BARK
470. OXALIC ACID FROM WASTE VEGETABLES
471. OXYGEN GAS PLANT
472. OXYGEN GAS PLANT (AIR SEPERATION METHOD)
473. PARA-AMINO BENZOIC ACID
474. PARA-AMINO PHENOL
475. PARA TOLUENE SULPHONIC ACID
476. PECTIN FROM RAW PAPAYA
477. PERFUME (LEMON & OTHERS)

CRUDE NAPHTHA
570. TRIMETHYL AMMONIUM CHLORIDE
571. TRIPHENYL PHOSPHITE (T.P.P)
572. ULTRAMARINE BLUE (LIQUID)
573. UREA FORMALDEHYDE & MELAMINE FORMALDEHYDE POWDER
574. UNDECYLINIC ACID
575. VINYL ACETATE MONOMER
576. VITAMIN C
577. VITAMIN E
578. WASTE WATER TREATMENT PLANT FOR INDUSTRIAL SECTOR IN INDIA (ONLY MARKER SURVEY)
579. WIRE DRAWING LUBRICANT
580. WIRE ENAMEL
581. XANTHATES
582. YELLOW DEXTRIN
583. ZINC CHLORIDE
584. ZINC OXIDE
585. ZINC PHOSPHATING BY COLD PROCESS
586. ZINC SILICATE
587. ZINC STEARATE
588. ZINC SULPHATE
589. ZINC SULPHATE MONOHYDRATE
590. ACID BLACK
591. AURAMINE'O'
592. AZO DYES STUFF
593. DYE & DYE INTERMEDIATE
594. DYE INTERMEDIATES
595. MALACHITE GREEN
596. METHYLENE BLUE
597. PHTHALOCYANINE BLUE
598. PHTHALOCYANINE BLUE & GREEN
599. REACTIVE DYES
600. SULPHUR BLACK DYE
601. VAT DYES
602. WATER CHILLING PLANT
603. WADDING OIL (100%) FOR WADDING OF COTTON HOSIERY CLOTH IN THE DYEING PROCESS
604. WHITE OIL
605. WAX FLOOR POLISH

ELECTRICAL, ELECTONICS, COMPUTERS AND INFOTECH/IT PROJECTS

606. AIR CONDITIONING
607. ALUMINIUM ALLOY CONDUCTOR
608. ALUMINIUM CABLE
609. ALUMINIUM ELECTROYTIC CAPACITORS
610. AUDIO CASSETTE ASSEMBLING & RECORDING
611. AUDIO CASSETTES DUPLICATING RECORDING
612. AUDIO CASSETTES & AUDIO STUDIO
613. AUDIO CASSETTES PLANE & RECORDED
614. AUDIO MAGNETIC HEADS
615. AUDIO MAGNETIC TAPE
616. AUDIO/VIDEO CASSETTES
617. AUTO BULB/LAMPS
618. AUTOMATIC VOLTAGE STABILIZER
619. BATTERY PLATES
620. BACK OFFICE (Rs. 5000/-)
621. B/W TV & COMPUTER MONITOR PICTURE TUBE
622. BREAD BOARDS
623. CALL CENTRE
624. CAMERA (35 MM)
625. CAPACITORS
626. CARBON ELECTRODE USED FOR BATTERY CELL
627. CARBON POTETIOMETERS
628. CEILING FAN
629. CERAMIC INSULATOR
630. CHILDREN INFOTECH TRAINING INSTITUTE (Rs. 5000/-)
631. CHOKE AND PATTI
632. CHOKE AND STARTER
633. CHOKE USED FOR FLUORESCENT LAMPS
634. COLOUR TELEVISION
635. COLOUR AND BLACK & WHITE TELEVISION
636. COMPACT DISC
637. COMPACT DISC PLAYER (AUDIO/VIDEO)
638. COMPUTER EDUCATION INSTITUTE
639. COMPUTER ASSEMBLY
640. COMPUTER HARDWARE
641. COMPUTER KEYBOARD
642. COMPUTER PERIPHERALS
643. COMPUTER PRINTERS
644. COMPUTER RIBBON
645. COMPUTER RIBBON REINKING OR REFILLING
646. COMPUTER STATIONERY
647. COMPUTER STATIONERY &

IMPORTED HARDWARE PARTS
648. COMPUTER TERMINALS
649. COMPUTERISED WASHING MACHINE (AUTOMATIC)
650. COMPUTER SOFTWARE
651. CONDENSER FOR MOTOR USING MPP FILM
652. CONTENT DEVELOPMENT CENTRE (EOU) (Rs. 5000/-)
653. CONTROL PANEL BOARD
654. COOLING COIL FOR AIR CONDITIONERS
655. COPPER STRIP COIL FROM SCRAP
656. CORDLESS TELEPHONES
657. CYBER CAFE
658. CYBERKIOSK (Rs. 5000/-)
659. DATA PROCESSING CENTRE (Rs. 5000/-)
660. D.C. MICRO MOTORS
661. D.G.SETS
662. DISH ANTENNA AND CABLE T.V. NETWORK EQUIPMENT
663. DISTRIBUTION TRANSFORMERS & REPAIRS
664. DOMESTIC ELECTRICAL APPLIANCES- ROOM COOLER, WASHING MACHINE, WATER HEATER, ELECTRIC ROOM HEATER
665. E-SCHOOL
666. E-COMMERCE/BUSINESS
667. ELECTRIC ENERGY METER
668. ELECTRIC FANS
669. ELECTRIC HORN FOR AUTOMOBILE
670. ELECTRIC LAMP/GLS (INCANDESCENT LAMP)
671. ELECTRIC MIXER
672. ELECTRIC MOTORS UP TO 10 HP. REWINDING OF ALL TYPES OF MOTORS WATER PUMPS
673. ELECTRIC MOTOR WINDING (FOR FAN, MIXIES, ETC.)
674. ELECTRIC STEAM IRON
675. ELECTRICAL APPLIANCES
676. ELECTRICAL FIXTURES
677. ELECTRICAL STAMPING
678. ELECTROLYTIC CAPACITORS
679. ELECTROMAGNETIC RELAY
680. ELECTRONIC BALAST/CHOK
681. ELECTRICAL CHOKE
682. ELECTRONIC DIGITAL WATCHES
683. ELECTRONIC DIGITAL WEIGHING MACHINE
684. ELECTRONIC FIRE ALARM
685. ELECTRONIC GAS STOVE LIGHTERS
686. ELECTRONIC PRESSURE INDICATORS, ELECTRICALS, ELECTRONIC LIQUID LEVEL INDICATORS, ELECTRONIC TEMPERATURE INDICATOR, DIGITAL TACHOMETER
687. ELECTRONIC TELEPHONE INSTRUMENTS
688. ELECTRONIC TOYS
689. ELECTRONIC WATCHES & CLOCKS
690. FAX MACHINES
691. F.H.P MOTORS
692. FLOPPY DISKETTES
693. FLUORESCENT LAMP STARTER
694. FLUORESCENT TUBULAR

Above all the "Detailed Project Reports" are available at *"ENGINEERS INDIA RESEARCH INSTITUTE"*. 4449, Nai Sarak (D), Main Road Delhi - 110 006 (India) ● Ph : 91-11-23918117, 2391 6431, 2384 0361 ● Fax : 91-11- 2391 6431 ●E-Mail : eirisidi@bol.net.in ● WebSite : www.eiriindia.org

LAMPS WITH INTRODUCTION TO MERCURY VAPOUR LAMP
695. FRANCHISEE COMPUTER EDUCATION CENTRE (Rs. 5000)
696. GAS DETECTOR (L.P.G)
697. GENERATOR SET & PUMP SETS
698. GENERATOR (BATTERY OPERATED)
699. GIS SERVICE CENTRE (GEOGRAPHICAL INFORMATION SYSTEMS)
700. HARDWARE FITTING FOR TRANSMISSION LINE (OVERHEAD LINE MATERIAL
701. HEADERS FOR TRANSISTOR ICS SEMI CONDUCTOR
702. H.T & L.T INSULATORS
703. H.T & M.V INDUSTRIAL CUBICAL SWITCH BOARD
704. INFORMATION MOVING DISPLAY (L.E.D TYPE)
705. INSURANCE CLAIM PROCESSING CENTRE (EOU) (Rs. 5000/-)
706. INTEGRATED CIRCUITS
707. INTERNET BASED STOCK TRADING (Rs. 5000/-)
708. INTERNET SERVICE PROVIDER (I.S.P.)
709. JELLY FILLED TELEPHONE CABLES
710. LAP TOP COMPUTERS
711. LEAD ACID BATTERIES
712. LEAD ACID BATTERY PLATES AND ASSEMBLING OF BATTERY
713. LEGAL TRANSCRIPTION & SECRETARIAL SERVICES CENTER (EOU)(Rs. 5000/-)
714. LIGHT EMITTING DIODES (L.E.D)
715. LINEAR ICS TRAINER KIT
716. LOUD SPEAKER
717. L.T TRANSFORMER REPAIRING
718. MEDICAL TRANSCRIPTION CENTRE
719. METAL FILM RESISTORS
720. METALLISED POLYPROPYLENE, POLYESTER FILM CAPACITOR
721. MICA BASE ELECTRONIC COMPONENTS
722. MICA PAPER WASTE PAPER FROM MICA WASTE
723. MICRO PROCESSORS TRAINER KITS BASED ON MICRO PROCESSORS
724. MINI COMPUTER (PERSONAL COMPUTER)
725. MINIATURE CIRCUIT BREAKER (M.C.B)
726. MINIATURE WATCH BATTERIES (BUTTON CELL)
727. MIXER/GRINDER (MIXI)
728. MONO CHROME COMPUTER MONITOR
729. MOTOR START ELECTROLYTIC CAPACITOR
730. MULTI LAYER P.C.B
731. MULTIPLE RELAY FOR LOW VOLTAGE
732. NEON INDICATOR
733. NEON SIGN MANUFACTURE
734. OPTICAL FIBRE CABLES
735. ON LINE SHOPPING MALL (Rs. 5000/-)
736. OPTO MECHANICAL & ELECTRICAL EQUIPMENTS
737. PHOTO COLOUR LAB
738. PICTURE TUBE (B/W)
739. PLAIN PAPER COPIER
740. PLASTIC FILM CAPACITORS
741. POLYESTER CAPACITORS
742. PORTABLE GENERATOR SET
743. PORTAL
744. PORTABLE TELEVISION(TV)
745. POWER CAPACITORS
746. POWER INVERTERS
747. POWER PLANT
748. POWER TRANSFORMERS UP TO 600 KVA
749. PRINTED CIRCUIT BOARD
750. PVC WIRES & CABLES
751. RE-CONDITIONING OF PICTURE TUBE
752. RESIN CAST CT & PT (1 KV)
753. SEMI CONDUCTOR DEVICE
754. SEMI CONDUCTORS FOR TRANSISTORS & DIODES
755. SETTING UP OF A VIDEO STUDIO
756. SMOKE DETECTORS
757. SOLAR CELLS
758. SOLAR MODULES
759. SOLAR PHOTO VOLTAIC SYSTEM
760. SOLDER FLUXES
761. SOLAR WATER HEATING PANELS
762. STEEL FURNITURE & ELECTRICAL APPLIANCES
763. STEREO AMPLIFIERS
764. STEREO CASSETTE RECORDERS/PLAYERS
765. STREET LIGHT FITTINGS SURGE SUPPRESSOR
766. TANTALUM CAPACITORS
767. TEFLON COATED ELECTRIC CABLE
768. TELEMEDICINE (DISTANCE HEALTH CARE) (Rs. 5000/-)
769. TELEPHONE CORD/CABLE
770. TELEPHONE (PUSH BUTTON TYPE)
771. TELEPHONE (PUSH BUTTON & CORDLESS)
772. TELEVISION (CTV & B/W)
773. TELEVISION (3-D)
774. TELEVISION DEFLECTION COMPONENTS
775. TELEVISION SIGNAL BOOSTERS
776. TELEVISION TUNERS
777. TRACTION BATTERIES
778. TRAINING INSTITUTE OF MEDICAL TRANSCRIPTION
779. TRANSFORMER FOR B/W TV
780. TRANSFORMER FOR VOLTAGE STABILIZER & E.H.T
781. TRANSMISSION POWER LINE FITTING
782. TRANSMISSION TOWER FITTING
783. TV AUDIO EQUIPMENT CABINETS & THEIR ASSEMBLING UNIT
784. UN-INTERRUPTED POWER SUPPLY (U.P.S)
785. VARIABLE FREQUENCY
786. VARIABLE VOLTAGE A.C. DRIVE
787. VIDEO CASSETTES (COMPLETE MANUFACTURING & ASSEMBLING)
788. VIDEO CASSETTES RECORDER (V.C.R)
789. VIDEO FILM STUDIO
790. VOLTAGE REGULATOR FOR AUTOMOBILES
791. VOLTAGE STABILIZERS
792. VOLTAGE STABLIZER & T.V. GAIN BOOSTER
793. WAX AND CHEMICAL COATED, BRAIDED TINSEL WIRE
794. WEBSITE DESIGN & E-MAIL REGISTERING
795. WELDING ELECTRODES
796. WIND ENERGY POWER PROJECT (10 MW) WIRE WOUND POTENTIOMETERS

FOOD, AGRO FOOD, PROCESSED FOOD, AGRO PLANTATION , CULTIVATION, FARMING, DAIRY/MILK, TOBACCO/PAN MASALA, BREWERY & DISTILLERY, EDIBLE OILS, EOU FOOD PRODUCTS AND ALLIED PRODUCTS

797. ALCOHOLIC BEVERAGES & VENEGAR FROM COCONUT WATER
798. ALCOHOL DRINKS FROM ETHYL ALCOHOL BY MIXING OF VARIOUS FLAVOURS
799. ANTI SCALE COMPOUND FOR ADDING INTO SUGAR JUICE BOILING
800. APPLE JUICE CONCENTRATED & DEHYDRATED FRUIT & VEGETABLES
801. ARTIFICIAL FISH MEAL FOR POULTRY FEED
802. AUTOMATIC BISCUIT PLANT
803. BABY CEREAL FOOD AND MILK POWDER
804. BACTERIA FOR CANE JUICE
805. BAKER'S YEAST
806. BAKERY INDUSTRY
807. BANANA PUREE
808. BEER & WINE
809. BEER PLANT (BREWERY)
810. BIDI
811. BIDI & CIGARETTE
812. BISCUIT PLANT

813. BREAD (AUTOMATIC PLANT)
814. BLACK PEPPER (SPICES)
815. BREAD AND BISCUITS
816. BREEDING FARM
817. BROILER CHICKEN
819. BUTTON MUSHROOM CULTIVATION & PROCESSING
820. CANNING OF RASAGULLAS IN METAL CANS
821. CAFFEIN FROM TEA WASTE
822. CANNING OF FRUITS & VEGETABLES
823. CASEIN AND BY-PRODUCTS
824. CASHEW FRUIT JUICE FROM CASHEW FRUIT APPLE
825. CASHEWNUT KERNEL EXTRACTION FROM CASHEWNUT FRUIT
826. CASHEWNUT SHELL LIQUID & KERNEL PROCESSING
827. CASHEW FENI
828. CATECHEU (BY CHEMICAL PROCESS)
829. CATTLE FEED FROM TAPIOCA
830. CHEWING & BUBBLE GUM
831. CHICKEN/SHEEP MEAT PROCESSING
832. CHOCOLATE (MILK)
833. CIGARETTE AND BEEDIES
834. COCOA BUTTER FROM COCOA MASS
835. COCONUT PRODUCTS & BY PRODUCTS PROCESS COMPLEX
836. COLD/SOFT DRINKS
837. COLLECTION OF MILK AND MILK MAKING POWDER
838. COLLECTION OF MILK AND PACKING IN POLYTHENE POUCH (1/2 KG.1 KG. & 2 KG.)
839. CONDENSED MILK (SWEETNED)
840. CONFECTIONERY INDUSTRY (TOFFEE & CANDY, SEMI-AUTOMATIC PLANT)
841. COUNTRY LIQUOR FROM MOLASSES
842. CIGARETTE
843. DAIRY FARM AND DAIRY (MILK) PRODUCTS (PASTEURISED MILK, BUTTER, GHEE, PANEER)
844. DAIRY FARM TO PRODUCE MILK & PACKING IN POUCHES (50%) & CAN(50%)
845. DAIRY FOR MILK PROCESSING
846. DAIRY FARM (BUFALO)
847. DAL (PULSE) MILL UNIT
848. DEHYDRATION OF CARROT & GARLIC
849. DEHYDRATION & CANNING OF FRUITS & VEGETABLES
850. DEHYDRATION OF FIGS
851. DEHYDRATION OF FRUITS AND VEGETABLES
852. DEHYDRATED ONIONS AND ONION POWDER
853. DRY ICE BY BREAKING OF AIR
854. DRYING OF RED CHILLIES, HALDI, DHANIA, AND GREEN PEAS
855. EGG POWDER (40,000 EGGS PROCESSING PER DAY)
856. EXPORT OF PROCESSED FOODS AND MARINE PRODUCTS
857. FISH CANNING & POUCHING
859. FISH FARMING (PRAWN & OTHER MARINE PRODUCTS)
860. FISH MEAL
861. FLOUR MILL AND MUSTARD OIL
862. FOOD COLOUR & ORASTED GROUNDNUT GRAM PEAS, ETC IN POUCHES
863. FROG LEGS PROCESSING
864. FROZEN MEATS PROCESSING
865. FOOD FLAVOURS (WHISKY) VODKA, GRAPE, BUTTER SCOTCH)
866. FOOD PRODUCTS COMPLEX (DEHYDRATED ONIONS, GARLIC POWDER & FLAKES, CATTLE FEED, TOMATO POWDER, TOMATO PRODUCTS, CANNED FRUITS & VEGETABLES, TOMATO PURE, GROUN NUT OIL, REFIND OIL, DEHYDRATED GRAPES, BANANA POWDER & WAFFERS)
867. FRUIT JUICE, JAM, JELLIES & ALLIED PRODUCTS
868. FRUIT JUICE, PICKLES PROCESSING AND CANNING
869. FRUIT JUICE MAKING & PACKING IN PLASTIC CONTAINER/POUCHES
870. FRUIT PROCESSING (JAM & JELLIES)
871. FRUIT PULP & JUICE CONCENTRATES
872. FRUIT & VEGETABLE DRYING (FREEZE DRYING METHOD)
873. GOAT & SHEEP FARMING
874. GRAM DALL/PULSE MILL
875. GRAPE DEHYDRATION
876. HARD BOILED CANDY (TOFFEE & CANDY)
877. HERBAL CIGARETTES
878. HONEY PROCESSING & PACKAGING
879. ICE CREAM OF DIFFERENT FLAVOURS
880. ICE CREAM STABILIZER
881. ICE MAKING PLANT
882. INDIAN MADE FOREIGN LIQUOR (I.M.F.L)
883. INSTANT FOOD (IDLI MIX, DOSA MIX, GULAB JAMUN MIX)
884. INSTANT FOOD (INSTANT FOOD & FAST FOOD PARLOUR)
885. INSTANT NOODLES
886. INSTANT TEA
887. INSTANT TEA FROM BLACK TEA
888. INTEGERATED STARCH BAKING POWDER/YEAST INDUSTRY
889. IODIZED SALT
890. IODIZED SALT (ORDINARY MOISTURE-LESS/FREE FLOWING IN PLASTIC BAGS AND CONTAINERS)
891. JAM, JELLIES, FRUIT JUICE & ALLIED PRODUCTS
892. KATHA AND CUTCH
893. KHANDSARI SUGAR
894. KHANDSARI SUGAR & IMFL
895. LACTIC ACID FROM WHITE SUGAR BY FERMENTATION PROCESS
896. LACTOSE & BY PRODUCTS PROCESSING FROM MILK
897. LIQUID GLUCOSE AND ITS BYE PRODUCTS
898. MACRONI AND VERMICILLI
899. MALT EXTRACTION FROM BARLEY
900. MANGO PROCESSING (MANGO PULP, JUICE & SLICES)
901. MAYUR BRAND TYPE CHEWING TOBACCO
902. MINERAL WATER
903. MILK PRESERVATION & MARKETING TO WHOLE SELLERS (INPOUCH PACKING BY UHT TECHNOLOGY)
904. MILK PROCESSING AND PACKAGING OF MILK PRODUCTS
905. MILK PRODUCTS (CASEIN, LACTOSE, GHEE & WHEY POWDER)
906. MILK TOFFEE
907. MINI FLOUR MILL
908. MINI SUGAR PLANT
909. MISRI (PEARL SUGAR CANDIES)
910. MODERN RICE MILL
911. MURABBA
912. MUSTARD OIL EXTRACTION & REFINING
913. MUTTON TALLOW
914. NAMKEEN INDUSTRY (BHUJIA, CHANA CHUR ETC.)
915. NAMKEEN & SWEETS
916. NON-BASMATI RICE FROM PADDY
917. OLEORESIN, ESSENTIAL OIL, DYES & POWDER OF SPICES
918. OLEORESIN EXTRACTION FROM DIPTERO-CARPUT TURMINATUS AND PINUS KHASYANA
919. OLEORESIN EXTRACTION FROM CHILLI
920. PAN MASALA AND POUCH

1059. BUFFALO HORN TIP, HOOF
1060. BANQUET HALL
1061. BUTTON
1062. CALCINED PETROLEUM (C.P) COKE
1063. CANVAS SHOES
1064. CANVAS SHOES, JUNGLE BOOTS
1065. CARBON BRUSH, BRUSH HOLDER & SLIP RING
1066. CEMENT SHEETS WITH COIR FIBRE & OTHER SEGMENTS
1067. CERAMIC TILES (GLAZED) BY DOUBLE FIRING/HEATING
1068. CHILDREN RECREATION CENTRE
1069. COAL BRIQUETTES
1070. COLD STORAGE & ICE
1071. COLD STORAGE FOR FRUITS AND VEGETABLES
1072. COMPRESSOR (HERMETIC) FOR AIR CONDITIONER
1073. COSTUME JEWELLERY/ IMITATION JEWELLERY
1074. DECORATIVE LAMINATED SHEET (SUNMICA)
1075. DIAMOND CUTTING & EXPORTS
1076. DRINKING STRAW FROM PROPYLENE
1077. ENGINEERING COLLEGE
1078. ENTERTAINMENT CLUB
1079. FASHION TECHNOLOGY INSTITUTE
1080. FAST FOOD PARLOUR
1081. FAST FOOD (INSTANT FOOD & FAST FOOD PARLOUR)
1082. FIRE EXTINGUISHERS (SODA ACID TYPE)
1083. FISH NET
1084. FLORICULTURE (CUT FLOWER ROSE) WITH GREEN HOUSE
1085. FLOOR COVERING SHEET
1086. FILM STUDIO (VIDEO)
1087. FLUSH DOOR, CHIP BOARD, WOOD WOOL & OTHER INSULATING BOARDS
1088. GAS DETECTORS OF L.P.G
1089. GEMS MANUFACTURING
1090. GLASS BOTTLE BY SCRAP
1092. GOAT & SHEEP FARMING
1093. GOLD ELECTROPLATING
1094. GOLD JEWELLERY (E.O.U)
1095. GOLD PLATED SILVER JEWELLERY & CUTLERY
1096. GRANITE SLAB AND TILES
1097. GREEN HOUSE
1098. HARD CHROMIUM PLATING
1099. HEALTH CLUB AND BEAUTY PARLOUR CUM HAIR SALOON WITH SONA BATH
1100. HEALTH CLUB CUM BEAUTY PARLOUR TRAININGINSTITUTE
1101. HORN TIP,HOOVE BUTTON
1102. HOSPITAL
1103. HOSPITAL (100 BEDS)
1104. HOSPITAL (200 BEDS)
1105. ICE MAKING PLANT
1106. IMITATION AND COSTUME
1107. JEWELLERY (NECKLACE, EARRINGS EAR TOP ETC.)
1108. INITMATE SCENT CHEMICALS FROM ALL TYPES OF FLAVOUR
1109. INVESTMENT CASTING
1110. JUTE, COIR, GLASS ROPE/ SUTLI
1111. JUTE TWINE
1112. L.P.G BOTTLING PLANT
1113. L.P.G REGULATOR (DOMESTIC PURPOSE)
1114. LAMINATED PARTICLE BOARD & HARD BOARD
1115. LAMINATED SAFETY AND TOUGHENED GLASS
1116. LEASING & HIRE PURCHASE
1117. LICHEN (CHARILA)
1118. MANILA ROPES
1119. MEDICAL COLLEGE
1120. MATCH UNIT FROM WAXED PAPER
1121. MEDIUM DENSITY FIBRE BOARD
1122. MELAMINE CROCKERY
1123. MINERAL WATER
1124. MINI CEMENT PLANT
1125. MIRROR SILVER, GOLDEN, PINK, BLACK & SMOKES
1126. MODERN ADVERTISING AGENCY WITH DTP & FILM STUDIO
1127. MOTEL/SMALL HOTEL
1128. MULTI COLOUR PRINTING
1129. MULTI STOREY COMMERCIAL COMPLEX ALONGWITH RESIDENTIALAND DELUX FLATS FOR FOREIGN TOURISTS & REVOLVING RESTAURENT AT THE TOP
1130. MULTIPLE LAMINATION INDUSTRY
1131. MUSHROOM GROWING AND PROCESSING (BY DEEP FREEZING METHOD)
1132. NEWS PAPER PRINTING
1133. NICKEL LINED INDUSTRIAL SCREEN
1134. OFFSET COLOUR PRINTING PRESS (SIX COLOUR)
1135. OFFSET PRINTING PRESS
1136. P.C.C ELECTRIC POLES
1137. PHOTOGRAPHIC DEVELOPER & FIXER
1138. PVC EXTRUSION PROFILE (DOOR & WINDOWS)
1139. POP-CORN
1140. PHOTO ETCHING OF S.S.
1141. PRE STRESSED CEMENT CONCRETE PIPES
1142. PILFER PROOF CAPS
1143. PILFER PROOF CAPS AND CROWN CAP
1144. POUCH MAKING & GRAVURE PRINTING (ROTO PRINTING)
1145. POULTRY & FISH FARMING (INTEGERATED UNIT)
1146. PRINTING OF TIN SHEETS
1147. READYMADE GARMENTS
1148. RESTAURANT
1149. ROSE PLANTATION AND ROSE OIL EXTRACTION
1150. ROTOGRAVURE PRINTING
1151. SAFETY BELTS
1152. SAFETY MATCHES
1153. SHOE LACES
1154. SILK COCOON CULTIVATION (GROWING OF SILK COCOON WARM)
1155. SILK SCREEN PRINTING FORMULATIONS FOR PLASTIC, PAPER & CLOTH
1156. SPIKENARD (JATAMANSI)
1157. STENCIL COATING SOLUTION
1158. SUGAR CANDY (MISRI)
1159. SUGAR CANE PLANTATION
1160. SUGAR CANE JUICE PRESERVATION
1161. SURAT ZARI
1162. SYNTHETIC SHOES & SOLES
1163. TEA PACKAGING INDUSTRY
1164. TENNIS BALLS
1165. THREE STAR HOTEL
1166. TRAVELLING AGENCY
1167. TRAYS, TROLLEYS FOR HOSPITAL WITH SCRATCHLESS COATING
1168. WAX EXTRACTS (TANNING POWDER)
1169. WIRE ROPE SLINGS
1170. WOOD WOOL SLAB
1171. WOODEN CANE FURNITURE WITH EXPORT POTENTIAL
1172. WOODEN FURNITURE
1173. WOODEN PANEL INCLUDING KILN SEASONING
1174. WOODEN FURNITURE
1175. WATCH CASE BUFFING
1176. WATCH DIAL
1177. WRIST WATCHES
1178. WATCHES (ELECTRONIC)
1179. ZEDOARY (KACHUR)

EDIBLE OILS, ESSENTIAL OILS LURICATIING OILS, GREASES, VEGETABLE OILS, WAXES, CAMPHOR, PERFUMES & PERFUMERY COMPOUNDS AND REFINED OILS ETC.

1180. AROMATIC PERFUMERY COMPOUND
1181. AEROSOL
1182. AGARBATTI PERFUMERY COMPOUND
1183. BEES WAX MANUFACTURE
1184. CAMPHOR
1185. CARDANOL FROM CASHEW NUT SHELL LIQUID
1186. CASTOR OIL
1187. CASTOR OIL DERIVATIVE OLEORESINS
1188. CHILLI OIL
1189. CITRONELLA OILS
1190. CLOVE OIL
1191. CONCENTRATE OF ROSE JASMINE & LILY ETC.
1192. COLOURED FLAME CANDLE

1193. CANDLES (SEMI-AUTOMATIC)
1194. CORN OIL (MAIZE OIL)
1195. DEHYDRATED CASTOR OIL
1196. EUGENOL FROM CINNAMON LEAF OIL
1197. EXTRACTION OF ESSENTIAL OIL (CARDAMON, JEERA, AJOWAN, GINGER OILS ETC. & PACKAGING OF GROUND SPICES)
1198. EXTRACTION OF JASMINE ESSENCE
1199. EXTRACTION OF ESSENTIAL OILS BY SUPER CRITICAL FLUID METHOD FROM FLOWERS, HERBS & SPICES
1200. EUCALYPTUS OIL
1201. EXTRACTION OF OIL FROM OIL SEED EXPANDEREXTRUSION TECHNOLOGY)
1202. FAT LIQUOR SULPHATED OIL
1203. FLAVOURS FOR FOOD
1204. GARLIC OIL & POWDER
1205. GINGER OIL, SANDALWOOD OIL AND NAGARMOTHA OIL
1206. GINGER OIL
1207. GINGER OIL & GINGER DUST
1208. INTEGERATED WAX COMPLEX
1209. IONONE FROM LEMON GRASS OIL
1210. JASMINE & LILLY FLOWER OIL
1211. LEMON GRASS OIL
1212. LIQUID PARAFFIN
1213. LUBE OIL & GREASE
1214. LUBRICATING OIL
1215. MENTHOL CRYSTALS
1216. MENTHOL OIL & CRYSTAL
1217. MICRO CRYSTALLINE WAX
1218. MUSTARD OIL (EDIBLE OIL)
1219. OIL FROM ARTEMISIA HERBS
1220. PALM OIL CRUSHING UNIT
1221. PAN MASALA
1222. PARAFFIN WAX
1223. PARAFFIN WAX FROM SLACK WAX
1224. REFINED OIL-SUN FLOWER OIL, GROUNDNUT OIL, STAFF FLOWER OIL & COTTON SEED OIL
1225. REFINED VEGETABLE OIL
1226. RECLAMATION OF USED ENGINE OIL
1227. RICE BRAN OIL (R.B.O)
1228. ROSE OIL EXTRACTION
1229. SMOKE LESS CANDLE
1230. SPICE OIL & OLEORESINS
1231. SOLVENT EXTRACTION PLANT (OIL CAKE BASED)
1232. SYNTHETIC ALMOND OIL
1233. SYNTHETIC TALLOW
1234. SYNTHETIC GHEE
1235. VEGETABLE OIL EXTRACTION & REFINING
1236. WADDING OIL (100%) FOR WADDING OF COTTON HOSIERY CLOTH IN DYEING PROCESS
1237 WAX EMULSION FOR TEXTILE
1238. WAX FLOOR POLISH

PAINT, ENAMEL, SOLVENTS, THINNERS, INKS & VARNISH

1239. ACRYLIC EMULSION PAINTS
1240. ALUMINIUM PAINT
1241 AUTOMOBILE PAINTS
1242. BALL POINT PEN REFILL INK
1243. BITUMINIOUS ROAD EMULSION
1244. BITUMEN
1245. BITUMINIOUS FELTS FOR WATER & DAMP PROOFING
1246. BITUMINIOUS ROAD EMULSION RAPID MEDIUM & SLOW SETTING
1247. BUFFING & POLISHING
1248. CEMENT PAINT FOR WHITE & GREY CEMENT

1249. DISPERSANT
1250. DRY DISTEMPER
1251. DRY DISTEMPER & CEMENT PAINT
1252. DUPLICATING INK BLACK FOR GESTNER DUPLICATOR
1255. EMULSION PAINTS (WATER BASED)
1256. HAMMERTONE PAINT
1257. INSULATING VARNISH & WIRE ENAMEL
1258 IRON OXIDE PIGMENTS
1259. INSULATING VARNISH (POLY VINYL BUTYRAL BASED, FFC GRADE)
1260. LIME COLOUR (CEMENT COLOUR)
1261. SYNTHETIC RED OXIDE FOR FLOORINGS
1262. SOLVENT & THINNERS
1263. MARKING INKS (WATER PROOF)
1264. METAL NAPHTHANATE (AS DRIER FOR PAINTS)
1265. N.C.PUTTY
1266. OFFSET PRINTING INK
1267. OIL BOUND DISTEMPER PAINT
1268. PAINT BRUSHES
1269. PAINT REMOVERS
1270. PAINT INDUSTRY
1271. PAINT & VARNISH
1272. PICTURE VARNISH
1273. POWDER COATING PAINT
1274. PRINTING INKS (OFFSET, FLEXO & ROTO GRAVURE)
1275. PRIMER PAINT & ENAMEL PAINT
1276. PUTTY & WATER PROOFING PAINT
1277. PRINTING INKS (FLEXO-GRAPHIC INK)
1278. PUTTY (METAL CASEMENT)
1279. RED OXIDE PRIMER (ANTI CORROSIVE)
1280. REFRECTORY PAINT (GRAPHITE BASED)
1281. SCREEN PRINTING INKS
1282. SILK SCREEN PRINTING INK FORMULATION FOR PLASTIC, PAPER, CLOTH
1283. STAMP & PAD INK
1284. STOVING PAINT
1285. SPIRIT SOLUBLE MALEIC RESIN
1286. TEXTURE PAINT
1287. THINNERS AND ITS ALLIED PRODUCTS
1288. TONER INK
1289. VARNISH THINNER (SOLVENT)
1290. VACUUM METALLIZING LACQUERS
1291. WOOD PRIMER

PHARMACEUTICAL, DRUGS, AYURVEDIC/HERBAL COSMETICS & MEDICINES, HOMOEOPATHIC MEDICINES, DISPOSABLE SYRINGE, DENTAL COLLEGE & FINE CHEMICALS ETC.

1292. AROMATIC PILLS
1293. ASPIRIN
1294. AYURVEDIC PAIN BALM OINTMENTS
1295. AYURVEDIC CHURAN AND TABLETS
1296. AYURVEDIC TABLETS (HAJMOLA TYPE)
1297. AYURVEDIC/HERBAL PHARMACY
1298. AYURVEDIC SHERBATS
1299. AYURVEDIC PRODUCTS
1300. BULK DRUGS (E.O.U)
1301. BLOOD BAGS
1302. CALCIUM GLUCONATE
1303. CAPSULE, TABLET & INJECTION WITH MODERN INSTRUMENTS
1304. CASHEW FENI
1305. CHLOROQUINONE PHOSPHATE (BULK DRUGS)
1306. CLINICAL THERMOMETER
1307. DENTAL CLINIC

Above all the "Detailed Project Reports" are available at *"ENGINEERS INDIA RESEARCH INSTITUTE"*. 4449, Nai Sarak (D), Main Road Delhi - 110 006 (India) ● Ph : 91-11-23918117, 2391 6431, 2384 0361 ● Fax : 91-11- 2391 6431 ●E-Mail : eirisidi@bol.net.in ● WebSite : www.eiriindia.org

1308. DENTAL COLLEGE
1309. DENTAL GRADE EUGENOL
1310. DEXTROSE MONOHYDRATE, LIQUID GLUCOSE
1311. DEHYDRATED ONION & ONION POWDER
1312. DEXTROSE POWDER (ANHYDROUS FROM STARCH)
1314. DEXTROSE SALINE SOLUTION
1315. DISTILLERY (I.M.F.L)
1316. DISPOSABLE NEEDLES FOR SYRINGES
1317. DISPRIN
1318. DISTILLED WATER
1319. EMPTY HARD GELATINE CAPSULES
1320. FILLING & PACKING OF CAPSULES
1321. GLUCOSE - D - POWDER
1322. GLYCERINE
1323. HERBAL COSMETICS
1324. HERBAL SHAMPOO
1325. HERBAL HAIR OILS (AYURVEDIC)
1326. HOMOE & BIO-MEDICINES WITH MOTHER TINCTURE
1327. HOMOEPATHIC MEDICINES
1328. HYPODERMIC NEEDLES
1329. I.V. FLUIDS
1330. IBUPROFEN
1331. INFUSION & TRANSFUSION SETS (I.V. SET)
1332. INJECTABLE FOR PHARMACEUTICALS
1333. INJECTION AMPOULES PACKAGING BOX
1334. INTEGERATED SURGICAL COTTON
1335. ICE MAKING PLANT
1336. ICE & COLD STORAGE
1337. LACTOSE & BY PRODUCTS PROCESSING FROM MILK
1338. LICHEN (JATAMANSI CHARILA)
1339. LIQUID GLUCOSE AND ITS BY-PRODUCTS
1340. L-LYSINE MONOHYDRO CHLORIDE
1341. LIQUID GLUCOSE FROM POTATOES
1342. MEDICAL COLLEGE
1343. NICOTINE FROM TOBACCO WASTE
1344. OINTMENT-AYURVEDIC (YELLOW & WHITE)
1345. PHARMACEUTICAL AND FOOD GRADE GELATINE
1346. PHARMACEUTICAL INDUSTRY (TABLETS, CAPSULES, LIQUID, GEL, OINTMENT POWDER INJECTABLE)
1347. PHARMACEUTICAL UNIT (EOU) WITH FORMULA TIONS, INJECTABLES, ETC. PYRIDINE & DERIVATIVES
1348. SALT (IODIZED SALT)
1349. SALINE & INJECTION WATER
1350. SALINE WATER & DEXTRCSE SOLUTION (I.V.FLUID IN PLASTIC BOTTLES)
1351. SORBITOL
1352. STARCH (MAIZE)
1353. SURGICAL ADHESIVE PLASTER
1354. SURGICAL BANDAGES
1355. SURGICAL GLOVES
1357. SURGICAL COTTON
1358. SURGICAL COTTON AND BANDAGE
1359. SYNTHETIC CAMPHOR POWDER
1360. TABLETS & CAPSULES
1361. TISSUE CULTURE
1362. TINCTURE FROM RECTIFIED SPIRIT
1363. TRIMETHOPIME
1364. VETERENARY MEDICINES (ONLY FORMULATIONS)
1365. VITAMIN 'C', SORBITOL' ANHYDROUS DEXTROSE, STARCH

PULP, PAPER, STRAW/GREY BOARD, KRAFT PAPER, PACKAGING, PAPER CARRY BAGE, PAPER FROM AGRO WASTE & STATIONERY ETC.

1366. AMMONIA PAPER
1367. AUTOMATIC BOOK BINDING
1368. ADHESIVE (FEVICOL TYPE)
1369. ALL PIN & GEM CLIPS
1370. CARBON PAPER
1371. CARD BOARD
1372. CARBON LESS PAPER
1373. CELLPHANE PAPER
1374. COMPUTER FORMS & SECURITY PRINTING PRESS
1375. CORRUGATED BOARD & BOX (PRINTED & LAMINATED)
1376. CORRUGATED BOARD AND BOXES FROM FROM CARD BOARDS
1377. CORRUGATED CARTONS FROM PLAIN PAPERS
1378. CORRUGATRED PACKING & MATERIAL (BULB & TUBES PACKING)
1379. DESK TOP PUBLISHING
1380. DEFOAMING AGENT FOR PAPER PLANT
1381. DRINKING STRAW PAPER
1382. D.T.P CUM OFFSET PRESS
1383. EGG TRAYS
1384. EXERCISE NOTE BOOK, REGISTER AND PAD
1385. FLEXOGRAPHIC INK
1386. GREETING CARD BY OFFSET PRESS
1387. HAND MADE PAPER FILTER PAPER
1388. HARD BOARD
1389. INJECTION AMPOULES PACKAGING BOXES
1390. INSULATIING PAPER
1391. KRAFT PAPER
1392. KRAFT PAPER FROM BAGASSE
1393. LAMINATED PACKAGING PAPER WITH PRINTING
1394. LAMINATION & COATING ON PAPER
1395. M.G. PAPER FROM WASTE PAPER
1396. MILL PAPER FROM WASTE PAPER
1397. MILL BOARD FROM RICE & WHEAT STRAWS
1398. MILL BOARD FROM WASTE PAPER
1399. MINI PAPER PLANT FROM SISAL
1400. MINI PAPER PLANT
1401. MULTI WALL PAPER SACKS
1402. NEWS PAPER FOR CHILDREN
1403. NEWS PRINT PAPER FROM RICE STRAW BAGASSE
1404. NEWS PAPER CHILDRENS
1405. NEWS PRINT PAPER
1406. OFFSET AND TREADLE TYPE PRINTING PRESS
1407. MILL BOARD BASED ON RICE STRAW
1408. PAPER AND BOARD FROM STRAW
1409. PAPER & PAPER PRODUCTS
1410. PAPER ENVELOPES
1411. PAPER CARRY BAGS
1412. PAPER BOARD CARTON
1413. PAPER CONES FOR LOUD SPEAKERS
1414. PAPER FROM AKRA
1415. PAPER FROM BAGASSE WITH CORRUGATED BOARD & BOXES
1416. PAPER FROM BAMBOO
1417. PAPER GLASSES FOR BEVERAGES
1418. PAPER FROM RICE HUSK & WHEAT HUSK
1419. PAPER FROM TREE BARK, EUCALYPRUS WOOD
1420. PAPER PRODUCTS
1421. PAPER PLANT (WHITE WRITING & NEWS PAPER FOR PULP & WASTE PAPER)
1422. PAPER PLATES, PAPER GLASS
1423. PAPER CONES & TUBES
1425. PAPER PLANT WITH DTP & PRINTING & PUBLISHING UNIT
1426. PAPER BASED PHENOLIC SHEET
1427. PAPER CUP FOR ICE CREAM
1428. PAPER TUBES SPIRAL WINDING COMPOSIT CONTAINER
1429. PAPER LABLE FOR BEER BOTTLES
1430. PARTICLE BOARD & BLACK BOARD WITH SANDING & LAMINATION OF PARTICLE BOARD
1431. PARTICLE BOARD FROM RICE HUSK
1432. POUCH FILLING & MAKING FOR TOMATO SAUCE
1433. POUCH MAKING &

GRAVURE PRINTING
1434. PROCESSING OF PAPER FOR FEEDING IN COMPUTER
1435. PULP FROM BAMBOO & WOOD
1436. PAPER FILES
1437. PLAYING CARDS
1438. ROSIN SIZING AGENT (FOR PAPER PLANT)
1439. SAND PAPER
1440. SANITRY NAPKINS
1441. SILICON COATED PAPER
1442. STENCIL PAPER
1443. STRAW BOARD AND GREY BOARD
1444. STRAW BOARD & MILL BOARD
1445. STRAW BOARD AND PAPER BOARD
1446. TISSUE PAPER FACIAL
1447. TISSUE MOIST TOILETERY CLEANSING TISSUE AND RELATED PRODUCTS
1448. TISSUE PAPER ROLLS
1449. TETRA PACK FOR MILK PACKAGING, GHEE & OTHER LIQUIDS
1450. TOILET PAPER ROLLS
1451. TOILET PAPER & NAPKINS
1452. WAX COATED PRINTED PAPER
1453. WET FACE FRESHNER TISSUE
1454. WHITE WRITING & PRINTING PAPER
1455. WRITING & PRINTING PAPER (PAPER MILLS)

PLASTIC, B.O.P.P, ACRYLIC, DISPOSABLE PLASTIC PRODUCTS, PET PRODUCTS, P.V.C, H.D.P.E, P.P, L.D.P.E., P.U, A.B.S, THERMOFOARMING, MASTER BATCHES, & POLYMER AND RUBBER PRODUCTS, TYRE, TUBE, ADHESIVE, SHEET, COIR & MANY OTHERS

1456. ABS GRANULES FROM ABS SCRAPS FROM OLD T.V. CABINETS, WHITE GOODS ETC.
1457. ACRYLIC BEADS
1458. ACRYLIC COPOLYMER EMULSION
1459. ACRYLIC LATEX
1460. ACRYLIC SHEET
1461. ACRYLIC SHEET & MOULDED PRODUCTS
1462. ACRYLIC TEETH
1463. AUTO TUBES
1464. AUTO FLAPS FOR TRUCKS & BUSES
1465. AUTO TYRES & TUBES
1466. BABY BOTTLES (PLASTIC) WITH WHITESILICON RUBBER NIPPLES
1467. B.O.P.P. FILM
1468. B.O.P.P. PRESSURE SENSITIVE SELF ADHESIVE TAPE
1469. BABY NIPPLE (SILICON)
1470. BABY NIPPLE (BIG SIZE)
1471. BALLOON PLASTIC ADVERTISING
1472. BLISTER FILM PVC
1473. BLISTER PACKAGING & POUCH PAKAGING
1474. BLOW MOULDING PLASTIC CONTAINER
1475. COATING ON METALIZED POLYESTER FILM/METALISED PAPER/ ALIMINIUM FOIL
1476. COATING ON PLASTIC (ELECTROLYSIS) & GLASS
1477. COIR FOAM (RUBBERISED)
1478. COLOUR COATING ON PLASTICS
1479. COLOUR MASTER BATCHES FOR VARIOUS PLASTICS
1480. CYCLE TYRES AND TUBES
1481. DISPOSABLE PLASTIC CUPS GLASSES, ETC.
1482. DISPOSABLE PLASTIC SYRINGES & NEEDLES
1483. DISPOSABLE PLASTIC SYRINGES
1484. DOUGH MOULDING COMPOUND (D.M.C)
1485. EPOXY RESIN
1486. EXPANDED POLYESTRENE MOULDING (THERMOCOLE)
1487. F.R.P AUTO,SCOOTER ROOFS & CEILINGS
1488. F.R.P PRODUCTS (HELMET, WASHBASIN SHEETS, ROOFING SHEETS)
1489. FIBRE REINFORCED PLASTIC (HIGH PRESSURE MOULDING WITH SMC BMC AND DMC)
1490. FIELD RUBBER CONVERTED TO THE 60% LATEX RUBBER
1491. FLEXIBLE P.U. FOAM
1492. FORMALDEHYDE CROCKERY & OTHER ITEMS
1493. FORMALDEHYDE RESIN (UREA, PHENOL,MELEMINE)
1494. GASKET SHEET
1495. GUM BOTTLE (PVC)
1496. GLASS BEADS
1497. HDPE COATED PAPER SACK
1498. H.D.P.E. BAGS
1499. H.D.P.E. CONTAINERS (BLOW MOULDING)
1500. H.D.P.E. CONTAINER, POLY JARS BY INJECTION MOULDING (FOOD GRADE)
1501. H.D.P.E. JERRY CANS
1502. HDPE MANUFACTURING FROM ETHYLALCOHOL
1503. H.D.P.E PIPE AND FITTINGS
1504. H.D.P.E. PIPES
1505. H.D.P.E PRINTED BAGS
1506. H.D.P.E TWINES AND ROPES
1507. H.D.P.E. & L.D.P.E PIPES AND FITTINGS
1508. H.D.P.E/PP BOX STRAPPING
1509. H.D.P.E/PP WOVEN SACKS USING PLAIN LOOMS
1510. HOLOGRAM STICKERS-3D
1511. H.M BAG PLANT WITH PRINTING UNIT
1512. HAWAI CHAPPALS (RUBBER)
1513. I.V PLASTIC BOTTLE
1514. ICE CREAM CUP (PLASTIC)
1515. INJECTION MOULDED AUTO COMPONENTS
1516. INJECTION & BLOW MOULDED PLASTIC PRODUCTS
1517. INJECTION MOULDED PLASTIC PRODUCTS
1518. INTEGERATED COMPLEX ESTER'S & ALLIED PRODUCTS (D.O.P,D.B.P, & ETHYL ACETATE, BUYTL ACETATE, WIRE ENAMELS, JELLY CABLE COMPOUND)
1519. L.D.P.E. (LOW DENSITY POLY ETHYLENE) GRANULES FROM VIRGIN (L.D.P.E. RESIN)
1520. INTEGERATED SURGICAL RUBBER GOODS INDUSTRY
1521. INJECTION MOULDED PLASTIC BALLS
1522. L.D.P.E FROM ETHYL ALCOHOL
1523. LDPE MOULDED PRODUCTS
1524. LAMINATION OF COEXTRUSION MULTILAYER FILM IN ROLL FORM
1525. LATEX RUBBER
1526. LATEX RUBBER CONDOM
1527. MASTER BATCHES (COLOURED, P.V.C, L.D.P.E, H.D.P.E, ETC.)
1528. MELAMINE FORMALHYDE RESIN
1529. MOULDED LUGGAGE
1530. MULTI-LAYER (3 LAYER BAGS)
1531. MULTI-LAYER (3 LAYER) FILM WITH LAMINATION & PRINTING
1532. OIL SEAL
1533. PET BOTTLE/CONTAINERS
1534. PET BOTTLES FROM PRE FORM
1535. PET BOTTLE & MINERAL WATER
1536. PET PRE-FORM FROM PET RESIN
1537. PET PRE-FORM CUM PET BOTTLES
1538. PET PRE-FORM PET BOTTLES CUM MINERAL WATERS
1539. POLY CARBONATE RESIN
1540. PTFE COMPONENTS
1541. PU/PVC SOLE FOR SPORT SHOE BY IMPORTED M/C.
1542. PVC BATTERY SEPARATOR
1543. P.V.C COMPOUNDS (FRESH)
1544. P.V.C COMPOUNDS (SCRAP)
1545. P.V.C ELECTRICAL INSULATING TAPE
1546. P.V.C. EXTRUSION PROFILES
1547. P.V.C FITTINGS
1548. P.V.C FLEXIBLE FUSIBLE POWDER HEAT FUSIBLE POWDER
1549. P.V.C GRANULES (FOR

INSULATION & SHEETS GRADES)

1550. P.V.C GRANULES FROM PVC SCRAPS (WITH POLLUTION CONTROL)
1551. P.V.C HOSES
1552. P.V.C LEATHER CLOTH
1553. P.V.C FLEXIBLE PIPES
1554. P.V.C PIPES AND FITTINGS
1555. POLYTHENE BAGS (PRINTED)
1556. PVC PLASTICS FILM SHEET SOFT/RIGID
1557. PVC RESIN AND COMPOUND
1558. PVC RULAR
1559. PVC STABLIZERS (SINGLE PACK SYSTEM)
1560. PVC WIRE AND CABLES
1561. PAPER BASED PHENOLIC SHEET FOR ELECTRICAL
1562. PHENOL FORMALDEHYDE RESIN
1563. PHENOLIC RESIN
1564. PLASTIC BEADS FROM PLASTIC SCRAPS
1565. PLASTIC BUTTONS
1566. PLASTIC CANS
1567. PLASTIC COLLAPSIBLE TUBE
1568. PLASTIC CORRUGATED SHEET & BOXES
1569. PLASTIC FILM AND SHEETS WITH PRINTING FLEXO & ROTO/LDPE/HDPE/PP/HM/PVC
1570. PLASTIC FILTER MASTER BATCH & OTHER MASTER BATCHES FOR VARIOUS PLASTICS
1571. PLASTIC JERRY CANS
1572. PLASTIC GRANULES OR POWDER FROM PLASTIC SCRAP
1573. PLASTIC INJECTION MOULDED T.V. CABINETS
1574. PLASTIC ITEMS MANUFAC TURE FROM POWDER MELAMINE
1575. PLASTIC GOODS
1576. PLASTIC PIPES & TARPAULINES
1577. PLASTIC SHEET FROM SCRAP
1578. PLASTIC PLANT (BLOW MOULDING & INJECTION MOULDING)
1579. PLASTIC PRODUCTS (GOLD, SILVER, NICKEL)
1580. PLASTIC TOYS
1581. POLYESTER BEADING
1582. POLYESTER FILM
1583. POLYTHENE BAGS & AUTOMATIC PRINTING
1584. POLYTHENE PRINTED BAGS
1585. POLYURETHANE FOAM AND ITS PRODUCTS
1586. PROPYLENE FILM (PRINTED) & BAG MANUFACTURING
1587. PLASTIC MATS
1588. RAINBOW COLOUR ON PVC FILM & SHEET
1589. RED MUD PVC PIPES AND FITTINGS
1590. RE-RUBBERISED OF SOLID TYPE
1591. RESIN COATED SAND REXINE
1592. REXINE CLOTH & ALLIED PRODUCTS
1593. RUBBER ADHESIVE
1594. RUBBER AUTO PARTS
1595. RUBBER BELTING
1596. RUBBER MOULDING UNIT INCLUDING LINING RUBBER SHEETING
1597. RUBBER RECLAIMING
1598. RUBBER ROLLERS FOR TEXTILE MILLS & PAPER INDUSTRIES
1599. RUBBER & PLASTIC SHEETS, MATS & FLAPS
1600. RUBBER SHEET AND ALLIED HOSPITAL RUBBER GOODS
1601. RUBBERIZED PVC GASKET
1602. RUBBERISED COIR
1603. RUBBER COMPOUND FOR AUTOMOBILES
1604. SAFETY BELTS
1605. SILVER AND GOLD PLATING ON PVC AND NYLON-6
1606. SILICONE RUBBER NIPPLES/ TEATS
1607. SPECTACLE FRAMES (PLASTIC)
1608. SPUNGE RUBBER
1609. SURGICAL EXAMINATION GLOVES
1610. SYNTHETIC PEARL COATING ON POLYSTYRENE BEADS
1611. SYNTHETIC RUBBER ADHESIVE
1612. TEFLON MANUFACTURING
1613. TEFLON TAPE
1614. TEFLON TAPES & CABLES
1615. THERMOCOLE SHEET AND MOULDED PRODUCTS EXPANDED POLYESTERENE EXTRUSION PROFILES
1616. THERMOFORMED PACKAGING (BLISTER PACKAGING & POUCH PACKAGING)
1617. THERMOPLASTIC POLYURETHANE
1618. THERMOFORMED CUPS, PLATES & GLASS WITH HIPS SHEET
1619. THERMOCOLE
1620. THERMOCOLE BASED DISPOSABLE GLASS, CUPS & PLATES
1621. TOOTH BRUSHES
1622. TOY BALLOON, DECORA TIVE & INDUSTRIAL BALLOONS
1623. TREAD RUBBER
1624. TYRE RETREADING (HOT)
1625. TYRE RETREADING BY COLD PROCESS
1626. TYRE TUBES & FLAPS
1627. TYRE & TUBES
1628. UNSATURATED POLYESTER FOR REXINE
1629. V-BELT AND FAN BELT
1630. VINYL ASBESTOS AND PVC WALL PAPER
1631. VITON (FLUORO ELASTOMER)

SOAP, COSMETICS & PERFUMS

1632. ACID SLURRY, SYNTHETIC DETERGENT POWDER
1632. ACID SLURRY
1633. AGARBATTI SYNTHETIC, PERFUMERY COMPOUND
1634. AFTER SHAVE LOTION
1635. ANTISEPTIC CREAM
1636. BETA IONONE
1637. BLEACHING POWDER
1638. BLUE DETERGENT POWDER
1639. CLEANING POWDER (VIMTYPE)
1640. COLD CREAM
1641. COLOURED FLAME & PERFUMED CANDLES (RED, BLUE, GREEN FLAME)
1642. COSMETIC INDUSTRY (MODERN)
1643. COSMETIC INDUSTRY (SHAMPOO, SPRAY PERFUME, TALCUM POWDER
1644. DETERGENT POWDER (ARIEL TYPE)
1645. DETERGENT POWDER (NIRMA TYPE) FULLY AUTOMATIC PLANT
1646. DETERGENT WASHING POWDER
1647. FISH OIL SOAP
1648. GLYCERINE TRANSPARENT SOAP
1649. HAIR REMOVING CREAM
1650. HERBAL COSMETICS
1651. HERBAL SHAMPO & CREAM
1652. HERBAL/AYURVEDIC COSMETICS
1653. INCENSE POWDER, INCENSE STICKS & INCENSE CAKE
1654. OPTICAL WHITENERS
1655. ROSE OIL EXTRACTION
1656. SHAMPOOS (COCONUT OIL BASED COLD PROCESS)
1657. SHAVING CREAM
1658. SINDUR (KUMKUM)
1659. SOAP COATED PAPER
1660. SPRAY DRIED DETERGENT POWDER
1661. STAIN REMOVER
1662. TALCUM POWDER (FACE & TOILET POWDER)
1663. TOILET AND HERBAL SOAP
1664. TOOTH PASTE & POWDER
1665. WASHING DETERGENT POWDER AND WASHING SOAP
1666. WASHING POWDER LIQUID DETERGENTS, LOTION & SHAMPOO

Above all the Detailed Project Reports are available at *"ENGINEERS INDIA RESEARCH INSTITUTE"*. 4449, Nai Sarak (D), Main Road Delhi - 110 006
●Ph : 91-11-23918117, 2391 6431, 23840361, 31082370 ●Fax : 91-11-2391 6431
●E-Mail : eirisidi@bol.net.in

TEXTILE INDUSTRIES, READYMADE GARMENTS, COTTON, DYEING, BLEACHING, CLOTH, HOSIERY, POWER LOOM, HAND LOOM, WOOLLEN, SILK, SOCKS, SURGICAL COTTON & MANY OTHERS

1667. ANGORA RABBIT WOOL
1668. BUCKRAM
1669. CANVAS SHOES, JUNGLE BOOT, BOOT RUBBER KNEES & BOOT COMBAT
1670. CARPET FROM COTTON WASTE
1671. CERAMIC THREAD GUIDE
1672. COTTON BUDS/SWABS
1673. COTTON FROM WASTE YARN
1674. COTTON ROLLS
1675. COTTON SPIDERS FOR LOUD SPEAKERS
1676. DENIM CLOTH
1677. DENIM CLOTH (INTEGERATED UNIT WITH BLEACHING, DYEING AND PRINTING)
1678. DISPERSENT FOR TEXTILE
1679. DYEING & BLEACHING
1680. DYEING OF HANK YARN
1681. EMULSIFIER FOR WOOL BATCHING OIL
1682. EMBROIDERY ON FABRICS
1683. GARMENT DYEING, WASHING & STITCHING (JEANS, JACKETS, SKIRTS & SHIRTS)
1684. GOVES KNITTING
1685. GUNNY BAGS
1687. HDPE WOVEN SACKS
1688. HDPE TARPAULINS USING PLAIN LOOM WITH LAMINATION
1689. HDPE/PP WOVEN SACKS USING CIRCULAR LOOMS
1690. HOSIERY CLOTH (COTTON) PROCESSING (BLEACHING, DYEING, FINISHING OF CLOTH)
1691. HOSIERY INDUSTRY
1692. HOSIERY MERCERISING
1693. HOSIERY PRODUCTS LIKE VEST, BRIEF, T-SHIRTS & SOCKS
1694. JACQUARD FABRICS
1695. JUTE COIR, GRASS ROPE/ SUTLI MAKING
1696. JUTE FELT
1697. JUTE TWINES
1698. KNITTED FABRICS
1699. LAMINATED JUTE BAGS
1700. LAMINATION OF HDPE WOVEN CLOTH (JUTE,COTTON, PAPER)
1701. NYLON YARN CRIMPING, DOUBLING AND BLEACHING
1702. PIGMENT BINDER FOR TEXTILE PRINTING
1704. POLYESTER RESIN FOR WIRE ENAMEL
1705. POLYESTER RESIN
1706. POLYESTER YARN FROM WASTE POLYESTER ZIP FASTENERS
1707. POWER LOOM
1708. READYMADE GARMENTS & HOSIERY
1709. READYMADE GARMENTS MERCHANDISE
1710. READYMADE GARMENTS & COVERS
1711. READYMADE GARMENTS & EMBROIDERY OF GOWNS, SHIRTS, BLOUSES, T-SHIRTS ETC. (ONLY LADIES)
1712. READYMADE SALWAR SUIT
1713. RECOVERY OF NYLON FROM NYLON WASTE
1714. ROTARY PRINTING AND DYEING ON COTTON, SYNTHETIC TEXTILE
1715. SANITARY NAPKINS
1716. SCREEN PRINTING ON COTTON CLOTH
1717. SEWING THREAD REELS & BALLS MAKING INDUSTRIES
1718. SCREEN PRINTING ON COTTON, POLYESTER & ACRYLIC
1719. SHAWLS (WOOLLEN)
1720. SHOE LACES
1721. SILK FABRICS ON HANDLOOM
1722. SOCKS KNITTING
1723. SPINNING, DOUBLING DYEING MERCERISING & BLEACHING OF COTTON YARN
1724. SPINNING & CARDING OF WOOL INTO YARNS
1725. STARCH BOOK BINDING CLOTH
1726. SURAT JARI
1727. SURGICAL COTTON & BANDAGE
1728. SYNTHETIC TEXTILE INDUSTRY(SUITING, SHIRTING, SAREES) TERRY CLOTH
1729. T-SHIRTS
1730. TOWELS, BED SHEET COVERS
1731. TERRY TOWEL
1732. TERRY FABRICS WEAVING UNIT
1733. TEXTILE AUXILLIARIES & CHEMICALS
1734. TEXTILE BLEACHING, DYEING & FINISHING & PRINTING OF COTTON FABRICS
1735. TEXTILE (HOSIERY)
1736. TEXTILE MILL
1737. TEXTILE DYEING & PRINTING
1738. TEXTILE PRINTING (JOB WORK)
1739. TEXTILE PIGMENT PRINTING BINDER
1740. TOWEL (TERRY)
1741. VELVET CLOTH BY FLOCKING PROCESS
1742. VISCOSE STAPLE FIBRE
1743. WADDING OIL (100%) FOR WADDING OF COTTON HOSIERY CLOTH IN THE DYEING PROCESS
1744. WEAVING OF DASUTI CLOTH WITH PRINTING, DYEING, EMBROIDERY & FINISHING
1745. WASHING OF JEANS & OTHER GARMENTS
1746. WORSTED WOOLLEN YARN CLOTH
1747. ZARI GLITTER SALMA SITARA OF PLASTIC FILM

INFOTECH/IT, HOSPITALITY, HOSPITAL, COLLEGE, SCHOOL, MEDICAL, ENTERTAINMENT CLUB, WARE HOUSING & REAL ESTATE, PROJECTS

1748. AMUSEMENT PARK
1749. AMUSEMENT PARK CUM WATER PARK
1750. BANQUET HALL
1751. CALL CENTER (DOMESTIC)
1752. CALL CENTER (INTERNATIONAL)
1753. CHILDREN RECREATION CENTRE
1754. COLD STORAGE
1755. COMMUNITY HALL
1756. COMPUTER EDUCATION INSTITUTE
1757. COMPUTER SOFTWARE
1758. COLLEGE
1759. CYBER CAFE
1760. DENTAL CLINIC
1761. DENTAL COLLEGE
1762. DIAGONOSTIC CENTRE
1763. E-COMMERCE/BUSINESS
1764. E-SCHOOL (Rs. 5000/-)
1765. ENGINEERING COLLEGE
1766. ENTERTAINMENT CLUB
1767. ENTERTAINMENT CLUB, HOLIDAY RESORT, 4 STAR HOTEL, AMUSEMENT PARK CUM WATER PARK, MUSHROOM & ITS PRODUCTS, FISH FARMING, LAKE FOR BOATING, DEER PARK
1768. FASHION TECHNOLOGY INSTITUTE
1769. FAST FOOD PARLOUR
1770. FIVE STAR HOTEL
1771. FOOD PARLOUR
1772. FRANCHISE TRAINING PROGRAMME FOR IIT & ENGINEERING ENTRANCE EXAMS.
1773. GOLF COURSE
1774. HEALTH CLUB, BEAUTY PARLOUR
1775. HEALTH CLUB AND FITNESS CENTER
1776. HEALTH RESORTS
1777. HOLIDAY RESORTS
1778. HOLIDAY RESORT CUM

Above all the Detailed Project Reports are available at *"ENGINEERS INDIA RESEARCH INSTITUTE"*. 4449, Nai Sarak (D), Main Road Delhi - 110 006

● Ph : 91-11-23918117, 2391 6431, 23840361, 31082370 ●Fax : 91-11-2391 6431

●E-Mail : eirisidi@bol.net.in

ENTERTAINMENT CLUB WITH 4 STAR HOTEL
1779. HOSPITALS
1780. ICE CREAM PARLOUR
1781. INTERNET SERVICE PROVIDER (I.S.P.)
1782. MEDICAL COLLEGE
1783. MEDICAL COLLEGE, HOSPITAL & RESEARCH INSTITUTE
1784. MEDICAL TRANSCRIPTION CENTRE
1785. MENTAL RETARDATION HOSPITAL & CEREBRAL PALSY
1786. MOTEL/SMALL HOTEL
1787. MULTISTOREY COMMERCIAL COMPLEX
1788. MULTISTOREY RESIDENTIAL COMPLEX
1789. NURSERY SCHOOL
1790. NATURE CARE CENTRE
1791. NURSING HOME
1792. ONLINE SHOPPING MALL (RS. 5000/- REPORT)
1793. PORTAL
1794. REHABILITATION CENTRE FOR AGED & NEEDY PERSONS
1795. RESIDENTIAL CUM COMMERCIAL COMPLEX
1796. RESTAURANT
1797. RESTAURANT WITH PUB
1798. SCHOOL (PRIMARY)
1799. SCHOOL (HIGHER SECONDARY)
1800. THREE STAR HOTEL
1801. TOURIST CLUB
1802. TRAINING INSTITUTE FOR MEDICAL TRANSCRIPTION
1803. VIDEO FILM STUDIO
1804. WARE HOUSE
1805. WEBSITE DESIGN & E-MAIL REGISTERING

AGRO BASED INDUSTRIES

1806. COAL BRIQUETTES FROM AGROWASTE
1807. FURFURALFROM RICEHULL
1808. MUSHROOM CULTIVATION & PROCESSING (BUTTON)
1809. MUSHROOM GROWING & PROCESSING WITH AIR CONDITIONING
1810. MUSHROOM CULTIVATION & PROCESSING UNIT DEHYDRATION & PACKAGING OF OYSTER & PADDY STRAW MUSHROOMS
1811. ORGANIC MANURE
1812. PAPAYA CULTIVATION
1813. PAPAYA & TOMATO CULTIVATION
1814. PROCESSING & UTILISATION OF COCONUT
1815. PROCESSING OF SHEEP HAIR TO PRODUCE WOOL

BAKERY, CONFECTIONERY & FOOD PRODUCTS

1816. AGROLACTOR SOYA MILK
1817. APPLE FRUIT JUICE WITH CANNING BOTTLING
1818. AYURVEDIC SHARBAT
1819. BAKERY UNIT (PASTRIES, BREAD, BUNS, CAKE, TOFFEE ETC.)
1820. BAKING POWDER
1821. BANANA & ITS BY PRODUCTS
1822. BANANA POWDER
1823. BANANA WAFERS
1824. BANANA CULTIVATION
1825. BEER INDUSTRY
1826. DEHULLING OF JAUN FOR BEER
1827. BEER & WINE
1828. BEER, ALCOHOL, IMFL
1829. BESEN PLANT
1830. BISCUIT PLANT
1831. BREAD & BISCUIT PLANT
1832. BOTTLING PLANT COUNTRY LIQUOR FROM RECTIFIED SPIRIT
1833. BRANDY
1834. BREAD RUSKS
1835. CANNED FRUITS & VEGETABLES
1836. CANNING & PRESERVATION OF MEAT
1837. CANNING & PRESERVATION OF VEGETABLES
1838. CANNING OF MANGO PULP & MANGO SLICES
1839. CARBONATED BEVERAGS
1840. CASHEW FENI
1841. CASHEW NUT (DRIED & FRIED)
1842. CATTLE BREEDING
1843. CATTLE BREEDING & DAIRY FARM TO PRODUCE MILK
1844. CATTLE FEED FROM TAPIOCA
1845. CHEWING GINGER & AMLOKI
1846. CHEWING GUM
1847. CHILLI SAUCE
1848. CHILLI POWDER
1849. CHOCOLATE
1850. CIDER PLANT
1851. COCOA POWDER
1852. COCOA BUTTER & COCOA POWDER
1853. COCONUT SHELL POWDER
1854. COCONUT WATER
1855. COCONUT SWEET (WATERY)
1856. COCONUT MILK POWDER (DEHYDRATED)
1857. COCONUT PRODUCTS & BY PRODUCTS (INTEGRATED PLANT)
1858. COLD DRINK
1859. CURRY POWDER
1860. DAIRY FOR MILK PROCESSING (GHEE, BUTTER & PANEER)
1861. DAIRY PRODUCTS
1862. DAIRY PRODUCTS MILK PACKAGING IN POUCH (GHEE, BUTTER, ETC.
1863. DAIRY FARM TO PRDUCE MILK WITH PACKAGING (COW)
1864. DAIRY FARM TO PRDUCE MILK WITH PACKAGING (BUFALLOE)
1865. DAIRY FARM & MILK PRODUCTS
1866. DAL MOTH, CHANACHUR & BHUJIYA
1867. DEHYDRATION OF FRUITS & VEGETABLE
1868. DESICCATED COCONUT POWDER FROM COCONUTS
1869. DEHYDRATION & CANNING OF FRUITS & VEGETABLES
1870. DRY FRUIT ROASTING & PACKAGING
1871. DRYING OF RED CHILLIES, HALDI, DHANIYA, PEAS & GROUND NUT
1872. EGG POWDER
1873. FISH CANNING IN TIN & POUCHES
1874. FISH DEHYRATION (DRYING OF FISH)
1875. FISH MEAL
1876. FISH PROCESSING (BEAST FREEZING PROCESSES)
1877. FLAVOURS FOR FOOD INDUSTRIES
1878. FLOUR MILL (ROLLER)
1879. FROZEN MEAT
1880. FOOD DEHYDRATION (FRUITS & VEGETABLES)
1881. FRIED & ROASTED GROUND NUT, GRAMS, PEAR ETC.
1882. FRUIT JUICE MAKING & PACKAGING IN PLASTIC CONTAINER
1883. FRUIT JUICE IN TETRA PACK (DRINKS)
1884. FRUIT JUICE, SQUASHES, SAUCE & KETCHUP, JAM, JELLY, VINEGAR ETC.
1885. GARLIC FLAKES
1886. GARLIC POWDER
1887. GHEE & BUTTER
1888. GINGER (PULVERISED)
1889. GINGER GLAZING & PRESERVATION
1890. GINGER STORAGE
1891. GINGER PROCESSING
1892. GINGER OIL & GINGER DUST
1893. GINGER POWDER (DRY) & OLEORESIN
1894. GRAPE DEHYDRATION
1895. GRAPE CULTIVATION
1896. GRAPE JUICE
1897. HONEY PROCESSING & PACKAGING
1898. ICE CREAM & ICE CANDY
1899. ICE CUBE
1900. INVERT SUGAR
1901. IDLI MIX, DOSA MIX SAMBHAR MIX, VADA MIX, GULAB JAMUN MIX
1902. INSTANT COFFEE & INSTANT TEA

1903. INSTANT NOODLES
1904, INSTANT SOUPS
1905. IODIZED SALT FROM CRUDE SALT
1906. JAM CHUTNEY PICKLES & SQUASHES
1907. KATHA MANUFACTURING
1908. LECITHIN (SOYA BASED)
1909. LEMON & ITS PRODUCTS
1910. MACARONI MANUFACTURING
1911. MACARONI, SPAGHETTI, VERMICELLI & NOODLES
1912. MAIZE & ITS BY PRODUCTS MALTING PLANT
1913. MANGO PAPPAD (AAM PAPPAD)
1914. MANGO POWDER RIPE
1915. MANGO POWDER
1916. MANGO PROCESSING & CANNING (MANGO PULP)
1917. MEAT PROCESSING (CHICKEN MUTTON)
1918. MEAT PROCESSING (BUFFALO)
1919. MENTHOL BOLD FROM MENTHOL FLAKES
1020. MILK POWDER
1921. MILK POWDER & GHEE
1922. MILK POWDER, GHEE & SPICES
1923. MILK PRESERVATION & MARKETING TO WHOLE SELLERS
1924. MILK PRESERVATION & MARKETING TO WHOLE SELLERS (IN POUCHES)
1925. MILK TOFFEE MANUFACTURES
1926. MINERAL WATER
1927. MINERAL WATER IN POUCHES
1928. MINI FLOUR MILL ATTA MAIDA, SUJI & WHEAT BRAN
1929. MITHAI/HALWAI (SWEET & NAMKEEN)
1930. MUTTON PROCESSING
1931. PAN MASALA (MEETHA, SADA, ZARDA) MAKING & PACKING
1932. PAN MASALA AND POUCH MAKING
1933. PANEER (CHEESE)
1934. PAPAD & BARIYAN
1935. PAPAD PLANT
1936. PEPSICOLA IN POLYTUBES
1937. PETHA PACKAGING
1938. PICKLES
1939. PIGGERY/MEAT/CHICKEN PROCESSING
1940. PINE APPLE JUICE CANNING
1941. POTATO & ONION POWDER
1942. POTATO & ONION FLAKES
1943. POTATO CHIPS
1944. POTATO GRANULES
1945. POUCH FILLING FOR SAUNF SUPARI ILAICHI ETC.
1946. PRESERVATION OF RAWS MANGO JUICE
1947. PROCESSED CHEESE & MARINE PDTS.
1948. PULP FROM TARMARIND
1949. READYMATE PROCESSED FOOD
1950. RICE & CORN FLAKES
1951. RICE BASMATI (TRADING)
1952. RICE POLISHING & PACKAGING IN POUCH
1953. ROASTED/SALTED/MASALA/ CASHEW NUTS ALMONDS & PEA NUT
1954. ROLLER FLOUR MILL

INFOTECH/IT PROJECTS

1955. MEDICAL TRANSCRIPTION
1956. E-COMMERCE
1957. CYBERCAFE
1958. INTERNET SERVICE PROVIDER (ISP)
1959. COMPUTER EDUCATION CENTRE
1960. PORTAL (WEBSITE DESIGN)
1961. CALL CENTRE

TERMS AND CONDITIONS

FOR INDIA

1. Please ask for Quotations of Each *Market Survey Cum Detailed Techno Economic Feasibility Report.* Payable in advance through Draft/M.O./Cash in favour of 'ENGINEERS INDIA RESEARCH INSTITUTE', Delhi. Delivery by Regd.post within 2 Days. (Postage Free)

2. Ask for the Hi-Tech Projects Monthly magazine. Each Magazine covers many Project Profiles for selection of Industry.

FOR OVERSEAS

1. Please ask for Quotations in US $ of Each *Market Survey Cum Detailed Techno Economic Feasibility Report.* Payable in advance through Draft/M.O./Cash in favour of 'ENGINEERS INDIA RESEARCH INSTITUTE', Delhi. (Payable in India) Delivery by Regd.post within 4 Days.

2. Ask for "Hi-Tech Projects" Monthly magazine. Each Magazine covers many Project Profiles for selection of Industry.

ENGINEERS INDIA RESEARCH INSTITUTE

Add: 4449, Nai Sarak (D), Main Road, Delhi - 110 006 (India)
Ph:. 91-11-23918117, 23916431, 23840361, 98114-37895
Fax: 91-11-23916431 E-Mail : eirisidi@bol.net.in
Website:www.eiriinia.org
Also at : 4/27, Roop Nagar, Near Roop Nagar No. 1 School, Delhi - 110 007 (India) Ph:. 23840361